HISTORY OF THE COMMUNIST PARTY
OF GREAT BRITAIN 1927–1941

HISTORY OF
THE COMMUNIST PARTY
OF GREAT BRITAIN
1927–1941

★ ★ ★

NOREEN BRANSON

LAWRENCE AND WISHART
London

Lawrence and Wishart Limited
39 Museum Street
London WC1A 1LQ

First published 1985
© Noreen Branson, 1985

Photoset by Type Practitioners, Sevenoaks, Kent
Printed and bound in Great Britain by
Oxford University Press

Contents

Illustrations

Introduction

James Klugmann was responsible for writing the first two volumes of the history of the Communist Party of Great Britain. Published in 1968 and 1969, they covered the period 1919 to 1926, including the Party's activities during the General Strike. He was planning a further volume; sadly, he died before it was written.

In 1978 I offered to continue with the Party history from 1927, the date at which James's second volume ended. My proposal was discussed with the Communist Party's Political Committee and was put before the Executive Committee; my offer was accepted, and it was agreed that I should take full responsibility for any opinions expressed. This I gladly do. Any views put forward or judgements made are my own, and it must not be assumed that they represent the views of members of the Executive Committee of the Communist Party, either individually or collectively.

Like James, I have tried to place this history within the context of the political events of the period, and to explore the relationship of the Party with the labour movement in general, and with the Labour Party in particular. I have also examined the role of the Communist International at certain key periods and the part played by the British Party within that body before it was finally dissolved in 1943.

During the years covered by this volume, the Party was subject to considerable police harassment, and faced a continuing threat of being declared illegal. For this reason, it was customary to keep secret the names of those elected to the Party's Central Committee, and to destroy minutes and records of committee meetings other than those taken by hand to the headquarters of the Communist International in Moscow. When planning his third volume, James Klugmann went to study the British material in the archives of the Communist International. He brought back with him hand-written notes on the political discussions within the British Party during the years 1927–32, and also some more general material derived from later years. I was given access to these Klugmann papers, and, as the reader will see, I have made extensive use of them in the earlier chapters. Where the 1927–32 notes are used, I have indicated this by the reference to 'JK folder –'; information from the CI archives relating to later years is listed as coming from the 'JK papers'.

I must place on record my grateful thanks to all those who have helped me in writing this book. Four people read the completed manuscript: Margot Heinemann, Yvonne Kapp, George Matthews and Margaret Morris. Their comments and suggestions were extremely useful to me. So were those of Bill Alexander and Jim Fyrth who read the chapter on the war in Spain. Monty Johnstone read the parts of the draft relating to Trotskyism, and gave me much valuable information both on this subject and on other matters relating to the Comintern and to the French Communist Party.

Betty Reid, who, with George Matthews, is in charge of the Communist Party Archive, has given me unfailing assistance, supplying me with old leaflets and documents on request, and sometimes drawing my attention to material that I did not know existed. I have also received much help from the staff of the Marx Memorial Library – in particular, from its librarian, Andrew Davies and his predecessor, Charles Hall.

In the course of my researches, I have had interviews with many people. My thanks are due to Robin Page Arnot, Ted Bramley, Idris Cox and Andrew Rothstein, all of whom served on the Party's Central Committee for many years, and whose recollections were very important to me. Kay Beauchamp told me a great deal – particularly about the early days of the *Daily Worker*; Isabel Brown spoke to me about the Reichstag Fire trial and the Aid for Spain movements; Charles Hoyle recalled for me his early days in the engineering industry; Ralph Bond told me all about the 'National Left Wing Movement' in the 1920s and lent me a unique collection of cuttings on the subject; Hymie Fagan, who worked for the Party in different capacities for many years, discussed his experiences with me; Phil Piratin recalled for me the events leading up to the 'Battle of Cable Street'; Tamara and Wogan Phillips talked to me of their wartime activities. Three people with whom I had interviews are, sadly, no longer with us: George Aitken, Jack Cohen and Hilda Vernon.

I am much indebted to Edmund and Ruth Frow for important information concerning the role of individual Party members in the engineering industry; to Reuben Falber for material relating to the 'Class against Class' period; to Doris Allison for sending me the pamphlet on the trial of George Allison in 1931.

I would like to thank the Communist Party for permission to

reproduce all the illustrations used in this book, with the exception of the *Daily Worker* Cable Street supplement, the first page of which is reproduced by kind permission of the Marx Memorial Library.

On two occasions the Communist Party History Group enabled me to present papers for discussion, and its secretary, Geoff Ferres, put me in touch with others working in related fields. Members of the group who gave me special help include John Attfield, Allan Merson, Bill Moore, A.L. Morton and Willie Thompson.

Finally, I must once more stress that none of the people listed above are responsible in any way for the views expressed in the course of this book.

September 1984

CHAPTER 1

The Great Purge
(1926–28)

After the 1926 General Strike the leaders of the Labour Party and the Trades Union Congress opened up a new drive to outlaw the Communists and isolate them from the rest of the labour movement. The Communist Party was still very small; at the end of 1926 it had no more than 7,900 members. But its influence was wider than such numbers would suggest, since it had initiated several important movements. One was the Minority Movement through which trade-union activists came together to campaign for more militant policies. Another was the National Unemployed Workers' Committee Movement which mobilised the jobless for action around the slogan 'work or full maintenance'. At the same time, nearly 1,500 Communists were active inside the Labour Party itself, joining with other left-wingers in the fight for socialist policies in place of those which offered no real challenge to the capitalist system.

The Communist Party was only six years old, having been founded in 1920 when various groups of revolutionary socialists had come together for the purpose. For decades, Marxists had been trying to convince others that capitalism was the cause of oppression, hunger and war, and that only by ending the system could the emancipation of working people be achieved. But the Russian Revolution of 1917 meant that socialist theories were at last being put to the test. 'Social revolution, formerly but an empty phrase, has become a real live force' said a 1920 manifesto calling for the formation of a Communist Party in Britain. In Russia, it said, socialism could be seen in action and 'no longer in the clubroom and coffee houses'.

Socialists all over the world had been similarly inspired, and, responding to the initiative of the Russian Bolshevik Party, had jointly formed the Communist International (CI) – or Third International – with its headquarters in Moscow. The Communist Party of Great Britain was proud to designate itself the British

Section of the Communist International, an organisation which aimed to mobilise working people in every country for the overthrow of their capitalist oppressors. In the words of the revolutionary marching song: 'The International unites the human race.'

The 1926 General Strike had appeared to underline the need for a Communist Party in Britain. For nine days, two million workers had responded to the call of their trade-union leaders and, at considerable personal sacrifice, had downed tools, not on their own behalf, but in support of the miners who had been locked out for their refusal to submit to a wage cut. But just as the strike was going from strength to strength, the TUC leaders had called it off, leaving the miners to fight on alone for a further seven months until hunger brought defeat. Meanwhile, humiliating agreements were imposed on transport workers, railwaymen, seamen and printers on their return to work, while the Conservative government introduced draconian measures to weaken the trade unions.

To Communists, the event had given a glimpse of something new. It had shown that some, at least, of the ingredients for social revolution were present, including a growing class solidarity in place of the old craft sectionalism, and a rising determination to challenge, not only the employers, but the ruling class itself. But it also seemed to prove that if and when confrontation took place between the working class and the capitalist class, the trade-union and Labour leaders would betray the cause and desert to the side of the enemy.

To the trade-union leaders, the lesson of the General Strike was equally clear: it was 'Never Again'. They had not wanted the strike in the first place, but had been pushed into it by a combination of unforeseen happenings. They had called it off as soon as possible, and a few months later succeeded in persuading the majority of union executives that their actions had been reasonable, and that the miners had only themselves to blame for their predicament. Meanwhile, the event had helped to clarify their ideas on an alternative path. They believed that if they cooperated with the employers in the reorganisation of industry, and in measures to increase efficiency, their members would reap the reward in the shape of trade union recognition and a share in the resulting industrial prosperity.[1]

So, in 1928 they entered discussions with a group of employers headed by Sir Alfred Mond on such matters as rationalisation and methods of avoiding industrial disputes. They did this at a time when Britain was heading for the worst economic crisis yet known. In this context 'rationalisation' meant speed-up, sackings, wage cuts.

For the Labour Party leaders, the lesson of the General Strike was the same. More and more they set their faces against any kind of 'direct action'; increasingly they made clear their belief that change must be brought about gradually through Parliament. Simultaneously they toned down their election programme, hoping to make it more acceptable to the middle-class voter. On many immediate issues they trimmed their sails to the Conservative breeze. For example, in 1927 the Labour representatives on a government committee (the Blanesburgh Committee) jointly signed a majority report which, contrary to trade-union policy, advocated reductions in unemployment benefit.

In their drive for conciliation and industrial peace, the Labour and trade-union leaders could expect trouble from their left wing, and how to deal with the trouble-makers became a major preoccupation. Inevitably, their chief target was the Communists. The Labour leaders concentrated on expelling them from the Labour Party, the TUC General Council on smashing the Minority Movement and trying to prevent the election of Communists to office in trade unions. Both leaderships endeavoured to isolate and discredit the National Unemployed Workers' Committee Movement.

Arguments used against the Communists in this long-drawn out attack can be summarised as follows: firstly, they were said to be aiming for armed insurrection; secondly, they were accused of believing in the 'dictatorship of the proletariat' instead of in the democratic rule of Parliament; thirdly, it was alleged that the Communist Party was not a free agent, since it was subject to 'orders from Moscow'. The detailed answers given by the Communist Party to these objections will be examined in the course of this book.[2] In brief, its reply to the first objection was that socialism could not be achieved through Parliament, since the real power of the capitalist class was outside it. To the second objection, the Party argued that the dictatorship of the proletariat meant real democracy for the vast majority – the workers – whereas the parliamentary system was a disguised dictatorship of the minority – the capitalists. As to the third objection, the Party took pride in its membership of the Communist International which was struggling to follow the call in the original *Manifesto*: 'Workers Of All Countries, Unite.' Obviously, the CI met in Moscow because that was the only place where it could do so without police interference.

In practice, of course, it was not so much Communist views concerning the advance to socialism or the seizure of power which aroused the hostility of the Labour leaders as the Communist attitude to the immediate struggle. Whenever a compromise agreement was being negotiated with the employers, the Communists rushed in urging the rank and file to resist. Moreover, they did not mince their words when criticising policies of class collaboration. To Labour and trade-union leaders, who wanted a docile rank and file, the Communists were a terrible nuisance. They undermined the image of respectability that the leaders were anxious to promote, since any alleged association of Labour with Communists was habitually publicised in the press. Inevitably 'disruption' became the main charge against Communists.

The Exclusion From the Labour Party

Moves to exclude Communists from the Labour Party had been going on for some years. Unlike the social-democratic parties on the Continent, the Labour Party, originally created by the trade unions to give them a voice in Parliament, was a loose federation of affiliated bodies comprising both trade unions and socialist societies. The latter (of which the Independent Labour Party was the most important) had the right to argue for their point of view at annual conferences, though when the votes were taken at such conferences, the trade unions had a decisive majority. Soon after its formation, the Communist Party had applied to the Labour Party for affiliation. There was no constitutional reason why its application should not have been accepted, as had that of the British Socialist Party, its avowedly Marxist predecessor. But the Labour leadership resisted the request, and the rejection of the Party as an affiliated society had been endorsed by annual conferences in 1921, 1922, 1923 and 1924.[3]

However, rejection of affiliation did not in itself prevent Communists participating in Labour Party activities. There was no rule to stop members of the Communist Party becoming individual members of the Labour Party as well. And trade unions could elect

Communists as delegates to Labour organisations and meetings. The Labour leaders were determined to put an end to such Communist participation.

The decision that Communists should not be entitled to individual membership of the Labour Party was first taken at the 1924 Labour Party Annual Conference, and was reaffirmed at the Liverpool conference in the autumn of 1925. At the same time, trade unions were asked not to nominate Communists as delegates to Labour organisations. It was easier said than done. At the end of 1926, out of the Communist Party's total membership of 7,900, as many as 1,544 still belonged to the Labour Party as individuals, and another 242 were trade union delegates to Labour organisations.

By this time, the process of disaffiliating local Labour parties who refused to expel their Communist Party members had been inaugurated. Within the next three years, 27 such local bodies were to be outlawed, 'official' parties being set up in their place. They were listed as follows at successive Labour Party conferences:

1926: Battersea Trades Council and Labour Party (TC&LP); Bethnal Green TC&LP; South-West Bethnal Green Divisional Labour Party (DLP); Greenock Trades and Labour Council (T&LC); Springburn DLP; Stratford (West Ham) DLP; East Lewisham DLP; Westminster LP; Chelsea TC&LP; Holborn TC&LP; Bridgeton (Glasgow) DLP; Gorbals (Glasgow) DLP; Kelvingrove (Glasgow) DLP.

1927: Hackney Trades Council and Borough Labour Party (TC&BLP); North Islington DLP; East Ham BLP&TC; Southwark TC&BLP; Lewisham BLP&TC; Rhondda BLP; Rhondda East DLP; Rhondda West DLP; Camberwell TC&BLP; Poplar TC&LP.

1928: Edgbaston (Birmingham) DLP; Moseley (Birmingham) DLP; Kelvingrove (Glasgow) DLP.

1929: Southport TC&LP.

The list of 27 was confined to organisations of borough or divisional status which had to be dealt with directly by headquarters. It did not include ward parties and subsidiary bodies expelled or dissolved by local borough parties.

The drive against the Communists began in London where some 434 Communists out of a total London membership of 1,105 were active in their local Labour Parties or as delegates to them.[4] The attack was launched by Herbert Morrison, secretary of the London Labour Party, whose political stance was summed up in the Communist paper *Workers' Life* as follows:

> When the workers of London are prepared to lead, we of the London Labour Party will possibly consider whether it is desirable, or convenient, or respectable, or constitutional to follow.[5]

He had indeed been trying to stamp out the left-wing tradition of some of the London Labour parties ever since the unconstitutional action of the Poplar Council, led by George Lansbury in 1921. By 1928 Morrison was being described as 'our chief witch-finder' at the Labour Party Annual Conference.[6] Top of Morrison's hit-list was the Battersea Party which had the distinction of choosing as their local Labour MP a man who was not only a Communist but the first Indian ever to sit in the House of Commons: S. Saklatvala. After defying Morrison's demands that they should expel their Communist members, the Battersea Party was disaffiliated and official Labour Parties set up instead. 'The people who have started rival Labour parties in Battersea are the very ones who are always complaining that the Communists are "splitting the movement"' commented Saklatvala. 'Here we have an example of the lengths to which the official clique are prepared to go in their efforts to show the bosses that the Labour Party means them no harm.'[7]

Simultaneously with the disaffiliation of Battersea came that of Bethnal Green. Here the former mayor, Communist Joe Vaughan, an electrician by trade, was active as a councillor; he alleged that people were referring to the 'moderate' Labour parties set up under Morrison's guidance in his area as 'pudding clubs'.[8] The policy of setting up 'official' parties in the areas where the former parties had been expelled continued throughout 1926 and 1927; for some time they existed side by side with the outlawed ones.

It was Joe Vaughan and his Bethnal Green Party which had been responsible for inaugurating the National Left Wing Movement. For two and a half years this organisation led and co-ordinated the activities of disaffiliated Labour parties, others threatened with disaffiliation, and groups of left-wingers within the Labour Party. Its origin had been a conference called in November 1925 'to discuss ways and means of bringing the Party back to the idealism and fighting spirit of Keir Hardie.' At this conference a 'National Left

Wing Provisional Committee' was set up; it issued a programme which argued that the Labour Party had been formed to 'fight for the interests of the working class as against those of the master class', that the left wing of the party sought to keep this tradition alive, but that the right wing were 'trying to transform it into an organisation which will serve the master class'.[9] Beginning as a London movement it constituted itself as a national body at a conference in September 1926 attended by delegates from 52 Labour parties, and 40 from left-wing groups in other Labour parties.

The headquarters of the National Left Wing Movement were at the Grays Inn Road premises of the *Sunday Worker*, a paper which had been launched early in 1925 on Communist initiative, and was intended as a voice for the left wing, both Communist and non-Communist. The paper's shareholders included miners' lodges, ILP branches, local Labour parties and trades councils, though, according to documents seized in a police raid on the Communist Party headquarters at 16 King Street in 1925, the Party had allocated £4,000 to its running costs out of a grant of £16,000 from the Communist International. The editor of the *Sunday Worker* was William Paul, a foundation member of the Party, and among those on its staff was Walter Holmes, who had worked on the labour newspaper, the *Daily Herald*, in its early days. Unlike some Communist Party literature it was lively and readable; by the beginning of 1926 it had a stable weekend circulation of 85,000, and its sales frequently topped 100,000. From the start it acted as spokesman for the Left Wing Movement.

From early in 1927 until 1929, the secretary of the National Left Wing Movement was Ralph Bond, a young Communist who, in later life, was to be well known in the workers' film movement. He issued a call for a network of left-wing groups to be formed within wards and individual sections of the Labour Party.[10] The object was to 'secure the adoption by the Labour Party of a militant socialist policy in place of its present policy of compromise with capitalism.'[11] And in view of the tendency (both then and now) to portray the Communist Party as a conspiratorial body, it should perhaps be recorded that these proposals for groups within the Labour Party were launched in no surreptitious fashion but loudly proclaimed.

The leadership of the National Left Wing Movement consisted of activists from the localities. Prominent among them were Will

Crick, a tramwayman, chairman of Manchester and Salford Trades Council, and Joseph Southall, of the ILP and Vice-President of the Birmingham Borough Labour Party. Communists in the leadership included Joe Vaughan, Dr Robert Dunstan of Birmingham, and C.J. Moody from Richmond Trades Council who was in process of being excluded from the general council of the National Union of General and Municipal Workers by that union's leaders. On the Left Wing Movement's Advisory Council were some well-known trade unionists. The non-Communists among them included Alex Gossip, Secretary of the Furnishing Trades Association; J.J.W. Bradley, Secretary of the firemen's union; S.O. Davies, Vice-President of the South Wales Miners and Will Lawther of the Durham Miners' Executive. The Movement's programme included nationalisation of industry without compensation; the introduction of a legal £4 minimum wage; a capital levy on fortunes over £5,000; a 'socialist programme for the abolition of the British Empire'; a scheme for educational reform, including the elimination of imperialist and militaristic teaching, and self-government by pupils, parents and teachers' councils.

During 1927 several large district conferences were held by the Movement. One in Newcastle was presided over by Will Lawther; the Durham Miners' Executive, of which he was a member, nevertheless circularised miners' lodges telling them not to send delegates. Despite this, it was attended by representatives of 16 Durham miners' lodges, 3 Northumberland miners' lodges, 25 other trade union branches, 32 Labour parties and trades councils, 3 Labour party women's sections and 15 Left Wing groups within Labour parties.[12] When the Movement's first annual conference took place in September 1927, 120 organisations were represented including 54 Labour parties and some ILP branches; the rest were mainly left-wing groups which were reported to number about ninety throughout the country.

By this time, the drive from on high had reached a new stage. Originally concerned with excluding Communists, those at headquarters were now busy expelling people who were not Communists but wanted to work with them. They were characteristed by Herbert Morrison as 'elements it is not desirable to mix with.'[13] Thus in September 1927 several left-wingers were excluded from the General Committee of the South East St Pancras Labour Party on the grounds that they had associated with the

Greater London Left Wing Committee. They protested to headquarters at Eccleston Square, saying that none of them were Communists, and there was nothing in the Labour Party's constitution to prevent them associating with the Left Wing Movement. But Eccleston Square turned a deaf ear to their protests. Again, under threat of disaffiliation, Tottenham Trades Council and Central Labour Party expelled nine non-Communist delegates who were associated with either the Left Wing movement, the Minority Movement or the International Class War Prisoners' Aid.

It was in 1927 that matters came to a head in Birmingham. Here a well-known local Communist, Dr Robert Dunstan, had stood as parliamentary candidate since 1924 in the Tory controlled constituency of West Birmingham. He had the support of a left-wing committee composed of both Communists and non-Communists. But after the Liverpool decision, an 'official' Labour candidate was adopted for the constituency. This led to considerable local protest and indeed to strong objections by National Executive member George Lansbury who said that the decision to oppose Dunstan was 'a disgusting procedure . . . I would be glad to support Dr Dunstan's canditature at any time. The Communists are not our enemies but our friends.'[14] Many Labour members continued to support Dunstan and in 1927, the Birmingham Borough Labour Party decided on a majority vote to recommend the expulsion of these supporters. But the expulsions had to be carried out by the Divisional parties concerned. There were six of these, and four of them refused to obey. In particular, the Edgbaston Party refused by 50 votes to 19 to expel the well-known Dunstan supporter, Joseph Southall. In the end, an official enquiry was conducted from Labour Party headquarters; it was chaired, ironically by none other than George Lansbury who had, for that year, been elected chairman of the Labour Party NEC. The Edgbaston and Moseley Parties refused to conform and in 1928 were disaffiliated.

Earlier, the proceedings at the 1927 Labour Party Annual Conference had revealed that the leaders were still some way off achieving their object. A number of Communists were present as delegates from their respective trade unions. They included Harry Pollitt, from the Boilermakers Union, who expressed his fears that the Labour programme for the next General Election would be one with which the Liberal Party would agree; Peter Kerrigan, of the Amalgamated Engineering Union, who criticised the tactics of the

Parliamentary Labour Party in relation to the Trade Disputes Bill; and Arthur Horner, of the Miners' Federation, who got the platform into an awkward corner over whether Communists should be asked to pay the political levy to the Labour Party.[16]

Disquiet at the attitude of the Labour Party leadership found expression in a Manifesto issued jointly in June 1928 by A.J. Cook, the Secretary of the Miners' Federation, and James Maxton, MP, Chairman of the Independent Labour Party. 'As a result of the new conception that socialism and capitalism should sink their differences,' it said, 'much of the energy which should be expended in fighting capitalism is now expended in crushing everybody who dares to remain true to the ideals of the movement.'[17] They ran a series of well-attended public meetings with the support of the National Left Wing Movement. But at the Labour Party Annual Conference in October 1928, the left wing failed to persuade the leaders to change course.

At this conference, the National Executive introduced a new series of recommendations under the heading 'Party Loyalty'. These debarred trade unions from electing Communists as delegates to Labour Party meetings, either nationally or locally. And Clause 3 laid down that local parties must refrain from 'inviting to or permitting on their platforms, members of political parties not eligible for affiliation, including the Communist Party, or any individual who opposes constitutionally selected Labour candidates.'[18] Thus not only Communists, but non-Communist members of the Left Wing Movement, were debarred from sharing platforms at public meetings convened by Labour Parties.

Ironically, in the 1928 Report, signed by the National Executive, one very prominent Communist was listed among those who had sadly passed away. He was Alfred Augustine Watts, to whom tribute was paid for his 'years of steady, ungrudging work' as a councillor and guardian. The tribute did not mention that he had been a Communist, but the truth was that his local Labour Party – Bow and Bromley, to which George Lansbury belonged – had never expelled him, and he had held both a Communist and a Labour Party card until his death in 1928.

In 1929, the 'loyalty clauses' were to be elaborated so as to exclude not only Communists but also members of organisations 'ancillary or subsidiary' to the Communist Party. And soon after, the Executive sent out a circular listing seven such organisations: the

Left Wing Movement, the Minority Movement, the National Unemployed Workers' Committee Movement, the League against Imperialism, Workers' International Relief, International Class War Prisoners' Aid, and the Friends of Soviet Russia.[19] The new ruling meant that no members of any of the organisations concerned could be in the Labour Party, nor could they be elected as delegates to Labour Party meetings.

The Minority Movement and the NUWCM

Long before this, the drive to isolate the Communists and their left-wing allies was under way in several trade unions. The main target was the Minority Movement (MM), founded on Communist initiative in 1924 as a co-ordinating body for militant movements in a number of industries. The MM was affiliated to the Red International of Labour Unions (RILU), an organisation formed in 1921 with the aim of building up a militant trade union movement in contrast to the International Federation of Trade Unions which was thought to be dominated by class collaborators. (The RILU was often referred to as the 'Profintern.') According to a pre-1926 Minority Movement leaflet:

> Most of the Unions today are supporters of the capitalist system. We hold that it is the duty of the Unions to stoutly resist the continuous encroachments of the Employing Class and aim definitely at the OVERTHROW OF THE CAPITALIST SYSTEM.

At its 1927 Conference, the Minority Movement's aims were listed as follows: 1) to fight against the capitalist offensive on wages, hours and trade union rights. 2) 'to fight any tendency to leave or split the unions, and to wage an energetic campaign for a 100 per cent trade union movement.' 3) to expose the role of the capitalist state. 4) to fight for unification of workers in factories, trade union branches etc., and 'to agitate for one union for each industry, a centralised General Council and a single Trade Union International.' 5) to build up Minority Movement groups in every industry so that MM policy would become the policy of the trade union movement as a whole. It declared that 'The Minority Movement itself is not a trade union; it consists of militant members of existing trade unions, who aim at making the trade unions real militant organs in the class struggle.'[20]

The MM was composed of affiliated organisations and individual members who came together as groups within various industries. At its 1927 conference there were 718 delegates representing 319 trade union branches, 20 trades councils, 26 co-operative guilds. Also represented were 28 branches of the National Unemployed Workers' Committee movement and 61 Minority Movement groups. It was a two-day conference and part of the time was devoted to sectional meetings: for miners, metal workers, transport workers, building workers and so forth.

A year earlier, the TUC General Council had ruled that local trades councils must not affiliate to the Minority Movement, a ruling upheld at the 1926 Bournemouth Congress by 2,710,000 votes to 738,000, after A. Conley, Secretary of the Tailor and Garment Workers Union, had expressed fears that if trades councils were allowed to affiliate to the Movement, the 'Minority' might in a short time become the 'Majority'.

It was the signal for action in some unions. In February 1927, the Executive of the National Union of General and Municipal Workers suspended a Communist member of its General Council, C.J. Moody, and seventeen other members. Five branches were then disenfranchised, and it was decided that no member of the Minority Movement or the Communist Party might stand for any union position. Branches were prohibited from sending delegates to Minority Movement conferences.

In December 1927, the General Secretary of the TUC, Walter Citrine, launched a sustained attack on the Minority Movement in the pages of the magazine *Labour*; his series of articles was later issued in pamphlet form under the title *Democracy or Disruption*. According to this, the lines of future development of the trade union movement should run 'in the direction of making the workers' organisations an integral part of the economic machinery of society.' To allow the trade unions to be used as instruments of social upheaval would be 'fatal to our hopes of ordered progress.' But the object of the Communists was 'to capture the trade union movement and exploit it for a revolutionary subversive purpose.' From the outset, the purpose of the Minority Movement 'was to set the rank and file of the working-class movement in bitter opposition to its elected and responsible representatives.' In pursuit of the policy of 'Don't trust

WHAT IS THIS MINORITY MOVEMENT?

1D

Published by the N.M.M., 38 Great Ormond Street, London, W.C.1. February, 1928.

your leaders', the MM, alleged Citrine, misrepresented the policy of the official movement.

This call from Citrine did not go unheeded by the leaders of some important trade unions. The Executive of the Boilermakers Union decided that Communists must not be elected as delegates to TUC or Labour Party conferences; later Communists were banned from holding office within the union. By June 1928 both the Shop Assistants Union Executive and the Executive of the print union NATSOPA had decided not to allow Communists or MM members to stand for office; the Executives of the National Union of Railwaymen and the Transport and General Workers Union both told their branches they were to have nothing to do with the Minority Movement; the Executive of the Electrical Trades Union quashed the election of three MM members to its London District Committee; the Painters' Society Executive forbade its branches to affiliate to the MM and the AEU Executive considered taking similar action. Officials of the Boot and Shoe Operatives' Union and of the Bakers' Union decided to take disciplinary action against any member who criticised their policy. In May and June 1928, Communists were expelled from various weavers' associations.

In one place, however, Conley's fears were realised, and the Minority became the Majority. This was among the miners of Fife and Lanark. In Scotland a loose federation of county miners' unions had come together to form the National Union of Scottish Mineworkers, in turn affiliated to the Miners' Federation of Great Britain (MFGB). In 1927, Communists were elected by ballot vote to a series of important position in both the Fife and Lanarkshire County Unions. But the Executive of the Scottish Mineworkers refused to recognise the election of the Communists concerned, and delayed convening the annual conference at which they should have taken their seats. Moreover, when the Miners' Federation of Great Britain conference took place in July 1928, four properly elected Lanarkshire delegates were denied admission because the Scottish Executive would not endorse their credentials.

Simultaneously with the attacks in the trade unions came the endeavour to isolate the National Unemployed Workers' Committee Movement (NUWCM). In 1923 a Joint Committee composed of representatives of the General Council of the TUC and the NUWCM had been appointed. But in the autumn of 1927 the TUC decided to sever its links with this Communist-led movement of the unemployed. In November 1927 a miners' march from South Wales to London took place with Communist Wal Hannington as its chief marshall. The march had originally been proposed by A.J. Cook, Secretary of the Miners' Federation of Great Britain, and himself a member of the TUC General Council. But Cook did not succeed in getting MFGB support for the march, and this gave Walter Citrine his chance to intervene. He circularised local trades councils along the route where reception committees were busy arranging hospitality for the marching miners, telling them that the TUC could not recommend support for the march. And, though Cook's intention had been to draw attention to the appalling conditions of unemployed miners in the South Wales valleys, certain trade-union leaders tried to persuade the world that this was not its real purpose: it was a sinister Communist plot designed to recruit members for nefarious purposes.

At the 1928 Trades Union Congress in Swansea, the decision to outlaw the Minority Movement was confirmed; moreover a resolution from the Railway Clerks Association was carried calling on the General Council to 'institute an inquiry into the proceedings and methods of disruptive elements within the trade union movement.'

Thus, after two years strenuous endeavour, the leaders of the Labour Party and TUC succeeded in isolating the Communists and, in the process, putting down their own left wing.

[1] *TUC Report 1928*, p.209 *et al.*
[2] See, in particular, Chapter 8.
[3] See James Klugmann, *History of the Communist Party*, Vol. I, London 1969, pp.166–81. See also 'Labour Communist Relations 1920–39', the fifth quarterly number of *Our History*, published by the History Group of the Communist Party in 1957. The verbatim report of a meeting of Labour Party representatives with those of the Communist Party on 29 December 1921 was reproduced in the *Bulletin of the Society for the Study of Labour History*, No.29, Autumn 1974.
[4] JK folder 4. Party Census, January 1927.
[5] *Workers' Life*, 2 December 1927.
[6] W.J. Brown, General Secretary of CSCA, *Labour Party Annual Report 1928*, p.207.
[7] *Sunday Worker*, 11 July, 1926.
[8] *Sunday Worker*, 3 July 1927.
[9] *The Left Wing: its Programme and Activities*, pamphlet issued by the National Left Wing Provisional Committee, 1926.
[10] *Sunday Worker*, 20 March 1927.
[11] *Sunday Worker*, 2 October 1927.
[12] *Sunday Worker*, 24 July 1927.
[13] *Workers' Life*, 2 December 1927.

[14] *Sunday Worker*, 19 September 1926. See also life of Joseph Southall, *Dictionary of Labour Biography*, Vol. V.
[15] *Labour Party Annual Report 1927*, p.183.
[16] Ibid., pp.195–6.
[17] *Sunday Worker*, 21 June 1928.
[19] *Labour Party Annual Report 1930*, p.29.
[20] Final Agenda of 4th Annual Conference of the Minority Movement, 1927.

CHAPTER 2

The New Line
(1928)

The defeat of the Communists in the great purge was inevitable. They could not have withstood the determined efforts of the right wing to exclude them during those days of depression and demoralisation ,following the General Strike. Nevertheless, in its final stages in 1928–9, the purge was made easier for the right by a change in the line of the Communist Party itself. This new line – which came to be known as 'Class against Class' – was a disaster. It alienated former allies, and made it much harder for the Party to recover lost ground in later years. And though exclusion of Communists had begun before its introduction, it was used by the right wing to justify anti-Communist vendettas for many years after it had been abandoned.

The new approach did not emanate from within the British Party, but from the Communist International.

As mentioned in the last chapter, the Communist Party of Great Britain ranked as a Section of the Communist International which according to Clause I of its constitution was 'a World Communist Party'. The International and its Sections were 'built up on the basis of democratic centralism' which meant the 'election of all the leading committees of the Party . . . by general meetings of Party members, conferences, congresses and international congresses', and 'decisions of superior Party committees to be obligatory for subordinate committees.'

Policy could be discussed throughout Party oranisations until a decision was taken by the appropriate body – e.g. by Congresses of the Communist International, or by Congresses of the Sections, or by leading committees of the Comintern and of its various Sections. But once a decision was taken it must be carried out even if some of the party membeers disagreed with it. The supreme decision-making body of the Comintern was the World Congress, which, according to Clause 8, must meet every two years. In between Congresses the Executive Committee of the Comintern (ECCI) had

17

the right to give instructions to all Sections. 'The Sections have the right to appeal against decisions of the ECCI to the World Congress, but must continue to carry out such decisions pending the decision of the World Congress.'[1]

Democratic centralism thus had two aspects. One was the participation of the membership in policy making and in the election of higher committees. The other was the obligation to act as a united body in carrying out Congress decisions, or, between Congresses, decisions of the leading committees. The argument for loyal implementation of decisions even by those who disagreed with them was that the Comintern's task was to lead the working class into action and this made it necessary to speak and act as a united body.

In 1928 the British Party had three representatives on the ECCI which comprised 60 members representing many countries; it also had two members among the 42 candidates to the ECCI and one on the International Control Commission numbering 22.[2]

British Party members as a whole were proud to belong to the Communist International. They believed it was an organisation which would one day lead the world working class to victory. Since the leading Marxists from every country were represented in it, they assumed that its decisions were more likely than not to be correct in any given situation; certainly they were wedded to the idea that the implementation of these decisions was their bounden duty. And until 1927 they had seen no reason to question this attitude. The British Party leaders had found discussions with other sections of the International enormously helpful; the British Party might be tiny, but some of the Parties involved were huge, like that of Germany; while the biggest Party of all, the Russian, had shown itself capable of leading the people to victory. The sense of belonging to such an international body was inspiring. Moreover the leaders of the British Party had always been fully consulted on issues of policy which affected them, and had found no major differences of opinion. It was this situation that was about to change.

First intimation that the ECCI wanted a different political line was contained in a telegram to the British Party which was sent off before the Party's Ninth Congress, but did not arrive until after it was over. The Ninth Congress was held at Salford on 8–9 October 1927; despite the witch-hunt from which the Party was suffering, no change in the attitude to the Labour Party emerged at this Congress. Thus a resolution was adopted calling for a struggle to bring down the Conservative government and its 'replacement by a Labour government pursuing a working class policy under the control of the labour movement.' And it demanded the adoption of 'a more definite Socialist programme' by the next Labour government.

But the Congress was no sooner over than the telegram arrived, followed by a letter from Bukharin, President of the Comintern, which made clear that the attitude of the parties to their respective social democratic parties was to be reconsidered. Two months later, on 15 December 1927, the Presidium of the ECCI held in Moscow a small meeting on the British situation at which it was argued that the demand of the British Party for the election of a Labour government was wrong, and should be replaced with a slogan for a 'revolutionary Labour government'.[3] Representing the British Party at this meeting were Albert Inkpin and William Gallacher. Inkpin was a member of the British Party's Secretariat, being in practice its chief administrator; a quiet, unassuming man, he had been Secretary of the British Socialist Party before the CP was founded. Gallacher was well known for his leadership of the shop stewards' movement on Clydeside during and after the First World War.

On his return, Gallacher gave the British Central Committee an account of the meeting. He alleged that on arriving in Moscow in November, he found that the British position had already been discussed and certain conclusions reached. Gallacher reported that these conclusions

> were thrown at us quite unexpectedly and had the appearance of coming from nowhere. . . The conclusions had the appearance to us of having no relation whatever to the situation actually in existence in Britain. . . We objected to the conclusions and had several discussions there as a consequence.[4]

The outcome was a special Commission set up during the Ninth Plenum of the ECCI in February 1928 to review the tactics of the British Party in relation to the Labour Party. In preparation for this event, the Central Committee of the British Party adopted a special Thesis.[5]

The Majority View

The British Party was facing a problem which was new at the time but has beset left-wing socialists and Marxists in Britain ever since. A Labour government had held office in 1924 and had made clear that, despite assertions that socialism was its ultimate goal, minor tinkering with the capitalist system was the most that could be expected of it. In such a situation, should the Communist Party continue to advocate support for Labour, while fighting to get it to change course? Or should it, on the contrary, withdraw any vestige of support, and come out as an opponent of these collaborators with capitalism, so as to emphasise that if the system was ever to be overthrown, the working-class movement must follow a different road? The Comintern was rapidly moving towards the second alternative strategy. The majority of the Central Committee of the CPGB wanted to continue with the first.

Any change in strategy would require new decisions on a host of practical questions, three of which seemed particularly urgent. They were 1) should the Communist Party, now being hounded out of the Labour Party, go on struggling to stay inside it? 2) In the coming general election, should the Communist Party go on calling for the election of a Labour government? 3) Should the Communist Party put up candidates against Labour candidates now that Communists could no longer be adopted by local Labour parties?

The answers to these questions as expressed in the Thesis of the British Central Committee were as follows: 1) Yes, the Party should go on fighting for the restoration of its rights within the Labour Party. 2) Yes, the Party should help to get another Labour government elected. 3) Therefore Communist candidates should only contest where a) they have contested before, or b) in double-member constituencies where there is only one Labour candidate, or c) if chosen by a disaffiliated Labour Party, or d) in constituencies so overwhelmingly proletarian that a split vote would not let in a capitalist candidate.

In support of these aims, the Thesis argued that the British Labour Party, despite its social-democratic programme and its 'completely putrified leadership' was not yet a social-democratic *party* in the accepted meaning of the term. It remained a loose federation for parliamentary purposes of reformist political parties and trade unions in which the latter had numerical predominance and a jealously preserved autonomy. And it quoted Lenin who, in 1920, had argued that the British Communist Party should try to stay inside the Labour Party:

It is not a Party in the ordinary sense of the word. It consists of the members of all the trade union organisations which means four million members. . . Such peculiar conditions prevail now in England that a political party which really desires to be and can be a revolutionary workers' party, nevertheless can be united with this strange workers' organisation of four millions of workers of half trade union and half political character, which is led by the bourgeoisie. Under these circumstances, it would be the greatest mistake for the best revolutionary elements not to do all in their power in order to remain in this party.[6]

Moreover, continued the Thesis, in 1920 Lenin had urged Communists to help a right-wing Labour government into office so that the masses should learn from experience what this meant.

To the argument that Lenin's advice was now obsolete because the workers had since then experienced a Labour government, the Thesis rejoined that the experience of the 1924 government was too short and incomplete to convince the masses that the Communists were right. Moreover, it asserted that 'objectively the situation in Britain in 1927 is not so revolutionary as in 1920.'

The Thesis had been drafted by John Ross Campbell who had become prominent as a left-wing socialist when still a shop assistant in Paisley before the First World War and had since made his name as editor of the Communist *Workers' Weekly*. He was much respected for what Gallacher described as his 'clear, logical reasoning'.[7]

On 7–9 January 1928, Campbell's Thesis was the subject of a three-day debate by the members of the Central Committee of the British Party. Campbell, who was well aware of the desire of the Comintern to change the line, said: 'I think we should examine the whole situation, and not be afraid of labels, and go for the correct policy though the heavens fall.' He admitted that the attempts of the Labour bureaucracy to smash the party had led some members to say 'Let's fight the b. . .s and have it out with them.' But, said Campbell, a leftist attitude meant once again becoming a 'socialist sect'. 'We might get a larger membership amongst proletarian intellectuals desirous of making the CP a socialist monastery, but we would lose our influence in the working class immediately.'[8]

But it transpired in the course of the discussion that some members of the Central Committee were far from convinced by Campbell's arguments and believed that the time was ripe for a

change of direction. The most formidable among these was Harry
Pollitt, national Secretary of the Minority Movement. Pollitt was
still working in the shipyard, and as a delegate from the
Boilermakers Union to Labour Party Annual Conferences had
borne much of the brunt of right-wing hostility; he was now about
to be banned from holding office by the Boilermakers Executive.
Early in 1927 he had disagreed with a decision of his Party colleagues
to retreat in face of the TUC's move to outlaw trades councils
affiliated to the Minority Movement, arguing that trades councils
should be urged to defy the TUC.[9] He now told the Central
Committee that when in Moscow the previous October (in
connection with a libel case over some seamen) he had had
discussions, including one with Stalin and Bukharin, who had
argued for a break with the existing policy. He asked why this break
had been initiated from outside. It was 'because we damped it down
at home.' But feeling had been growing, he said, against turning the
other cheek. The Labour Party was by this time a third bourgeois
party, but the workers would not express resentment against it
unless we gave them the opportunity. The miners in Fifeshire and
Lanarkshire had shown that the workers would vote against the old
bureaucracy if given a chance. He urged that the policy of
Communist affiliation to the Labour Party be abandoned and that
the Left Wing Movement be liquidated, because 'it stands as a barrier
between our party and the masses.'[10]

Even before Pollitt's statement, some other members had
expressed doubts about Campbell's Thesis. They included
Saklatvala, the Battersea MP, Helen Crawfurd from Scotland (one
of the Party's best known women members) and William ('Willie')
Allan who had just been elected in a ballot of Lanarkshire Miners as
their General Secretary. Later J.T. Murphy, formerly a toolmaker
and leader of the wartime shop stewards' movement in Sheffield,
also contended, like Pollitt, that the Labour Party was now the 'third
party of the bourgeoisie'.

But Campbell's Thesis received majority support. Those in
favour of it included Andrew Rothstein, one of the Party's leading
intellectuals, who said that Lenin had believed that affiliation to the
Labour Party provided the Party with a link with the masses ('he had
in mind what the working masses thought about it, not what we, as
Communists, thought about it'); T.A. Jackson who had come to
left-wing politics when a printer's apprentice and was well-known

as an orator and writer, ('what on earth is the use of us mistaking our own subjective emotions for the revolutionary feelings of the proletariat?'); the Scottish veteran, Bob Stewart ('if we are placed in a position whereby we seem to be helping Baldwin to retain power it is going to put us into an invidious position from which it will take years to recover'). Wal Hannington, the leader of the NUWM, Bill Rust, and Walter Tapsell, both of whom represented the Young Communist League on the Central Committee, and Tom Bell, foundation member and iron-moulder by trade were also among those who supported the Thesis and it was adopted by 17 votes to 6.[11]

The Minority View

Pollitt, however, decided to put in a minority statement – indeed he drafted one and signed it on 24 January 1928. It was short and simple. It stated that, whereas in 1920 the Labour Party programme still embraced many working-class demands and its practice allowed affiliated parties to have their own policy, by 1928 it had become a third capitalist party, had 'surrendered socialism', i.e. given up socialism, while the introduction of disciplinary measures meant there was no longer opportunity for affiliated parties to put forward separate programmes. So he proposed that the Party should stop trying to affiliate to the Labour Party, should refuse to vote for Labour candidates unless they agreed to support the Party's policy, and should put up candidates against leaders like MacDonald and Henderson. The Left Wing Movement should be liquidated and left-wingers in disaffiliated Labour parties be invited to join the party. 'Whilst I do not think we could get them all, I believe we could get a good proportion.'[12]

But Pollitt was at that time distrustful of his own ability as a theoretician – no doubt that was one reason why he paid so much heed to the opinions of the Comintern leaders – so he sent a copy of his statement to R.P. Dutt, asking him to draft an alternative Thesis.

Dutt had not attended Central Committee meetings for some time because he was suffering from TB of the spine and was temporarily living in Brussels. From there he sent regular letters to the Committee analysing the political situation and giving his views on what should be done. Unlike most of the Central Committee of the Party, who were skilled industrial workers in origin, Dutt was an intellectual, half-Indian and half-Swedish by birth, who had gained a double first at Oxford. In 1922 he had been one of the founders of the magazine *Labour Monthly* in which, by means of his regular 'Notes of the Month', he had rapidly established a reputation as a Marxist political commentator of outstanding ability.

Now, on receiving both the majority Thesis and Pollitt's document he proceeded to draw up a much more elaborate alternative Thesis, and sent this back to Pollitt. 'You'll will find the statement follows your points' he wrote in an accompanying letter dated 25 January.[13]

On one point only he disagreed with Pollitt. 'You can't say "liquidate the National Left Wing" as a slogan,' he wrote, because 'it's like murdering a baby'; a left-wing fraction was necessary in a social-democratic party; and finally because the Party could not go to left-wingers and say 'please liquidate'. On receiving Dutt's document Pollitt withdrew his own, and put in Dutt's instead. It was entitled 'Alternative Proposals to the Thesis of the Central Committee' and was signed jointly by Pollitt and Dutt.[14]

The document challenged the analysis on which the majority Thesis was based. It disagreed with the assertion that the situation in 1927 was 'not so revolutionary' as in 1920, saying that this failed to recognise the significance of events such as Black Friday and the General Strike and 'the further arising Left wave now visible, all leading to the continuous *revolutionisation* of the British working class.' Indeed the experience of the mass movement and the exposure of the reformist leadership 'makes the present stage of revolutionary development *higher* in the total line of development of the British working class than the temporary boom point of 1920.' (This argument – that the working class was becoming more revolutionary – was not one used in Pollitt's original document. It was, however, one that was to be repeated over and over again in the coming months, particularly by those who were furthest away from the actual struggle.)

Dutt's document contended that the Labour Party was in process of being transformed into a reformist machine. It therefore proposed that in the next election the Communist Party should *not* assist the official Labour Party leadership to return to office but should 'lead the revolutionary working-class fight in open opposition to both the capitalist reaction and to the official Labour Party leadership.' The maximum number of Communist candidates should contest, and where there was no Communist candidate and the Labour candidate refused the Party's united front demands, the Party should call on the workers to 'refuse to vote'. Once the independent fight was launched said the statement, the basis for trying to affiliate to the Labour Party would cease to exist.

One other member of the Central Committee put in minority proposals. This was J.T. Murphy, who also urged abandonment of the old line in favour of mobilising opposition to the Labour Party. But he advocated something which no other member wanted; the transformation of the National Left Wing Movement into a new national anti-capitalist party.

The Ninth Plenum and After

In practice, Murphy's document hardly figured in the debate at the Ninth Plenum held in Moscow in February 1928; the real argument was between the supporters of the majority Thesis and those of the Dutt-Pollitt alternative.[15] The main spokesman for the majority Thesis was J.R. Campbell, supported by William Gallacher. Neither Dutt nor Pollitt was present, but they had a spokesman for their alternative policy in Robin Page Arnot, a man who, like Dutt, had had a university education. (He had been one of the Communist leaders imprisoned in 1925, but had been released in time to play a leading role in the North East Joint Strike Committee. Before that he was secretary of the Labour Research Department and had worked closely with A.J. Cook of the Miners' Federation.)

Representatives of a number of Communist parties from various countries took part in the discussion on the British situation at the Ninth Plenum. Campbell and Gallacher fought a tenacious and skilful rearguard action in defence of their majority Thesis, but they were up against a view widespread in the international movement: that since, in all countries, the social-democratic parties had unmasked themselves as bodies endeavouring to hold back the workers' struggle, it was now necessary to come out against them so as to draw the workers away from their influence and into the direct struggle against the capitalist class. 'The problems of the British labour movement are the centre of the problems of the international Labour movement' said 'Ercoli' (or Togliatti) the Italian leader.

If Campbell and Gallacher had represented a united Central Committee they might well have defended their Thesis to the bitter end and, if defeated, have taken the matter to the coming World Congress. Campbell himself had initially suggested that they should 'go for the correct policy though the heavens fall.' But they faced the fact that there was a formidable minority, headed by Pollitt and Dutt, and including Arnot and Murphy, who disagreed with their Thesis. Once the rest of the Central Committee realised that the minority had the backing of the leading figures in the CI, the minority might soon turn into a majority, not so much because the ECCI had the constitutional right to insist on a certain line, but because of a deep-rooted conviction that the collective opinion of the world's leading Marxists was more likely to be correct than not. For Campbell and Gallacher to have maintained their stand would, in these circumstances, have split the British Party. The upshot was that they retreated and agreed to a resolution which appeared on the surface to be a compromise but which, in reality, supported the change in policy demanded by both the CI and the Dutt-Pollitt proposals. Thus after stressing the need to 'adopt clearer and sharper tactics of opposition' to the Labour leaders, it laid down that the slogan in favour of a Labour government be abandoned and replaced by the call for a 'Revolutionary Workers' Government' and it asserted that the Labour leaders were endeavouring to convert Labour organisations into 'auxiliary apparatuses of the bourgeoisie', stating that it was 'absolutely necessary' to put up candidates against the dominant leaders of the Labour Party.

On two crucial questions, however, the Dutt-Pollitt proposals were not accepted. First the resolution laid down that it was 'inexpedient as yet' to abandon the slogan of Communist affiliation to the Labour Party. And second, the proposal to urge the workers to abstain from voting Labour where no Communist or left-wing candidate was standing was not adopted. And indeed, in view of all that happened later, it should be emphasized that throughout the sittings of the British Commission, the majority was against the tactic of abstention.

When the results of the Plenum were reported back to the Central Committee over the weekend 17–18 March 1928, one member, T.A. Jackson, expressed his doubts; the new policy, he said, contained the possibility of extreme danger. Up to now we have drawn a distinction between the leadership of the Labour Party and the Labour Party itself as an expression of proletarian struggle, potential if not actual. We have claimed our right to be with the rank and file in the struggle against the leadership. We have on that basis built up the whole of left-wing policy, and it is now changed.

It followed, he said, that the Communist Party would now go forward to oppose the Labour Party as such. 'The change could not be greater.' 'I have expressed my opinion,' he said towards the end of his statement 'and will submit loyally to the decisions if they are passed.'[16]

They were passed, unanimously, after some members had welcomed them and others had accepted their correctness, though expressing concern about how the decisions would be implemented in practice.[17] Some clearly foresaw the difficulties that would face them in this respect.

What nobody foresaw was the rapid development of the new policy and the extreme lengths to which it would be carried. The Plenum of February 1928, during which the first somewhat tentative and very confused decisions were taken, largely around the issue of electoral tactics, was only the start of a process which was to gather momentum. By the summer of 1928 when the Sixth World Congress took place, the new policy had been elaborated and laid down as a guide for the parties of every European country, and electoral tactics were only a minor aspect of a whole strategy. In the resolution adopted there, not only was right-wing social democracy denounced but left-wing social democracy was also attacked on the grounds that in carrying out a counter-revolutionary policy 'the left wing is essential for the subtle deception of the workers.' Thus the very people who had hitherto been regarded as left-wing allies of Communists were now characterised as 'the most dangerous faction in the social democratic parties.' At the same time 'social fascist tendencies' among social democrats were attacked.[19]

At the Tenth Plenum of the CI held in the summer of 1929, the change in policy went further still. By this time not only the Labour Party but the trade unions were classified as enemy organisations – part of the apparatus of capitalism. Thus at the 11th Congress of the British Party in the autumn of 1929, the 'reformist' trade unions were characterised as 'social-fascist agencies of capitalism'.[20]

Originally, the decisions of the Ninth Plenum were accepted by most British Communists as a move to assert the Communist Party's independence and to stop 'trailing behind' the right-wing Labour Party policies. No one at that time envisaged that the new line would involve treating the unions as enemy organisations – least of all Pollitt, who had been one of the members most convinced of the need for a change of attitude towards the Labour Party. And, as will be shown, when the new approach to trade-union work was advocated, the British Party dragged its feet as long as it could, and at the end of 1931 was the first Party to insist on a reversal of this aspect of the policy.

The new line – which was misnamed 'Class against Class' – was a disaster in every country, and the question that requires examination is how it ever came to be adopted by the Comintern. Its basis was an analysis of the economic situation which was in the main sound. According to this, there was developing in all capitalist countries a trend towards rationalisation, the growth of trusts and a tendency for these to merge with the State. The reverse side of this process was the more ruthless exploitation of the workers, the closing down of numerous enterprises, with chronic unemployment on a scale never before witnessed. In most European countries social-democratic parties held the commanding position as leaders of the organised workers. They preached socialism, but everywhere were in practice collaborating with the capitalist class. Several countries had by this time experienced social-democratic governments; they had brought socialism no nearer, but had strengthened the capitalist framework, while the workers had been betrayed.

Such was the view taken of the objective situation by the leaders of the Comintern; there was little in it that was not in accordance with the facts. But the assumptions made on the basis of this analysis were, as it turned out, unfounded.

The new line assumed that, as the economic situation worsened, there would be an automatic intensification of the class struggle. It assumed that industrial workers inevitably respond to attack with increasing militancy. Yet history has shown many times that this is not always the response to an employers' offensive; if there is any great degree of unemployment, wage cuts and speed-up are just as likely to create divisions and despondency. In the two years that followed the introduction of the new line such a mood was in the ascendant. Despite this, instead of examining the facts – the first requirement for anyone claiming to be a Marxist – the alleged 'radicalisation of the workers' was elevated to an article of faith, it became customary to refer to 'the rising revolutionary upsurge' and any Communist who failed to notice this 'upsurge' was likely to be accused of 'tailing behind the masses'.

Even more damaging than these false assumptions about the mood of the masses were those concerning the role of social democracy. The social-democratic parties began to be regarded as monolithic parties of reaction. The divergent tendencies within them were ignored. Instead of concentrating on the *policies* of the leaders and trying to win rank-and-file support for a change in direction, social-democratic parties, and indeed, in the end, the 'reformist' unions, were treated as a single, unified reactionary bloc. And this attitude, in turn, led to another: a denial that social-democratic parties and 'reformist' unions could ever be different. It led to a fixed belief that, because a worker's organisation in practice at some given moment fulfills a role supportive of the capitalist state, or is used on some occasion or in some capacity to further the interests, not of its own members, but of the ruling class, this is its true function, and it will continue as an instrument of the capitalist class for all time.

As we have seen, the new line was initially imposed by the Comintern; whose influence within that body was primarily responsible for its introduction remains obscure. Some writers have suggested that it reflected the Russian domestic situation, since it came at a time when the kulaks were being liquidated and the new line was officially known as 'Class against Class'. But the truth is that the name of the new line had almost nothing to do with its content.

Most writers tend to associate the introduction of the new line with the rise of Stalin. There is certainly evidence that Stalin agreed with it; there is little that he was responsible for initiating it. And the fact is that a line of extreme sectarianism is one to which Marxists have been prone ever since Karl Marx himself fought against it. When under pressure, an isolationist and ultra-left posture has often been the outcome. In the late 1920s it had become clear that the previous strategy had failed. The majority of the workers accepted the leadership of the social democrats, who had betrayed them and in every country were hounding the Communists as enemies, in practice, defeating them. In such a situation the symptoms of what Lenin once referred to as 'Left-Wing Communism: an infantile disorder' are only too likely to appear. It has been proved many times in the half century since 1928 that you do not need a Stalin for this disorder to reveal itself.

The influence of Stalin had certainly begun to be felt in the Comintern by 1928, but it manifested itself less in the line adopted than in the methods of carrying it through. For there can be no doubt that from the Sixth World Congress onwards, the approach of those at Comintern headquarters was far more authoritarian, the dealings with affiliated parties more dictatorial, while heresy-hunting began to be practiced, instead of arriving at policy by the free exchange of views. Despite the rule in the constitution that World Congresses should be held every two years, it was seven years before the next one took place. This meant that if a Party wanted to challenge aspects of the new line its opportunities were very limited.

[1] International Press Correspondence, referred to below as *Inprecorr*, 28 November 1928, p.1600.

[2] *Inprecorr*, 21 November 1928, p.1547. At the Sixth World Congress in 1928 the British representatives elected were: *ECCI*, J.R. Campbell, Tom Bell, William Rust; *Candidates to ECCI*, Harry Pollitt, Arthur Horner; *Control Commission*, J.T. Murphy.

[3] JK folder 8.

[4] JK folder 11, no.6.

[5] See *Communist Policy in Great Britain*, The Report of the British Commission of the Ninth Plenum of the Comintern, 1928.

[6] *Communist Policy in Great Britain* p.138.

[7] William Gallacher, *Revolt on the Clyde*, London 1948 (reprinted 1978), p.16.

[8] JK folder 11, no.2.

[9] JK folder 10, no.1.

[10] JK folder 11, no.2.

[11] JK folder 11, no.2. Also '1929 Documents': letter to Locals, see p.173 18 November 1929, loc. cit.

[12] JK folder 11, no. 5.

[13] Dutt correspondence. CP Archive.

[14] *Communist Policy in Great Britain*, p.153.

[15] The report of the debate is in *Communist Policy in Great Britain*.

[16] JK folder 11, no.6.

[17] See '1929 Documents': letter to Locals 18 November 1929, loc. cit.

[18] *Inprecorr*, 31 December 1928, p.1754.

[19] *Inprecorr*, 4 September 1928, p.1039.

[20] See foreword, signed 'W.T.', to *Resolutions of the 11th Congress*, pamphlet, n.d.

CHAPTER 3

The Impact of 'Class Against Class' (1928–29)

It quite soon became clear that, however convincing the new line sounded in theory, in practice it raised appalling difficulties. In fact, the attempt to implement it threw up so many contradictions, that for nearly two years the members of the British Party were embroiled in argument.

The New Attitude to the Labour Party

According to the new policy, the Labour Party was in process of becoming an 'auxiliary apparatus of the bourgeoisie'. For some Communists the logical response was to treat it as such. They advocated dropping the demand for Communist affiliation to the Labour Party and opposition to payment of the political levy; they argued that trade unions should be urged to disaffiliate from the Labour Party, and that voters should be told *not* to vote Labour in elections.

Most Party members did not react in this way, and indeed the resolution adopted at the Ninth Plenum had stopped short of such extremes. However, the practical implications of the new line were in constant debate on the Central Committee whose members, for the first time, found themselves seriously at odds with one another.

In April 1928 a memorandum prepared by J.T. Murphy was issued to Districts proposing that the fight for Communist affiliation to the Labour Party be continued, but converted into a 'political offensive' against the Labour Party.[1] Not surprisingly the rank and file of the Party failed to find this approach convincing, and the London District Committee responded with a resolution urging that the affiliation fight be abandoned, a view once again supported by Harry Pollitt at a Central Committee meeting in June 1928. But Campbell and Gallacher both urged continuation of the 'offensive' fight for affiliation and, when a vote was taken, the meeting was split down the middle, 9 for and 9 against, as follows:

For continuing the fight for affiliation: E.H. Brown, Campbell, Gallacher, Horner, Inkpin, Joss, Loeber, Rust, Tapsell.
Against: Allan, Crawfurd, Elsbury, Glading, Hannington, Pollitt, Murphy, Watkins, Wilson.[2]

The issue of the political levy aroused even greater controversy. A method whereby trade unions raised political funds, this levy was used to pay the affiliation fee to the Labour Party, as well as for other political purposes, including financial support for trade-union sponsored Labour MPs. Since the 1927 Trade Disputes Act, the political levy could be collected only from those who decided to 'contract in' and the Communist Party had been urging all workers to do so. Now the Ninth Plenum called for a campaign for *local control* of the political levy. However, the Central Committee felt obliged to warn Party members that if such local control were arbitrarily decided on by a trade union branch, it could expect legal action from its national executive for misappropriation of union funds.[3] Obviously, the campaign for local control was not likely to get very far, and immediately some Party members suggested that trade unionists should be urged *not* to pay the political levy. In the end, the Central Committee set up a commission to consider the matter.

The most acute disagreement arose over the attitude to Labour candidates in by-elections. On this, Pollitt again argued that if the Labour candidate rejected the Party's united front demands, electors should be urged *not* to vote for him or her. Only three other members of the Central Committee agreed with him. But when it was moved that the vote be given 'against the Baldwin government as a general line' they were again split 9 against 9.[4]

The isolating implications of the new policy were dramatically revealed over the Cook-Maxton Manifesto, which, as explained in the first chapter, came out in June 1928, denouncing the Labour leaders for making peace with capitalism and for expending energy on 'crushing everybody who dares to remain true to the ideals of the movement.' A.J. Cook, Secretary of the Miners' Federation, had played an outstanding part as a left-wing miners' leader, and had always been regarded by the Communist Party as one of its closest allies. And, ironically, the Party had played a major role in bringing this Manifesto into being. It had started with conversations between

Gallacher and the two ILP leaders, Maxton and Wheatley. Gallacher had put Maxton in touch with A.J. Cook, and had participated in all the subsequent discussions between the two, together with other Communist Party representatives. As Murphy told the Central Committee, the Cook-Maxton Manifesto 'came out as a result of our pressure.'[5] But, by the time it appeared, the new line had been introduced. This impelled Party headquarters to issue a statement which, while welcoming the Manifesto, nevertheless criticised it as 'weak and sentimental' and challenged Maxton and Cook to state specifically what they stood for, saying that unless they did this

> their declaration becomes nothing more than the effort to create a pseudo-left opposition in the parliamentary Labour Party and trade union bureaucracy, resulting in diverting the workers from the real struggle. We warn the workers against such a manoeuvre.[6]

Even this did not satisfy some Party members who were arguing that the attitude to left-wing leaders should no longer be one of 'critical support' but of 'ruthless exposure'.

By November 1928, opinion on the Central Committee had crystallised on certain issues. Another Party Congress was to be held in January 1929 in Bermondsey, and draft resolutions for it were brought before the Central Committee on 18–19 November. It was decided, this time unanimously, that the demand for Communist Party affiliation to the Labour Party be dropped, and that trade unions be urged to disaffiliate from the Labour Party. It was agreed by 15 votes to 2 that workers be encouraged to continue payment of the political levy with the aim of gaining local control of it in due course, and by 13 votes to 4 to continue support for the National Left Wing Movement.[7]

These draft resolutions were sent to the Comintern for comment, but no reply was received until just before Congress opened, when it emerged that the ECCI did not yet approve of its left turn being followed to its logical conclusion, and was opposed to both the decision to drop the Communist affiliation demand and to the recommendation to trade unions to disaffiliate from the Labour Party. In practice, most of the resolution on relations with the Labour Party had already been withdrawn owing to an over-full agenda, and affiliation to the Labour Party was not discussed at the Congress though a vague statement about 'the necessity of preparing the Party for the abandonment of the affiliation tactic' was incorporated in the main Thesis.[9]

When the Congress opened, J.R. Campbell was in the chair. 'We know that some of our enemies may be speculating upon divisions in our ranks,' he said in his opening speech. 'We have had a sharp, vigorous and on the whole good humoured discussion.' As the Congress proceeded, however, the good humour wore thin. The delegates were only too well aware that membership was falling, and their frustration was apparent. Yet no voice was raised against the new line; on the contrary, the leadership's hesitation in applying it was held to blame.

There were so many accusations of 'lack of self-criticism' that Harry Pollitt, the member of the Central Committee most convinced of the correctness of the new policy, was moved to protest. 'Don't let Congress become slaves of phrases' he said. 'Self-criticism is only useful when it is accompanied by practical suggestions'.[9]

The atmosphere at Congress impelled T.A. Jackson to write a lighthearted article in the February 1929 issue of *Communist Review*, observing that for most comrades, self-criticism appeared to mean taking it for granted that the centre was bound to be 'right' (and therefore wrong) and any opposition to it necessarily 'left' (and therefore right). He poked fun at 'the perspiring concern of certain comrades to root out (or more usually to "liquidate") the "right danger" – a "danger" that, to use their own jargon they "fail to concretise with any sharpness"'. He suggested that the 'next task' of the Party was to liquidate the process of 'Inprecorrisation' and thereby restore plain English and common sense to their rightful place. This article was shortly afterwards the subject of some controversy.

The Sunday of the Congress weekend was spent entirely in closed session debating two of the most complicated issues: the political levy and the Left Wing Movement. On the first of these, the policy submitted by the leadership was that it was 'not expedient' to abandon payment of the political levy, so Communists must oppose its use for reactionary purposes, and demand local control of it. But the Party must at the same time avoid creating the illusion that it was possible to reform the Labour Party and force the leaders to fight: 'we continue to pay the political levy only in order more effectively to work for the break-down of this bourgeois party.'[10] Speaking of the eventual necessity for the withdrawal of the trade unions from the Labour Party, it held that it would be premature immediately to place this demand on the agenda of trade-union conferences. In the event the recommendation to continue support for payment of the political levy was carried by 100 votes to 22.

On this issue the decision of the Central Committee was upheld. This was not to be the case with the other contentious issue, that of the Left Wing Movement. Here the leadership's recommendation for continued support of the Movement was opposed by Idris Cox, the young South Wales organiser, Vice-Chairman of the disaffiliated Maestag Labour Party, and a former miner. He was in favour of the liquidation of the Left Wing Movement saying:

> 'It is quite a new proposition to me, that in order to bring sympathetic workers into the Communist Party we must build a special lane for them . . . have a kind of preparatory school in the form of a National Left Wing Movement before they can become members of the party.[9]

He was supported by none other than Ralph Bond, secretary of the National Left Wing Movement itself, who stressed that the majority of people in the Movement were by now no longer inside the Labour Party, but in disaffiliated parties. Therefore the Movement had ceased to serve a useful purpose. No fewer than 43 speakers wanted their say on this issue, and when the vote was taken, those who favoured disbanding the Movement carried the day against the recommendation of the Central Committee by 55 votes to 52.

On the issue of the election of the new Central Committee (CC), the leaders made a tactical blunder which brought them into conflict with the Comintern. The usual procedure was for the retiring Central Committee to recommend a limited list of nominees and then ask for further nominations from the floor. On this occasion the CC put forward 24 names and as usual invited further nominations. But two former members of the Central Committee were omitted from the list of 24. They were Robin Page Arnot and William Rust, both of whom were representing the British Party at Comintern headquarters in Moscow. The Central Committee had excluded them on the ostensible grounds that their international commitments prevented them from participating in Central Committee sessions. Just before the Congress the Political Bureau had proposed that in view of the expense, neither Rust nor Arnot should journey to London to attend it. However, both Arnot and Rust arrived at the Congress and protested at the way they had been treated. Rust who had previously been secretary of the Young Communist League had been elected to the ECCI at the Sixth World Congress.

> I contend that it is unheard of in the history of the Comintern that a comrade who is elected to the Executive of the Comintern should be deemed unfit . . . to be a member of the Central Committee of his own Party,

he said. He told Congress he wanted his name to go forward for re-election. Arnot associated himself with Rust's remarks. However, when the election took place, Arnot secured re-election to the Central Committee, but Rust failed to win enough votes.[9]

Rust returned to Moscow. With him was a member of the German Party, Lenz, who had attended the British Congress as representatives of the Comintern. He gave a very adverse report of the Congress to the ECCI Political Secretariat, which thereupon held an inquest. For this, which took place in February 1929, three representatives of the British Party were present. They were Tom Bell, Harry Pollitt, and the man on the spot, William Rust.

Tom Bell expressed his disagreement with – and indeed resentment at – Lenz's criticisms of the British Congress. He was supported by Pollitt who said that the Congress had been the best in the history of the Party; that the delegates had been overwhelmingly workers from the localities and factories and that no single delegate had dissented from the new line. But Rust then went into the attack, saying that he agreed with the Lenz report of the Congress and its view that the attitude of the Central Committee had been one of 'veiled resistance' to the decisions of the Comintern.[11]

The upshot was a 'closed letter' dated 27 February from the ECCI Presidium to the Central Committee of the CPGB in which were listed numerous criticisms, many of them similar to those made by Rust. It said that Congress had 'disclosed serious deficiencies in the leadership which made a number of mistakes, among them right mistakes'; that active Party members were more prepared for the change in line than the Central Committee which had shown an absence of self-criticism and a conciliatory attitude to the right danger. It said that the reservation concerning Arnot and Rust 'may be interpreted as a demonstration against the Comintern.' It denounced the 'philistine twaddle' about self-criticism in the article in the *Communist Review* by T.A. Jackson, and ended with a series of exhortations to put an end to vacillation.[12] The letter was ·discussed at the Central Committee meeting on 23 March 1929 and caused further divisions. In the end it was decided to distribute it to the Districts.

There was a much more crucial matter on the agenda: the attitude of the Party to the Labour candidates in those areas where Communists were not standing in the coming General Election. Discussion of this matter had been avoided at the Congress. Delegates had merely been reminded that in April 1928 the Central Committee had rejected a proposal in favour of abstentionism.[13] Moreover, abstentionism had not been agreed to at the Ninth Plenum, despite its advocacy in the Dutt-Pollitt document.

Now on this last occasion, though neither Dutt nor Pollitt was present, Bob Stewart advocated abstention, saying that at the time of the Ninth Plenum, the transformation of the Labour Party into a bourgeois party had not been completed, but since then there had been the 'loyalty' resolution at the 1928 conference. Referring to the capitulation of the trade-union bureaucracy to Mondism, the imperialist speeches of Labour statesmen, the hostility to strikes, the sabotage of the unemployed miners' march, Stewart forecast that the 'next Labour government will serve capitalism just as faithfully as the Tories have done.' In such circumstances 'it would be fatal for the future of our Party to encourage any illusions as to the character and the role of the Labour Party, or to give any support whatever to it.'[14]

Stewart was answered by Campbell who warned the Committee against being stampeded by a 'right danger bogey'. He said that they all agreed that indignation against the Labour Party was justified but indignation was sometimes a poor basis on which to build a political line. The ,tactics of struggle against the Labour camp must be different from those against the Tory camp. He believed that if the Party advocated no votes for Labour candidates, it would be creating a barrier between itself and the left-wing workers.

After a prolonged discussion, Campbell was defeated, and Stewart's recommendation for abstentionism was adopted by 18 votes to 5 as follows:

For abstentionism: Stewart, Gallacher, Hannington, Cox, Kerrigan, Marjorie Pollitt, Ferguson, Joss, Allan, Wilson, Beth Turner, Crawfurd, Murphy, E.H. Brown, Tapsell, Watkins, Webb, Glading.

Against: Campbell, Rothstein, Aitken, Inkpin, Bright.[14]

So the Communist Party went into the General Election armed with a Manifesto which said:

> The Labour Party is the third capitalist party. It is now no longer possible for the Communist Party or the trade unions to bring pressure to bear on the Labour Party from within. It is a completely disciplined capitalist party.

The General Election took place on 31 May 1929. There was an unprecedented shift to Labour which emerged for the first time as the largest party in the House, having received 37.1 per cent of the vote. Clearly trade unionists in great numbers now looked upon the Labour Party as *their* party; they might grumble about it, but Labour was 'us' and other parties 'them'. This close identification with 'Labour' on the part of manual workers was relatively new at the time, but was to prevail throughout the ensuing decades.

For the Communist Party, the election was a major set-back and Campbell's warnings were justified. The Party had put up only 25 candidates and their total vote was 50,000, averaging 5.3 per cent of the poll in the areas where they stood. Even Saklatvala, who had been MP for North Battersea for many years, failed to retain his seat when opposed by an official Labour candidate. Meanwhile, the advice to voters *not* to support Labour in the areas where no Communist was standing was to be held against the Party by left-wingers for years to come.

The Attitude to the Trade Unions

For the whole of 1928 the majority of the Central Committee resisted pressure for a changed attitude to the trade unions. This pressure came in the main from the Red International of Labour Unions, an organisation set up in 1921 to which the Minority Movement was affiliated.

The guiding aim of the Party and the Minority Movement had been to build up the existing unions, while working to win them away from policies of class collaboration and so transform them into organisations genuinely fighting in the interests of the working class. But the new idea emerging from RILU circles was that it was no longer possible to change existing unions, since they were fast becoming part of the capitalist apparatus. This meant that the Party and the Minority Movement must develop 'independent leadership' on the factory floor which would, when the time was ripe, lead to the creation of alternative revolutionary trade unions; unless and until this happened, work must continue within the 'reformist' unions, but only in order to expose the treacherous leaders and win over the rank and file to the new revolutionary trade union opposition.

This attitude to the trade unions was not an inevitable corollary of the changed approach to social-democratic parties. Indeed, the chief initiator and supporter of the new line in Britain, Harry Pollitt, had thought the ultimate aim should be to win the existing trade unions to transfer allegiance from the Labour Party to the Communist Party. Though the relationship of the unions to the Labour Party had been discussed at the Ninth Plenum in February 1928, almost nothing had been said about the role of the Party in the trade union field. Had it been suggested at this Plenum that the way forward was the creation of revolutionary unions, it is safe to say that the British delegation would have disagreed unanimously. Nevertheless, shortly after the February Plenum, the British Central Committee received the first signs and portents of danger in the form of a report-back from the Fourth Congress of the RILU in April 1928.

The report was given by Arthur Horner, leader of the Miners' Minority Movement and already a well-known figure in the South Wales Miners' Federation. He said that at the RILU Congress, the General Secretary, a Russian named Lozovsky, had shown 'a tendency to treat all reformist unions as having actually become units of capitalist production.' 'We had to fight against a tendency to drive us into setting up independent unions,' he said.[15] He added that the Minority Movement was criticised for its 'inferiority complex' and that British delegates had been urged to drop the idea that the MM must be regarded as 'a permeating force and never an independent organisation.'

On the whole Lozovsky's efforts were resisted successfully by the British at this Congress. The statement adopted there on the 'Tasks of the British Minority Movement' set out a policy which differed little from the previous one, though couched in somewhat more strident language. Thus it talked of 'transforming the trade unions into effective weapons of class struggle', stressing the need to campaign for changes in leadership and to prepare MM members for election to positions of responsibility within the unions. And it called on the MM to fight for the slogan 'No splitting the unions'.[16] This continued to be the line at the Minority Movement's Annual Conference held in August 1928 – a conference which showed that despite the attempts of the trade union leaders to destroy it, the MM was still very much alive. Indeed, the number of trade-union organisations represented (287 trade union branches and 19 trades councils) was hardly less than that of the previous year.

Meanwhile, at the Sixth World Congress of the Comintern held in Moscow in July 1928, no decisions had been taken which would necessitate a change in trade-union strategy for the British Party. However, some members of the British delegation, after talks with members of the Russian trade unions, had returned to Britain with changed ideas, having become convinced that the fight to transform the existing unions into organs of genuine struggle was no longer the way forward. This led to a protest from the British Political Bureau to the Comintern; in a statement signed on their behalf by J.R. Campbell, the latter complained that some members of the British delegation had 'come back with what can only be described as a new union complex. . . This is complicating our work at the present time.'[17]

At a discussion on trade-union strategy at a Central Committee meeting in September 1928 Campbell referred to the 'loose talk . . . about the time arriving when the Party must contemplate the organisation of Red Unions in this country – that is absurd.'[18] E.H. Brown said he was perturbed at the discussions on Red Unions at Birmingham and Bradford District Committee meetings: 'We must make clear that this is *not* our policy.' Harry Pollitt, still Honorary Secretary of the Minority Movement, said that the Party must try to get unorganised workers to join the existing trade unions and must stop workers dropping out because the leadership was rotten. Campbell wound up by stressing that the Ninth Plenum had not changed the Party's trade union policy. In America, he said, organising those not in trade unions could mean setting up new unions, but that did not apply to Britain.

The British Party had already refused to implement a proposal for the formation of a new seamen's union. The National Union of Seamen, which had long been involved in strike-breaking activities, was about to be expelled from the TUC, and it was known that when that happened the existing Transport and General Workers Union intended to set up a seamen's section. On the recommendation of Pollitt, the Political Bureau decided they were opposed to the creation of a 'revolutionary seamen's union' and decided that their aim should be the formation of a seamen's section of the Minority Movement. This decision was adhered to despite continued pressure from the RILU.[19]

The Central Committee's trade union policy was re-asserted in a Thesis put before the Tenth Party Congress in January 1929. Stating that the TUC General Council's campaign alleged 'disruption' was designed to 'provoke splits from our side', the Thesis warned of the danger of 'dropping trade union work because of the objective difficulties which that work is encountering'; another danger was the tendency to 'talk about the necessity for establishing new unions'. 'This policy,' said the Thesis, 'would only lead to the isolation of the revolutionary workers from the great mass of the organised workers and play into the hands of the bureaucracy.'[20]

Just after this Congress came a new development which helped to persuade some Party members that a change in trade union policy was desirable. It concerned the Scottish miners. Here, as already mentioned in the first chapter, Communists had been elected to official positions in two county unions, Fife and Lanarkshire. But the unseated former secretary of the Fife Union, a right-winger named Adamson, responded to his defeat by forming a new breakaway union in August 1928. In February 1929 this breakaway union was recognised by the Scottish Executive of the Miners' Federation in place of the existing Fife Union in which Communists had won positions. Moreover, the Scottish Executive continued to refuse recognition to the elected Communist officials in the Lanarkshire County Union, including its Secretary, William Allan. The initial response of the Communists to Adamson's right-wing breakaway had been to call a conference and set up a 'Save the Union Council'. But official recognition of the breakaway forced their hand. In April 1929, following another 'Save the Union Council' conference, the United Mineworkers of Scotland was formed with Willie Allan as Secretary. The whole affair appeared to confirm the argument growing up in the Party that the trade-union bureaucracy would inevitably split the unions if their control was threatened, and this would mean setting up new unions.

The formation of the UMS was inevitable. Much more controversial was the creation of the United Clothing Workers Union in London. This arose out of a strike by members of the Tailor and Garment Workers Union at Rego Clothiers in Edmonton in North London. The Executive of the union refused to make this strike official, and after holding an investigation, dismissed from his post a leading London organiser, Sam Elsbury, who had supported the strike. Elsbury was a co-opted member of the Communist Party Central Committee. The London Executive of the Union refused to accept his dismissal, and convened a meeting of the London membership, where a proposal to form a new union was enthusiastically adopted.

Unlike the UMS, the establishment of the UCWU aroused misgivings among the Party leadership. Pollitt was abroad at the time, and said on his return that had he been present he would have opposed its formation.[21] In fact, Elsbury was one of the Party members who favoured the 'new union' idea; he had early on conveyed the impression that splits in the union should be expected and welcomed.[22] The new union was quickly involved in further strikes which were complicated by inter-union quarrels and, in the autumn of 1929, Elsbury attacked the Party leadership for 'blowing hot and cold'; by December he had resigned from the Party and was thereupon expelled.

By the late spring of 1929 many of the younger Party members had become convinced that the perspective of *changing* the existing unions was a dangerous illusion. Thus John Mahon wrote about the new stage in which the reformist leadership had 'definitely and irrevocably' become part of the capitalist apparatus and had begun 'to transform the trade unions into organisations indistinguishable from company unions.[23]More and more Party members were ceasing to be active in the existing unions, and were even leaving them.

A document on 'Strike Strategy and Tactics' adopted at an RILU conference held in Strasburg in January 1929 had considerable influence, though initially distributed to a limited circle – it was not published in Britain until 1931. It sought to draw lessons from various strikes, in particular one in Poland in 1928 where the leaders of the official trade unions and of the social–democratic party had played a strike-breaking role. In this document, the need for 'independent leadership' to replace that of the 'reformist traitors' was stressed. It was considered no longer desirable to recruit unorganised workers into existing trade unions; on the contrary, the emphasis was on strike committees democratically elected by all workers in the firm concerned, both organised and unorganised. The impression was given that joining a 'reformist' union would be a drawback; it was taken for granted that any trade-union officials involved would be strike-breakers; 'official representatives of the reformist unions should on no account be admitted to strike committees.'[24]

In August 1929 at the Sixth Annual Conference of the Minority Movement the principle of 'independent leadership' and of organising strikes under the direction of committees of action 'uniting organised and unorganised workers' was at last endorsed. The number of trade union branches and trades councils represented was less than half that of the previous year. It signified the beginning of the end for the Minority Movement. It was also the moment when Harry Pollitt left his job in the shipyards together with his post as Honorary Secretary of the Movement in order to take up a position at Party headquarters.

Reorganisation and the Tenth Plenum

The decision that Pollitt should come to work at 16 King Street had been taken a couple of months earlier. Immediately after the General Election in May 1929 Comintern representatives held a meeting in Berlin with a delegation from the British Party; at this meeting it was proposed that Pollitt should become a full time member of the British Party's secretariat. It was not surprising that the CI representatives wanted to see Pollitt at Party headquarters since he had led the fight for the new line from the beginning so far as the Labour Party was concerned, even though he had resisted the RILU line in the trade unions. Moreover he was undoubtedly very popular throughout the Party, and had established himself as an outstanding mass leader and work-place organiser.

At the time, the Party leadership was made up of three elements. There was a Secretariat consisting of J.R. Campbell, who was 'political secretary', Albert Inkpin, business manager, and Bob

Stewart, treasurer. The day-to-day administration was in the hands of these three; they were assisted by a Political Bureau (PB) of ten members of the Central Committee who met weekly and were in turn responsible to a Central Committee numbering 31 which met every month or so. The Berlin proposal was that the new Secretariat should consist of Campbell (to be responsible for 'general ideological activity') and Pollitt (whose function would be 'organisational') together with *either* Inkpin or Stewart. Simultaneously it was proposed that the Political Bureau be reduced from ten people to seven; among those to be dropped would be Inkpin. What the proposals really meant was that Pollitt should be brought in as a full-time official with a leading political role; Inkpin should be eased out of political responsibility and become purely an administrator.

These proposals were brought before the Central Committee on 15–16 June when they created considerable argument and cross-voting, not so much in relation to Pollitt (indeed the majority was much in favour of him coming to headquarters) but in connection with the choice of members for the PB. What finally emerged was a Secretariat precisely as proposed in Berlin – Campbell, Pollitt, Inkpin – and a Political Bureau to which Inkpin was re-elected but from which two other former members were dropped. They were Gallacher and Murphy.[25] Walter Tapsell the representative on the Central Committee of the Young Communist League, had wanted Gallacher and Murphy to be on both the Secretariat and the PB; he voiced his indigation to the YCL Executive which wrote to the PB expressing consternation that 'left and self-critical elements' in the persons of Gallacher and Murphy, had been removed from the PB. The designation of Gallacher as a 'left' element was curious since it was only with difficulty that he had managed to reorientate himself in the direction of the 'new line'; moreover Tapsell himself was soon to denounce him for putting up 'a smokescreen of left phrases' and as a man who could 'pull the right-wing chestnuts out of the right-wing fire.'[26] However, Tapsell's complaint was forwarded to the delegation attending the Tenth Plenum in Moscow which opened on 3 July and was used by Rust to mount another attack on the leadership of the British Party.

At this Plenum, all the ideas about social democracy were carried further, and elaborated, social democrats now being characterised as 'social fascists'.[27] The British Party came in for much criticism. The

Party's dismal performance at the 1929 General Election was commented on, but no one was prepared to suggest that this might in part be attributed to the new line. On the contrary according to the leading Russian Party member, Manuilsky, who gave the main report on behalf of the ECCI it was not the 'Class against Class' tactics that were wrong, but the fact that the British Party had 'not employed these tactics with sufficient energy and firmness'. The whole Party, he said, 'was for a long time wavering before it adopted these tactics. Many of you have accepted them out of your loyalty to discipline and not because you were convinced of their correctness.'[28] This view was supported by Ulbricht of the German Party, who did not see how the struggle could be carried on against the Labour Party if the majority of the PB had thought that workers should vote Labour when there was no Communist candidate.[29]

Losovsky of the RILU and Gey of the German Party criticised the British approach to the trade unions, including an alleged delay in forming the United Mineworkers of Scotland and the Party's attitude to unorganised workers which, Gey said, was 'modelled after the worst reformist samples.'[30] Early on during the Plenum Rust made clear that he sided with the critics; he denounced the elimination of Gallacher and Murphy from the PB, he brought up once more the issue of the earlier attempt to exclude himself and Arnot; he accused the British leadership of stifling the criticisms of the membership, and attacked Campbell and Rothstein for supporting the idea that the workers should be urged to vote Labour in the absence of a Party candidate.[31]

Both Pollitt and Tom Bell defended the actions of the British Party, but towards the end Manuilsky came back with a lengthy denunciation of the British leadership. Campbell had told him, he said, that

> it is not the tradition of the British Communist Party to divide the Party into goats and sheep, into those who defend the Party and those who do not defend it, that they are all united in the fervent desire to carry out the general line.

'I am not acquainted with the British custom,' said Manuilsky. 'Possibly it is so. But I am going to ask our British friends: when you will have the revolution in your country, it will be perhaps necessary to chop some heads off.' Manuilsky complained of the British Party's 'excessive insularity'. Speaking of the passionate discussions taking place in the German Party he said:

> The German comrades carefully weigh every word spoken by anybody. They allow no deviation from the line, they attack the least deviation, respecting no persons. . . Yet in the British Communist Party there is a sort of special system which may be characterised thus: the Party is a society of great friends. . . We welcome the solidarity existing in the British Party but it seems to me that a little breach ought occasionally to be made in this solidarity.[32]

The Tenth Plenum speeches appeared in *Inprecorr* during August and September 1929. It was clearly Manuilsky's aim to stir up the rank and file against the leadership. He succeeded.

The rank and file Party members had been doggedly trying to swim against the stream for a long time. Often targets for victimisation at work, they were now being witch-hunted by trade-union and Labour Party leaders. They had been offered a new line, one which plausibly suggested there should be no more trailing behind the right wing; the Party should strike out as an independent force. Since then, those who could not stand the isolating results of the new line, its strident criticism of former left-wing allies, had drifted out of the Party. For the shrinking number still in the Party, the outlook was horribly depressing. Frustrated and dejected, the members responded to the insistence from the Comintern that it was not the new line that was wrong, but the hesitations and vacillations by the leadership which had never whole-heartedly agreed with it. The main danger in the Party was the 'right danger', in other words the people who resisted the full-blooded operation of the new line. Such people must be removed from leading positions.

On the return of the delegation from Moscow, the Central Committee sent out a document to the membership admitting that the chief cause of the critical situation in the Party was the right-wing mistakes made by the leadership. This was followed by another reshuffle: Inkpin was dropped from both the Secretariat and the PB and Gallacher was brought on in his place; Rothstein was also dropped from the PB. These alterations did not satisfy Rust who, back from the CI in crusading mood, said: 'These are only temporary changes – the beginning of an attempt to cleanse the leadership of the Party from top to bottom.'[33]

And indeed, at District conference after conference, calls were heard for further changes. Thus the London District issued a lengthy statement about the leadership's mistakes, and singled out Rothstein (who had voted against the abstention policy in general elections) as one of their chief targets. At the Scottish conference a delegate complained that Campbell was one of those primarily responsible for 'right' mistakes but no action had been taken against him; a YCLer demanded that Gallacher be exposed as the author of the Cook–Maxton Manifesto; another delegate attacked Rothstein, Campbell and Gallacher, declaring that the Central Committee 'was dying of old age and needed burying.' E.H. Brown, acting Scottish Organiser (and soon to be dropped himself) implored conference not to ask for a 'clean sweep'.[34] The Liverpool Sub-District thought the changes in the PB were inadequate; Birmingham demanded to know the voting record of every CC member.[35] Tyneside District conference passed a resolution criticising the delegates to the Tenth Plenum, and Tom Bell in particular, for retaining an 'old line mentality'. Gallacher, who was present, deplored the 'wholesale condemnation' of the Central Committee made at this meeting. 'Surely', he asked, 'there is at least one member of the Central Committee who could have been chosen out as worth saving?' For example, Rust was 'a very strong critic of the leadership.' To which Lily Webb (herself a member of the Central Committee on which she often found herself voting in a minority of one) interjected: 'Rust? He's not a critic, he has capitulated to the right.' 'What about Tapsell?' asked Gallacher. 'He's not a critic, either.' 'What about Dutt then?' To which Lily Webb replied, 'Yes, we accept Dutt.'[36] Indeed Dutt was one of the few members of the Central Committee to escape censure at this period, perhaps because he was away in Brussels and only communicated by post.

One of the few regions where a desire to attack the Central Committee failed to take root was the Rhondda in South Wales. Here, at an aggregate meeting of 35 members called to discuss 'The New Line and the Right Danger' only 8 of those present participated in the discussion after an opening by the district organiser Len Jeffries. Lewis Jones, the Welsh Regional Secretary, wrote that

> This, considering the gravity of the matter, was probably the worst aggregate from every point of view that has been held in the Rhondda for some considerable time. . . The level of discussion was particularly low, and there was not manifested any too clear a knowledge of the New Line and the Right Danger.[37]

On the Central Committee, one member openly disagreed with the findings of the Tenth Plenum; this was T.A. Jackson, who said after the delegation's return: 'I now feel that the fundamental stand which I took some time ago, which incurred me the distrust and suspicion of the International was an honest and justifiable one.' He added that he did not think there was any fundamental political division in the ranks of the Party, 'though Comrade Tapsell has worked like a hero to create one.'[38] But as the District conferences proceeded, Central Committee members began to feel they were on trial. Arthur Horner said angrily at a Central Committee meeting on 21 September that 'much of the criticism taking place is of the most unscrupulous kind that ever has been practiced in the history of the Party.' Saying that at the Scottish Conference Pollitt had been referred to as a right winger, 'which was a libel', he ended by demanding that he, Horner, be relieved of all duties at the Party headquarters. A little later he insisted that his demand to be relieved of duties be put to the vote. The demand was defeated by 16 votes to 3.[39]

The Leeds Congress

It had become clear that a new Party congress was necessary; it took place in Leeds at the end of November 1929. In the eighteen months since the new line was first mooted, the membership of the British Party had fallen from over 7,000 to under 3,000.[40] Yet the view persisted that this could not be because the line was wrong; it must be because of vacillations and mistakes – particularly on the part of the leadership. So the resolutions which came before Congress reiterated the New Line in its most extreme form, particularly in relation to the trade unions. Thus the resolution on economic struggles said that the 'ever-growing fascisation of the trade union apparatus' would give rise to conditions necessitating the formation of new unions.

> The problem of unorganised workers is not one of recruitment into the reformist trade unions. . . The Party and the MM must develop an independent campaign to establish representative factory committees of both organised and unorganised, and expose the slogan of 100 per cent trade unionism as a means in the hands of the trade-union bureaucracy to carry through their policy of class collaboration.[41]

It was already apparent that this new approach to the trade unions had induced a certain paralysis. Indeed, apart from remarks which revealed confusion concerning the role of the Minority Movement, the discussion on industrial work was unusually generalised. Here and there doubt was thrown on the proposition that a process of radicalisation was taking place among the workers. Dai Lloyd Davies, a miner from South Wales who had been president of his 2,500-strong lodge, admitted bluntly:

> When comrades speak of the radicalisation of the masses and the great wave of insurrection, I want to tell you that in my experience – which is not small – I have not seen a ripple of it. [42]

An engineer from a Coventry factory, Bill Stokes, said that those who spoke of the revolt of the workers were 'living in a fool's paradise.' But Tom Bell, speaking for the Central Committee, insited that radicalisation was a fact.

The main resolution at Congress was introduced by Harry Pollitt, who went out of his way to accept responsibility, along with his colleagues, for the errors of the Central Committee. And indeed the need to elect a new leadership dominated the minds of many delegates.

This question had taken up considerable time in the deliberations of the Central Committee before the Congress opened. The previous practice had been for the retiring Central Committee to recommend a short list as a nucleus, and to call for further nominations from the floor. However, a system in which the opinion of the retiring Central Committee exerted a major influence was clearly not going to be acceptable to the membership in its present mood. It was decided that the task of drawing up a recommended list should be handed over to a Panels Commission appointed by Congress. The majority of this Commission – ten out of fourteen – consisted of delegates nominated by the various Districts; only four out of the fourteen were appointed by the retiring Central Committee which, after much argument, chose Rust, Gallacher, Robson and Joss. Tapsell tried to stop the nomination of Gallacher, and his objection was carried to the floor of Congress where a London delegate moved that Gallacher should not be appointed; however when put to the vote, Gallacher was narrowly supported by 41 votes to 35. The London delegation also objected to the appointment of Campbell to the Political

Commission (which was responsible for dealing with amendments to resolutions), but Campbell survived by 50 votes to 46.

Such was the atmosphere at the Congress that Arthur Horner said:

> I am afraid this congress is being approached by some of us as we would approach a cup-tie football match. Everybody appears to have come with the intention of carrying through a particular team into a successful position in the struggle. [42]

And with Rust chairing the Panels Commission, and such a mood among the delegates, it was not surprising that, when the Commission finalised its list of 35 recommended names, only 12 should be those of the previous Central Committee. Rothstein, Horner, Hannington, Tom Bell, Lily Webb, Frank Bright, E.H. Brown, Bob Stewart, were all among those removed.

Rust called for a unanimous vote from Congress for his list as a whole. But the ensuing discussion showed that Congress was far from unanimous, and the panel was adopted by only 56 votes to 32 on the understanding that additional nominations could also be voted on. There were then six additional nominations, but only one of them received a majority of the votes. This was Wal Hannington, leader of the National Unemployed Workers' Movement, who had earlier made a challenging speech to Congress, stating that he was 'not standing on the penitents form because it happens to be fashionable, because I believe my line has been a left line all the time.' He was re-elected to the Central Committee by 52 votes to 30. Arthur Horner was also nominated but failed to get on by 25 votes to 56, an outcome which was inevitable since he himself had told Congress he did not want to be on the Central Committee – 'I would rather do anything than stop there.' Two other former Central Committee members, Tom Bell and Lily Webb, were also nominated but defeated.

After all this, a delegate moved that there should be voting for *exclusions* from the recommendation list, whereupon demands for the exclusion of, among others, Campbell, Gallacher, Rust and Tapsell, were raised from various parts of the hall. After some commotion, the proposal to allow a vote on individual exclusions was turned down by 43 votes to 25. In the end the list with the addition of Hannington was adopted by 78 votes to 7. [42]

The Leeds Congress revealed that Manuilsky had momentarily achieved his purpose. The former 'society of great friends' had temporarily deteriorated into a collection of warring groups, and a great many active and dedicated Party members had been attacked and blamed for a situation which was none of their making, but which arose from the imposition of an ultra-left political line.

[1] JK folder 11, no. 10.
[2] JK folder 11, no. 23. Details of how members of the Central Committee voted on many occasions are contained in two documents in 'Documents of 1929', loc. cit. One is dated 18 November 1929 and sent to Locals; the other was issued to delegates attending the 1929 Leeds Congress. These documents are referred to below respectively as DA and DB
[3] JK folder 11, no. 20.
[4] JK folder 11, no. 23. See also DA.
[5] JK folder 11, no. 24.
[6] See *Birmingham Post*, 22 June 1928.
[7] JK folder 11, nos. 33 and 34.
[8] *The New Line*, printed documents of the Tenth Congress, January 1929, p. 81. Also JK folder 12, no. 6.
[9] JK folder 6. Report of Bermondsey Congress.
[10] *The New Line*, pp. 82–3.
[11] JK folder 12, no. 4.
[12] 'Closed Letter'; see 'Documents of 1929', loc. cit.
[13] *The New Line*, p. 23.
[14] See DB.
[15] JK folder 2, no. 2.
[16] RILU Report of Fourth Congress pp. 99–103.
[17] JK folder 2, no. 9.
[18] JK folder 2, no. 5.
[19] JK folder 2, no. 6.
[20] *The New Line*, pp. 91, 92.
[21] JK folder 2, no. 7.
[22] JK folder 2, nos. 5 and 7.
[23] *Labour Monthly*, June 1929.
[24] *Strike*, pamphlet published in 1931, p. 14.
[25] See DB. See also JK folder 4. Meeting 15–16 June 1929.
[26] JK folder 12, no. 42.
[27] See Kuusinen, *Inprecorr*, 20 August 1929, p. 848.
[28] Ibid., p. 855.
[29] *Inprecorr*, 11 September 1929, p. 1029.
[30] *Inprecorr*, 9 October 1929, p. 1225.
[31] *Inprecorr*, 20 August 1929, p. 885.
[32] *Inprecorr*, 25 September, 1929 pp. 1139–40.
[33] JK folder 12, no. 23.
[34] JK folder 12, no. 28.
[35] JK folder 12, no. 26.
[36] JK folder 12, no. 32.
[37] JK folder 12, no. 30.
[38] JK folder 12, no. 23.
[39] JK folder 12, no. 33.
[40] JK folder 12 and 9. Misc & Org.
[41] *Resolutions of the 11th Congress* (printed), pp. 22–3.
[42] JK folder 7. Report of 11th Congress.

CHAPTER 4

The Birth of the 'Daily Worker' (1930)

The Leeds Congress left the Party smaller and more isolated than ever before or since. Yet it had a few positive results. The most important was the founding of the *Daily Worker*.

The need to establish a daily paper had long been accepted by members of the Party, and the failure to achieve this was taken at the Leeds Congress as yet one more symptom of the 'right danger' on the Central Committee. A proposal was made that the Party's daily paper should be launched without fail on New Year's Day 1930. On this matter, Harry Pollitt had certainly appeared to hesitate. Dismayed at the low level of organisation and, in particular, the disastrous financial position of the Party which had become only too clear to him at the Secretariat meeting in August, he was determined that the membership should face up to the difficulties involved. So he argued that the proposed date was premature. But the mood of Congress was such as to sweep aside all such hesitations. January the first 1930 it had to be.

On that day, despite seemingly insuperable difficulties, the *Daily Worker* appeared, with a banner headline 'Workers of the World Unite' and the emblem of the hammer and sickle incorporated into its title. It was to be the only left-wing daily newspaper published in Britain during the ensuing thirty years.

The odds were heavily against its survival. Everyone had seen what had happened to the *Daily Herald*, which had made its mark as a crusading left-wing newspaper of the labour movement in the years just after the war. Its existence had become more and more precarious until, in 1929, it had been taken over by Odhams Press. Now, insofar as it dealt with political and trade-union matters, it reflected the right-wing stance of two of its trade-union directors: Ernest Bevin and Walter Citrine. Socialist themes were liable to be soft-pedalled so as not to offend the advertisers, and matters concerning the labour movement were often tucked away in the inside pages. Most space was devoted to the sort of 'human interest' news which dominated all the other Fleet Street papers intended for popular consumption. It was before the days of television, even radios were few and far between, and a fierce circulation battle was developing in which Fleet Street newspapers vied with one another in offering inducements to those who made new readers.

Such was the world into which the *Daily Worker* was born, with no money and little chance of attracting any of the advertising revenue on which all other newspapers depended. For editorial offices, the Party secured the lease of an old warehouse at 41 Tabernacle Street, London. The ground landlords were the Ecclesiastical Commissioners who held up the arrangements for obtaining possession, so that the handful of people appointed by the Central Committee to get the paper out were only able to move in a few days before the first number was due. They were initially without lighting, heating, telephone or tape machine.

The team was headed by William Rust who was still only twenty-six years old. 'It must be said that my experience of daily journalism was practically nil,' he recalled subsequently.'[1] He had left school at fourteen and, while still a boy, had worked in the office of the Hulton Press. Later he had edited the *Young Worker* for the Young Communist League for a brief period. Nevertheless, it was a shrewd move to give him chief editorial responsibility since, apart from his undoubted abilities as an organiser, he had been the former leadership's most determined critic, and the new position would give him a chance to prove himself in a more positive role. The team included only one journalist who had ever worked on a daily newspaper and that was Walter Holmes, once employed on the *Daily Herald*, and later editor of the *Sunday Worker*. Also from the *Sunday Worker* were Tom Wintringham and the young Frank Brennan Ward, a former Durham miner. Bill Shepherd, a woodworker, came on to the paper straight from a building site and soon rose to be its chief sub-editor. Kay Beauchamp, who had started out as a teacher and had worked for *Labour Monthly*, was initially put in charge of the women's page but, early on, became the paper's business manager. Three months after the paper was launched, the staff was joined by G. Allen Hutt who, like Holmes, had previously been with the *Daily Herald*. The main characteristic of the editorial staff was its youth and inexperience.

Arrangements were made to print the paper at the Utopia Press in Worship Street. This was not far from Tabernacle Street, but the fact that the editorial offices were not housed on the same premises as the press added to the complications of getting the paper out; moreover, the political attitude of the owners and management of the Utopia Press was soon to cause difficulties.

In Fleet Street, the arrival of the *Daily Worker* was regarded with scepticism. The paper reported on its second day that

> The *Daily Herald* is very disappointed. Yesterday, just before our Scottish edition went to press, they telephoned up to ask if we were bringing out a second number. Undoubtedly, they were quite down-in-the-mouth when we told them the *Daily Worker* has come to stay.

On its first day, the *Daily Worker* printed a message from the Communist International greeting the appearance of a paper which would be 'the standard for rallying the working class for the counter-offensive against capitalist rationalisation', the 'rallying point for the fight against speeding-up, wage cuts, overtime and unemployment' and 'against the Labour government of . . . anti-Soviet intrigues, colonial brutalities and preparations for another imperialist war.' It said:

> The *Daily Worker* comes as a strong antidote to the poison gas of the bourgeois and pseudo-Labour press, and as an instrument for enlightenment and the organisation of the proletariat in the fight for the revolutionary workers government.

Although this message was identical with the type of statement regularly appearing in the Party's former weekly, *Workers' Life*, it was made the pretext for an enormous fuss in other newspapers, headed by *The Times*, which denounced the CI as the 'General Staff of the World Revolution.' Three and a half weeks later, when it had become clear that the *Daily Worker* was not going to die, organised steps were taken to kill it. The Provincial Wholesalers Federation decided to boycott it, with the result that wholesalers in Lancashire, Birmingham, Newcastle, Leicester, Nottingham, Bradford and South Wales cancelled all orders. In May 1930, the Federation of London Wholesalers informed the paper they would no longer handle it. In July, the Scottish wholesalers followed suit, and the boycott was complete.

This meant that the *Daily Worker* had to set up its own distributive machinery. It could not have been done without the active participation of the rank and file of the Communist Party, something that was to continue at a remarkable level for the next ten years. In the provinces, rotas of volunteers were organised to get up in the small hours, collect parcels at the local railway station and deliver them to retailers. In London, a network of 'dumps' was set up from which the distribution was arranged. This involved persuading newsagents to take the paper, organising its delivery to them and the regular collection of returns and cash. The Communist Party members took over this job with enthusiasm; indeed, the challenge which faced them as a result of the wholesalers' boycott in some ways acted as a tonic. The despondency of 1929 began to be dispelled, the comradeship which had been somewhat undermined during the inner-party struggle was re-established in the battle to beat the ban. Fortunately, the Retail Newsagents Federation always stood out against the wholesalers' boycott.

A major difficulty in the early days was that the *Daily Worker* was not at all easy to read, and thus put off many potential supporters. A regular sale of at least 25,000 a day had been hoped for, based on previous experience with *Workers' Life* and the *Sunday Worker*. In practice, after some good initial sales, its daily readership settled at about 11,000. From the start there was a lot of controversy about the paper's contents. One correspondent argued that 'to interest the mass of the workers, more topical news must be introduced.'[2] 'Humour is missing' alleged another, who also complained that workers did not understand terms like 'social-fascist', 'bureaucracy' and 'sham-left'.[3] One of the paper's strongest critics was Pollitt. The workers did not want a 'daily edition of *Inprecorr*' catering only for the 'militant faithful' he said.[4] He wanted the paper to cover topical news and to include sport and racing tips. But the majority was against racing tips as being one of the things which 'doped the workers.' And Rust argued that the 'so-called "general news" has no place in our columns' and that the main aim was worker-correspondents.[5]

However, the idea that a daily paper could avoid 'topical news' and base itself mainly on worker correspondents turned out to be an illusion. There were two reasons for this. One was that the majority of industrial workers were not continuously thinking about, or preoccupied by, the class struggle. They might take an uncompromisingly class-conscious line when involved in a show-down with their employer, but that did not mean they thought about nothing else. The idea that they would buy every day a paper which devoted itself largely to discussing the happenings on someone else's workshop floor was not based on reality. Indeed, as the owners of the Fleet Street newspapers were all too well aware, most workers bought a paper which afforded them some entertainment and enabled them to escape from the dreariness of their work; this was the last thing they wanted to be reminded of in their short leisure hours. The second difficulty was, of course, that there were not enough workers on the shop floor who wanted to communicate information. This was mainly because, despite all assertions that the workers were moving to the left, the situation was somewhat stagnant; except in textiles, industrial activity was at a low ebb in 1930. The kind of ferment which the country had experienced just before the General Strike, and which might well have induced a growth of worker-correspondents, was conspicuous by its absence. As will be shown, the paper did, in the end, establish a wide network of worker-correspondents, including both activists in factories and people in trade-union positions. But that day still lay ahead.

Meanwhile, for some years, the *Daily Worker* failed to achieve the hoped-for circulation. By the end of 1932, it had reached 20,000 daily with 30,000 on Fridays and 46,000 on Saturdays.[6] Thereafter, the new political situation in 1933 and a changed political line encouraged further growth. By 1934 the paper was beginning to recruit some very talented journalists onto its staff – one of whom was Claud Cockburn – together with some outstanding cartoonists. It started to allocate proper space to sport, and even to racing tips; the topics covered became much broader. By November 1935 it had a daily circulation of 30,000 and weekend sales which sometimes topped 100,000. By 1939 its daily sales were between 40,000 and 50,000 and its weekend sales averaged 75,000 to 80,000.[7] In view of the fact that the wholesalers' boycott continued throughout the entire period, such sales were no mean achievement.

Despite its difficulties, the *Daily Worker* acted as a mobilising force for left-wingers from the very first day of its inception. During its first six months, four major political issues dominated its pages. First, was rising unemployment and the activities of the National Unemployed Workers' Movement which, despite bans by the official Labour and trade-union leadership, continued to mobilise thousands for action, and mounted another National Hunger March in the spring of 1930. A second crucial issue was the employers' drive to force down wages in the textile industry. A third point of concentration was the Soviet Union; the defence of the only country in the world which had abolished the capitalist system was seen as a paramount responsibility and the Soviet Union received regular, committed support from the paper. The fourth major concern was with colonial liberation and the role of the armed forces used to hold down the colonies.

Despite its small circulation, the authorities clearly regarded the *Daily Worker* as a threat. So, throughout the 1930s the paper was subject to continuous police surveillance and was involved in numerous court cases. Many of its staff served prison sentences. It was for this reason that the names of those who were appointed as chief political editor were never officially made public. William Rust was the first; he was succeeded in 1933 by Jimmy Shields. In 1935 Idris Cox took over; in 1936, R. Palme Dutt; in 1938, Dave Springhall; in 1939, shortly before the outbreak of war, J.R. Campbell.[8] And then, in October 1939, Rust returned in circumstances which will be explored later.

[1] William Rust, *The Story of the Daily Worker*, London, 1949.
[2] *Daily Worker*, 7 January 1930.
[3] *Daily Worker*, 8 January 1930.
[4] Statement issued to Political Bureau 19 June 1930. CP Archives.
[5] *Daily Worker*, 28 January 1930.
[6] JK folder 17. Report of 1932 Congress, p.35. Figures from JK papers.
[7] 1935 figures are from the Political Bureau Meeting on 21 November 1935, JK papers. But see also Pountney papers which show that the average weekly sale in February 1939 was 315,000; that in April 1939 377,000. The Pountney papers are in the CP Archive.
[8] The information on the successive editors was supplied to the author by Idris Cox.

CHAPTER 5

Conspiracy and Incitement to Mutiny
(1929–31)

During the period of the 1929–31 Labour government many Party members were imprisoned for activities connected with two highly sensitive issues. One was the struggle for colonial freedom; the other the attempt to build up influence in the armed forces. The two were in practice often linked, since a major function of the armed forces was the maintenance of British rule over the colonial territories.

The British Empire had a population of about 445 million, nearly one quarter of the human race. Most of the territory had been won by conquest, and 85 per cent of the inhabitants had no democratic rights, but were subject to dictatorial rule by British administrators, backed up by a massive British army and navy.

From the beginning, the Communist Party had stood uncompromisingly for the liberation of colonial peoples. It had tried to expose the 'hideous foundation' on which the wealth of the British ruling class rested, and had argued that the enemies of the British and colonial workers were one and the same.

> Whether in the sugar fields of the West Indies, or the jute mills of India, in the rubber plantations of Africa, or the blast furnaces of Middlesbrough, the toiling masses slave away to build up the colonial fortunes of the City and the West End.[1]

But the Party had found it was no easy task to arouse interest in the struggle for colonial freedom, since most people believed what they had been taught at school: that the Empire was a glorious thing, and the British had a mission to bring civilisation to backward peoples.

Situated as it was at the heart of the Empire, the British Party had a two-fold aim. One was to deliver the anti-colonial message, to try and bring about understanding among British workers. Much of the activity was channelled through the League against Imperialism, set up in 1927 in collaboration with certain Labour and ILP leaders. But by 1930, the Labour Party had outlawed the League as a Communist organisation.

58

The Meerut Conspiracy

The second aim was to give direct help to liberation movements in British-owned territories. In pursuit of this, various British Party members went out to India where there was growing discontent among the people. Most Indian workers were unorganised, and the main activity of British Communists had been to help establish some militant trade unions, particularly in the industrial centres of Calcutta and Bombay. This was something that Party members were singularly well-equipped to do. Two such were Philip Spratt and Ben Bradley. The latter had been a member of the London District Committee of the Amalgamated Engineering Union. As a result of their initiating work both were elected members of the Executive Committee of the All-India Trade Union Congress.

In March 1929 Spratt and Bradley were among 31 people arrested on a charge of conspiracy. The 29 others were nearly all executive members of trade unions based in Bombay or Calcutta; there were also one or two members of the Workers' and Peasants' Party. Three months later another Englishman, was arrested. He was Lester Hutchinson, a left-wing English journalist who had offered his services to one of the trade unions deprived of its leading members.

It was perfectly obvious that the intention behind the arrests was to behead the newly-established fast-growing and militant trade-union movement. But since those leading it were not thereby infringing the letter of the law, some other pretext for taking them into custody had to be found. So the 32 prisoners found themselves charged with 'conspiracy' to 'deprive the King-Emperor of Sovereignty over British India'. They were taken to an out-of-the-way military station, Meerut, to be tried without a jury by a District Judge (in reality a British civil servant). The prosecutor's initial speech amounted to a discursive and somewhat inaccurate lecture on the Russian Revolution, the Soviet government, the Communist International and the theories of Marxism-Leninism. 'It is the case for the prosecution that the accused are Bolsheviks,' he said.[2]

The proceedings dragged on for nearly four years during which most of the prisoners were in jail in appalling conditions. When finally found guilty in January 1933 sentences of unprecedented severity were imposed on them. Among them, Spratt was condemned to 12 years' transportation and Bradley to 10 years. This meant being taken to a notorious penal settlement in the Andaman

Islands. The sentences provoked international public protest and, on appeal, several prisoners were acquitted and the remainder were released shortly afterwards.

In the eyes of British Communists, the behaviour of the Labour government over the Meerut trial proved, as nothing else could have done, that all Labour's talk of 'democracy' was a sham.

The arrests of the trade unionists had taken place just before Labour took office. The new government could have shown its mettle by insisting on their release. Instead, a further 'conspirator', Hutchinson, was arrested and imprisoned. Far from relaxing the oppressive Indian régime. the Labour government presided over its continuance for two and a quarter years. At the 1929 Labour Party Annual Conference an attempt to protest at the Meerut proceedings was frustrated. It was not until the spring of 1933, long after the Labour government had fallen, that the National Council of Labour at last issued a statement asserting that the whole Meerut affair from beginning to end had been 'indefensible'.[3]

In contrast, the *Daily Worker* from its very first appearance on 1 January 1930 had given prominence to news about the Indian liberation struggle. A manifesto headed 'Long Live Indian Independence' appeared on 14 May 1930. It asserted that British Imperialism was 'face to face with the day of reckoning.' On Empire Day, officially celebrated every year on 24 May, the Party called for 'Down with Empire' demonstrations. In the South Wales town of Porth, the police tried to close down an open-air meeting in support of the Indian workers. Resistance during and after this event led to the arrest of fourteen Party members, seven of whom were sentenced to between two and four months' hard labour. Among them was young Will Paynter, who was one day to become Secretary of the National Union of Mineworkers.

Meanwhile, unrest in India was spreading. In the spring of 1930 there was not only a wave of strikes but a civil disobedience campaign. Then came risings in Peshawar and Sholapur; a crack Hindu regiment refused to fire on demonstrators, and the two towns were held by insurgents for two weeks until re-occupied by British troops. At the time, the British Army numbered nearly 200,000, of whom about 68,000 were normally stationed in India. They were reinforced by Indian troops commanded by British officers; it was these troops which were now becoming unreliable.

In this situation, the British Party did not confine itself to generalised propaganda; it deliberately tried to influence the soldiers who might be sent out to India to crush the disturbances. It was obvious that anyone engaged in this activity would be in trouble with the courts, the police, the government. And so it proved.

The Party and Servicemen

The Party had for many years tried to break down the barrier between 'workers in uniform' and those in industry. A penny pamphlet, *The Soldiers' Programme* published in 1928, called for servicemen to have the right to join political parties and to attend political meetings. Leaflets were distributed outside barracks, usually concentrating on the lack of democratic rights in the army and the bad conditions. In some barracks, soldiers took the leaflets in and passed them round surreptitiously, or left them lying about for others to see. The same approach was made by the Party to the Navy and the Air Force, but here there was less direct contact.

Every now and then, Party members would be arrested for distributing leaflets outside barracks; they were usually charged with 'insulting behaviour' and fined.

With the news of Indian uprisings, and the Party's call on soldiers not to take part in putting them down, the situation changed. On 25 May 1930, two Communists were arrested and charged with 'maliciously endeavouring to seduce soldiers from their duty' under the 1797 Incitement to Mutiny Act. They had been distributing a leaflet to soldiers outside barracks in Brecon, Wales. The leaflet was headed 'We must not murder the workers and peasants of India', and argued:

> If the imperialist Labour government sends us to India, and calls on us to shoot down the heroic Indian workers and peasants, we must refuse. . . Our guns must be turned against our real enemy – the thieving, robbing, British ruling class and its lackey, the Labour government. (See Appendix at the end of this chapter.)

The leaflets had been delivered in closed envelopes, on the outside of which was printed 'Lee's tip for the Derby'. The two Party members involved were from Dowlais. 44 year-old Arthur Eyles was an unemployed miner, a widower with four young children, who lived on £1 12s a week unemployment benefit. 28 year-old John Ryan was an unemployed labourer. He was married but had no

PRICE 1ᴰ·

Published by

A. Massie, 38 Gt. Ormond St., London,
W.C.1

children and received £1 6s unemployment pay. The two were sent for trial at the Brecon Assizes.

When the case came before a jury, the judge, Mr Justice Roche, informed them that the leaflet which had been distributed 'was an extraordinarily foolish one' and that 'no one with any idea of the history of India and of this country would believe it.' 'The people of India were not ground down and oppressed,' he said, 'but were protected against the periodic invasions they had experienced before, by English rule.' The prosecuting council (who was acting on instructions from the Director of Public Prosecutions) asked the judge whether he could read the leaflet out in court. He was given permission to do so after the judge had again stressed that it was 'extraordinary rubbish, but the sort of rubbish that might prove mischievous.' The leaflet was thereupon read out and reproduced word for word in the *Brecon County Times*, thus giving it far more publicity than it would otherwise have achieved. Half-way through the reading the judge interrupted to ask what was meant by the term 'imperialist government'. 'Does it mean the British Government?' Counsel replied: 'I don't know, my Lord, but I presume so.'

The prisoners had decided to plead guilty, but this did not help them very much, since the judge was quite unable to believe that anyone should distribute such leaflets for any but mercenary reasons. (This, incidentally, was an assumption very widespread among members of the establishment who evidently found it hard to believe that any other motive could exist.)

'Can you give any idea where the money for these pamphlets comes from?' the judge asked the prosecuting counsel. 'Are these men being subsidised, and if so by whom?' He said that unless the accused made a clean breast of the whole thing, he would not show much leniency. The defence counsel said the accused did not know the man who had given them the leaflets, but he came from Cardiff, and that they had received 6s each which, as the judge commented, did not cover their railway fare from Dowlais to Brecon; 'what the prisoners have said is an insult to my intelligence.'[4] But he failed to get any further information, and a fortnight later sentenced Eyles to 12 months' hard labour and Ryan to 8 months, saying 'Let everybody understand, I am not punishing you for your opinions.'[5] (Both Eyles and Ryan joined the British Union of Fascists after their release from prison.)

Meanwhile a similar case had come up at Aldershot. Here on 30

May a 35 year-old electrician, Edward J. Thomas, had been arrested and later charged with incitement to mutiny. Thomas had himself previously served twelve years in the army and had done duty in Iraq, Egypt, India and China. His experiences had made a deep impression on him, and when he came out of the army he joined the Communist Party. Like the Dowlais members, he had for several days been handing out the leaflet in envelopes marked 'a tip for the Derby'. The case came up at the Winchester Assizes before Mr Justice Rigby Swift, a former Conservative MP who had, in 1925, tried and sentenced 12 Communist leaders on a charge of seditious conspiracy. Thomas was found guilty and on 5 July 1930 sentenced to 18 months' hard labour.

For some time the Government had been under fire in the House of Commons for prosecuting only the people who delivered the leaflets and not doing anything to track down those really responsible. In fact, the Party member in charge of anti-militarist activity for most of this period was a member of the Party's full-time staff, George Aitken, a skilled engineer and one of the organisers of the Clyde Workers' Committee during the First World War; he had been on the Party's Central Committee until 1929. The leaflets distributed to the armed forces were printed on a secret press in the cellar under a cobbler's shop in Junction Road, near Tufnell Park in north London. Most of these leaflets were delivered in batches by Aitken himself to contacts inside barracks. When volunteers distributed them from outside they were not, of course, paid for their activity and did not expect to be.[6] The authorities were unable to locate this printing press, so it was never raided by the police, as were so many other Party premises. But the Thomas case gave them the chance to do the next best thing. They took action against the *Daily Worker* for contempt of court.

The paper's report of the Thomas trial, which was headed 'Eighteen months hard labour for fighting war', was accompanied by a leader describing the judge as a 'bewigged puppet', it also referred to the 'strong class bias' of the judge and jury. It was for this passage that the *Daily Worker* was summonsed for contempt. Sir William Jowitt, the Attorney General in the Labour government, conducted the case in person.

The offending passage had in fact been written by Rust, whose feelings concerning the judge were understandable since he was one of those whom the latter had sent to jail in 1925. But Rust's identity as editor was being kept a close secret, so those prosecuted had to be three people who had agreed to stand as 'partners' in the Workers' Press (the nominal publisher of the *Daily Worker*), together with the paper's business manager and the non-Communist proprietor of the Utopia Press. 'I felt somewhat ashamed that I was not in the dock along with my comrades,' recalled Rust later.[8] When they appeared in Court, the partners were unrepentant. Frank Paterson, who came from Glasgow and was the paper's cashier, said that the prosecution was 'a cover for the attack of the Labour government against the Communist Party'; a young journalist, Frank Brennan Ward said the paper's statement had been

> a truthful political commentary on Mr Justice Swift and on the entire capitalist legal machinery which is not a fair and impartial machinery but part of the capitalist dictatorship.

Frank Priestly, business manager, who had been prominent in the shop stewards' movement in Sheffield during the First World War, would not apologise for one word because 'what it said was true.'[9]

The Lord Chief Justice, Lord Hewart, found that the words in the *Daily Worker* constituted a 'gross and outrageous contempt of court' and that Priestly, Paterson and Ward had 'aggravated the contempt', since they stood by the words printed. They were sentenced respectively to nine, six and five months' imprisonment. Later the police managed to track down the third 'partner', Bob McIlhone, and when he appeared in court in January 1931, he too refused to apologise and was sentenced to six months.

Wilkinson, the non-Communist managing-director of the Utopia Press, apologised to the court and was fined £250 plus £25 costs. Apprehensive of similar court actions in the future, he began to exercise censorship over the paper's contents, arbitrarily deleting passages which might be dangerous. A manifesto from the Party's political bureau appeared on 17 July with large blank spaces in it.

There were now a dozen Communists in jail for activities associated with the Indian liberation struggle. Others were not deterred. On 19 July 1930, a 25 year-old jute worker from Dundee, Duncan Butchart, was arrested at Leuchars in Fife while handing out leaflets to RAF men. He was charged with distributing material 'likely to create disaffection amongst members of the Royal Air Force.' As before, when the accused appeared at Cupar Sheriff Court, long extracts from the offending leaflet were read out and reappeared in the *Fife Herald* of 15 October 1930, thus obtaining a much larger readership than would otherwise have been the case. The leaflet called for a day of demonstration against war and in defence of Soviet Russia; it proposed the election of barracks committees, and said:

> Above all see that every soldier knows the truth about India. Who wants to shoot Indian workers and peasants? . . . The interests of the British workers lie in helping the Indian workers to overthrow British rule.

An RAF commander testified that he had 20 men who were required to go East – to India, Egypt, or Mesopotamia – and the words of the leaflet might result in some of them refusing to obey orders.

Butchart defended himself in Court. He was cross-examined by the Procurator Fiscal who asked him if he approved of the words 'Down with the murderous Labour government', to which Butchart replied 'Yes'. 'Why is it a murderous government?' 'We maintain that the Government is responsible for the shooting of Indian workers.' 'Is "murderous" the common word for Communists to use?' 'It is the common word for most people when someone commits murder.'[10]

Addressing the jury, Butchart stated that soldiers as well as civilians were entitled to take part in political activity; soldiers should not be isolated from other members of their own class. He was found guilty. The Sheriff said that in view of Butchart's youth he would exercise leniency; he sent him to prison for five months.

In February 1931 a Bristol Communist, 26 year-old William Fairman, was arrested and charged with 'incitement to mutiny' and with 'uttering a seditious speech.' The police alleged that, while addressing an open-air meeting of about 100 people, Fairman said:

> The Labour government call themselves a peace party, but make no mistake they are as much a war party as any other party. Look how they ordered the bombing of the Indian workers for making peaceful demonstrations. Comrades, another war is inevitable. When that war comes, tell your friends who are in the Army and Navy that, when they are issued out with rifles, not to shoot down the working classes but to turn their rifles onto the capitalist class who gave them the rifles. I myself have been among the soldiers

at Horfield Barracks and the Royal Air Force at Filton advising them the same.[11]

Fairman conducted his own defence at the Bristol Assizes. Explaining to the jury that he was a plumber and not a lawyer, he alleged the evidence was a frame-up. In the end the jury found Fairman not guilty of 'incitement to mutiny' but guilty of uttering a seditious speech. He was lucky enough to be bound over to keep the peace for twelve months after agreeing not to make further seditious speeches. As before the remarks of which he was accused were given much publicity and quoted at length in the *Western Daily Press*.

Most of the Party propaganda to the troops was distributed via a paper called *The Soldiers' Voice*. On 9 May 1931, John Gollan was caught handing it to troopers in the 16/5th Lancers stationed at Redford Barracks, Edinburgh. Gollan, a 20 year-old apprentice painter and sign-writer, was charged with the usual offences involving 'sedition', 'disaffection' and 'incitement to mutiny'. At the trial at Edinburgh Sheriff Court on 17 July a military police witness expressed the opinon that such a pamphlet was not fit to be published and distributed among the troops since 'it might cause mutiny.'[12]

Gollan conducted his own case and addressed the jury for an hour and a half. In the end the jury found him 'not guilty' on the sedition charge, but guilty of that invoking 'disaffection' and he was sentenced to six months' imprisonment.

Gollan was a young man who had already made his mark in the Edinburgh labour movement, and his case was the focus for considerable local agitation. While he was awaiting trial, a local defence committee was formed, petitions for his release were circulated, there were demonstrations and police baton charges. An appeal for funds was launched; these were needed not only for defence costs but to help support Gollan's family – he had seven brothers and sisters and an ailing father, and his earnings had been crucial to their support.

Both the Fairman and the Gollan cases revealed that Communist activities in connection with the armed forces had a certain impact on the local labour movement. There is little evidence of much impact on the armed forces themselves. Yet the officers, the government, the judiciary and, indeed, the whole establishment appeared to be preoccupied with worries about subversion. And these fears were shortly to seem justified by an event unprecedented in British history: the naval mutiny at Invergordon.

Invergordon

In August 1931, the month when Gollan appealed unsuccessfully against his sentence, a government crisis was imminent. Working people had by this time reason to be disillusioned with the Labour government, having suffered wage cuts and a huge rise in unemployment. Economies in social services were threatened and reductions in the pay of public servants. There was a failure to agree in the Cabinet to cuts in unemployment benefit, and the Labour government resigned. Whereupon it was announced on 24 August 1931 that the Labour Prime Minister, Ramsay MacDonald, had formed a coalition government with Conservatives and Liberals in order to implement the dreaded economies.

To the average labour voter, it was the final let-down after months of disappointment. To Communists, it seemed as though everything they had said about 'reformists', all their allegations concerning betrayals by Labour leaders, all their denunciations of them as the servants of the capitalist class, had at last been proved true in a fashion that *no one* could ignore. And indeed, as the newly formed National Government proceeded to rush through economy measures by a process of Emergency Act and Orders-in-Council, it almost began to seem as though the doom-laden prophecy of the Communists that Great Britain, the oldest capitalist power, was 'hastening headlong to collapse', was about to be fulfilled.[13] It was in this situation that news came on 15 September of a mutiny in the Atlantic Fleet in Cromarty Firth.

The sailors who took action had not been lured from their allegiance by revolutionary leaflets. They had been suddenly informed of a 25 per cent cut in pay. There was an angry meeting on shore in the naval canteen at Invergordon. Speeches were made, one of them by Len Wincott who later joined the Communist Party, but at the time knew nothing of politics; indeed, he did not even know how to conduct a meeting. 'We must strike like the miners,' he said. And that is what happened. For two days 12,000 sailors stayed on board their warships refusing to turn to for duty. They signalled their action from ship to ship by cheering. On board the cruiser *Norfolk*, Wincott drafted a manifesto which was taken across to the other ships where it was endorsed by their crews. It began:

> We the loyal subjects of His Majesty the King, do hereby present to My Lords the Commissioners of the Admiralty our representative, to implore them to amend the drastic cuts in pay which have been inflicted on the lowest paid men of the lower deck.

After two days, an Admiralty statement was issued which was rightly construed as a climb-down, the strike was called off, the Atlantic exercises were abandoned, and all the ships departed for their home ports.

The staff of the *Daily Worker* was as much surprised by the Invergordon 'strike' as everyone else; however, on 17 September the event was headlined and it was forecast that the movement would spread throughout the Navy and out to the Army and RAF. On 18 September the manifesto issued from the *Norfolk* was reproduced in a box, and workers in and out of uniform were called upon to support the sailors. With this, an article appeared which was later used as evidence to support charges against the paper of 'incitement to mutiny'. It said that when the ships of the Atlantic Fleet reached their home ports – Devonport, Portsmouth, Chatham and Sheerness – 'the crews should be greeted by workers and helped to raise in those ports precisely those questions which were raised at Invergordon.' It called on all sections of the armed forces – soldiers, sailors and airmen – to make common cause around the slogan 'Not a penny off the pay'; there was an item explaining 'How cuts hit sailors hard; officers lightly' and a call: 'Now reader, what about handing this copy to a sailor, soldier or airman. Pass it on.' On 21 September the paper reported an interview with some sailors from the *Valiant* and the *Repulse* when they arrived at Sheerness.

Inevitably the blow fell. On 25 September the *Daily Worker* premises were raided by detectives from the Special Branch who, though they had no search warrent, ransacked the building and removed piles of papers. On the same day Wilkinson of the Utopia Press was arrested and charged under the Incitement to Mutiny Act. He was released on bail on the understanding that as printer of the paper he would allow nothing to appear in it concerning the armed forces. Thereafter for some weeks, the pages of the Daily Worker were spotted with blank spaces containing the words 'censored by printer'.

This time, Wilkinson did not escape with a fine; he was jailed for nine months. 'This is not a political case,' counsel for the prosecution told the jury at the Old Bailey trial. 'You must put political views out of your minds.' And the judge emphasized that 'one of the things we are most proud of as English people is the absolute freedom we have in expressing our opinions.'[14] Soon after Frank Paterson and Frank Priestly both of whom had served sentences for 'contempt' in 1930 were again arrested. Patterson got two years' hard labour and Priestly three years' penal servitude.

Meanwhile the security services (including Naval Intelligence and MI5) had set up a hasty organisation to sort out the suspected ring-leaders of the Invergordon mutiny and avert a further mutiny which, with no evidence to suggest its likelihood, was nevertheless expected and dreaded.[15] As part of its activities, a trap was laid and resulted in the arrest of two Party members, George Allison and Bill Shepherd. Allison, aged 36, had been a miner in Fife; he was now on the Party's Central Committee and Secretary of the Minority Movement. Shepherd, aged 24, was a woodworker by trade, but now working as a sub-editor on the *Daily Worker*. As was mentioned earlier, the *Daily Worker* had urged its readers to contact sailors who had been involved at Invergordon when they came on shore in their home ports. Following one such encounter, a message was sent to Allison who travelled to Portsmouth accompanied by Shepherd to be introduced to some sailors. One of them, named Boutsfield, asked to have a leaflet printed calling out the fleet again. Boutsfield was in reality acting on the instructions of his officers, and the proposed leaflet was drafted with their collaboration; the draft was given to Allison who was not happy with it, but made an appointment to meet Boutsfield again to hand over a printed version. The object of this exercise, set up by the security services, was to catch Allison red-handed with the seditious leaflets on him. The exercise failed because Allison had become suspicious and, after consultation with George Aitken, had arrived at the appointed time to meet Boutsfield *without* any leaflets on him. He was, nevertheless, arrested, and so was Shepherd a little later.

Since there were no incriminating leaflets to use as evidence, the charges against Allison and Shepherd depended on the evidence of Boutsfield and his companion. In their defence Allison and Shepherd characterised the two sailors as *provocateurs*. They had posed as leaders of the Invergordon mutiny (which they were not); they had produced a draft leaflet written in consultation with their officers, and had asked Allison and Shepherd to print it. But the judge rejected this argument and Allison was sentenced to three years' penal servitude and Shepherd to 20 months' hard labour.[16]

That month, 36 sailors, alleged to have been 'ring-leaders' were dismissed from the Navy. They included Len Wincott and Fred Copeman, both of whom later joined the Communist Party. Neither of them had previously had any contact with the Party, but it was not surprising they should now be drawn towards the one organisation which had backed them in their 'strike'.

On 27 October 1931, just before the Allison-Shepherd trial, a General Election took place. The Conservatives stood everywhere as patriotic 'National' candidates in support of a coalition government headed by Labour's defector, Ramsay MacDonald, and were returned with an overwhelming majority. The Communist Party's 26 candidates received between them 75,000 votes. Five of these candidates were in jail and the Party's election appeal to 'workers, sailors and soldiers' appeared in the *Daily Worker* of 14 October with, as usual, several of its passages censored by the printers.

Among the Communist candidates was a Meerut prisoner named Shaukat Usmani who had already spent two and a half years in jail during the trial and was, as he put it, separated from the voters by 6,000 miles and prison bars. He sent a message asking for support 'in the cause of the freedom of the colonial masses'. 'The British and Indian workers are engaged in a common struggle against a common enemy,' ran an accompanying appeal from the CPGB. 'As long as India remains under British imperialism, the workers of Britain can never be free.' Usmani received only 332 votes. Nobody had expected him to get more. Everyone knew that in trying to build a movement for colonial freedom the Party faced the most difficult task of all.

Appendix

Since there are no copies in the Communist Party archives of the leaflet about India distributed to the troops, we reproduce below the version that was printed in the *Brecon County Times* on 12 June 1930. It was headed: 'We must not murder the workers and peasants of India' and ran as follows:

Comrades,

India is ablaze. The great national revolutionary movement is sweeping the country. Ground down for centuries by the blood-sucking British capitalist, hundreds of millions of Indian workers and peasants are breaking their fetters and striking mighty blows for freedom.

Indian troops are going over to their side. They refuse to fire on their brothers and are being replaced by British troops. Already the call has gone out for more British soldiers. At any moment, thousands of us may be shipped off to India.

Comrades, if the imperialist Labour government sends us there, what must we do? Must we obey the orders of the parasites who, for centuries, have battened on the blood of the Indian masses? Must we do the foul work which the Indian soldiers have so heroically refused, and murder the masses fighting for bread and national freedom?

No, a thousand times, no! The fight of the Indian workers and peasants is our fight too.

The capitalists who have battened on the misery and want of the Indian coolies, and who wish to continue to do so, are our enemies too.

They have kept us and our kin in poverty. When we were miners, dockers, engineers or cotton workers, they forced starvation on us after long weeks of industrial struggle. Today they are attempting to do the same thing with our brothers and sisters in the woollen industry of Yorkshire.

They forced us into their armed forces through unemployment. When they have finished using us for their foul work against their colonial slaves and the workers at home, they will throw us to starvation once again.

Our course is clear. If the imperialist Labour government sends us to India, and calls on us to shoot down the heroic Indian workers and peasants, we must refuse. Our class duty, alike in the interests of ourselves, the workers and peasants here and in India, is to fraternise with the Indian workers and peasants.

Our guns must be turned against our real enemy – the thieving, robbing, British ruling class and its lackey, the Labour government.

[1] See CPGB statement quoted in James Klugmann, op. cit., vol. 1, p. 159.

[2] Most of the prosecutor's speech was printed in *Labour Monthly*, January, February and March, 1930.

[3] See *Meerut: Release the Prisoners*, pamphlet published jointly by the TUC, the Labour Party and the Parliamentary Labour Party in May 1933.

[4] *Brecon County Times*, 12 and 19 June 1930.

[5] *Brecon County Times*, 3 July 1930.

[6] This information was given to the author by George Aitken in an interview in 1979, shortly before he died at the age of 85.

[7] *Daily Worker*, 8 July 1930.

[8] See William Rust, op. cit., p. 18.

[9] *Daily Worker*, 16 July 1930.

[10] *Fife Herald*, 15 October 1930.

[11] *Western Daily Press*, 7 and 8 July 1931.

[12] *Scotsman*, 18 July 1931.

[13] *Daily Worker*, 15 August 1931.

[14] *Daily Worker*, 22 and 23 October 1931.

[15] See David Divine, *Mutiny at Invergordon*, London 1970, pp. 188 et seq.

[16] *The Times*, 27 November 1931.

CHAPTER 6

The Party and the Unemployed
(1930–35)

When the Labour government was elected in May 1929, unemployment was already high at 1.1 million insured workers, or just under 10 per cent of the workforce. Following the Wall Street crash, and the onset of the most severe world economic crisis yet known, the number out of work rose inexorably, reaching 2.8 million in 1931 when the Labour government fell and Ramsay MacDonald formed his National government. Unemployment remained at just under 3 million – or 20 per cent of insured workers – throughout most of 1932.

Inevitably, the composition of the Party reflected this situation. Thus in November 1930, when membership reached its lowest level – 2,555 – no less than 845 – one third – were out of work.[1] In 1931 when the membership shot up again to around 6,000 the majority of the new recruits were unemployed. One reason they joined was that the Party offered them something positive – the chance to get into action – which no other political party did. The Party's work among the unemployed was in the main channelled through the National Unemployed Workers' Movement (which had been known as the National Unemployed Workers' Committee Movement until 1929).

Throughout the whole of the inter-war period, the NUWM was the body chiefly responsible for mobilising the jobless, and organising resistance to hunger and persecution. It showed a remarkable capacity for survival despite all attempts from outside to destroy it. These attempts included the decision of the Labour leadership and the TUC to proscribe it, as well as continual interference and general harrassment.

Moreover, after the Leeds Congress in 1929 the NUWM suffered, as did the Minority Movement, from the inhibiting effects of the Class-against-Class policy. Yet, unlike the Minority Movement which, as we shall see, faded away under these pressures, the NUWM lived on. In the spring of 1930, soon after the Labour Party

74

National Executive had sent out a circular prohibiting any association with it, the NUWM had a dues-paying membership of 20,000. By the autumn of 1931 this had risen to 37,000; a year later it was put at 50,000.[2]

The main objects of the NUWM, as laid down in a revised constitution adopted at its annual conference in 1929, were to lead the struggle for 'work or full maintenance at trade-union rates'; to fight for higher benefits and the removal of grievances connected with their administration; to unite employed and unemployed, and so prevent the latter being used to undermine wages; to compel payment of trade-union rates on work schemes for the unemployed; and to struggle 'against the danger of peaceful toleration of poverty'. The final clause in the constitution read:

> Capitalism is the system which inevitably creates unemployment; we declare therefore that our movement shall keep before itself the ultimate goal of working-class power for the overthrow of capitalism and the establishment of the Workers' Socialist Republic.

Membership of the NUWM was open to all unemployed workers, male and female, who accepted these principles and who paid 2d for a membership card and 1d a week thereafter. Employed workers were eligible as associate members; they paid 6d for their entrance card and 4d a month thereafter.

The members were grouped in branches which numbered between 200 and 300 in 1930–31, rising to 386 in 1932. If four or more branches existed in one district, they were entitled to form a District Council for the purpose of co-ordinating the work. In 1932 there were 32 such District Councils composed of branch delegates; each of the councils elected a representative to the National Administrative Council which met quarterly. This appointed a headquarters advisory committee to carry out its decisions. The NAC had always had a majority of Party members on it, but after the Labour and TUC bans, there was a greater preponderance of Communists.

One of the problems facing the NUWM was its floating membership. Except in the distressed areas, where many people had been continuously out of work for years on end, the membership tended to be in a state of flux, since most members would drop out when they found work. But to offset such losses, new recruits were continually flocking in. The movement's vitality arose partly from the fact that most branches were organised around the Labour Exchanges. To collect benefit, the unemployed had to sign on at the local Exchange as often as required – usually two or three times a week. The signing-on process involved queuing up in the street, sometimes for an hour or more. The NUWM activists would conduct open-air meetings within sight and sound of these queues. Many Communists were experienced open-air speakers. They were accustomed to putting up a platform on a street corner – or even standing on a chair – and holding forth to anyone who would stop and listen. They spoke without microphones (which only began to make an appearance here and there in the late 1930s) and many developed into highly gifted orators who could hold the interest of large crowds. Most NUWM branches had one or two members who could perform in this fashion and they offered opportunities to any who wanted to learn the art and themselves become speakers.

Propaganda meetings outside Labour Exchanges were a regular event in most industrial areas, and some NUWM branches went even further; they conducted their branch meetings in the open. At such meetings, committee members would be elected, and activity for the coming week would be discussed, including, for example, demonstrations and marches to the local Public Assistance Committee, the mobilisation of members to sell the *Daily Worker*, invitations to help block the eviction of an unemployed family, arranging for squads to chalk slogans in the streets, and so on.

The importance of the Labour Exchange as the focal point for building the NUWM was only too well understood by the authorities; at the end of 1931, Lord Trenchard, Commissioner of the Metropolitan Police imposed a ban on meetings outside the Exchanges in London. Those who tried to break this ban were arrested, and there was conflict with the police here and there; London branches of the NUWM were obliged to spend much time devising ways to beat the ban.

From November 1931 to the end of 1934 the local Public Assistance Committees (PACs), appointed by the County Councils and Borough Councils, were responsible for fixing the scale rates of 'transitional benefit', i.e. the benefit to which the unemployed had to resort once their national insurance unemployment benefit was exhausted. The PACs were also responsible for the operation of the 'household means test'. The maximum scale rate which the PACs were allowed to award was low enough and meant, at best, terrible deprivation, at worst, hunger; but local PACs could – and often did – fix scale rates far below the maximum. The household means test meant that the earnings of young boys and girls were used to reduce the allowances of unemployed parents; conversely, parents in work were forced to maintain the young unemployed teenagers living at home. Nearly half the unemployed were on 'transitional benefit' and it rapidly became clear after 1931 that local agitation and propaganda, local deputations and marches stirring up public opinion, could have a great influence in persuading the councillors who served on the PACs to provide the highest scale of benefit permitted, and to modify the harshness of their local means test. Thus many NUWM branches could claim that their activities had achieved important practical results.

It was this that led to police violence in Birkenhead in 1932. Here the NUWM had led a peaceful march to the local PAC to secure an increase in the scale of transitional benefit. They achieved their object; the PAC, after receiving a deputation, made some concessions. But at subsequent demonstrations, the police went into action; they clubbed down many demonstrators, and followed this up by raiding workers' homes at midnight, smashing windows, beating up the inhabitants, arresting all the local NUWM leaders and taking them away in a Black Maria.

As well as agitating for concessions, the NUWM gave advice and guidance to individual members on their rights. Most NUWM branches had a 'Claims Secretary', aided by a committee, who helped members to avoid being cut off benefit under one rule or another, saw to it that they got as much as they were entitled to and, if necessary, went with them to state their case in front of Courts of Referees, or other local adjudicating machinery. Appeals to the 'Umpire' – whose decisions were published as case law, and therefore binding on other similar cases – were handled by NUWM headquarters where a Legal Department, financed by a special levy of 1s per week per branch, not only arranged for Umpire appeals, but gave advice to branches on legal questions.

Most local branches had one or two members who became expert on unemployment insurance and on how to sidestep the more punitive regulations. They were thus able to offer advice to the members, helping them to avoid the worst penalties imposed under the means tests or, in earlier years, under the 'not genuinely seeking work' regulations, the Anomalies Act (which denied benefit to many married women), the regulations concerning 'task work' and so forth. Under the NUWM rules, branch officials might not defend the claims of non-members before the authorities concerned; any non-member who wanted help in stating a case had to take out a card and pay a month's contribution in advance.

Controversy Over the NUWM's Role

The NUWM's activities on individual claims provoked some argument within the Party. As has already been indicated, the NUWM was less affected by the 'Class against Class' line than most other spheres of Party activity. This did not mean that in the atmosphere prevailing after the Leeds Congress, the leaders of the NUWM could escape criticism. At the first Political Bureau meeting in January 1930, R.W. Robson, then District Secretary of the London Party, spoke of the tendencies towards 'legalism' in the NUWM's work, by which he meant that the organisation spent too much time on detailed help to individuals, and acting as spokesmen for individual cases. Robson was supported by others who criticised the concentration on legal work rather than mass agitation. Later, at another Political Bureau meeting on 21 March 1930, there was a long discussion, mostly critical of Hannington who, as NUWM National Organiser, was in attendance. Among others, R.P. Arnot deplored 'the tendency of the NUWM to become a kind of specialised trade union.'[3] Arnot was reflecting the view widely held in RILU circles that the constitution and structure of the NUWM and, in particular, the insistence on dues-paying membership, inhibited the mobilisation for action of the mass of unemployed workers. There were, after all, 2 million unemployed workers, yet the NUWM had a membership of only 20,000–40,000. It was argued that the payment of dues deterred people from joining.

Hannington himself thought that, in some NUWM branches, concentration on defence of individual cases distracted the branch leaders from other activities. There were some members who believed that fighting such cases was the most important aspect of the NUWM's work; Hannington thought they were wrong, arguing that such work should not be regarded as an end in itself.[4] But he fiercely resisted the proposals emanating from the RILU that the NUWM should cease to be a tightly organised, dues-paying body. 'I don't believe that the unemployed in Britain prefer to have an organisation they don't pay for,' he told the Central Council of the RILU at a special session held in December 1931.[5]

He did not elaborate on that occasion, but in truth the NUWM *was* a kind of 'specialised trade union', as Arnot had alleged, and that was not its weakness but its strength. It was not that the membership dues were crucial as a source of income; much more could be, and was, raised by collections. But for the jobless people who joined it, payment of dues meant self-respect. Instinctively, those who built up the organisation had adopted a framework that bore many resemblances to their trade unions, and that was part of its appeal.

For NUWM members, life was bleak. The majority of those who joined were young men in the 25–34 age group. A large part of their time was spent loafing about on street corners, bored, aimless and without hope. Work and money had disappeared, and with them their former social life. They could no longer meet their friends at the local pub, because they had not the cash to stand a round. In the NUWM it did not matter so much that you had no money and your clothes were getting shabbier every day, because everyone else was in the same boat. The NUWM provided interest, some excitement perhaps, a chance for everyone to participate. The least articulate could make themselves indispensable by assuming responsibility for one or other of the manifold activities associated with campaigns – leafleting, chalking, carrying the platform to the meeting place, and so on. The NUWM offered them something that unemployed people always need: a purpose in life and a sense of belonging.

In the end, the RILU dropped the proposal to abandon dues-paying, but concentrated instead on urging that broad unemployed councils be set up at every Labour Exchange, the membership of which would not be confined to members of the NUWM and which would draw employed workers into activity. This proposition was reiterated in the 'January resolution' adopted by the ECCI on 29 December 1931. It had been urged most strongly by the German representatives on the RILU.[6]

But however applicable such a strategy was in Germany, it was a non-starter in Britain. It was accepted by the British Party as an aim, and was reiterated in the resolution adopted by the Twelfth Congress of the Party in November 1932, but except in isolated instances, such councils were not set up. It soon became clear that the overriding aim of the British Party leadership – unity between employed and unemployed – could not be achieved in this way.

Marches and Demonstrations

The NUWM became famous for its organisation of Hunger Marches. These could be local or regional, and designed to last a few days only, or they could be national, in which case contingents starting from various parts of the country would head for London. The earliest contingent to take the road would be Scottish because it had the greatest distance to travel; in the following weeks other groups would in turn start off, all of them timed to converge on London on a given day, usually to be met in Hyde Park by a massive demonstration of welcome. During the period 1929–36 five such national Hunger Marches took place.

They required weeks of preparation. Everyone who wanted to march had to undergo a medical check-up. Money had to be collected, initially to provide each marcher with boots, socks and a kitbag, and sometimes other clothing, since people on unemployment benefit could seldom afford to replace worn-out clothes. At each town or village through which the marchers passed, they collected money for the next leg; the aim was to arrive by late afternoon at some town where a meeting would be held and the crowds addressed. In areas where there was a strong labour movement tradition, reception committees would have prepared a meal, and – with luck – secured the loan of a hall or other public building where the marchers could spend the night. Where no such preparation had been made the marchers would head for the workhouse, where they would invariably refuse treatment as 'casuals' and cause enough trouble to persuade the authorities to make concessions.

The least successful march was that in 1930 which took place during the period of the Labour government. It had been hurredly organised and numbered no more than 350 marchers, though there was one important innovation: for the first time, there was a women's contingent. This reflected the fact that unemployment among women was growing fast in the textile areas. But on this march the hostility of the Labour leaders combined with the sectarian slogans of the 'Class against Class' policy resulted in the reception arrangements being totally inadequate in most towns.

Most of the accommodation was provided by the workhouses.

Very different was the march in 1932. For though the hostility of the Labour leaders was no less, the attitude in the localities had begun to change, and the 2,000 marchers, organised in seventeen contingents, who took to the road in September and October of that year were given a warm welcome by local trade union and Labour Party members in many of the towns through which they passed.

It was on this march that police harassment and indeed police violence was very marked. It culminated in baton charges by mounted police in London in which many demonstrators were injured, and in a raid on the NUWM headquarters and the arrest of the four NUWM leaders: Hannington, Sid Elias, Emrys Llewellyn and Tom Mann.[7] By the time the Hunger Marches of 1934 and 1936 took place the police were acting with more restraint, and on the latter occasion a crowd of over a quarter of a million was present to welcome it in Hyde Park.

By 1934 the government had decided that the PACs which had been so susceptible to pressure from local unemployed agitators were to be relieved of their responsibility for fixing transitional benefit. This function was to be taken over by a newly formed central body, the Unemployment Assistance Board, which would in future administer the means test on a uniform basis. The new arrangements came into force in January 1935, and it immediately transpired that at least half the unemployed were to get harsher treatment from the UAB than they had from their local PAC.

That month the NUWM call for action received an unprecedented response. 300,000 people came out on demonstrations in Wales; there were large scale protests in Glasgow and other parts of Scotland and in the North of England. In Sheffield, 40,000 people participated in a march to the Town Hall, resulting in a hurried deputation to Parliament from the City Council led by the Lord Mayor. By 5 February 1935 the government was in full retreat; a Standstill Order was announced under which applicants were to get either what they would have got under the previous PAC assessment or an allowance in accordance with the new UAB regulations, whichever was the higher. The Standstill Order became an Act which remained in force for nearly two years.

'We have scored one of the greatest victories in the history of the British working-class movement', a circular sent out to branches by NUWM headquarters on 6 February, 1935 declared:

The National Government, in face of the tremendous storm of working-class demonstrations and mass action, led by the NUWM, has been compelled to màke a humiliating retreat to restore the cuts. This is what mass action has been able to do. . . It is an emphatic answer to those tame reformist labour leaders who have consistantly told the workers that they must wait till the next General Election before they can remedy their grievances.[8]

[1]See *Inprecorr*, 19 May 1932, p.446.
[2]Wall Hannington, *RILU Magazine*, 1 February 1932. See *Pollitt's report, The Communist International*, October 1932, p.619.
[3]JK folder 9.
[4]JK folder 15.
[5]Hannington, art. cit.
[6]See, for example, Fritz Heckert, *Inprecorr*, 10 September 1931, p.884; F. Emrich, *RILU Magazine*, 15 November 1931. See also G. Evers, *RILU Magazine*, 15 September 1931.
[7]The hunger marches are well described in *The Hunger Marchers in Britain, 1920–1940* by Peter Kingsford, London 1982. The behaviour of the police and the activities of the police informers and Special Branch is dealt with in detail.
[8]Hannington papers, Circular no D 39, 6 February 1935; the Hannington papers are in the CP Archives.

CHAPTER 7

Industrial Struggles: How the Line Was Changed
(1930–35)

In 1931 some 75 per cent of those employed were manual workers. Communist Party members came mainly from among them: miners, engineers, furniture workers, building workers, shipyard workers, railwaymen, dockers, and so on. Party members took it for granted that the main challenge to the employing class must come from industrial workers. They believed that economic strikes would one day develop into political strikes, and finally to all-out revolution. The first, elementary step towards this was to establish solidarity at the workplace through trade union organisation. Already many Party members had made their mark as outstanding trade-union activists.

But between 1929 and 1931 the Party's former base in the trade union movement faded away. The trade-union leaders had tried to destroy the Party; ironically, 'Class against Class' had made their job much easier.

In theory the new line had laid it down that Party members and Minority Movement supporters must go on working within the 'reformist' unions. But, in practice, few could face the kind of task expected of them. No longer must they hold out hope of transforming the unions into genuine instruments of struggle. This was thought to be an illusion, since the reformist bureaucracy would split the unions before this could happen. In other words, the former perspective of joining with others to try and change the unions from within had vanished. Instead, Party members were called upon to exercise 'independent leadership'.

The meaning of 'independent leadership' in practice was illustrated during the woollen strike in Yorkshire in the spring of 1930. Here there were about 250,000 woollen workers, 60 per cent of them women, with a high proportion not organised in trade unions. Employment was dispersed among many hundreds of mills, the largest single concentration being around Bradford, which became the focal point of Party activity during the strike.

The employers were trying to enforce big wage cuts, and the union leaders, after unsuccessfully offering smaller wage reductions as a compromise, told their members to stop work if and when the threatened large reductions were imposed. These started in April 1930 and the stoppage quickly spread.

In anticipation of coming events, a conference was called in Bradford on 23 March under the auspices of the Minority Movement. 125 people attended and a Committee of Action was elected which, a few days later was converted into a 'Central Strike Committee'.[1] It included unemployed woollen workers and sympathisers outside the industry who wanted the workers to win. Those members of the Committee who were strikers had not been elected by the workers from their respective mills; they were present on their own initiative, and not as delegates. In line with the Strasburg resolution, the 'Central Strike Committee' issued a continuous call for the formation of rank-and-file committees in each mill. There was no response.

Despite this failure, the 'Central Strike Committee' made a remarkable contribution towards maintaining solidarity. Among other things, it was responsible for organising much of the picketing, for collecting money, for arrangements to feed the strikers, for marches to the Public Assistance Committees, and so on. The Party's best organisers and propagandists were mobilised to help, including Pollitt, Gallacher and Murphy and two women, Lily Webb, who came down from the Tyneside to participate, and Isabel Brown, already recognised as an outstanding speaker and organiser; her husband, Ernest Brown, was the Party District Secretary in Yorkshire. Meetings were held outside mill gates; many were broken up by police, there were reports of police brutality; a number of Party members, including Isabel Brown, were arrested.[2] Between March and June 1930, the membership of the Party in Bradford rose from 66 to 300.

At the beginning of June, the union leaders authorised separate negotiations with individual employers for wage reductions, following which the strike quickly crumbled. The 'Central Strike Committee' issued a call to continue the strike; not a single mill did so. A little later it was discovered that half of the 240 new recruits to the Party in Yorkshire had already left.

The woollen dispute furnished some lessons which had in the end to be reluctantly accepted. One was that rank-and-file committees did not, as a rule, spring up as a result of a generalised call from outside; one individual worker inside a workplace with a clear grasp of what was needed, and able to initiate group activity, was worth countless propaganda meetings outside, no matter how talented the speakers.

Another lesson was that industrial or workplace organisation which was separate from the existing trade unions did not provide a basis on which to build up strength for the future; such organisations could be thrown up in the heat of battle but tended to melt away as soon as the particular conflict was over.

Horner and the South Wales Miners

This lesson was to be underlined most devastatingly in the 1931 South Wales miners' dispute. The background to this was the Labour government's 1930 Coal Mines Act which reduced hours per shift from eight to seven-and-a-half. Coal owners and union officials failed to reach agreement on how the new rules were to be applied and on 1 January 1931 the employers arbitrarily announced new rosters involving wage reductions and spreadover of hours. There was a spontaneous downing of tools; the miners struck and stayed out for over a fortnight. With government help, the union officials secured a temporary compromise while the matter went to arbitration. This compromise was endorsed by 169 votes to 72 at a South Wales Miners' Federation (SWMF) conference on 17 January, after which most pits returned to work. The end result of the arbitration was a 6 per cent wage reduction announced in March. The SWMF leaders reluctantly advocated acceptance of this award, and at a SWMF conference on 20 March a motion for strike action against the reduction was narrowly defeated on a card vote by 787 to 747.

Unlike previous occasions, the Party members and the Minority Movement played almost no part in influencing the events just described. Indeed, the Minority Movement hardly existed any longer, except on paper. The secretary of the miners' section of the Minority Movement was now Arthur Horner, who had only taken up the position a few weeks earlier. As previously recounted,

Horner had not been re-elected to the Party Central Committee in 1929, largely as a result of his own wishes. He had subsequently spent most of 1930 working with the RILU and had only returned to Britain in December.

In response to the spontaneous downing of tools on 1 January, the Minority Movement convened a conference in Cardiff on 10 January attended by 55 delegates, said to represent 20,000 miners (about 12 per cent of the workforce) and a 'Strike Committee' was set up with Arthur Horner as chairman. But at the SWMF conference held a week later on 17 January, when the proposal to return to work was endorsed, there was only one party member present. According to Horner, this was the smallest representation at such a conference in the Party's history, and since 90 per cent of the delegates were elected direct from the collieries via the lodges, it demonstrated the fact that Party members now regarded work in the 'reformist unions' as of no account.

When the decision to resume work was taken, a furious row broke out between Horner and his colleagues on the Welsh District Committee. The so-called 'Strike Committee' of which he was chairman issued a call to continue the strike, but only one pit stayed out (and this was over a separate issue), whereupon Horner asked to be relieved of his position as chairman of the 'Strike Committee.' Writing a letter of complaint to the miners' section of the RILU, he said that the tactics employed to continue the struggle after 17 January had been 'infantile'.[3]

> The role of the SWMF was practically disregarded, artificial strike committees, really MM groups, were set up as alternatives to the Lodges without mass content, resulting only in our isolation.

The response of the Party leadership was to issue a statement criticising the mistaken idea that the machinery of the South Wales Miners Federation was the decisive factor determining the Party's strategy and tactics. A series of articles appeared in the *Daily Worker* analysing the weaknesses shown in the strike, one of which was 'a deep-rooted conviction' that it was impossible to carry on the struggle independently of the Miners' Federation. This weakness was termed 'trade union legalism.'[4]

At a series of aggregate meetings of Party members in South members in South Wales, the line of the leadership received majority support. But Horner refused to attend any of them. On 26 February a statement from the Political Bureau appeared, drawing attention to the 'refusal of Comrade Horner to recognise the defeatist role that he played as chairman of the Central Strike Committee' and saying that he had 'deserted his post at a vital moment.'

The Minority Movement continued to hold conferences in South Wales and there were some well-attended mass meetings. After the SWMF meeting on 20 March when the proposal to strike was narrowly defeated, the 'Central Strike Committee' issued a call for strike action. But only six pits responded and came out. After this it was clear that an all-out strike was no longer feasible.

The argument with Horner continued, however. Throughout, Horner was careful not to question the validity of the line of 'independent leadership' which had been adopted by the Leeds Congress. What he did was to underline the artificial and non-representative character of the so-called 'Central Strike Committee' which he attributed to the absence of 'preparatory mass work' and for which he blamed the Party leadership. By May he was threatened with expulsion from the Party, but was called to a meeting of the Central Committee to explain his conduct before any decision should be taken. In the course of a long report concerning the events in South Wales, he made the following statement:

> It has been queried about whether I am still a Communist . . . I believe that no individual can be a revolutionary member of the working class if they are outside the ranks of the Communist Party . . . therefore the suggestions which have been made for my expulsion from this movement have a very, very serious meaning for me. Because after all, comrades, I want you to understand that my association with the revolutionary movement in this country is not something of yesterday or even the day before. Though only 36 years of age I have been for more than 20 years actively connected, taking an active part in the revolutionary struggle in this country . . . I regard this matter as a vitally serious matter to me – it is life and death for me . . . in the sense that to be outside of the revolutionary working-class movement is something that I have never thought about when thinking about living in the future.[5]

In the end it was decided that Horner should go to Moscow. There prolonged discussions took place, and in September 1931 he made a statement agreeing that his political line had been mistaken. He arrived back in Britain in time to stand as Communist candidate for East Rhondda in the October General Election. He polled 10,359 votes (against 22,000 for the Labour candidate), a higher vote than for any other Communist candidate.

At this election Conservative candidates, calling themselves 'national' and headed by Labour's defector, Ramsay MacDonald, were returned by an overwhelming majority. But the assumptions of the CI that once the social democrats had exposed themselves, their supporters would turn to the Communists was shown to be quite unfounded. It is true that Labour's vote slumped by 1¾ million, but these former Labour voters did not vote Communist – most of them failed to go to the polls at all. The Communist Party's 26 candidates won between them 75,000 votes. The average percentage of the poll received by Communists was 7.5, an improvement, certainly, on the 5.3 per cent achieved in 1929, but not as large as that hoped for. Indeed the election revealed a trend which was to be seen many times in subsequent years: disillusioned Labour voters do not necessarily swing left.

Change and the International Movement

The British Party leaders had not really expected to make major electoral gains, so the results did not come as a surprise except at Comintern headquarters, where another British Commission was convened in December 1931. And here, at last, Harry Pollitt was able to convince the ECCI that the attitude to the trade unions in Britain must be changed. Thus, the British Party was at last enabled to begin extricating itself from the 'independent leadership' trap as laid down at the Leeds Congress.

The main battle took place at an RILU Central Council session where Pollitt challenged Losovsky's formulations on the future work of the Minority Movement. The underlying idea, said Pollitt, had been that the Minority Movement should be built up on the lines of the revolutionary trade union opposition in Germany. In the opinion of the British delegation, on the contrary, the need was to encourage every manifestation of revolt *inside* the existing unions. Giving as examples the Members' Rights Committee Movement in the Amalgamated Engineering Union and the Builders Forward Movement, in both of which Party members had been closely involved, he criticised the theory emanating from the RILU that

such organisations were barriers to the advance of the MM, and that
the Party had been making a mistake in encouraging them. 'This
point of view is wrong,' asserted Pollitt.

> Our task, far from stifling these movements, is to encourage and
> stimulate them. . . We want to state openly that we will not be
> able to achieve this drive into the reformist unions unless there is
> a change of attitude both on the part of the militant workers under
> our influence in England, and on the part of the Profintern.[6]

The upshot of the 'British Commission' was a statement adopted
by the ECCI, published at the beginning of 1932, which became
known as the 'January resolution'. This reiterated many of the
unfounded assumptions concerning the 'radicalisation of the masses'
but, in respect of trade-union work, it made a significant change in
direction. In Part IV it spoke of the need to fight for the
'transformation of the trade union branches from organs of class
collaboration into organs of class struggle.'

Pollitt lost no time on his return. He told the Political Bureau that

> there must be a relentless combatting of the theory that the unions
> are played out and this 'new union' psychology must be strangled
> . . . the theory that the trade unions are now schools of capitalism
> and we are in them to destroy them is absolutely false.[7]

Publication of the 'January resolution' was followed up by a series
of eleven articles in the *Daily Worker* on how to build up organisation
in the place of work. Much of the guidance revealed the weak state
of trade-union organisation then prevalent. The articles were
attributed to 'the Secretariat'; most were obviously written by
Pollitt. They began by stressing the need to know what the issues
were in any given workplace: the conditions of work, wages, hours,
methods of speed-up, canteen arrangements, lavatory
accommodation, etc.

> To be able to listen to a conversation in the canteen, or in the
> tram, or in the place where the workers go to, pinch two whiffs
> at a Woodbine, and then be able to sense what is the grievance in
> that factory, what needs putting right, that is the big thing. We
> must be able to seize on an issue immediately it arises, perhaps to
> get a protest meeting called after the buzzer has gone, or a
> resolution passed and sent to the management.[8]

Party members who were active only in their leisure hours were criticised:

> It is rather a pronounced habit in our party only to be Communists when we have got our working clothes off and are hurrying up with our tea so as to go to some local meeting in connection with other party members. Until we are firmly convinced that we must be Communists in our daily work in the factories on the basis of the issues that arise there and not what we are too often inclined to manufacture, we cannot take even the first steps towards winning the majority of the working class.[9]

One article poked fun at the comrade who held forth fluently on questions like 'Do you think England will finish with Free Trade?' or 'Things are looking black in Manchuria' but was not concerned with the day-to-day issues around which workers could be mobilised for action.[10] Several articles dealt with the wrong attitudes to work in the trade unions; 'we have only seen the TU leaders, and not the masses who are organised inside the TUs.'[11] There were some withering remarks about the Party's previous strike tactics, and a strong welcome for the new rank-and-file movements which were springing up.

Gradually, the new approach bore fruit. It was uphill work partly because Party members had too often dropped out of trade union activity. Neither in the 'January resolution' nor in the subsequent lead from British Party headquarters was it suggested that there had been anything wrong with the new line as formulated at the Leeds Congress and subsequently. The weaknesses in the industrial work were initially attributed to sectarian distortions of the new line. However, the contradiction between the new approach, led by Pollitt, and that of the Leeds Congress could hardly be overlooked and, indeed became the subject of controversy in the discussion leading up to the Party's 12th Congress to be held in the Autumn of 1932.

The discussion was launched by Pollitt in an article on trade union work which appeared in the *Daily Worker* on 20 August. Pointing out that of the 700 delegates to the forthcoming Trade Union Congress *only two* were Party members, he said that the Party must 'try and make the trade union organisations of the workers strong and powerful weapons in their daily fight.' The Party was *not* out to disorganise and disrupt the trade unions, he wrote, it was out to smash the power of the trade-union leaders who had made the unions allies of the employers in conniving at wage cuts and rationalisation. Stressing the contribution Party members could have made in a recent Lancashire cotton dispute if they had had members on the Weavers Union committees (since they would have known how to organise mass meetings, and get workers together from different mills, and so on) he said the Party should try to win the lower trade-union officials for its policy.

Pollitt's line was challenged by R. Palme Dutt who, on 14 September, voiced 'a very strong protest against a recent tendency to reverse our whole trade-union line' and followed it up with an article on 19 September on the danger of returning to the old, pre-Leeds Congress policy on trade unions. On Pollitt's statement that the Party aimed to strengthen the trade unions, Dutt said:

> Of course, Pollitt means that it is essential to win the lower organs of the reformist unions. . . But many readers might easily misunderstand this expression as meaning that we are to win the reformist unions as a whole and so make them powerful weapons in the daily fight.

He criticised Pollitt's statement that the Party was not out to destroy the unions but to destroy the influence of the trade union leaders. He argued that when Pollitt said 'we have to work to win these union organisations' he really meant that we should 'win the rank-and-file organs of the reformist unions'. Quoting Pollitt's assertion that 'the Communist Party is for a powerful united trade unionism,' Dutt said that, on the contrary, 'we stand for a powerful, united, revolutionary trade union opposition.'

In a letter the following week, published on 26 September Pollitt refuted Dutt's somewhat patronising suggestions that he had not really meant what he said, but something different. The article, said Pollitt, 'represents quite accurately my opinions, which were carefully and deliberately formulated.' 'To add to my other heresies,' he wrote, 'I hate the phrase "revolutionary trade union opposition", firmly believing that the word "opposition" in England is widely understood to be opposition to trade unionism.'

He agreed that the policy of the trade union leaders was 'social fascism', 'but that is a vastly different thing from labelling the whole of the trade unionists social fascists.' He poured scorn on Dutt's argument that, while it was essential to win the lower organs of the unions, it was wrong to imply that we aimed to win the unions as a whole

> We can strengthen the branches and District Committees for our revolutionary line and then full stop. Thus far and no further is the motto. Anything that happens after that, anything which is forced through a reformist union machinery, suddenly becomes a cunning manoeuvre.

For the next few weeks the controversy continued. Gallacher criticised Dutt, declaring 'I am all the way with Pollitt.'[12] Dutt's other critics included the miner and UMS leader Willy Allan and – significantly – young Jimmy Shields who had been the British representative in Moscow since the turn of the year. But Dutt had the support of Rust and John Mahon. The Tyneside District Party Committee passed a resolution supporting Dutt and attacking Pollitt and Gallacher.[13] The response to this was a lengthy resolution from the Scottish District Committee which, without mentioning Dutt by name, challenged his whole stand on work in the trade unions, asserting that it was nonsense to regard the trade unions and even the union apparatus as 'one indivisible whole'. It said: 'We must make it understood beyond doubt that we are in favour of building the trade unions, not of disrupting them.'[14]

It was now a few days before the congress, and Pollitt having made his point, deemed it wise to strike a conciliatory note. The discussion had shown, he said, that 'I made certain unclear formulations that might be used to distort the line of the workers' independent fight'; he had not been trying to revise the line of the Party but 'the rotten sectarianism that is paralysing our work in the unions.' And he pointed to a hopeful sign: the development of a whole series of rank-and-file movements.[15]

At the ensuing 12th Congress held on 12–15 November, Pollitt called for 'an end to all this useless talk about whether we can win the apparatus or whether we cannot' and said, to applause, that the main issue before Congress was what the Party was going to do in the factories and trade unions in order to win them.[16] In the resolution that was passed, the various rank-and-file movements were characterised as 'important phases in the development of independent leadership', while the words of the January resolution concerning the need to carry on work in the 'reformist unions' were adopted together with a call to make a 'decisive change in our work' in this respect.

Rank-and-File Movements

In point of fact, the change had already begun. It had shown itself in the formation of the Members' Rights Movement in engineering which Pollitt had defended at the RILU. The origin of this Movement was a decision in the summer of 1931 by the Executive of the Amalgamated Engineering Union to sign an agreement with the employers for wage reductions without consulting the union's members. After some indignant resolutions and protest meetings called under the auspices of the Minority Movement, a number of Party members were expelled from the Union, including Joe Scott, Percy Glading and Alec Herman of London; Bill Ward of Sheffield; Tom Sillars of Glasgow; William Stokes of Coventry and a big group in Manchester including Steve Nuttall and Edmund Frow. Those expelled did *not* try to form another union; on the contrary, they formed the Members' Rights Movement aiming at reinstatement; it launched petitions, organised branch resolutions and started a special monthly paper, *The Monkey Wrench*. The campaign succeeded; in July 1932, the Union's Final Appeals Court reinstated those expelled.

Another rank-and-file movement which was, by 1932, meeting with some success was the Railwaymen's Vigilance Movement. This concentrated on issues in the rail depots, but saw to it that they were brought to the branches for discussion and action. The movement's monthly paper the *Railway Vigilant* had a circulation of some 12,000.

The most effective of the 'rank-and-file' movements initiated by the Party at that time was that of the London busmen which came into existence in the late summer of 1932, just when the debate in the *Daily Worker* was reaching its climax.

London busmen, numbering nearly 25,000, belonged to the giant Transport and General Workers' Union, but had their own 'trade group' status, including a Central Bus Committee with a full-time secretary. The General Secretary of the T&GWU was Ernest Bevin, a determined enemy of Communists, and the Central Bus Committee had shown no signs of being anything but Bevin's obedient servant until the events of 1932. These began when the London General Omnibus Company made it known that it was about to impose wage cuts. Union officials started negotiations.

The Communist Party had no more than twelve members in the London bus fleet; six months earlier they had started a duplicated paper entitled *Busmen's Punch* at the Cricklewood Garage. The paper failed, but now, on 12 July 1932, a new version was launched claiming that it had been 'taken over by a group of militant busmen from a number of London Garages.' About a fortnight later, the news leaked out that the union officials were to recommend acceptance of the company's new terms. A group at Chelverton Road garage summoned an unofficial meeting to discuss the terms; 33 garages were represented and it was decided to set up a delegate committee, later to be known as the Rank and File Committee. The prime mover in getting this meeting called was Bert Papworth, who had previously worked closely with the Party and later became one of its leading members. The meeting coincided with the publication of the second issue of the new re-titled, *Busman's Punch* in which the company's terms were analysed, and there was a call to turn them down.

Shortly afterwards, they were rejected in a four-to-one ballot, and the Central Bus Committee was forced to call an official strike. At this, the company withdrew its threatened wage reductions and dismissals. It was a resounding victory, and the Rank and File Movement claimed the credit. It was soon decided to keep the Rank and File Committee in existence and every garage was asked to elect six delegates (to allow for shifts and inside staff) to attend monthly meetings. The Committee took over responsibility for the *Busman's Punch*, setting up an editorial board and appointing Emile Burns (a leading Communist by this time working at 16 King Street) as the Technical Editor.[17] By November, the paper was being printed and throughout the next five years, it had a regular monthly readership among busman of about 10,000.

The Rank and File Committee was a genuine example of collaboration between left-wingers of different ideas. Its secretary was a member of the Independent Labour Party, Bill Jones, who afterwards joined the Communist Party. Among the Party members on the Committee were Bill Ware from Enfield and B. Sharkey from Willesden. The latter was elected to the Central Bus Committee in November 1932, and this was the start of a gradual replacement of the existing Central Bus Committee members by a majority of Rank and File Movement nominees. By the end of 1932, membership of the Communist Party in the fleet had risen from 12 to 40; in the next three years it was to reach 100.

In South Wales, the Party was slowly emerging from the isolation imposed upon it during the 1930–31 period. In 1933 it was resolved to try and build a 'rank-and-file' movement; sympathisers were circularised, conferences called, and a rank-and-file paper, *South Wales Miner*, was started in June 1933 with Arthur Horner as its editor. One of its objectives was 100 per cent membership of the South Wales Miners' Federation. Though it had no more than 3,000 readers, its influence was marked, as was shown by the election of Horner by ballot vote in the autumn of 1933 to the position of miners' agent for the Anthracite District of the SWMF. By the beginning of 1935, the Party had 352 members in the SWMF, mostly in responsible positions.[18]

The new approach of the Communist Party to the trade unions was exemplified during a series of strikes in 1933 and 1934, some of which began as spontaneous walk-outs against speed-up on the part of unorganised workers. Guided by its new concept of 'independent leadership' the Party made recruitment to the appropriate union its top priority. But, simultaneously, it revealed that in practice its members knew far better than most how to conduct a strike, and the essential guidelines to be followed which included the need for a democratically-elected and representative strike committee; close daily contact between this committee and those who had elected it by way of regular strike bulletins, frequent mass meetings and, in certain cases, encouragement of strikers to be present during the committee's deliberations; the organisation of picketing and deterrence of strike breakers; mobilising support from other trade-union bodies and labour-movement organisations in the locality; the raising of funds in support of the strikers; and running a food kitchen to feed the strikers (who were probably without strike pay, since they had not been in a union before). Above all, attempts by the union officials to get the strikes called off while they went into negotiations with the employers had to be resisted.

Among the strikes in which Communists played a crucial role in 1933 and 1934 was that against the Bedaux system (a time-and-motion study system brought in from the USA) at the Henry Hope window manufacturers in Smethwick, which Tom Roberts, the Birmingham Communist Party organiser, helped to run; the strike at the Firestone Tyre Factory in West London in which leading London Communist, Ted Bramley, was the moving spirit; a successful strike against wage cuts at the Ford Motor works in Dagenham in which the chief organiser was a Party member working in the toolroom, Jack Longworth. In 1934, when a strike broke out at Pressed Steel company works at Oxford – again a largely unorganised factory – a deputation of strikers went to the local Communist Party premises to ask for help, with the result that Abe Lazarus, the district Party organiser, emerged as the acknowledged leader of the strike, which ended by winning the most important demands with 98 per cent of the strikers organised into their appropriate union.[19]

The Party also made some contribution towards the most difficult job of all: the organisation of women. A big influx of girls into the engineering industry was just beginning. Their low pay served to undermine the wages of the skilled men. The vast majority of the women were not in a trade union, and one of the problems was that the skilled men's unions – particularly the Amalgamated Engineering Union – refused to admit women, so that their only resort was the general workers unions.

The Communist Party had always stood for equal pay for men and women, and for the organisation of women into the same unions as the men. These aims had been incorporated into the Class against Class election manifesto of 1929; in relation to the engineering industry, the question was discussed in some detail at the 13th Communist Party Congress in February 1935. Here a resolution was adopted, pointing out that

> the skilled workers' unions refuse to organise women workers, while the general labour unions are largely indifferent. Communist Party members in the unions must take a leading part in breaking down the hostility to the organisation of women workers.

It called for adequate rates of pay, and for the election of women shop stewards representing the unions in the factories.

One example of Party endeavour in this field was at the Lucas factories in Birmingham where some 15,000 – mainly girls – were employed. Here the Party had initiated resistence to the Bedaux system, after which the firm introduced its own 'Points system'. One of the Party members who led the movement against these systems and in organising women into the union was Jessie Eden who became a shop steward. She was, in 1935, elected to the Central Committee of the Communist Party

The growing influence of Communists in the trade unions

LIGHT on LUCAS

AN EXPOSURE OF THE POINT SYSTEM

impelled the TUC General Council in 1934 to issue what became known as the 'Black Circular' forbidding Trades Councils to accept Communists as delegates from trade-union branches. At the same time, the General Council asked its affiliated unions to prohibit the nomination of 'members of disruptive bodies' for any official positions. The response to this request was mixed, and showed that the positive contribution that Communists were making had brought about a certain change in the attitude of union members. Unions that opposed the TUC request included those of the miners, the two main ralway unions, and the Amalgamated Engineering Union which, only three years earlier, had expelled those Communists who had signed a protest against acceptance of wage cuts, and had then been forced to reinstate them.

At the Thirteenth Party Congress in February 1935, the changed approach to industrial and trade union work was clearly demonstrated. Out of 294 delegates, 234 were trade unionists, and of these 34 were national or district officials of unions, and 82 were branch officials. At this Congress, the Party's growing industrial base was referred to by Pollitt as 'a revolution within the Party'.[20]

[1]JK folder 9.
[2]See May Hill, *Red Roses for Isabel*, London 1982, pp.32–41.
[3]JK folder 14.
[4]*Daily Worker*, 26, 28 and 29 January 1931; 3 February 1931.
[5]JK folder 14.
[6]*RILU Magazine*, Vol.2, Nos 1 and 2, February 1932.
[7]JK folder 15.
[8]*Daily Worker*, 13 January 1932.
[9]*Daily Worker*, 15 January 1932.
[10]*Daily Worker*, 18 January 1932.
[11]*Daily Worker*, 19 January 1932.
[12]*Daily Worker*, 21 September 1932.
[13]*Daily Worker*, 30 September 1932.
[14]*Daily Worker*, 10 November 1932.
[15]*Daily Worker*, 7 November 1932.
[16]JK folder 17. Report of 1932 Congress proceedings.
[17]Burns was at this time working closely with Pollitt at 16 King Street. He had formerly been general secretary of the Labour Research Department which had already printed two pamphlets on behalf of the Busman's Rank and File Committee.
[18]See *The Fed*, Hywel Francis and David Smith, London 1980, pp.190–1, 208, 269.
[19]Recollections of the Pressed Steel Strike and of the role of Abe Lazarus are contained in Part II of 'Morris Motors in the 1930s', Arthur Exell, *History Workshop Journal*, No.7, Spring 1979.
[20]*Daily Worker*, 6 February 1935.

CHAPTER 8

Which Road to Socialism?
(1935)

At the Party's Congress in February 1935 there was a prolonged discussion on long-term aims and the way forward. A new programme was finally adopted, and later published under the title *For Soviet Britain*. In the space of thirty pages it provided a concise and clear exposition of Communist beliefs concerning the path to socialism and, indeed, what was meant by 'socialism'.

Some work on the subject had already been done by Emile Burns and had appeared in two books, *The Only Way Out*,[1] and *Capitalism, Communism and the Transition*.[2] The basic aim of all Communists was, of course, to get rid of the capitalist system in which, as Burns put it,

the means of production are owned by a relatively small class . . . the products are commodities for sale . . . [and the] motive of production is surplus value, created in the process of production by a propertyless working class or 'proletariat'.[3]

The abolition of capitalism would mean that

the means of production and transport are owned, not by any narrow class or group within society, but by the whole people; and therefore the product, the result of the social processes of production, will be at the disposal of the whole people.[4]

This would enable production and distribution to be *planned* and coordinated to the benefit of all.

Communists were convinced that once production for profit had given place to production for need, and a planned economy introduced, idle factories and mass unemployment would disappear. 'Poverty in the midst of Plenty' would be a thing of the past, and so, eventually, would the inequalities and injustices so rife in capitalist society. The abolition of capitalist contradictions and rivalries would mean the end of wars, and of colonial oppression. It would open up the prospect of satisfactory material conditions for

99

all. It would do more than this. It would mean rapid intellectual and cultural development on a scale unknown before, leading the whole human race forward to a higher stage. 'This is the new world for which many generations of British workers have struggled. It is for us in our generation to bring this new world into being.'[5]

Belief in the need to get rid of the capitalist system was shared by all socialists and indeed, constantly stressed by people who professed to be socialists, though their actions belied their words. But Communists differed from other socialists both in their ideas on how to reach the socialist goal, and in their conception of how a socialist society would function. Their ideas were largely based on Lenin's *State and Revolution* written just before the 1917 October Revolution which involved, among other things, an examination of Marx's work on the experience of the Paris Commune in 1871.

According to Lenin, the state machine, including parliament, was not a neutral power standing above society, but an organ of class rule, of oppression of one class (the working class) by another (the capitalist class). Therefore, the working class could not 'simply lay hold of the ready-made state machine and wield it for its own purpose' – it must smash it, and put in its place a system of direct democracy for the workers, i.e. Soviets. In *For Soviet Britain* this theory was expressed in terms of Great Britain.

It was argued in the first place that capitalism could not be ended through parliament. There were two basic reasons for this view. First, 'the capitalist class will never allow itself to be gradually expropriated by successive Acts of Parliament.' Second, parliament itself was not designed to administer a socialist system.

With regard to the first issue – the resistance which could be expected from the capitalist class if threatened with expropriation – it was recalled that twenty years earlier the Tory Party leaders had organised an armed rebellion in Ireland rather than submit to an Act bringing in Home Rule. Since then the rise of fascism in various countries had proved that 'the capitalists themselves will throw overboard all forms of democracy and resort to every kind of lawless violence to preserve their power and their profits.' To the Labour leaders, who declared that workers must choose between a 'peaceful, gradual way of abolishing capitalism' and the revolutionary way advocated by the Communists, the answer was: 'the workers have no such choice. There is no such "peaceful gradual" way.'

In short, violence could not be avoided because the capitalist class ('who are themselves already employing unceasing violence against the workers in every part of the world') would inevitably resort to it if challenged. How then was the capitalist class to be overthrown? 'The answer is that a workers' revolution can do it,' asserted the programme. 'Nor has the Communist Party ever denied that this overthrow must be a forceful one, for the capitalists are certain to resist with all their might.'

But the programme made clear that by 'revolution' was meant a continuous process, not 'a single spontaneous act, coming like a bolt from the blue.' It would begin with a united struggle by the workers for elementary demands, for example against wage cuts, high rents, speed-up, dismissals, and go on to embrace wider questions such as fascism and war and colonial liberation; bit by bit, the point would be reached when the workers must either be crushed by the capitalists or must overthrow them. Crucial in this process would be the attitude of the armed forces; as and when they were asked to perform more tasks of violence 'the capitalists will find that their soldiers, sailors and airmen are after all only workers in uniform.'

With regard to the second issue – parliament as an instrument for the administration of socialism – the programme asserted that once capitalism was overthrown, the British workers would not maintain the present parliamentary system, since this 'had not brought any real democracy to the overwhelming majority of the British people' but, on the contrary, was a form of political organisation which the capitalist class had devised to serve its own needs.

> While Parliament registers formal decisions, it is the whole elaborate machinery of government, from the Cabinet at the top to the Public Assistance Committees at the bottom, and including the Civil Service, the Military, Naval and Air High Commands, the judges, the magistrates and the police, by which the capitalist class manages its affairs and maintains its rule over the working class. How can this whole machinery, officered by the boss class, be expected faithfully to serve the interests of the working class?

'It is quite impossible for the workers to take over this machine and use it for their own entirely different purposes,' it was claimed.

If Parliament was to be abolished, what was to be put in its place? The answer was a 'Workers' Dictatorship.' This did not mean the abolition of democracy, since a workers' dictatorship meant real democracy for the workers, instead of sham democracy.

What form would this rule by the workers take? There would be

> Workers' Councils, made up of delegates elected democractically from every factory, workshop and mine, and from every other grouping of men and women of this country who have to work for their living. . . These Workers' Councils will break up the capitalist machinery of government and take the place of it.

Recalling the setting up of the Councils of Action in 1920 and 1926, and the experience of British workers in organising trade unions and co-operative bodies, shop committees and pit committees, it said that the Workers' Councils would run the affairs of their own localities, and

> these local Workers' Councils will chose their best members as delegates to the National Workers' Council, which will carry on the Government of the country as a whole.

Thus what was envisaged was a 'pyramid' in which each council was composed of representatives elected from the one below. It meant that people would be chosen by those who knew them personally, and worked with them.

Such Workers' Councils, it was argued, would mean for the vast majority, democratic rights and privileges to an extent unknown under capitalism because those who served on them would be elected from below and answerable to those they represented. The parliamentary system, in contrast, kept the mass of the people from participating in the administration of the country, despite the fact that in law they had equal rights. The programme argued that

> It is the absence of this genuine participation in the work of administration which makes the present capitalist form of 'democracy' so empty and useless from the workers' point of view.

In time, as former capitalists became transformed into workers, the need for dictatorship of one class over another would disappear, since classes would have disappeared, and there would come into being an all-inclusive workers' democracy in which everybody would participate. And then, in further course of time, when its laws and regulations had become the habit and custom of the whole people, the need for any state whatever, including 'democracy', would begin to disappear. (In this way, the concept of the 'withering away of the state' was introduced, a prospect explored by Engels in *Anti-Dühring* (1878) and further examined by Lenin in *State and Revolution*.)

Meanwhile, what exactly would the British Soviets, or Workers' Councils, do?

> They will take over, without compensation, the banks, the big factories, the mines, the transport concerns etc from their present owners. Then they will set all these industries to work in order to supply the needs of the people.

Describing the vast increase in production which would ensue, together with the improvements in services, the pamphlet pointed out that such an expansion would only be possible on the basis of a 'scientific plan for the whole economic and social work of the country.'

The need to take over the means of production without compensation was seen as crucial. It was one more issue on which the Communist Party disagreed with the Labour Party. Robin Page Arnot, who introduced the programme to the Party Congress on behalf of the Central Committee, reminded his audience that at its Southport Conference in 1934 the Labour Party had committed itself to compensate owners for industries taken over. Arnot argued:

> This Southport socialism will be introduced by buying out the capitalists. That is to say, capitalist industries are no longer to be nationalised without compensation (as used to be the programme, even of the Fabian Society). Who will provide the means? The answer is that the workers will provide the money. The workers will have to go on being exploited in order to provide money for the bondholders.[6]

The objection of Communists to 'gradualism' or, as Arnot put it, 'purchase by instalment', was two-fold. First it gave the capitalists time to mobilise and repossess themselves. Second, if nationalisation were carried out piecemeal it was hard to justify depriving former owners of compensation while others continued to enjoy the fruits of private ownership. But, if compensation were paid, it could not result in any redistribution of wealth (a criticism which was to be proved true many decades later).

For Soviet Britain ended by picturing the future when the burden of rent, interest and profit had been swept away, and industry and agriculture, under the management of Workers' Councils, would produce for need and not for profit. The programme was printed as a penny pamphlet and 60,000 copies were sold.[7] It was a coherent statement of the Communist Party's view of the way forward after its first fifteen years of existence.

The Impact of the Russian Experience

In this programme, and throughout the discussion around it, British Party members were, of course, assuming that the advance to socialism in Britain would follow the Russian pattern in certain important respects. This was not surprising, since Russia was then the only country trying to build a socialist society.

Less than twenty years earlier, there had been no such country. In 1917 had come the Russian Revolution, after which fourteen governments had sent their armies in to destroy the first socialist state. In Britain, socialists and left-wing shop stewards, inspired by a vision of workers like themselves seizing power, had gone into action demanding 'Hands off Russia'. Thereafter *defence* of the Soviet Union, the campaign to ensure the survival of the first socialist state in a hostile capitalist world, to rally support for it, had been seen by Communists as crucial to the advance of socialism elsewhere.

For although armed intervention by the capitalist powers against Russia ended in 1920, the same powers continued to regard that country as a threat. Not, of course, a military threat – Russian military capability was looked on with contempt; in that respect, the Soviet Union acquired 'great power' status only some twenty-five years later. The hostility of the capitalist world was based on the realisation that if the Russians could make a success of building socialism, workers in the rest of the world might be persuaded to take the same road and, in turn, overthrow their own capitalist class. So every instrument of propaganda in Britain – mainly the press, but to a growing extent, radio – was mobilised to denigrate the Soviet system, to express contempt for its incompetence and inefficiency, to sneer at the notion that industry could be run by workers, to pour scorn on efforts to modernise agriculture.

Initially this was not very difficult, partly because the wars of intervention had been followed in 1921 by the worst famine in living memory. But even without this, Russia at the time of the revolution against the Tsarist régime had been a weak, struggling, abysmally backward country. 80 per cent of the people could not read or write. The majority were peasants. Though the primitive agriculture was interspersed with small islands of industry, the latter lagged far behind their Western counterparts, so that many of the antiquated agricultural implements and machinery used had to be imported.

But a little later, during the mid-1930s, a different picture began to emerge. The land, the rich mineral resources, the means of production had been taken into public ownership, and output and distribution co-ordinated under a central plan. The result had been a vast development of natural resources combined with massive construction of up-to-date heavy industry. This had been accompanied by the introduction of large-scale collective agriculture, employing modern machinery. At a time when the Western capitalist economies were in deep recession, the Soviet Union was half way through its second Five Year Plan. Output was forging ahead, the workforce was establishing one record after another and, apparently, proving the truth of the Communist theory that it was capitalism which held back the forces of production, and that once the capitalist fetters were broken, there could be unprecedented advance. For though nobody pretended that living standards had yet reached those of the most advanced capitalist countries, or denied that there was still a severe shortage of consumer goods, it was clear that the foundations of an up-to-date economy had been established in record time and against overwhelming odds.

It was not just the economic achievements which were impressive. To those on the left, it seemed that a new kind of society was in the making. Unlike Britain, there were no unemployed in the Soviet Union, and workers who found a way of increasing output did not fear that it would lead to lay-offs or a reduction in piece-work prices; on the contrary, they were paid more for their increased output and encouraged to instruct others so that they could do likewise. While workers in capitalist countries were struggling against wage cuts, in the Soviet Union wages were increasing with every industrial advance. There was a legal maximum 7-hour day (6 hours for miners), a level below that prevailing in Britain.

It should be remembered that many of the improvements in social provision which are now taken for granted only came into force in Britain after the Second World War, which made the contrast between the social support provided in the Soviet Union and in Britain very marked. Thus, in Russia every worker was entitled to paid holidays, something only existing here and there in Britain at the time. Pensions and payments during sickness in the Soviet Union were much nearer to average wages than those received in Britain. Medical and hospital treatment were free; in Britain they were not.

In the Soviet Union basic illiteracy had been abolished and the younger generation had educational opportunities never available to their parents and, indeed, not generally offered in Britain. Thus any school leaver who reached a certain standard could go on to university with the help of a maintenance allowance from the state. In Britain only a very limited number of student grants were available.

The attitude to women appeared to be more advanced in the Soviet Union than in any other country in the world. Thus by law, Soviet women had equal rights with men, and were entitled to equal pay – no such law then existed in Britain. Women were employed in many jobs which, in capitalist countries, were considered a male preserve, such as driving trams or bricklaying at one end of the scale, and carrying on professional work as doctors and judges at the other. (In Britain, at the time, there were no female judges and few women doctors.) In the Soviet Union advice on contraceptives and family planning was freely available at state-owned clinics; every pregnant woman was entitled to four months off on full pay. Crèche and nursery facilities were provided at most workplaces; canteens and community restaurants were introduced in order to prevent women becoming kitchen slaves. In all these matters, the Soviet Union was far ahead of Britain at that time.

So, despite the backwardness that still prevailed, the shortages, the lack of decent housing, the low standards in clothing and consumer goods, the Soviet Union seemed to be building a new kind of society.

G.D.H. Cole, by no means a Communist, but a convinced socialist, was one of those who, during the 1930s recognised the influence that the Soviet achievement was having over the minds of many young people in Britain:

The Soviet Union, whatever it may have done amiss, has produced by far the greatest example of constructive achievement of our epoch; and it would be strange indeed if this magnificent creative triumph against tremendous difficulties had not fired the imagination of many of the best among the generation that has been growing up through these tragic, and yet inspiring, years. It is not necessary to be member of the Communist Party in order to recognise the generous impulses which have led many of the most intelligent young men and women towards it.[8]

In Britain, Communists attributed the Soviet Union's successes to two main factors: firstly, the rule of Workers' Councils or Soviets, and secondly, the leadership of the Communist Party. A large measure of corroboration of this view came from an unexpected quarter during 1935 with the publication of a massive book, *Soviet Communism: a New Civilisation?* by the two Fabians, Sidney and Beatrice Webb, hitherto regarded as the leading exponents of parliamentary gradualism. This book, which contained a detailed examination of the Soviet system, running to over 1100 pages, bore out the Communist contention that the Soviet system, far from being the autocratic and oppressive regime portrayed in the anti-Communist literature of the day, was *more* democratic in the sense of rule from below than any other system of government. Thus the Webbs spoke of the

widespread participation in government which seems to us one of the most characteristic notes of Soviet Communism. It is, more than anything else, this almost universal personal participation, through an amazing variety of channels, that justifies the designation of it as a multiform democracy.

And it held that the government of the USSR was 'the very opposite of a dictatorship.'[9]

As for the Communist Party which, in Russia, numbered between two and three million members, the Webbs devoted many pages to describing the 'voluntarily recruited membership of this remarkable companionship', how it had no legal authority over others, could give no orders, but influenced the policy of public authorities by persuasion. Over half the members were manual workers in factories, mines, farms, and so on; they had no financial incentives to join the Party since their pay was limited to a common maximum, their function was to influence those with whom they worked, leading their shifts, teams or brigades into 'socialist competition' with others working in the same field. 'They constitute, it is said, the vanguard of the proletariat . . . the spearhead of its activity in the building up of the socialist state.'[10]

In Retrospect

One day, British Communists were to realise that the Webbs' portrayal of Soviet society formed only part of the picture; that there were flaws in the system which permitted terrible injustices to occur. The crimes perpetrated under the Stalin régime were, in the end, to cause members of the Party to revise their ideas about democracy in the Soviet Union. But, in 1935, the famous trials of leading Russian Communists had not begun, and when they did, their significance was not understood.

There was, however, one thing which caused some misgivings already in 1935, and that was, as Dutt later put it, 'the cult of excessive adulation of Stalin.'[11] At the Seventh World Congress, the British delegation raised objections to this, with the result that there was a prolonged argument with the Comintern leaders.

Meanwhile, although the rise of fascism and the need to defend existing rights and liberties caused a certain modification in the attitude to parliament during the second half of the 1930s, it was not until the war was nearing its end that the British Party began to face up to the fact that the mechanical application of Soviet experiences and methods to Britain was actually an un-Marxist and un-Leninist approach. From then on, extra-parliamentary action ceased to be seen as an *alternative* to parliamentary action; on the contrary, it was realised that the way forward must involve a combination of the two. The object must be to transform and democratise the state machine, and to change the parliamentary system, not to 'replace' it. So began work on a different concept: that of a British road to socialism.

[1]Emile Burns, *The Only Way Out*, London 1932.
[2]Emile Burns, *Capitalism, Communism and the Transition*, London 1933.
[3]Ibid, p.33.
[4]Ibid, p.104.
[5]*For Soviet Britain*, pamphlet published by the Communist Party, 1935, p.46.
[6]Arnot's speech was reprinted as an introduction to the pamphlet *For Soviet Britain*.

[7]Central Committee Report to 14th Congress, contained in *It Can Be Done*, p.250.
[8]G.D.H. Cole, *The People's Front*, London 1937, p.44.
[9]Sidney and Beatrice Webb, *Soviet Communism: a New Civilisation?*, London 1935, pp.427, 436.
[10]Ibid, pp.341, 351.
[11]See letter from R.P. Dutt in *The Times Literary Supplement*, 5 May 1966.

CHAPTER 9

Fascism and the United Front
(1933–35)

In 1932, the British Communist Party had with difficulty extricated itself from the Class against Class guidelines for trade unionism and industrial work. But from 1933 to 1935, much of the theory upon which Class against Class had been built was discarded by the Communist International itself.

The cause for this change was the coming to power of Hitler in Germany. On 30 January 1933, he became Chancellor; on 5 March the Nazis won a majority in the general election.

In the weeks before this election there had been widespread intimidation, with Communists as the chief target. Police occupied the Party's headquarters, the Reichstag (parliament) building was set on fire, and Communists accused of arson. Many Party members were arrested or went into hiding. A little later, the Social Democratic Party and other political groups were dissolved, the opposition press closed down, trade unions suppressed. Soon liberal and Christian organisations were meeting the same fate. The doctrine of racial purity was officially adopted; Jews were persecuted; opponents of the régime ran the risk of arrest, torture, concentration camp, death. In short, a fully fledged fascist dictatorship had come into being.

Hitler's victory was the last thing expected by anyone in the world Communist movement. After the 1917 revolution in Russia, it had always been assumed that Germany would be the next country to have a successful socialist revolution. In many ways the German Communists had been the driving force within the Comintern. Their Party had a vast membership, second only to that of the Russians. Some of the Class against Class tactics had been based on the relationship of forces in Germany. Communists in other countries expected that it was here that the revolution would soon surge forward – this time to victory. Now this vision of the future was fading.

How had it happened? In November 1932 Communists had won

nearly 6 million votes in the German elections, compared with 7.2 million for the Social Democrats; the Nazis had received 11.7 million. Numerically speaking, the two working-class parties should have been able to ward off the Nazi menace. Instead, the disunity – and indeed, antagonism – between the two had enabled the enemy to charge in and smash them both. The initial responsibility for this had lain with the social democratic leaders who, as in Britain, had aimed at collaboration with the employers and had been just as anxious as they were to kill off the Communist Party. But the German Communists had failed to win over the followers of these Social-Democratic leaders, indeed their denunciations of the latter as 'social fascists' had helped to exacerbate divisions.

Faced with the collapse of all its hopes, the Comintern, little by little, embarked on a fundamental change in its approach to working-class unity.

The original concept of the 'united front' as introduced at the Third CI Congress in 1921, had involved a two-sided approach: firstly, and most importantly, the need to win non-Communist workers for united struggle on immediate issues; secondly, the aim of agreements between Communist Parties and non-Communist organisations for joint action. But from the time of the Sixth World Congress in 1928, the second of these ideas had not only been abandoned but also denounced, and the theory that the united front must be only from *below* had become an article of faith.[1] Yet, ironically, the prohibition on attempts at agreement at the top had in practice made unity among the rank and file much more difficult to achieve. Such was the dilemma in which the Comintern found itself in 1933.

Significantly, pressure for Communist-Social Democrat unity against fascism came initially from outside the Communist movement. On 4 February 1933, seven left-wing parties appealed to the Labour and Socialist International (LSI) and to the CI to summon a joint conference. One of the seven was Britain's Independent Labour Party.

The LSI responded on 19 February with a manifesto calling on 'the workers of all countries to cease their attacks upon each other, and to join together in the fight against fascism.' And it made a conciliatory gesture to the Comintern in the following terms: 'The Labour and Socialist International has always been ready to negotiate with the Communist International with a view to common action as soon as this body is ready.'[2]

The response of the ECCI was ambiguous; it showed simultaneously a determination to stick by its own guidelines and a desperate desire to be rid of them. A manifesto dated 5 March contemptuously brushed aside the idea of negotiations between the CI and the LSI.[3] But, at the same time, the ECCI called on all Communist Parties to do what it refused to do itself: to approach the leaders of the social-democratic parties in their respective countries 'with proposals regarding joint actions against fascism and against the capitalist offensive.'

The LSI's reaction to this attempt to by-pass it was predictable. It requested all its affiliated social-democratic parties to refrain from negotiations with their respective Communist Parties *until* results had been achieved from contact between the two Internationals.[2] So there was once more deadlock.

Not all Communist Parties agreed with the refusal of the CI to respond to the LSI's gesture. Gottwald, on behalf of the Czech Party, argued that the Comintern should try to negotiate direct with the LSI, and a similar view was pressed on the ECCI by the Central Committees of the British and the French Parties.[4] But the majority of the ECCI remained convinced that direct negotiations with the LSI would be a violation of previous decisions. It was not until mid-1934 that, under pressure from various parties, in particular the French, the CI at last approached the LSI with proposals for joint action,.

Meanwhile, however, the ECCI's call to Communist Parties to propose united action to social-democratic parties acted as a catalyst all over Europe. As movements for unity gathered strength, the old guidelines faded away.

The New Approach in Britain

Unlike the turn to Class against Class in 1928, which had provoked endless argument in the British Party and, indeed, considerable opposition, the call by the CI on 5 March, 1933 to approach other socialist parties met with an immediate response.

The first move was on 9 March 1933 when a special enlarged meeting of the Political Bureau took place to discuss a proposal that a united front should be offered to the Labour Party, the TUC, the Co-operative Party and the Independent Labour Party. It was quickly agreed and letters were sent the following day. A fortnight later, the Central Committee held a full dress discussion on the question.

In moving the proposal to offer a united front to the Labour Party, Pollitt did not suggest that the old line had been wrong. He simply argued that the new situation made it *permissible* to approach the social democratic leadership for a united front.[5] It was reported by Trevor Robinson, the Lancashire District secretary, that a number of comrades in his area thought the decision should have come three months ago; they could not see it was the product of a new situation, but thought the Party had taken a wrong line previously, and that the German Party in particular had been mistaken in its approach. This was not Robinson's own view, nor was it a common one. Kerrigan from the Scottish Party, said that the first reaction to the CI manifesto had been surprise, because comrades had been taught to believe that any united front from above with social-democratic organisations was wrong. But there was little in the way of dissent and, within a few months, the new initiative was bringing results such as had not been seen for over five years.

The letters, written to the Executive of the Labour Party, the TUC, the Co-operative Party and the Independent Labour Party proposed a meeting of representatives to plan united action in support of the fight against fascism and against the National Government. The response of the Labour Party and the TUC was, of course, total rejection. Moreover, fearing that some left-wingers might be tempted to associate with Communists once more (a fear which was to prove justified almost immediately) the Labour leaders issued a special statement on 24 March 1933, entitled 'Democracy and Dictatorship' which alleged that 'Communist dictatorship or fear of it had led to fascist dictatorship' and called on workers everywhere to 'strengthen the Labour Party, the spearhead of political power against dictators, fascist or Communist.' (Thus Communism was not only judged responsible for the rise of fascism, but was equated with it.) British Labour, said the statement, must stand firm by its democratic principles and its belief in the attainment of Socialism by peaceful means. A socialist society, it asserted, could be established 'so soon as the workers are sufficiently advanced in political wisdom as to place their own movement in the seat of Government.'[6] This argument that the promised land could be reached so soon as the workers could be persuaded to give Labour a majority – was some years later to be proved untrue. But, in the 1930s, it was constantly invoked to deter people from taking extra-parliamentary action.

With the Independent Labour Party, which had already made its own proposals for joint action by all parties, a quite different situation prevailed.

The ILP had disaffiliated from the Labour Party only a few months earlier, as a result of disillusionment with the experience of the 1929–31 Labour government. Until then it had been the largest of the affiliated socialist societies; it still numbered 20,000 in 1931. It included in its ranks many left-wing activists, crusading pacifists and anti-militarists. There was growing conviction that in a world in which capitalism was collapsing, gradualism was no longer possible; reformism must give place to revolutionary policies. A minority in the ILP insisted that parliament could not anyway function as the main instrument for socialist transformation. The result was the formation of an ILP Revolutionary Policy Committee, which became the driving force in a campaign to disaffiliate from the Labour Party. Its main base was in London; among its leaders were Dr C.K. Cullen and 22 year-old Jack Gaster.

Some ILP members had been full of expectation that once the ILP had broken free from the Labour Party and could go forward with a clear socialist line, the workers would swing behind it.[7] They were, in many ways, subject to the same illusions as those in the Communist Party who had fought for the new line. And, like the Communists, they discovered that the reality was something very different. A few joined the Communist Party at this time; more would have done so had they not been deterred by the Party's attitude. As Jack Gaster complained at the beginning of 1933, Communists constantly suggested that 'all who are not within the ranks of the CP are consciously and deliberately traitors to the working-class movement – bulwarks of the capitalist system – social fascists' and that the decision of the ILP to dissaffiliate from the Labour Party was simply a 'manoeuvre to deceive the workers.'[8]

Now such talk was on its way out. Discussions between the leaders of the Communist Party and the ILP began in March 1933. The first result was a joint demonstration against fascism in Hyde Park. 40,000 people turned up, a foretaste of things to come. The previous line had isolated Communist Party members from other left-wing enthusiasts, but now the sectarian practices were slowly discarded. The very process taught its own lesson. The 'united front from below' suddenly acquired a new meaning as more and more people were drawn into activity and became allies in the struggle.

The Reichstag Fire Trial Campaign

Initially a good deal of anti-fascist activity was centred round the Relief Committee for the Victims of German Fascism. At the first delegate conference called by this Committee in May 1933 Labour peer, Lord Marley, took the chair, and the Committee members on the platform included Ellen Wilkinson, a former Labour MP and now candidate for Jarrow, and the Committee's joint secretaries, Isabel Brown, a well-known Communist and Dorothy Woodman, Labour candidate for Wood Green. Two months later, when the Committee called a mass meeting at the Kingsway Hall in London, with leading Communist, ILP and left-wing Labour speakers, 2,500 queued to get in and some hundreds more were turned away. At its next meeting in September 1933, the audience numbered 4,000.

That autumn, the Committee's most spectacular activity concerned the Reichstag fire trial. The burning of the Reichstag had been used by the Nazis as a pretext for the bloody suppression of the German Communist Party. The Nazis had alleged that the fire was intended as a signal for Communist insurrection throughout Germany, and four leading Communists had been arrested and charged with the crime. As preparations went forward for a show trial, Hitler himself and his colleagues, Goering and Goebbels, made speeches denouncing the fire as a Communist plot and assuring the rest of the world that absolute proof of Communist guilt was in the hands of the German authorities.

Aware that a number of possible witnesses had escaped abroad, and could not go back to testify without risking arrest, the Relief Committee approached D.N. Pritt, a barrister and Labour candidate, and asked him to participate in a Commission of Enquiry to be composed of lawyers from several countries. Pritt agreed, and in the end presided over the Commission's proceedings which took place in Britain and included taking evidence from the witnesses in exile. The Enquiry not only found that the four Communist accused were innocent, but that there were grounds for suspecting that the Nazis had started the fire themselves. The British government made various attempts to frustrate the Enquiry but it received a lot of publicity helping to expose the true nature of the Nazi régime, towards which some British newspapers were not unfriendly.[9]

When the real trial took place in Leipzig starting on 21 September 1933, an event designed as a show-piece against Communists was transformed into an exposure of fascist tyranny, largely as a result of the remarkable courage and tenacity of one of the accused, the Bulgarian Communist, Georgi Dimitrov. Refused the lawyer of his choice, he decided to defend himself, though for him German was a foreign tongue. On his first day in Court, he proudly proclaimed himself a member of the Central Committee of the Bulgarian Communist Party and of the Executive Committee of the Communist International. Insisting that he was 'no mere terrorist adventurer' he described himself as 'an enthusiastic supporter of the proletarian revolution.' He then proceeded to cross-examine the prosecution witnesses and expose them as liars, and, despite the fact that he was frequently expelled from the Court, he challenged the judges and exposed them too. The culminating point was the appearance of Herman Goering as a witness. He also was subject to cross-examination. 'You are very afraid of my questions, are you not, Herr Minister?' taunted Dimitrov, at which Goering lost his temper and shouted, 'You wait till I get you out of the power of this Court.' By 23 December, when the Court was finally forced to acquit all four accused Communists, Dimitrov had become a hero in the eyes of people all over the world.

In Britain, the Labour leaders had done their best to stifle activities connected with the Reichstag fire trial. Pritt later recalled that, when he agreed to preside at the Commission of Enquiry, 'I met with frowns from the leadership of the Labour Party, who conveyed to me their disapproval of my "unwisdom" in doing anything that might be helpful to Communists.'[10] At the 1933 Labour Party Annual Conference, Dorothy Woodman was ruled out of order when she tried to move an emergency resolution expressing gratitude to the Commission of Enquiry and sympathy with those on trial at Leipzig. The labour leadership declared the Relief Committee for the Victims of German Fascism to be an 'organisation ancilliary or subsidiary to the Communist Party' which meant that if a member of the Labour Party belonged to it, or actively supported it, or appeared as a speaker at any of its meetings, he or she could be expelled. Moreover, any local Labour Party which sent a delegate to attend its meetings could be threatened with disaffiliation. By this time there were eleven such proscribed organisations:

> The League against Imperialism, Left Wing Movement, Minority Movement, Workers International Relief, National Unemployed Workers' Movement, Friends of Soviet Russia, National Charter Campaign Committee, International Labour Defence, British Anti-War Council, European Workers' Anti-Fascist Congress, Relief Committee for the Victims of German Fascism.[11]

The Labour leaders were, indeed, thoroughly alarmed at the response to the call for unity against fascism, and in September 1933 published a pamphlet entitled *The Communist Solar System* warning members against any association with what were termed 'Communist auxiliary organisations'. At the 1933 Annual Conference, Ellen Wilkinson, a former member of the Communist Party and now treasurer of the German Relief Committee, protested at the attitude of the leadership:

> That pamphlet that Mr Morrison is so proud of, *The Communist Solar System*, is a magnificent advertisement of the energy and drive of the Communist Party in this country. Why have these organisations flourished like this? Because our own Executive has not acted quickly enough, and has not acted in such a way as to appeal to the imagination. Take this question of the Reichstag fire . . . Why are not the great democratic forces of this country behind the efforts to unmask that great conspiracy of the Nazis which was used to destroy democracy in Germany? Why was it left to an unofficial Committee? If you just sit there and say, we will not have anything to do with the Communists or with the ILP or with anything that does not just keep on our tramway lines, I say the rank and file, whom we represent, will not listen.[12]

Mosley and the BUF

In several European countries, the Nazi victory had encouraged the growth of fascist movements. In Britain, many of the ingredients which had brought Hitler to power in Germany were present. Here was mass unemployment, widespread middle-class frustration, disillusionment among organised workers with the failure of two Labour governments to bring about promised changes. And here, too, finance and support for fascism was apparent in high places.

Sir Oswald Mosley formed his British Union of Fascists in 1932. Mosley, a wealthy man, had started his political life as a Conservative, but had later become a Labour MP. During the 1929–31 Labour government he made considerable impact by leading a campaign of dissidents and left-wingers against Ramsay MacDonald's policies, and forming a New Party, which was not to last.

Mosley now set up recruiting centres for his British Union of Fascists in all the major urban centres. Those who joined paid a shilling a month (unemployed, 4d) and bought a black shirt. The movement was given much publicity in the newspapers and by 1934 was alleged to have some 40,000 members.[13] Though among them were some unemployed with working-class backgrounds, the active membership was overwhelmingly middle class, including many former professional soldiers, particularly ex-officers. The BUF was organised on military lines. A big building in the Kings Road, Chelsea was converted into barracks for the BUF and became known as Black House.

Mosley's most influential supporter was Lord Rothermere, owner of the *Daily Mail* which had a circulation of 1½ million, as well as the London *Evening News* and the *Sunday Dispatch*. These papers ran a vigorous campaign in support of the BUF; Lord Rothermere himself launched it with a *Daily Mail* article entitled 'Hurrah for the Blackshirts', while the *Sunday Dispatch* offered a weekly prize to readers who sent in postcards on 'Why I like the Blackshirts.' Portrayed as an ally of the Conservative Party at a time of stress, the movement began to be regarded with favour by important members of the establishment.

Riding high on this wave of popularity, Mosley planned three giant rallies. The first was in the Albert Hall, London, in April 1934. The hall was packed out, and Mosley was wildly applauded, his speeches reported in the newspapers, in most cases favourably. There was little or no visible opposition inside the hall. Groups outside distributing anti-fascist leaflets were escorted away by the police.

The second rally was planned for 7 June, to take place at Olympia,

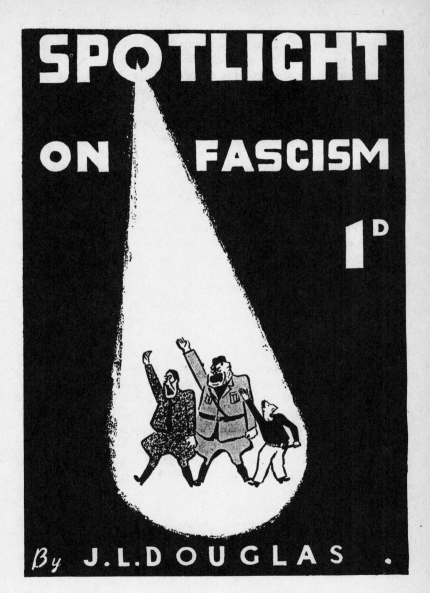

which could hold 13,000. The Albert Hall meeting, however, had provoked some discussion within the Communist Party, where it was argued that such meetings should not be allowed to take place without oppposition. Accordingly, on 17 May the London District Committee of the Communist Party issued a call for a counter-demonstration at Olympia. It invited the London Trades Council, the London Labour Party and the London ILP to cooperate. It also wrote to the London district committees of various trade unions.

The London Labour Party ignored the invitation, and at the London Trades Council a motion to participate in the counter-demonstration was ruled out of order. But a response did come from certain quarters. The London District of the Furniture Workers Union decided to participate; so did a newly-founded group, 'The Printing and Allied Trades Anti-Fascist Movement', which included the machine-minders on the two papers most ardently supporting Mosley, the *Daily Mail* and the *Evening News*. And, after hearing a speech by Ted Bramley, the workers on a big building job for Holland, Hannen & Cubitt passed a resolution of support. Meanwhile, tickets for the meeting were available only from the BUF; some 400 were acquired by various means (according to rumour, tickets for the gallery, where seats were not numbered, were forged.)

On the evening of the meeting, 2,000 people marched to Olympia shouting anti-fascist slogans and were met by a force of 760 foot and mounted police; the latter spent the evening riding roughly into the crowd to keep it on the move. But the police were not inside Olympia where there was an audience of some 12,000 including 2,000 uniformed blackshirts, 1,000 acting as stewards. Mosley stood under a spotlight and spoke with the aid of 24 amplifiers. The few hundred organised anti-fascists, scattered throughout the huge hall, and outnumbered five to one by uniformed fascists, began to heckle and shout slogans. Much of their shouting was inaudible except to near neighbours. However Mosley would pause, the spotlight would be swung onto the interrupter, a bunch of blackshirts would seize him, drag him to the passage outside, beat him up, kick him, perhaps throw him down the stairs and finally eject him from the hall. According to a policeman on duty outside the building 'all appeared to have been badly beaten prior to ejectment . . . many were bleeding profusely from face and head injuries.'[14] Women interrupters were handed over to groups of female Blackshirts who hit them and scratched them and tore their clothes off.

After a little, interrupters knew what faced them; courageously many persisted and paid the price. Some people who had come to listen protested at what was being done to their neighbours; they too were seized and knocked about. Outside, demonstrators concentrated on helping those thrown out to reach a nearby first aid post, hastily organised in a sympathiser's house. They were continually harassed by the mounted police who rode up on the pavement to stop them assisting the wounded. Some demonstrators begged the police to go inside the hall and stop the beatings; the police threatened with arrest those who spoke to them, and indeed some were arrested.

Within days of the Olympia meeting it emerged that the behaviour of the fascists had disgusted many of their potential followers. Some well-to-do people had gone to the meeting under the impression the BUF was a patriotic movement deserving of support. To many such the proceedings had come as a shock. The result was that Rothermere abruptly dropped Mosley who ceased to receive quite the favourable publicity he had been getting in the *Daily Mail*. Moreover the directors of the White City, which had been hired by Mosley for his third rally in August, hastily cancelled the booking.

To some on the left the lesson was clear. So long as there was no opposition, Mosley's movement went from strength to strength. In contrast, the challenge at Olympia, though it involved relatively small numbers, had achieved an important result. It had led the BUF to reveal itself in its true colours. It had brought home the ugly truth about fascism to many who had hitherto been barely conscious of the menace.

To Communists the lesson was also clear. Since Communists were always accused of wanting to 'foment disorder' and so equated with the fascists by the Labour leaders, it was essential that the organising of anti-fascist activities must be broadened to involve non-Communists. The upshot was a meeting on 25 July 1934 at the Conway Hall, London, at which a 'Co-ordinating Committee for Anti-Fascist Activity' was elected. Secretary of this Committee was John Strachey, former Labour MP, and one of the left-wingers who had been associated with Mosley in the New Party; he had broken away from Mosley, however, when the latter's fascist tendencies became obvious. Since then, his book, *The Coming Struggle for*

Power, had made a considerable impact, and he was now responsible for a regular column in the *Daily Worker*. The Co-ordinating Committee included Harry Adams of the Building Trade Workers; R. Briginshaw of Natsopa; Bert Papworth and Bill Jones of the Busmen's Rank and File; Leah Manning of the National Union of Teachers; the Labour peer, Lord Marley and, soon after its formation, Ellen Wilkinson and D.N. Pritt.

Shortly afterwards Mosley announced his intention of holding a BUF rally in Hyde Park on 9 September. The Committee responded with a call for a counter-demonstration on the same day. Sent as a circular to trade union and Labour organisations, and signed by the individual members of the committee, it said that since many workers would go spontaneously to Hyde Park to protest, and would thereby run the risk of attack by the fascists, the organisation and co-ordination of such workers was 'the one way in which the peace can be kept on 9 September.'

> We have no doubt that if this is done and the co-operation of all London working-class organisations is secured, the Fascist rally can be drowned in a sea of working-class activity.[15]

The circular asserted that a 'telling blow' could be struck at the BUF if Hyde Park were filled with hundreds of thousands of workers 'protesting their indignation with fascism', but that fascism would score a triumph if the BUF were allowed to stage a successful demonstration while the workers remained passive and inactive.

The Executive of the Labour Party and the TUC General Council immediately reacted with a joint statement calling upon their affiliated bodies to have nothing to do with the anti-fascist counter-demonstration. It alleged that the aim was 'a repetition on a wider scale of the tactics the Communist Party pursued at Olympia' which 'gave the BUF an opportunity for a display of violence.' Insisting that the 'organised Labour movement repudiates every form of organised interruption at public meetings', it forecast that the proposed counter-demonstration would 'lead to widespread disorder.'[16]

This statement illustrated a conflict of opinion between the Labour leadership and the left wing which was to prevail throughout the rest of the 1930s. The Labour leaders believed that the movement should make clear its opposition to fascism, should try to educate people to an understanding of fascism, so that they would vote against it at election times. *But* they wanted to keep people away from BUF meetings, believing that the best way of dealing with them was to ignore them. People who went and protested at BUF meetings were giving the fascists publicity and creating 'disorder'.

To the left wing, the lesson was exactly the opposite. It was argued that Mosley would gain support unless conscious anti-fascists mobilised against him. He had indeed *been* gaining support before the Olympia meeting undermined it. The Labour leaders, it was alleged, were adopting precisely the same attitude as that of the German social democratic leaders, and this had led to Hitler's triumph.

In defiance of their leaders' appeal, a considerable number of London trade union branches passed resolutions pledging support for the anti-fascist march to Hyde Park on 9 September; some decided to bring out their banners. Meanwhile, a quite unprecedented publicity campaign was mounted. A million leaflets were printed calling on workers to join the anti-fascist march and 'drown Mosley in a sea of working-class activity.' Some were issued under the auspices of the London Communist Party, others on behalf of some thirty other organisations.

At 16 King Street, the Party member in charge of propaganda, former miner Bert Williams, got together an *ad hoc* group to promote more unorthodox forms of publicity. The result was that the leaflets were not only distributed in normal fashion by the organisations that had ordered them, but were showered from roof-tops in Whitehall onto astonished passers-by. Banners appeared in the most unlikely places; a gigantic one was unfurled on a scaffolding round the law courts; an anti-fascist flag was flown from the top of the BBC building in Portland Place; at Transport House, headquarters of the Labour Party and the TUC, a banner was draped round the roof bearing the words 'The United Front from Below is on Top.' On several occasions, when dance music was being broadcast from restaurants, supporters commandeered the microphone and issued a call heard by millions over the radio. On the eve of the march chalking squads went out, and many streets, particularly in East London, were white with slogans.

It was emphasised throughout that violence was not the object of the counter-demonstration, and just before the march started word was passed down the ranks instructing marchers to make for the anti-fascist platforms when they reached Hyde Park, and not to turn towards the Mosley meeting. That, in fact, is precisely what happened. Some 10,000 anti-fascists were on the march, carrying with them a sprinkling of trade-union banners. There were large contingents from the London busmen and the Printers' Anti-Fascist Movement and, of course, the NUWM, the ILP and the Communist Party. There were no less than thirty sections of the Labour League of Youth on the march, in defiance of the Labour leaders' orders.

The marchers made for the anti-fascist platforms and found themselves greeted by a crowd of between 100,000 and 150,000 people. According to some newspapers, it was the largest crowd seen in Hyde Park in living memory. 'I shall never forget my elation when the contingent of which I was a member wheeled into the Park from the Bayswater Road,' wrote Allen Hutt. 'As we looked to the right . . . we could see nothing of the open sward which was entirely covered by what looked like a solid band of people.'[17]

But the Blackshirts had mobilised no more than 2,500. They stood in tight formation surrounded and protected by a cordon of 6,000 police. Outside this a jeering hooting crowd drowned the sound of Mosley's voice.

There was no violence, and all the prophets of doom were confounded. As the *Manchester Guardian* commented the next day:

> 'If this counter-demonstration, which outnumbered Mosley's by 20 to 1, could be gathered from such a small party as the Communists, with large numbers of Londoners acting on their own initiative, on what scale would the opposition have been had it had the whole force of oganised Labour behind it?'[18]

For the Communist Party it marked a new stage. From then on those who wanted to participate in anti-fascist activity found themselves, willy-nilly, associated with the Party.

The Seventh World Congress

On Saturday 8 September 1934, the day before the great Hyde Park demonstration, a message from Moscow was received at 16 King Street. It said that the Seventh Congress of the Communist International, scheduled to start that month, was to be postponed. The decision (which was taken at a meeting of the CI Presidium on

5 September) caused some inconvenience since one or two members of the British delegation were already on the way to Russia, though most of them were notified just in time to abandon their journey.[19]

The reason given for the decision was 'lack of political preparation' but the truth was that for months past there had been a growing demand from Communist Parties in various parts of the world for a revision of strategy and tactics, and this had revealed deep differences of opinion which were still not fully resolved in the summer of 1934. In the end the Congress was not held until July 1935. It is often portrayed as a watershed, the moment when the entire world Communist movement changed direction. In fact, to a large extent, it set the seal on policy changes already in existence, although it is true that by clarifying the political issues involved, it gave powerful impetus to movements already in existence.

One of those responsible for the changes was Georgi Dimitrov, who had gone to Moscow following his acquittal in Leipzig. In March 1934 he had a meeting with Stalin and Manuilsky and other CI leaders, where he urged drastic policy revisions. The point at issue was the whole theory upon which the 'Class against Class' tactics had been based. According to one account, Stalin at that time was 'still very attached to the old conception, little disposed to change (his) position, to accept the turn that his interlocutor was proposing.'[20] Manuilsky, alone among those present, supported Dimitrov. In the end, it took five months to convince the majority of the ECCI that change was necessary.

As we have seen, one of the assumptions upon which the Class against Class theory had been based was that a new 'revolutionary upsurge' was imminent. Even as late as 1933, the perspective of an imminent revolution had persisted. It was not until the summer of 1934, after weeks of argument, that the Comintern leaders at last faced reality. As Kuusinen admitted: 'previous formulations (had) suffered from a tendency to overrate the degree of maturity of the revolutionary crisis.'[21]

More important was a change in the analysis of fascism. By and large it had been regarded by Communists as simply another form of capitalist rule, an *open* dictatorship of the capitalist class in place of the *disguised* dictatorship operated by the capitalists under bourgeois democracy. And, although it was agreed that in one way fascism made revolutionary work more difficult (since workers' organisations were suppressed), in another way it was believed that it could *strengthen* the revolutionary forces, since it aroused the hatred of the workers for their rulers.[22]

Now it began to be recognised that this analysis was faulty, because it ignored the qualitative differences between fascism and other dictatorships; it ignored the influence that the Nazis had built up, not only among the lower middle class, but among a section of the workers. They had done this partly by representing themselves as National *Socialists*, by depicting themselves as a 'revolutionary movement' against the bourgeoisie on behalf of the whole nation. Their demagogy undermined and made much more difficult the struggle for socialist change. The lesson for the world Communist movement was clear: if further advances to socialism were to be achieved, the installation of fascist régimes must be blocked.

At the time, the fascist threat was very apparent in many countries. Events had shown that it could not be warded off if the anti-fascist forces were divided. Thus the establishment of unity between socialists, Communists and other anti-fascists had become a crucial question.

Dimitrov believed that the characterisation of social democracy as 'social fascism' was a mistake. This term had remained in use in the world Communist movement ever since 1929. In his book, *Fascism and Social Revolution* published in 1934, R. Palme Dutt showed that the theory of 'social fascism' was based on three main arguments: 1) that the social democrats, by betraying the workers' struggle, had directly led to the rule of fascism in various countries; 2) that both social democracy and fascism were different forms of capitalist rule and both were 'instruments of the rule of monopoly capital'; 3) that the social-democratic programmes for 'public corporations' were closely paralleled by the fascist policy of the 'corporate state'.[23] Dutt did admit that there was one major difference in this field: Lib–Lab proposals were based on incorporation of existing workers' organisations into the capitalist state, while the fascist corporate state was based on the destruction of the workers' organisations.[23] Despite this distinction, the tendency to equate social democracy with fascism, through the use of the concept of 'social-fascism', had been extremely damaging; it had alienated many possible allies in the socialist movement.

Another idea Dimitrov criticised was the theory that social democracy should always be regarded as the chief pillar of the bourgeoisie, since this led to the belief that social-democratic organisations could not be changed or won over. He spoke against the characterisation of left-wing social democrats as 'pseudo-lefts' who constituted the 'main danger' to the revolutionary movement. And he attacked the theory that the united front must only be 'from below'.[21]

In practice, the French Communist Party was already showing the way. In February 1934 the threat of a fascist coup in France had been successfully met and defeated by mass demonstrations and a general strike called jointly by Communists and Socialists. By July 1934 a formal agreement between the French Socialist Party and the Communist Party of France had been signed for a united anti-fascist front. By October of the same year the French Party had adopted a programme for an alliance of all proletarian and democratic forces under the slogan of 'Popular Front', an action not initially approved of by Stalin, who advised against it.[24]

In the intervening months, however, the members of the ECCI had come a long way towards changing their attitudes. One contentious issue was the future of the 'revolutionary unions.' The British Party had managed with difficulty to extricate itself from the RILU guidelines in 1932. Now the French Party had launched a campaign to amalgamate the 'revolutionary' trade unions with the 'reformist' ones.[25] Here again, Dimitrov was challenging the whole concept of 'new revolutionary trade unions'. He, too, argued that the object should be the *unification* of the 'reformist' and 'revolutionary' trade unions and the transformation of the 'reformist' unions into instruments of class struggle.[26] Though these proposals aroused opposition, particularly from the RILU leader Lozovsky, they were, in the end, approved by the majority of the Congress preparatory committee on 2 July 1934.

As for the theory that the united front must be only 'from below', the ECCI formally abandoned it on 10 October 1934. In response to pressure from the French Party, it proposed joint action to the Labour and Socialist International over the crisis in Spain.

When the Seventh World Congress finally took place in July and August 1935,[27] it was not openly acknowledged that the Class against Class policy had been wrong. Wilhelm Pieck from the German Party, who had been secretary to the ECCI, and who gave the opening report on its activities, dwelt on the 'mistakes' made by various parties since the Sixth World Congress, but he treated these for the most part as *wrong interpretations* of the Class against Class line, rather than as products of that line. Again, Dimitrov's report on 'The Working Class against Fascism' was in the main presented as a response to a new situation, not as a correction of the old line. Nevertheless, this report, and the resolution passed, left no doubt that the old line had been discarded.

Fascism was defined as the central issue facing the working class and was recognised as qualitatively different from other forms of capitalist rule. The answer to fascism was the establishment of the united front of the working class, and this meant agreements between all working-class organisations for joint action on a factory, local, district, national and international scale. Not only must Communists seek to establish unity with social-democratic organisations, they must try to bring about a wide anti-fascist *people's* front involving classes other than the proletariat, namely the peasantry and lower-middle class. The resolution declared support for the re-establishment of trade union unity. Finally, the Communist International declared itself prepared to enter into negotiations with the Second International.

Unlike the Sixth World Congress, this one was remarkably free from dissension and disagreements. In his report-back, Harry Pollitt pointed out that not one commission had to be appointed to consider internal quarrels. The political line of the Congress, he said, arose out of the experiences of comrades in Germany, Japan, the British Dominions, and elsewhere and was 'received amid scenes of enormous enthusiasm.'[28]

The British delegation returned home fortified by the knowledge that the decisions of the Congress were in tune with their experiences too. Unlike those of the Sixth World Congress which had led to endless difficulties, these were based on the realities of the situation, and opened up possibilities for advance of a sort not seen before.

[1] *Inprecorr*, 30 July 1928, p.735.
[2] *Labour Party Annual Report 1933*, pp.16 and 281. See also *Labour Research*, April 1933, p.91.
[3] *Daily Worker*, 8 March 1933.
[4] A.I. Sobolev et al, *Outline History of the Communist International*, Moscow 1971, p.334.
[5] JK folder. 1933 material.
[6] *Labour Party Annual Report 1933*, p.277.
[7] Fenner Brockway, *Socialism over Sixty Years: the life of Jowett of Bradford 1864*, London 1946, pp.301–6.
[8] *Labour Monthly*, January 1933.
[9] D.N. Pritt, *From Right to Left*, London 1965, p.56.

[10]Ibid, p.53.

[11]*Labour Party Annual Report 1933*, p.30; *Labour Party Annual Report 1934*, p.12.

[12]*Labour Party Annual Report 1933*, p.221.

[13]See Robert Skidelsky, *Oswald Mosley*, London 1975, p.331.

[14]See John Stevenson and Chris Cook, *The Slump*, London 1977, pp.235–6.

[15]*Daily Worker*, 15 August 1934.

[16]*Daily Worker*, 24 August 1934.

[17]Allen Hutt, *The Post-War History of the British Working Class*, London 1937.

[18]*Manchester Guardian*, 10 September 1934.

[19]Political Bureau minutes, 13 September 1934. JK papers.

[20]Jean Merot, *Dimitrov: Un Révolutionnaire de Notre Temps* , Paris 1972, pp.184–5. Dobring Michev, Institute of History of Bulgarian CP, June 1971.

[21]A.I. Sobolev et al, op. cit., pp.357–9.

[22]See Harry Pollitt, *Towards Soviet Power*, report on the 13th Plenum, pp.15–16, pamphlet, n.d.

[23]R. Palme Dutt, *Fascism and Social Revolution*, London 1934, pp.150–176, 203.

[24]See Monty Johnstone in *Marxism Today*, October 1975; he quotes G. Ceretti, *A L'Ombre des Deux T*, Paris 1973. See also *Outline History of Communist International* (op. cit.), p.361.

[25]Ibid, p.360.

[26]D. Michev and B. Kalaora (eds.), *Georgi Dimitrov and the Trade Union Movement*, Sofia 1976, p.210.

[27]The Seventh World Congress proceedings were reported in *Inprecorr* throughout the second half of 1935; some of the main reports and speeches were brought together in a single volume by Modern Books in 1936.

[28]*Labour Monthly*, November 1935.

CHAPTER 10

Attitudes to War
(1935)

At the time of the Communist Party's Thirteenth Congress in February 1935 membership still stood at only 6,500.[1] Within a few weeks, 2,000 new members were recruited, mainly as a result of the successful struggle against the cuts in unemployment benefit, culminating in the 'Standstill Act' (as described in Chapter 6). The movement had been led by the NUWM which was able to establish 84 new branches. However, as had happened only too frequently in the past, particularly with unemployed people, a proportion of the new recruits to the Party had joined on impulse and soon drifted away again, so that, by July 1935, the dues-paying membership was still only 7,700.[2]

Nevertheless, sales of the *Daily Worker* were mounting. By April 1935, though its regular daily readers still numbered under 30,000, its Saturday sales had risen to over 70,000.[3] The weekend sales were, of course, the result of activity by the Party members, who stood at street corners and at factory gates, or went on door-to-door canvasses on Sunday mornings. In London, they usually collected the Saturday edition on Friday evening so that people coming out of cinemas were met with the cry: 'Read tomorrow's *Daily Worker*'.

By now, the paper was readable and lively enough. Its editor in chief was Jimmy Shields, soon to make way for Idris Cox. Police surveillance was part of the scene. 'Every day for the past three weeks, members of the Special Branch have clustered round the Editorial Offices in Cayton Street,' it was reported on 28 February 1935, after unemployed demonstrations had been at their height.

The *Daily Worker* was (not surprisingly) the only newspaper to oppose the Royal Jubilee staged in 1935 to mark the 25th anniversary of the accession of George V to the throne. Under slogans such as 'Jubilee celebrations are War Preparations' the Party launched one of its more spectacular propaganda campaigns. The high spot was reached on Jubilee day itself, 6 May 1935, when the royal procession made its way across central London. The streets were festooned

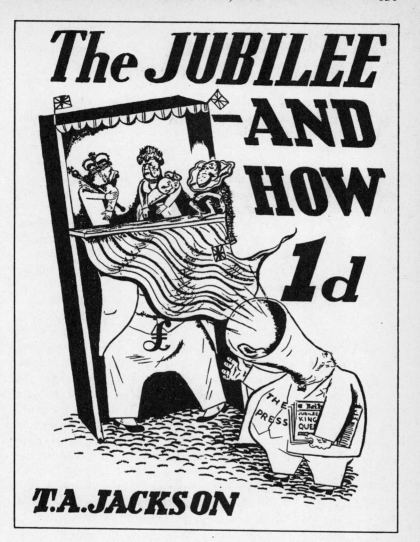

with flags, and a great banner inscribed with the words 'Long may they reign' was stretched across Fleet Street. But, as the royal coach passed beneath it, it fell open to display quite different sentiments:

TWENTY-FIVE YEARS OF HUNGER AND WAR

Communists knew that they were on the eve of war. They believed that the contradictions in the capitalist system inevitably led to war, and that the only way to lasting peace was to abolish this system. Their enemies frequently accused them of wanting war, so as to hasten the advent of revolution. There was never any truth in this accusation. The defeat of the imperialist war plans was seen as an integral part of the struggle against the capitalist class. By mobilising workers for action against war, this struggle could be raised to a higher level. To this end, they played an active role in anti-war movements, both locally and nationally. Such movements commanded considerable support, for the First World War, in which 800,000 British troops had been killed and 2 million wounded, was still fresh in the memory.

One aspect which was high-lighted was the role of the armament firms – the 'merchants of death', as they were called. In the spring of 1935, as a result of scandalous revelations from America, the government set up a Royal Commission to enquire into the Private Manufacture and Trade in Arms. To this Commission the Party put in a memorandum attacking the 'appalling traffic in weapons of mass murder', accusing the government of direct complicity in this traffic, and tracing the connections between the state apparatus and the armament trusts. The Memorandum was published as a penny pamphlet under the title *A Hell of a Business*. It was supplemented by Harry Pollitt's verbal evidence to the Commission, which was also issued as a pamphlet, *Dynamite in the Dock*.

The Party, in this evidence, alleged that the United Kingdom was the main centre of the world's armaments trade, and was responsible for about one-third of all arms exports. During 1931–2, when Japan was engaged in war on China, British firms had exported vast quantities of arms to Japan. The League of Nations had condemned Japan as an aggressor, and she had in consequence withdrawn from the League. But,

at the same time as the League of Nations was vainly endeavouring to check this flagrant violation of treaties and

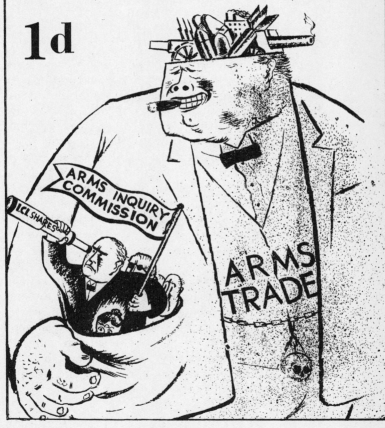

aggressive war of conquest, British armament manufacturers were supplying the means for it to be carried out.[4]

The Party in its evidence also accused the arms firms of rearming Germany since Hitler had come to power. It stated that the activities of the arms firms in fomenting war and helping to oppress colonial peoples were carried on with the active connivance of the British government. In his verbal evidence, Pollitt reminded the Commission that British arms had been used for the slaughter of British soldiers in the Dardanelles during the 1914–18 war.

The Role of the Fascist Powers

The aim of *preventing* war between nations had always been paramount. However, an associated question much discussed throughout the world Communist movement was what line to take should war break out, despite all endeavours. It had been laid down at various World Congresses that the attitude to any given war must be determined by an analysis of its role. At the Sixth World Congress in 1928, three main types of war had been defined. Firstly, open war between imperialist states, of which the First World War was the outstanding example. It was the duty of revolutionaries to do everything possible to prevent such a war, but if it broke out, the aim must be its transformation into civil war and the overthrow of the home government. The second kind of war was a counter-revolutionary war against countries building socialism, that is to say the Soviet Union. Such a war had already been witnessed only a few years earlier when the major capitalist powers, including Britain, had invaded Soviet Russia in the hope of overthrowing the new régime. To stop the repetition of such a war was seen by Communists as a first duty, but if, despite all efforts, it again took place, the aim was to be the defeat of the governments attacking the Soviet Union so as to ensure victory for the country building socialism. Thirdly, there were wars for colonial liberation; in these conflicts, those struggling against colonial oppression were to be supported.

This classification, and the appropriate response in each case, was in no way challenged at the Seventh World Congress. However, an important new element was introduced to take account of changes in the situation, which led to a major development in Communist theory concerning war, and how to struggle against it in a world dominated by capitalist states. This was the recognition that the fascist powers had become the spearhead in the advance to *any* of the three types of war. *They* were the powers most actively engaged in preparing a war for the redivision of the world; *they* were the ones adopting the most threatening attitude to the Soviet Union; *they* were the ones already engaged in, or preparing for, wars of colonial conquest. Thus it was stressed at the Congress that the aim of the anti-fascist struggle was not only to protect liberties and rights won by the working-class movement, but *also* to prevent war.

Recognition of the fascist powers as constituting the main danger to peace had been one of the factors involved in a changed attitude to the League of Nations. On this issue the British Party had already been engaged in argument with others on the left in the Labour movement, particularly in the ILP.

The League of Nations had been set up after the First World War and had initially been dominated by Britain, France, Italy and Japan. Ostensibly, the League's object was to prevent future wars by a system of 'collective security' which included the use of economic and military sanctions to deter aggressors, if possible, and stop them if they refused to be deterred. But since Lenin's day, the League had frequently been referred to by Communists as a 'thieves' kitchen' since it provided machinery for an alliance of capitalist states against the Soviet Union, and, at the same time, window-dressing to cover their warlike manoeuvres.

However, since 1932, the composition of the League had changed. In March 1933 Japan had been condemned as an aggressor and had left the League; in October 1933 Nazi Germany followed suit on the grounds that the League would not recognise Germany's right to rearm. One year later, in October 1934, the Soviet Union was admitted into the League. By this time, Germany had begun to rearm in earnest, receiving help from the British government in the form of war credits followed by an Anglo–German Naval Agreement in the Spring of 1935, giving Germany the right to build up a navy 35 per cent the size of the British navy.

The response of the Soviet Union to what appeared to be a threat from both Japan and Germany was to sign an agreement with France in May 1935 that if either country were the victim of unprovoked aggression, the other would go to its aid. This 'mutual assistance pact' was drawn up in accordance with the covenant of the League of Nations, and was intended to convince Hitler that if he attacked either of them, as he was constantly threatening to do, the other would not stand idly by.

To Communists, the changed composition of the League opened up the possibility that it might be used, however temporarily, to restrain the main aggressors: the fascist powers, who indeed left it precisely *because* it was an obstacle to their war plans. But the action of the Soviet Union in joining the League was denounced by some in the labour movement as a betrayal of socialist principle; even more ferocious were the criticisms concerning the mutual assistance pact between France and the Soviet Union. Foremost among those who voiced their disagreement was Fenner Brockway, chairman of the ILP, who, with good reason, had been highly critical of the Comintern's implacable hostility to other socialist parties during the Class against Class period, but who appeared to be anxious to stick to the guidelines laid down by the Comintern on international affairs in 1928, before the rise of Hitler or the Japanese invasion of China. 'Russia joined the League of Nations and began negotiations for a political and military alliance with the reactionary government of France', he wrote in retrospect:

> I believe I was the first person in Britain to criticise these developments from a socialist standpoint. I pointed out that Lenin had described the League as the 'thieves' kitchen' and that the Sixth World Congress of the CI had denounced alliances with capitalist governments because they would represent an alliance for the suppression of the proletarian revolution and of the national liberation movements of colonial peoples.[5]

Soon, he was accusing the Soviet Union and the Comintern of abandoning the class struggle and the cause of socialism in order to build alliances between Russia and other capitalist countries.[6]

The suggestion that by joining the League of Nations the Soviet Union was violating socialist principles was denied by among others Reg Bishop, a long-standing Party member and journalist, who quoted Lenin's words: 'We must know how to take advantage of contradictions and antagonism between the imperialists.'[7] Although he agreed that war was a product of capitalism, he pointed out that the two countries who most wanted to free their hands for war had left the League, and most of the capitalist states wanted to avoid it for the time being; it would be quite wrong of the Soviet Union not to make use of this contradiction in order to postpone war.

The 'thieves' kitchen' argument was taken up by J.R. Campbell who stressed that this definition was based on a concrete analysis of the role played by the League at a given moment, and requotation could not absolve socialists from enquiring into the role the League was now playing. The most dangerous thieves had left the kitchen, said Campbell, and not all those now in it were thieves.[8]

The suggestion that the Soviet Union was now relying on capitalist states and wanted a truce in the class struggle, seemed to most Communists to be absurd since they did not look on the use of the League as an *alternative* to independent working-class action; on the contrary use of the League, either to stop a war or to prevent war, *depended* on such action.

In practice the differences between the Communist Party and the ILP came to a head when the third major fascist power, Italy, invaded Abyssinia, an action which resulted in Italy's withdrawal from the League just as her allies, Japan and Hitler Germany, had done before her.

The Abyssinian War Controversy

The invasion of Abyssinia by Mussolini's Italy began in October 1935. Abyssinia was virtually the only independent state left in Africa; all the rest were colonies of the great powers, or subject to white settler régimes. For over two years, Italy had been preparing the invasion and buying arms from British manufacturers. Nevertheless, when the war started and Abyssinia appealed to the League of Nations, British government spokesmen professed to be in favour of upholding the system of 'collective security' laid down under the League's covenant. This meant the imposition of economic and/or military sanctions by League members against the aggressor.

By this time Conservative Baldwin had succeeded Labour defector, Ramsay MacDonald, in the post of Prime Minister, and all through the General Election in November 1935, government spokesmen continued to imply that sanctions would be imposed on Italy. After a joint appeal to return once more a 'national government' to office, Baldwin and the Conservative Party once again achieved a majority. It was not until the end of the year that the truth came out. A plan had been drawn up by the British and French Foreign Secretaries – Sir Samuel Hoare and Pierre Laval – to hand over two-thirds of Abyssinia to Italy. Outcry in Britain from all sides, including many in the Conservative Party itself, resulted in the withdrawal of this particular carve-up, and Hoare's resignation. But the sanctions that might have forced the Italians to retreat were not imposed, and, in the end, Italy emerged as the victor and conqueror.

What, in concrete terms, would 'sanctions' have meant? It was thought at the time that Italy could have been stopped by an oil embargo. This, of course, was never implemented. Had it been decided that military sanctions were required, this would probably have meant closing the Suez Canal and so severing the Italian army's supply route. The canal was under joint British and French ownership, and the British Mediterranean fleet was the dominant naval force in the area; experts believed there would be no problem in closing the canal. However, here again, there was discussion but no action taken; Italy's supply route through the canal continued uninterrupted to the end.

It was against this background that differences among socialists in Britain emerged. When the invasion of Abyssinia was imminent, the leaders of the TUC and the Labour Party issued a joint resolution calling on the British government, in cooperation with other nations in the League, to use all necessary measures to stop Italy's attack. And it pledged support for any action consistent with the principles and statutes of the League in enforcing peace. This resolution received overwhelming support when put to the vote at both the TUC and the Labour Party annual conferences in October 1935. At the latter conference, Hugh Dalton argued against those who said that sanctions would mean war. The threat of sanctions might be enough to prevent war, he said, whereas, if nothing was done, war was certain. He also suggested that the closing of the Suez Canal would not involve the use of force.[9]

The relatively small numbers opposing the resolution on the card vote obscured the fact that the opposition included some of the most influential people in the movement. They fell into two categories. First, the pacifists, led by George Lansbury, who believed that both the use of force and the threat of force was wrong. Lansbury resigned his leadership of the Parliamentary Party over the issue.

The second category of opponents were those on the left who had combined to form the Socialist League when the ILP disaffiliated from the Labour Party. The Socialist League was now an affiliated Socialist Society within the Labour Party and one of its spokesmen at the annual conference, William Mellor, argued that if the Party decided to support League sanctions, it would be 'going to the support of British imperialism in a conflict with other imperialisms' whereas the task of the workers was to fight their own enemy at home.[10]

The Independent Labour Party (though not, of course, represented at the Labour Party Conference, having disaffiliated some three years earlier) had by September decided to take a similar line to that of Mellor. So the *New Leader* criticised those who advocated sanctions by the League 'despite the capitalist character of the governments which dominate the League' and urged workers to 'apply their own sanctions'.[11]

The Communist Party disagreed with the ILP and the Socialist League. As already shown, Communists divided wars into three categories: imperialist, anti-Soviet, or colonial. The Italian invasion of Abyssinia was placed *not* in the first category, an 'imperialist' war, but in the third, a war for colonial conquest. In view of this the Party proclaimed its support for the Abyssinian people. The fact that these people were subject to an exceptionally backward régime, headed by an Emperor, was not believed to be the decisive issue. 'Millions of colonial people in India, Africa, and China are watching the progress of the events in Abyssinia,' wrote Harry Pollitt, arguing that if Mussolini's advance could be stopped,

> the whole colonial people all over the world will not only be glad of such practical international working-class solidarity, it will strengthen their fight against their imperialist exploiters.[12]

But there was also the new element, recognised at the Seventh World Congress, involved in the Italian invasion, As Emile Burns put it:

> The attack on Abyssinia is not *merely* an imperialist attack, but also a fascist attack. It is obvious that any victory for Italian aggression would be a tremendous encouragement to German fascism, already threatening the world with war. For Italy to gain any benefit from this war would be to make a new war, starting from Germany, an immediate certainty.[13]

In supporting action against Italy by the League, the Communist Party (unlike the leaders of both the Labour Party and the ILP) was under no illusions concerning the probable role of the British government. The party argued that the Government was trying to delude public opinion by posing, for electoral purposes, as a champion of the League, that the imperialist powers in the League were primarily concerned, not with the question of Italy and Abyssinia, but with utilising the situation to manoeuvre for position.[14] The Party press constantly recalled the bargain which the British government had earlier tried to strike with the Italians for a redivision of Abyssinian territory and warned that such a redivision was still the real policy of the Government.[15]

The Communist Party contended that since the Government was preparing to betray Abyssinia, the imposition of sanctions could not be left in government hands as was implied by the attitude of the Labour leaders; the workers must take direct action to impose such sanctions. Such action did occur here and there around the world. In South Africa, dockers in Capetown declined to load meat for the Italian Army; at Alexandria, Greek seamen refused to handle Italian supplies of war materials; Marseilles dockers held up the loading of an Italian transport; French dockers unions decided to boycott all Italian vessels. In Britain, action came from an unexpected quarter: the National Union of Boot and Shoe Operatives instructed its members to stop handling orders for boots from the Italian army. But when the Communist International approached the Second International urging common action on the grounds that only a powerful independent movement could force the governments in the League to act, the Second International refused, largely as a result of opposition from the representatives of the British Labour Party.

The contrast between the attitude of the Labour Party and the Communist Party was demonstrated during the general election. The *Daily Herald*, Labour's paper, implied early on that the election must be fought on domestic issues since on foreign policy and the attitude to the League of Nations there was no fundamental disagreement between Labour and Tory.[16]

And though the Labour 'Manifesto criticised the Government for the disastrous results of its foreign policy, it implied that what was wrong was the government's 'slow and half-hearted' action in support of the League. The Communist Party, in its manifesto, made no bones about it:

The National Government, which held back League action during the twelve months of open Italian military preparation, is now conspiring with Mussolini for the destruction of Abyssinian independence.

'A Vote for Baldwin is a vote for Mussolini' was the *Daily Worker*'s headline on the day of the General Election. 'The National Government is ready at any moment to double-cross the League of Nations and to double-cross Abyssinia if it can make a deal with Italy,' said William Gallacher in his maiden speech just after his election as a Communist MP.[17]

A fortnight later, the truth about the 'double-cross' was revealed with the publication of the Hoare-Laval Pact. It was by this time clear to Mussolini that talk about sanctions was an empty threat; the Italians continued their war of conquest until Abyssinia was vanquished. The lessons were not lost on other fascist leaders. As Gallacher himself said in retrospect, it was 'the green light for the fascists to go ahead.'[18]

ILP Members Join the Communist Party

The attitude to the Abyssinian invasion brought to a head the conflict of opinion within the ILP between those associated with the Revolutionary Policy Committee and the dominant leadership on the ILP National Council. The RPC had wanted the ILP to offer cooperation to the Communist International; the ILP leadership was opposed to this and, though forced by a Conference decision in 1933 to enter negotiations with the CI, was clearly unwilling that such negotiations should be successful. Simultaneously much material hostile to the Soviet Union had been appearing in the ILP's official journal, the *New Leader*, in which Russia's foreign policy had been attacked ever since the latter's entry into the League of Nations in 1934.

Despite these differences of opinion, there had been cooperation between the Communist Party and the ILP on immediate issues for over two years – in particular, in the campaigns against Mosley's fascists and against cuts in benefits for the unemployed. In the autumn of 1934 the Communist Party had proposed to the ILP that they should discuss practical steps towards unifying the two parties into one United Communist Party; this proposal was repeated at the

Communist Party's 13th Congress in February 1935, and raised by Pollitt in his speech as fraternal delegate to the ILP annual conference in April of that year. But it was clear that this proposal, like the one concerning cooperation with the CI, would be unacceptable to the ILP's leaders.

When the Abyssinian crisis arose, and the ILP leadership opposed sanctions against Italy, members of the ILP Revolutionary Policy Committee at last came to the conclusion that it was time to make a break. On 31 October 1935, the Committee publicly announced its decision to leave the ILP and join the Communist Party, and called on revolutionary workers inside and outside the ILP to follow it. Jack Gaster, one of the RPC leaders who was also on the ILP's National Council, said in a letter of resignation:

> The ILP, in face of the war menace, has abandoned struggle in support of Abyssinia, has refused to face up to the revolutionary implications of the fight against war, and adopted a line of opposition that is purely that of reliance upon individual pacifist resistance to war.[19]

The RPC issued a Manifesto which read: 'in the present war crisis, we declare our support for the Abyssinian peoples and of all subject peoples as well as in their struggle for independence from imperialist oppression.' The RPC, said the Manifesto, had worked for nearly four years 'to turn the Party on to a path of revolutionary struggle, based on Marxist principles.' It was now making this call because 'the policy of the ILP is leading to disunity of the workers' forces and is paving the way for reaction.'[20]

The Manifesto was signed by a number of well-known members of the ILP including Jack Gaster; Dr C.K. Cullen (former vice-chairman of the London Divisional Council of the ILP); Hilda Vernon (the London Divisional Council's former secretary); Alf Hawkins (former London chairman); D.J. Rosenbloom and Irma Gorniot (former EC members of the London Divisional Council); G.J. Jones of Wood Green, an area organiser, and T.S. Friedenson (industrial editor of the *New Leader*). The group brought with them quite a number of other ILP members. The ILP membership was in any case dwindling and by 1935 was already smaller than that of the Communist Party. After the exit of the RPC supporters, the ILP was to an increasing extent influenced by Trotskyists who, like Brockway, were extremely hostile to the foreign policy of the Soviet Union.

[1] *It Can Be Done*, 1937, Report of Central Committee to Congress, p.248.

[2] *Inprecorr*, 28 August 1935, p.1051.

[3] Report to Central Committee 26 April 1935, JK papers.

[4] *A Hell of a Business*, 1935 (pamphlet).

[5] Fenner Brockway, *Inside the Left*, London 1942, p.257. See also editorials in *New Leader* (Brockway was editor) on 27 July 1934, 21 September 1934, and the article by Brockway on 30 November 1934.

[6] See Fenner Brockway, *Workers' Front*, London 1938, pp.39, 60, 62–4.

[7] *Communist Review*, November 1934.

[8] *Labour Monthly*, November 1935.

[9] *Labour Party Annual Report 1935*, p.155.

[10] Ibid., pp.170–2.

[11] *New Leader*, 30 August and 6 September 1935.

[12] *We Can Stop War*, October 1935 (pamphlet).

[13] Emile Burns, *Abyssinia and Italy*, London 1935, pp.182–3, 210.

[14] 'Notes of the Month', R. Palme Dutt, *Labour Monthly*, November 1935.

[15] *Abyssinia and Italy*, p.189.

[16] *Daily Herald*, editorial, 15 October 1935.

[17] *Hansard*, 4 December 1935.

[18] William Gallacher, *Last Memoirs*, London 1966, p.250.

[19] *Daily Worker*, 5 November 1935.

[20] *Daily Worker*, 1 November 1935.

CHAPTER 11

Elections and Relations With the Labour Party
(1935–36)

In the General Election on 14 November 1935, William Gallacher was elected MP for West Fife. He was the only Communist between the wars to win a parliamentary contest against an official Labour candidate.

Communists who had become MPs in the early 1920s – notably Saklatvala – had been adopted as candidates of the local labour movement – no Labour candidates stood against them. But the bans and proscriptions enforced after 1926 put a stop to this. From then on, people who had ambitions to enter Parliament did not join the Communist Party, or, if they did, they did not stay in it very long. For Communist candidates were not only up against an anti-Communist prejudice fostered from on high. They were also trapped by an electoral system which was weighted against them.

Systems of proportional representation, or arrangements for second ballots, as in France, provided far more opportunities for minority party representation than Britain's 'first-past-the-post' method of voting which encouraged a two-party system. In such a situation, even ardent left-wingers who were opposed to the official Labour policies of class collaboration, and were sympathetic to the Communist point of view, were afraid that, if they voted Communist, it would split the anti-Conservative vote and let the enemy in. And Labour supporters in general harboured resentment against those who tried to divide the anti-Tory vote.

Another factor peculiar to Britain was the composition of the Labour Party itself. Unlike its social-democratic counterparts on the Continent, the Labour Party had been formed by the trade unions which still had the decisive voice in the making of its policy and programme. Thus, to the average trade unionist of that period, voting Labour meant voting for your own organisation, for your own side. Communists were beginning to play a leading part in

144

some of these trade unions; yet they could not participate, except indirectly, in the decisions of the party which belonged to them as trade unionists.

As shown in Chapter 8, Communists did not believe socialism could be brought about through parliament; the development of mass movements was seen to be the way of advance. They thought that the main advantage of getting a Communist into Parliament would be to stimulate such movements, but they also believed that it was important to contest elections because these provided a chance to publicise the policies for which the Party stood. Elections gave an opportunity to canvass on the doorstop and talk to people individually, even to make recruits to the Party. Though the vote received might be small, the results of an election campaign could be positive.

As we have seen, in the 1929 general election, the Party put up 25 candidates who averaged 5.3 per cent of the poll in the areas where they stood. In the 1931 general election, the Party put up 26 candidates who received 7.5 per cent of the poll. But in the 1935 election, when Gallacher got in, the Party withdrew all its candidates except two. This decision was the outcome of an argument within the Party about electoral tactics that had gone on for over a year.

The New Attitude to the Labour Party

The tactics adopted by the Party during the disastrous Class against Class period had involved denouncing the Labour Party as the 'third capitalist party' and telling the workers not to vote for Labour candidates but, if there were no Communist standing, to spoil their ballot papers. This policy had not only proved futile in the sense that nobody carried it out except dedicated members of the Party (and sometimes not even them); it had aroused much hostility among Labour supporters and potential allies. It had caused dissension within the Party when first adopted, and members here and there continued to raise objections to implementing it.

With the change in the political line at the beginning of 1933, and the approach to the Labour Party and ILP for a united front, a major revision of electoral strategy became inevitable. It began in preparation for the November 1934 municipal elections. The two-party system was not yet so rigidly entrenched in local government.

Many seats were still held by 'independents', and though splitting the vote could become an issue, Communists in some places had won support from the majority of voters and had been elected as councillors. In the mid-1930s there were about fifty such Communists councillors, mainly concentrated in the mining districts of South Wales and Scotland.

In the discussions preceeding the November 1934 borough council elections, it was decided that the Party should aim for an electoral understanding with the ILP to avoid rival candidatures. It was also agreed that, where an official Labour candidate was standing in a seat contested by either Communists or ILP-ers, the Party would try to persuade the Labour candidate to submit to a 'workers' selection conference' which would choose which candidate should run. But where there was no Communist or ILP candidate, the Party announced that it was prepared to support and work for those Labour candidates who would pledge themselves

> to fight on such questions as work schemes at trade union rates, lower rents, refusal to operate the means test, extra winter relief for the unemployed, withdrawal of the Sedition Bill, fight against Part 2 of the Unemployment Act, and for the united front against fascism and war.[1]

The results of this approach were predictable. It was not possible to get official Labour candidates to withdraw when faced with CP or ILP opponents, nor would they submit to proposals for 'workers' selection conferences'. On the other hand, where there was no CP or ILP candidate, quite a number of Labour candidates were prepared to support openly the list of 'united front' demands proposed by the Party; in return they reaped the benefit of active help from Communists in their election campaign.

And what of those places where the Labour candidate ignored or even rejected the 'united front' demands? The Party's election statement published on 20 October 1934 did not refer to such a possibility, but at the last movement, on 1 November, a leader in the *Daily Worker* calling for maximum support for CP, ILP and Labour candidates pledged to fight for united front action, went on to say:

> Where it has not been possible to make a united front approach, there, if the workers feel that the Labour candidate can be made to put up a fight on any issue or issues that will serve to strengthen

the unity of the workers, then their vote should be given to such a candidate.[2]

In other words, the policy of telling the workers *not* to vote for the 'third capitalist party' had been abandoned once and for all, even if the call to vote Labour was still hedged in with 'ifs'.

This was only the beginning. The municipal elections were followed by a prolonged discussion in the Party Central Committee on the attitude to be taken at the next General Election, whenever it came. Pollitt held the view that defeat of the National Government was imperative if the drift to war and fascism was to be stemmed, and that, though the Party's criticism of Labour's official programme must remain, the attitude to the question of a future Labour government should change. Millions of workers saw a Labour government as the only practical alternative. The aim should be the return of a group of Communist MPs and a majority of Labour MPs pledged to support a programme of immediate demands, and the formation of a Labour government on the basis of such a programme. This could be the starting point for further advance. To this end, he proposed that the Party should only run candidates in places where it had a real mass basis – half a dozen at most – and that everywhere else, Labour candidates should be asked to support the type of immediate demands that they would find difficult to refuse, with the object of developing a local movement around such demands.[3]

Foreseeing that members would ask whether such a change meant that the Class against Class policy had been wrong, Pollitt emphasized that policy and tactics must change when the situation changed.[4]

Not all members of the Central Committee agreed with this. Gallacher was strongly against any support for the return of a Labour government as such, though he wanted local campaigns to persuade Labour candidates to adopt immediate demands. Campbell was doubtful about the proposal to limit so severely the number of Communist candidates.

The outcome of the argument, which was continued right up to the eve of the Party's Thirteenth Congress in February 1935, appeared in a resolution passed at that Congress. This emphasised that the defeat of the National Government and the return of a Labour government could become 'a powerful impetus and strengthening of the fighting spirit and class consciousness of the workers for winning their demands.' *But* the statement was hedged round with warnings to the workers that the coming to power of Labour would not solve their problems. Nothing was said concerning any limitation in the number of Communist candidates, and, after the Congress, preparations went ahead to contest in about twenty constituencies.

But six months later, at the Seventh World Congress in Moscow, Pollitt declared on behalf of the British delegation that the formulations in the Thirteenth Congress resolution no longer met the demands of the situation. Speaking of the Abyssinian crisis and the pro-Hitler policy of the British government, he insisted that the main responsibility of the Communist Party must be to organise opposition to the National Government and bring about its defeat. The only way this could be achieved was by the election of a Labour government. Though the Party must not create illusions about the character of Labour's policy, a Labour government could be 'the means to an end through which the class fight of the workers is intensified and advanced to a higher stage.'[5]

This was finally the policy adopted. After the Congress the Communist Party wrote to the Labour Party asking for a discussion on how best to organise the campaign against the National Government and to avoid splitting the workers' vote. Not unexpectedly, the Labour Party refused to have any such discussions. After which, the Communist Party decided to withdraw all its candidates but two, and urged that in all other constituencies the Labour candidate should be supported.

1935 Election

When polling day came, on 14 November 1935, though Labour candidates succeeded in attracting as many votes as in 1929, they achieved far fewer seats, mainly because former Liberal supporters voted Conservative. The result was that the National Government – which now meant the Conservatives, led by Baldwin – was returned with a big majority. This was a great discouragement on the left, where it was only too well understood that another term for the National Government would accelerate the drift to fascism and war.

The Communist Party did well in the two constituencies where it ran candidates. Pollitt stood in East Rhondda for the seat previously contested by Arthur Horner. In a straight fight against a sitting Labour MP, he polled 13,665 votes, compared with Labour's 22,088.

In West Fife, the election of Gallacher came as a triumphant vindication of the Party's work in the mining industry in the face of persecution and attempts to ostracise it. Decisive to Gallacher's victory were members of the United Mineworkers of Scotland. It will be recalled that the UMS had been created in 1929 after Communists had been elected to posts in the official County Unions, but had been denied recognition by the Scottish Executive of the Miners' Federation. Instead, the Executive had recognised a right-wing breakaway, formed by Labour MP William Adamson. For six years the Communist-led UMS had battled away, up against both the coal-owners and the breakaway. Now, in this parliamentary contest, the UMS proved its strength.

Adamson, still secretary of the breakaway, had lost his seat to a Tory in the 1931 election. He was now, in 1935, once more the official Labour candidate, and fully expected to regain his seat. But the UMS went into action in support of Gallacher, with Alex Moffat, one of the union's officials, acting as Gallacher's election agent. Meetings were organised in every mining village; in every pit, the case for Gallacher was put. 'It was an inspiration to work with the UMS comrades' said Gallacher shortly afterwards.[6]

There was also support for Gallacher among railwaymen and busmen, while the NUWM, which had a big local branch, supplied a lot of help. According to Peter Kerrigan, it was above all the youth – 'the young miners, the young shop assistants, the young unemployed, the young cyclists, the youth everywhere' – that brought victory.[7] When polling day came, Gallacher was elected with 13,462 votes against Adamson's 12,869. Milne, the Conservative, received 9,677. That night, after the results of the poll had been announced, Gallacher was hastily driven to a meeting at the Valleyfield Miners Institute where he received a jubilant welcome; he went on to the village of Kincardine, and ended up at Lumphinans (once known as a 'little Moscow') where an all-night victory party was in progress. There was a big demonstration to welcome him in Glasgow the next day, and when he reached London to take his seat, the Shoreditch Town Hall could not accommodate the numbers who turned up to hear him speak.

The Affiliation Campaign

As soon as the election was over, the Party applied for affiliation to the Labour Party. In the early 1920s, the Party had aimed to become an affiliated body, as was its Marxist predecessor, the British Socialist Party, and had continued its efforts after 1926, despite the anti-Communist purge carried out by the TUC and Labour leaders. The Party had only discarded its affiliation policy in 1929, under the impact of Class against Class. Now it had once more become the obvious way forward.

As already indicated, the Labour Party was not a social-democratic party in the Continental sense; it was a loose federation of trade unions, individual members and socialist societies. The trade unions had the dominating voice and commanded over 80 per cent of the voting power at annual conferences. Thus the representation at the 1936 Annual Conference was as follows:

Organisations	Number	Delegates	Votes
Trade Unions	60	352	1,986,000
Labour Parties	285	292	414,000
County Federations of Labour Parties	6	6	7,000
Socialist Societies	8	8	12,000
Co-operative Society	1	6	36,000
	360	664	2,445,000[8]

The trade unions involved were affiliated on the basis of the number of members paying the political levy. This varied greatly from union to union. The Constituency Labour Parties, though they supplied a high proportion of delegates to the annual conference, had less than 20 per cent of the voting power. The same situation prevailed lower down. A Divisional Labour Party had not only individual members (usually organised in wards) but affiliated branches of local trade unions together with any eligible socialist and co-operative societies in the area. It would be governed by a management committee composed of delegates from these organisations. When it came to important decisions, such as choosing a candidate, local trade-union delegates would usually have the majority vote.

Had the Communist Party gained affiliation, it would have been in the group of 'socialist societies'. Until 1932, much the largest of these societies had been the Independent Labour Party; when the latter decided to disaffiliate, some of its members disagreed and formed the Socialist League. Numbering 3,000 this was now the largest of the affiliated socialist societies; among the others were the Fabian Society, the Social Democratic Federation and the Scottish Socialist Party. All these bodies had the right to table resolutions, argue for their point of view and be represented on the local management committees. The Communist Party hoped for the opportunity to participate in the same way.

The letter to Labour Party headquarters making formal application for the affiliation of the Communist Party to the Labour Party was dated 25 November 1935. It pointed out that the bitterest former opponents of Communist affiliation (MacDonald, Snowden, Thomas) had all since deserted to the class enemy, that the National Government meant attacks on workers at home and support for Nazi Germany abroad, and only united action could secure its defeat. In answer to the Labour Party's claim that, as a federal body, it already represented the united front of the working class, it contended that the Labour Party could not claim to be all-embracing if it excluded 'workers and organisations which hold the revolutionary standpoint.' The Communist Party, it said, would continue to uphold this position and would maintain its connections with revolutionary working-class parties in other countries (in other words it would stay a member of the Communist International) but would work loyally within the Labour Party on all current electoral and other campaigns.

> It is prepared to do this, not as a manoeuvre or for any concealed aims, but because it believes this would unite the working class and make it better able to face the immediate fight against the National Government, against Fascism and imperialist war.

The rejection by the National Executive Committee of the Labour Party, dated 27 January 1936, stated that no circumstances had arisen to justify departure from the decision of 1922; that the difference between the democratic policy of the Labour Party and the Communist Party policy of dictatorship was 'irreconcilable'; that the rise of fascist dictatorships abroad had been faciliated by Communist campaigns which had split the working-class movement; that the Communist Party sought to use Labour Party facilities for the promotion of Communist principles; that any weakening in the Labour Party's defence of democracy would assist the forces of reaction and retard the achievement of socialism in this country.[9]

The Communist Party then launched a campaign to win affiliation. Communists in trade union branches tabled resolutions; if these were carried they were sent to a higher committee and to the local Labour Party or trades council. Week by week the *Daily Worker* recorded the progress of the campaign. On 4 March it was announced that nearly 200 organisations had passed resolutions in favour of affiliation, including 100 trade union branches, 10 trades councils, 25 Co-op guilds, and 60 local Labour Party organisations (mainly ward parties). By the first week of May the list of organisations in favour of affiliation had reached 481; by mid-June it was 906.

By this time the most important socialist societies affiliated to the Labour Party, had come out in favour of communist affiliation. The Fabian Society declared itself in favour; so did the left-wing Socialist League whose leading members, Sir Stafford Cripps and Aneurin Bevan, had both made public declarations backing affiliation. On 13 June, another much-respected intellectual of the Labour movement, G.D.H. Cole, did so. He wrote in an article in the *New Statesman* that as the world was not obligingly standing still, but rushing helter-skelter towards a cataclysm, the continuation of traditional methods – 'this complacent patience' – was absurd; that in both the trade unions and the Labour Party, Communist influence was getting stronger, and that

> it would be wise, I believe, under these conditions, for the Labour Party to accept the affiliation of the Communist Party, and for the TUC General Council to stop its futile efforts to suppress Communism inside the trade unions and the local trades councils.

By September, over 1,400 organisations had passed resolutions supporting Communist affiliation, including 831 trade union branches, and 407 local Labour Party organisations. Three big unions had decided at their annual conferences to support the demand: they were the Mineworkers' Federation of Great Britain, the Amalgamated Engineering Union (the Executives of both these unions had some five years previously been trying to outlaw Communists) and the train-driver's union, ASLEF. Three small unions had also declared in favour: the Scottish Bakers, the National Union of Clerks and the Furnishing Trades Association. These six trade unions could between them command a vote of 490,000 at the annual conference, about one fifth of the total. However, some other major unions – for example, the National Union of Railwaymen and the distributive workers' unions – had rejected the demand, while it was obvious that the two giant general workers' unions (TGWU and GMWU), whose leaders were on the extreme right of the Labour movement, would vote against the proposal.

Despite the signs early on that the resolution for affiliation would fail to win majority support, the leaders of the Labour Party became very alarmed, and their fears were shared by the establishment. On 27 May 1936, *The Times* published a leader headed 'Railwaymen and Extremists' drawing attention to the increase in left-wing activities, both on the railways and among London busmen. It complained that the unions had diminished their 'watchfulness against the penetration of influences which seek to use them for their own final destruction.' It said that 'by the trade-union door, Communists and their friends are gaining access to positions of authority in the labour movement' and asserted that the TUC would not be able to ignore the issue.

The TUC leaders were in fact concerned that their 'Black Circulars' had not succeeded in retarding the growth of Communist influence, and in July a document under the title 'British Labour and Communism' was issued by the National Council of Labour (the joint body on which were represented the TUC, the NEC of the Labour Party and the Parliamentary Labour Party).[10] It reiterated the familiar objections to the Communists, and in a series of articles beginning on 29 July 1936, the *Daily Worker* answered many of them. Thus the document alleged that Communist efforts to promote revolutionary policies had 'stimulated fascist and Nazi reaction in some countries with disastrous consequences.' In response to this the *Daily Worker* pointed out that the military revolt against the Spanish Popular Front government (which had just begun) proved the exact opposite; there were no Communists or Socialists in this Government and

> the fascists in Spain were able to organise a military revolt, not because the Government was too 'revolutionary' but precisely because it believed (like the Labour leaders) that it could shape and adapt the State to its democratic purpose.[11]

The document accused the Communists of disruption in the trade unions, setting out its standpoint in characteristic fashion:

> Trade unions cannot enter into collective bargaining without accepting responsibility for carrying out their agreements. On numerous occasions, however, the executives of unions have been faced with unofficial strikes, deliberately fomented by Communists and directed, not so much against the employers as against executive authority and the unions themselves.

To this the Communist reply was that Communists were among the foremost in building up the unions, as was proved by the many Tolpuddle medals won by Party members. Referring to the growth of the Amalgamated Engineering Union, it said 'the record in recruiting in London is held by Joe Scott, London organiser and a Communist.' It pointed to the increasing membership of the South Wales Miners' Federation which had a Communist (Arthur Horner) as President and said: 'The real disrupters of trade unionism are those who try to apply Black Circulars in them, try to discriminate among the membership.'[12]

To the habitual charges of subsidies of Russian money, the article in the *Daily Worker* gave a two-fold answer. In the first place, it defended the right of the Communist International to give aid where it was needed. It upheld the principles of international solidarity, one of which was that the strong must help the weak. The article went on to show that the accusations about Moscow gold were in practice wide of the mark. Acknowledging that the Labour Party was largely financed by fees from affiliated unions, it stated that the Labour Party received less from its 400,000 individual members than did the Communist Party from its individual members in dues and donations combined. 'We challenge the National Council of Labour,' said the article. 'We are prepared to let the accounts be examined by independent persons, and we have no doubt what the result will be.'[13]

The National Council of Labour never accepted this challenge; had it done so it might well have found that the calculation was correct. At the time it was normal for the Labour Party's 412,000 individual members to subscribe not more than one shilling a year, of which 4d went to headquarters and amounted to less than £7,000 in the headquarters accounts.[14] Communist Party members, on the other hand, paid 3d a week, or 13s a year (of which one shilling went to the 'international levy', i.e. to the Communist International). By

1936 the membership had risen to over 11,000 so dues brought in about £7,000 a year, and most of the members made other donations, those to the *Daily Worker* amounting to £13,000 in 1935.[15]

'We have no fear of any investigation with regard to the source of our income,' Communist Evan J. Evans of the South Wales Miners told the Trades Union Congress.

> I am not saying this by way of idle boast, comrades; it is a fact, and I can prove it. I myself for the last two years have been voluntarily paying, not by order from Stalin or Russia, but of my own free will, from 5s to 10s a week for the maintenance of an organisation in South Wales.[16]

When the resolution on Communist affiliation came to be voted on at the Labour Party Annual Conference in October 1936 it received 592,000 votes with 1,728,000 against. Thus just over a quarter of the votes were cast in favour of affiliation.

The Impact of United Action

Throughout its campaign, the Labour leaders had constantly emphasised that the strength of the Communist Party was 'negligible'; that it was, what Citrine described as a 'fragment,' that its membership was 'pitiful'. But, as Rust suggested in *Labour Monthly*, if British Communism was such an 'abject failure', why then all the excitement, the agitated leading articles in the *Daily Herald*, the passionate denunciation of the 'united front'. 'The leaders of the British Labour Party have answered themselves,' wrote Rust. 'They are battering away so furiously precisely because Communism is *not* a negligible force.'[17] As the *Daily Worker* put it, unity was not a matter of arithmetic; it was a question of 'supplying a vital spark.'[18]

Hundreds of local Labour Party members were in process of discovering this. If they wanted to get into action on the great issues of the day – resistance to the means test, the fight against high rents, the battles against Mosley's fascists, help for Republican Spain – they invariably found themselves working side by side with Communists, who always seemed to be the keenest activists, the most dedicated distributors of leaflets, the most energetic canvassers, the most reliable attenders at meetings and, very often, the most convincing and accomplished outdoor speakers.

So the rock-like resistance of the Labour leadership to united action with Communists was in practice undermined all over the country in the years 1936–39. And more and more it appeared to the Labour left that the object of the bans and prescriptions imposed on Communists was to *stifle* any mass movements and *avoid* being involved in them. The Hunger March against the means test in the autumn of 1936 was a case in point. Before it was launched by the NUWM, efforts had been made to persuade the Labour leaders to sponsor such a march; they refused. Also rejected was a proposal for industrial action against the means test made at the Plymouth TUC in September 1936. In opposition to this proposal, Citrine, TUC General Secretary, treated the delegates to a lengthy dissertation on whether it was 'morally right' for a section of the community to subvert the will of Parliament by direct action. He didn't think it was.[19]

But when, in the absence of any action by the official labour movement, the NUWM launched its last great hunger march, local Labour parties and trades councils eagerly welcomed the marchers passing through their towns with meals laid on and offers of accommodation, while in London, for the first time, a reception committee was formed by the London Trades Council. The marchers' arrival was greeted by a crowd of 250,000 people in Hyde Park. 'Why should a first-class piece of work like the Hunger March have been left to the initiative of unofficial members of the Party and to the Communists and the ILP?' complained Aneurin Bevan in *Socialist*, the organ of the Socialist League.[20] Indeed, so great was the support for the march that the leader of the Parliamentary Labour Party, Clement Attlee deemed it wise to accept an invitation to speak at the Hyde Park rally. Just afterwards, H.N. Brailsford, another leading member of the Socialist League, voiced the widespread discontent within the Labour Party:

> The Labour Party has ceased to be the natural vehicle for the emotions and aspirations of the masses – their anger, their hope, their impulses of humanity and gallantry. It tends to become a mere electioneering machine . . . this jealous boycott of the Left impoverishes and narrows the Party.[21]

Just afterwards, as a result of discussion initiated by Stafford

Cripps, the Socialist League launched a 'unity campaign' jointly with the ILP and the Communist Party. There could be no uncertainty about the outcome of this action by the Socialist League. It was declared a banned organisation by the Executive of the Labour Party. After this the League dissolved itself.

Thus throughout the decade the Labour leaders fought desperately to maintain the isolation of the Communist Party, and so avoid being involved in any sort of direct action or struggle. They continued to follow the 'never again' guidelines laid down after the 1926 General Strike.

Inevitably, in such a situation, more and more local Labour Party members applied to join the Communist Party. Some of them were at this time encouraged to stay in the Labour Party and work to change it. Indeed, a number of them became Communists in secret; their Party cards were held for them, sometimes at 16 King Street, more commonly by the District Secretaries for the area in which they lived. This practice prevailed until after the outbreak of war in 1939. At that stage they were all asked to come out into the open as Communist Party members, and many of them did so; those who did not ceased to be members of the Communist Party.

Though no public statement was made on the matter, it was evidently concluded that to continue with such a practice would be a mistake. It laid the Party open to charges of 'conspiracy' and 'subversion' when its real strength was as an open, public campaigning force which could influence the ideas and actions of great numbers of Labour Party members. There was also the danger that it would undermine the campaign for the affiliation of the Communist Party to the Labour Party, which had always been based on the argument that Communists should be able officially to play a part in the Labour Party.

From that time on, it was always made clear to those Labour Party members who applied to join the Communist Party that they could not be individual members of both organisations.

---

[1] *Daily Worker*, 20 October 1934.

[2] *Daily Worker*, 1 November 1934.

[3] Meetings of Political Bureau, 15 November 1934, Central Committee, 14 December 1934, JK papers; see also article by H. Pollitt in *Communist Review*, December 1934.

[4] Ibid. See also Report to 13th Congress, p.29.

[5] Speech by Harry Pollitt at the Seventh World Congress.

[6] *Daily Worker*, 16 November 1935.

[7] *Daily Worker*, 5 February 1936.

[8] *Labour Party Annual Report 1936*, p.156.
[9] Ibid., pp.50–1.
[10] Ibid., p.296.
[11] *Daily Worker*, 29 July 1936.
[12] *Daily Worker*, 5 August, 1936.
[13] *Daily Worker*, 31 July 1936.
[14] *Labour Party Annual Report 1936*,, p.99.
[15] *Daily Worker* fighting fund total for 1935.
[16] *TUC Report 1936*, p.430.
[17] *Labour Monthly*, August 1936.
[18] *Daily Worker*, 11 September 1936.
[19] *TUC Report 1936*, pp.293–4.
[20] *Socialist*, November 1936.
[21] *Reynolds News*, 24 January 1937.

CHAPTER 12

'They Shall Not Pass!'
(1936–37)

Membership of the British Union of Fascists (BUF) had reached some 40,000 in the first half of 1934.[1] But after Olympia, and then the humiliation of 9 September in Hyde Park, the numbers fell away. Some of Mosley's rich backers, including Lord Rothermere, withdrew their support; members of the establishment cooled off; rank-and-file followers, who had climbed onto the bandwagon when it seemed to be rolling ahead, were now deserting it.

The Communist Party had been responsible for organising the counter-demonstrations at Olympia and in Hyde Park, and the results seemed to vindicate the contention that a fascist movement could not be defeated by ignoring its activities and allowing it to hold meetings and marches unopposed.

After the 1934 events, Mosley reorganised his shrinking forces, and attempted to win support in areas outside London. In Lancashire, he launched a campaign to 'save' the cotton industry by the simple process of excluding all foreign textiles from entry into the British colonies, especially India, which was to be prohibited from importing Japanese cotton goods, but obliged to remove its own tariffs against British textiles. Mosley addressed some big meetings in Lancashire in 1935, and was able to establish BUF branches in one or two places. He was supported by some of the employers, though the response from the hard-pressed cotton operatives was not particularly encouraging.

Even less successful were the efforts of the BUF in South Wales. On 11 June 1936, when one of Mosley's henchmen, an ex-miner named Moran, came with his van to Tonypandy, some 2,000 people participated in a hostile demonstration, and he was forced to leave. The police retaliated by arresting 36 Rhondda anti-fascists, most of them Communists. They were sent for trial and seven of them were given jail sentences, including Harry Dobson, who later lost his life fighting with the International Brigade in Spain.

It was in East London that the BUF established its most significant following after 1934: the basis for its support was anti-semitism. Until then, the movement's racial theories had been soft-pedalled; now the racist message was to go out loud and clear. For the first time Mosley's followers, who had largely consisted of disgruntled middle-class people, began, in East London, to include considerable numbers of young workers.

Almost half the Jewish population of Great Britain lived in East London. Most had been born and bred there, their parents having emigrated to England as refugees from pogroms in Eastern Europe in the late nineteenth and early twentieth century. Here, in East London, they formed a minority of the inhabitants living side by side with non-Jews, including considerable numbers of Roman Catholics, among them many Irish dockers.

Life was hard for people in East London; social surveys had revealed a far greater concentration of poverty here than elsewhere in London. Where there is unemployment and deprivation, it is not difficult to foster racial antagonism, and that is what Mosley and the BUF did. The cause of all grievances was attributed to the Jews. Unemployment was the fault of the Jews; the prevalent low wages and long hours were imposed by Jewish employers; it was Jewish landlords who forced up rents; wars were caused by 'international Jewish finance' which was trying to destroy world fascism because it had challenged the dictatorship of that finance. When Jewish refugees from Hitler Germany began to arrive in Britain (a much smaller number than went to other countries, largely because of the British government's restrictive rules), the Blackshirts created the impression that Britain was being 'over-run' by Jews, and demanded their deportation.

There was no law against incitement to racial hatred and the anti-Jewish message was delivered in unusually offensive language. Thus Jews of modest means were the lower echelons of a 'foul growth' that stretched to the City of London; 'the big Jew puts you out of employment by the million, the little Jew sweats you in Whitechapel.'[2]

It was 'Jew landlords with the money bags' who had put up rents. Blackshirt speakers talked of Jewish 'submen', and the 'sweepings of the ghetto'; they paraded the streets shouting 'Yids! Yids! We gotta get rid of the Yids!' They alleged that 'the Jews among us are a cancer and very foul disease'. Slogans such as 'Perish Judah' appeared chalked in the streets, and even 'Kill the dirty Jews'. By

1936, Jewish shopkeepers were being threatened and their windows smashed, and many cases of assaults on Jews were reported.

British liberal-minded people had all along regarded Hitler's persecution of the Jews with horror and disgust, and attempts to foment racial strife by Mosley's movement met with a similarly hostile reaction from such circles, when noticed. Communists held racialist movements in abhorence, but not simply because they violated human rights. They saw such movements as attempts by the ruling class to divide the workers, particularly when the capitalist system itself was threatened. 'Anti-semitism, the typical degrading expression of a tottering system, is developed by capitalism in its decaying stage in proportion as the class struggle grows acute', was how R. Palme Dutt characterised it in his book *Fascism and Social Revolution*.[3]

Unity of the working class against its common enemy was the paramount objective; it followed that anti-semitism must be fought. The question was, how? It was one thing to stage counter-demonstrations in London's West End, it was quite another to combat the unceasing racial propaganda which was spreading like a disease among the deprived people of the East End.

There were continuous arguments in the Stepney Communist Party over the tactics to be adopted in face of this menace. Members had begun by heckling the BUF speakers at their outdoor meetings whenever they were peddling their anti-semitic filth. They found, however, that they were liable to be pounced on by the police and hustled away; if they resisted, they could be arrested and charged with 'insulting words and behaviour'. Yet the police stood round, guarding BUF speakers, no matter how insulting their words were to Jewish people.

With this experience, some party members favoured the mobilisation of anti-fasicsts to shout down BUF meetings whenever they were held, in order to stop them getting a hearing. The trouble with this tactic was that it invariably resulted in fights, not with the fascists, but with the police. After which, Communists could be accused – and were – of 'fomenting disorder' and violence. In any case, these were customarily held by its enemies to be the Communist Party's chief objective.

Pollitt had foreseen this difficulty, early on:

It will be fatal for us if the Communist Party's opposition to Mosley is looked upon by the working class as in the nature of a brawl and not a real political struggle he told the Central Committee.[4]

The Battle of Cable Street

The Party, of course, was carrying on its own anti-fascist propaganda, but had become aware that this was not enough in itself. Phil Piratin, a young Stepney Communist, was among those who argued that the work should be concentrated less on street propaganda and more on building up organisation, whether at the workplace or in residential areas. If you could get people into action on their own problems, this would prove to them who their real enemies were. In time, the tenants' movements which arose in Stepney and Bethnal Green were to justify this stand. But meanwhile, in September 1936, the Stepney Party was suddenly confronted with an emergency. It was announced that, as the culmination of Mosley's summer-long anti-semitic campaign, a march of uniformed fascists was to take place through East London on Sunday 4 October. It was to start at Royal Mint Street, near Tower Bridge at Stepney's western border, go east through the heart of the Jewish quarter to hold a meeting in Salmon Lane, Limehouse, and then on again to Victoria Park, Bethnal Green, for a final rally. The first news of the proposed march (with as yet no details given) appeared in the *Blackshirt* newspaper only on Saturday 26 September, one week before the event was to take place.

During the next few days, urgent attempts were made to get the Home Office to ban the march. On Wednesday 30 September George Lansbury, MP for a Poplar constituency and, until 1935, leader of the Parliamentary Labour Party, asked the Home Secretary to divert the march; on Thursday a deputation of five East London mayors tried to persuade him to ban it; on Friday, a petition with 100,000 signatures was presented to the Home Office calling for the march to be stopped. The Home Secretary was reported to be 'considering' the matter; it was not until the evening of Saturday 3 October that it was definitely stated that the march was *not* to be banned.

The London District of the Communist Party had some days earlier arranged to support an Aid for Spain youth rally in Trafalgar Square on 4 October. Faced with the announcement of the Mosley march, it was initially proposed that demonstrators should go to East London to show opposition to Mosley at the end of the Spain rally. But after representations from members of the Stepney branch it was agreed that the march must take priority and that the youth should be asked to call off their meeting and to concentrate on action against the Blackshirts, and use the slogan 'The fascists shall not pass!' (This slogan echoed that of the Spanish Republican forces at that time defending Madrid against the fascist attack.) So on Friday 2 October 1936, the *Daily Worker* issued a call for 'the biggest rally against fascism that has yet been seen in Britain'.

By this time, the Labour leaders were imploring everyone to stay away. In Labour's *Daily Herald* a leader to this effect appeared on 1 October:

> **KEEP AWAY**
>
> 'I advise people to keep away from the fascist demonstration in the East End.' This is sound advice by Mr Lansbury. Fascist meetings are in themselves dull. The platform is dull, the speeches are dull. The 'message' is dull. The only attraction is the prospect of disturbances. Withdraw that attraction, and fascist meetings would die on the organisers' hands. Well, it can be withdrawn whenever the opponents of fascism are cool and disciplined enough to decide to do so.

Thus was reiterated the message of the Labour leaders – one which remained the same throughout the decade. Fascism could be defeated *provided* it was ignored. Anti-fascists who refused to ignore it were keeping it alive by creating 'disturbances'.

The Liberal *News Chronicle* also urged its readers to stay away, but on rather different grounds: those of free speech. 'The Communist has no more right to break up a fascist meeting than the fascist has to break up a Communist demonstration.'

The *Daily Worker* answered them. 'Haven't these people learned that you only increase fascist aggressiveness, fascist provocation, by retreating?' it asked. 'Haven't they learned that fascist appetite grows with eating?'[5]

There was indeed a rising number of people in the Labour movement and in the Jewish community who were utterly disgusted by the advice to turn their back on the enemy. To such people, the call to block Mosley's march seemed the only acceptable response.

In the end, the call was issued by both the London Communist Party and the Independent Labour Party, and received the active support of the Jewish Ex-Servicemen's Association. Hundreds of thousands of leaflets were distributed, the streets were covered with whitewashed slogans: 'They shall not pass', 'All out on October 4th'.

It was realised that if the fascist march was to be stopped there would have to be some careful organisation backing up the generalised call. To this end, the house in which Phil Piratin lived – No. 65 New Road, which was close to the eventual scene of operations – was used as a headquarters both before and during the event. Ted Bramley and John Mahon came down from the London District office to help map out the plan with the Stepney members, who included Phil Piratin himself, and others such as Sarah Wesker of the clothing workers' union and Lou Kenton who, a little later, went to fight in Spain.

A major problem was that the route that the fascists would take had not been announced; all that was known for certain was that they would assemble at Royal Mint Street at 2.30 p.m., parade there in front of Mosley and then march east to Salmon Lane, and from there make for Victoria Park Square in Bethnal Green. There were at least three routes which could be taken. The obvious choice was the one by way of Leman Street to Gardiner's Corner, Aldgate, where the march could swing right and proceed down the main thoroughfare, Commercial Road. But, if this route was blocked, the most likely alternative was Cable Street, though it was possible that a detour could be made along The Highway which was down near the docks. All three contingencies had to be allowed for. To this end, the *Daily Worker* in a special four-page supplement on Saturday 3 October, called on Londoners to rally at Leman Street, Gardiner's Corner and Cable Street. It published a map and instructions on how to reach these destinations. The supplement included a special section on anti-semitism.

> The fascists are pouring out unimaginable filth against the Jews. The attack on the Jews has been the well-known device of every bloodthirsty, reactionary, unpopular régime for centuries.

The issue, it said, was

> Not merely a question of elementary human rights . . . The attack on the Jews is the beginning of the attack to wipe out the socialist movement, trade unionism and democracy in Britain.[6]

Sunday, October 3, 1936   THE DAILY WORKER—Supplement

SAVE THE EAST END OF LONDON
FROM FASCISM
THRONG STREETS IN PROTEST

Wardens of democracy: London Communists' great parade a fortnight ago.

A woman weeps. . . . Fascism is at work in Spain.

NO LIBERTY FOR THE ASSASSINS OF LIBERTY

Let Gentiles And Jews Unite In Defence Of Freedom

WILL Fascism prepare civil war against the people? To-morrow, Sunday, Mosley leads his "officers in charge of Operation" in the streets of East London. His armed forces will parade for inspection in Royal Mint Street, prior to entering the workers' quarters.

Mosley, aristocrat and turncoat, seeks to rouse feeling against the Jewish citizens of this country. If he thus succeeds in splitting the people, then he will be able to go on to destroy all democratic institutions. Anti-semitism is the old ruling-class game of divide and conquer. Mosley praises the heroes of Fascism—Hitler, Mussolini and Franco. Remember the massacres of Badajoz and Irun! Remember the torture chambers and con-

centration camps of Hitler! Remember the bombing and gassing of the Abyssinian people!

Londoners, assert your rights and defend your freedom. Protest against the Fascist plans to destroy trade unionism, co-operative and labour organisations, cultural and intellectural freedom!

All support to the East End protest against Fascism on Sunday! By 2 p.m., fill Cable Street, Leman Street, St. George's Street, Gardiner's Corner with the protest of London's anti-Fascist people.

Against Fascism! For Freedom and Democracy! For the victory of the Spanish People! For the raising of the blockade which deprives them of arms! For Peace and Freedom in East London!

—Communist Party, London District Committee.
Young Communist League, L.D.C.

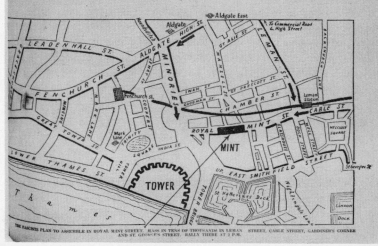

THE FASCISTS PLAN TO ASSEMBLE IN ROYAL MINT STREET. MASS IN TENS OF THOUSANDS IN LEMAN STREET, CABLE STREET, GARDINER'S CORNER AND ST. GEORGE'S STREET. RALLY THERE AT 2 P.M.

Behind the scenes, the Party had set up a tightly-knit organisation, including a team of cyclists and motor-cyclists to carry messages from those at the 'front' to those at headquarters and back again. There were also 'observers' placed at key positions from which they could telephone in information on Blackshirt movements, in particular possible changes of route. In practice, 'observers' found the telephone jammed and had to send messages by hand. Anti-fascist doctors and nurses were mobilised to serve at improvised first-aid posts.

Party members, though they might argue all evening about a given political line, were highly disciplined when it came to taking action. On this occasion, every Party branch in London was told where its members and supporters were expected to go. Bethnal Green members were instructed to stay in Victoria Park Square ready to put up a platform if Mosley got through. The Bethnal Green members were dismayed, but did what they were asked, and so missed the great event.[7]

The majority of London branches outside East London were asked to assemble with their supporters at Gardiner's Corner or at some nearby point at 2 p.m. In practice, many never reached their destination, for they found their way blocked by a crowd so huge that it filled not only Leman Street and Commercial Road, but all the streets leading into the area. It had in fact been assembling since early morning, and was later estimated at over a quarter of a million.

6,000 foot police and the whole of the mounted division had been drafted into the area; a police 'observation' plane circled overhead. The fascists arrived at Royal Mint Street in coaches, and were met by part of the hostile crowd which was kept at bay with difficulty by the police with baton charges; eventually, some 3,000 blackshirted BUF members were assembled and stood ready to march surrounded on all sides by the police.

Meanwhile, the mounted police were trying to clear the route up Leman Street with repeated baton charges, while cordons of foot police were thrown across every side street. They were not only met by a crowd solidly chanting 'they shall not pass' – there were other impediments. At Gardiner's Corner a tram had been abandoned by its anti-fascist driver; it was soon joined by others whose drivers got off and left them, thus raising an unexpected obstruction which the police could do nothing to remove. Gradually, after many heads had been broken, and some people had been pushed through shop windows, it became clear that though the mounted police might succeed by brute force in carving a narrow passage up Leman Street, the numbers with whom they would have to contend round the corner in Commercial Road would make progress impossible. At this stage it was decided to direct the march down Cable Street.

This was an eventuality which the Party had foreseen and for which special preparations had been made. In contrast to Leman Street and Commercial Road, Cable Street was relatively narrow. It could not be blocked by a large crowd and a different technique would be needed. So plans had been laid to put up barricades as soon as the signal was given. Many Irish dockers lived in or near Cable Street; they responded with enthusiasm to this plan, and when the moment came, showed their strength.

A lorry was driven up, pushed over on its side and on top of it were piled pieces of furniture and contents of a nearby builders' yard. As the police moved forward to dismantle this barricade, they were met by flying bricks. Marbles were thrown under horses' hooves, paving stones were pulled up, and bottles dropped from roof-tops. Gradually the police forced their way up to the barricade, and with difficulty pulled it down, only to find there was another one further up the street, and yet another.

By three o'clock, when Mosley arrived to lead the march, the police had spent hours trying to clear the route; many people had been hurt and many arrested. At 3.40 p.m., Sir Philip Game, Commissioner of the Metropolitan police, met Mosley at the assembly point and told him that the march must be abandoned. After which, instead of marching east, the fascists were ignominiously escorted west through a deserted City to disperse on the Embankment. It was Mosley's most humiliating defeat. 'The "sit-at-home" policy has been effectively rejected' the London Communist Party proclaimed in a special statement. The *Daily Worker* underlined the triumph:

> Mosley said he would march his militaristic columns through the East End of London. The police said yes; the Home Secretary said Yes; the Cabinet said Yes; but the workers said NO! and NO it was. Well done, historic East End of London!

The government's response was the Public Order Bill which received its Second Reading on 16 November 1936. Under this measure, the wearing of political uniforms was prohibited. Clearly such a ban would be disadvantageous to the British Union of Fascists, since their black shirts had, in some eyes, lent them glamour. But the rest of the Bill was regarded on the left as dangerous. There were two main objections raised by the Communist Party. First, it did nothing at all to ban racist propaganda, which meant that Mosley had complete liberty to continue with his anti-semitic campaign. (Incitement to racial hatred did not become illegal for another forty years.) The second criticism of the Bill was that it gave the police unprecedented powers to ban marches in general – not just racist ones. It was not difficult to guess how the police would use the Act. Time and again they were to invoke it to impose blanket bans on all processions, including May Day marches of trade unionists. For these reasons the *Daily Worker* described the measure as 'A Bill against Liberty'.[9]

Communists were not alone in recognising its dangers; the National Council for Civil Liberties argued that 'the persistent anxiety of government to afford yet greater powers to the police than those they already possess may well cause the greatest uneasiness'.[10]

To the dismay of many on the left, the Parliamentary Labour Party supported the Bill, and allowed its Second Reading to be carried without a division, explaining later that, though the Party had certain reservations concerning undue interference with rights of procession, 'there was a general feeling that its main provisions were necessary'.[11]

The significance of the Public Order Act was to be revealed only too soon. The BUF's anti-semitic activities in East London continued unimpeded; indeed, it was alleged that the police used the Act to protect the fascists from hecklers. But after plans had been announced for a fascist march from Limehouse to Trafalgar Square, an order was issued prohibiting *all* political processions in East London and parts of North London. The order, announced on 21 June 1937, remained in operation for twelve weeks. Among the events affected was a trade-union recruiting demonstration planned by Bethnal Green Trades Council.[12]

Bermondsey

However, when Mosley announced a march through Bermondsey in South London on 3 October, 1937, the Public Order Act was not invoked, and there was no ban. Immediately, all the issues faced twelve months earlier arose.

Bermondsey was an impoverished riverside borough with a solid Labour council. Many of its inhabitants worked in the docks, among them, large numbers of Catholics of Irish descent. There were, however, very few Jews living in the area. This was one of the arguments used to justify permission for the march to take place. But it also posed a question for the anti-fascist movement. It was obvious that Jewish people were consciously anti-fascist. What nobody knew was how far anti-fascist understanding had penetrated other sections of the London working class. On 3 October Bermondsey was to provide the answer.

As in October 1936, resolutions were passed by many organisations requesting that the march be banned. A deputation, headed by the Mayor of Bermondsey and the President of the local Trades Council, accompanied by Ben Smith, Labout MP for Rotherhithe (one of the Bermondsey constituencies), Dan Lewis, the South London organiser of the Communist Party, and various local churchmen, went to the Home Office to ask for the march to be stopped. The request was turned down. This news was reported to two mass meetings at Bermondsey and Rotherhithe Town Halls.

A few days earlier, Ben Smith and another Labour MP, Fred Montagu had both urged the boycott of the fascist procession if the Home Office refused to ban it. 'The proper answer to the fascists is self restraint and boycott, not hysteria or the other side of the fascist medal' said Montagu.[13]

But the conviction that you do not fight fascism by turning your back on it had grown since 1936. The Bermondsey Trades Council adopted a resolution calling once more for the march to be banned, but ending with the following words: 'We pledge ourselves to demonstrate on 3 October against fascism, and urge all London workers to do the same.'[14] Meanwhile, the London Communist Party put out 150,000 leaflets calling for a universal protest against the march, while on Saturday 2 October, the *Daily Worker,* all too conscious that a direct call for a counter-demonstration could result in proceedings under the Public Order Act, nevertheless made its meaning clear under the heading 'Bermondsey's Zero Hour':

The fascist march is due to start from Millbank, Westminster at 3 p.m. Reports from South London yesterday indicated that long before 2 p.m., thousands of people would be assembled along the route and particularly at the corner of Borough High Street and Long Lane, close to Borough Tube Station.

The anti–fascists got the message. Indeed some observers estimated that the numbers who turned out to oppose the march exceeded the crowds in East London twelve months earlier.[15]

The fascist marchers assembled at Millbank and started off across Westminster Bridge some forty minutes late. There were about 3,000 of them accompanied on either side by police, and headed by a posse of thirty mounted police, a riot van and a flying squad car. Hundreds more police were drawn up in side streets.

To sustained booing and shouting, the march went along York Road, past Waterloo Station (where the gates were closed and blocked by another big police contingent) and got to the end of Southwark Street. It had been intended to march down Long Lane, a broad thoroughfare which went through the heart of Bermondsey. But it was here that anti–fascists had been urged to assemble, and for over an hour and a half, mounted and foot police had been trying unsuccessfully to clear a passage. Early on, a barricade consisting of notice boards, ladders, costers' barrows, metal ovens and planks had been thrown across Long Lane at its western end. Surmounting it were red flags and behind it was a solid block of people shouting 'They shall not pass'; others were singing, the strains of the 'International' alternating with 'Land of Hope and Glory'.

When the police tried to pull down the barricade, pieces of scrap metal were thrown at them. Mounted police then came charging down a side street into the crowd, drove them back and tore down the barricade, only to find that another had been erected a hundred yards further down Long Lane. This time it consisted of trees pulled from the roadside, a huge water tank which had been taken from a disused factory, and packing cases. Again, the police hacked their way through with their truncheons and managed to demolish the second barricade. But the demonstrators, many of whom were dockers and used to handling heavy loads, were ready with a third barricade of planks and iron railings. Bus loads of reserve police were then rushed in. They swarmed over the barricade and managed to tear it down. Finally the mounted police charged the whole length of Long Lane, clearing it, only to find that the crowd, which had scattered down side streets, had gathered again and that the thoroughfare was once more blocked by thousands.

It was at this stage that the police sent an urgent message to those escorting Mosley that the planned route must be changed. So the fascist procession was diverted to Tooley Street, a narrow uninhabited road creeping between warehouses down by the riverside. Once the crowd in Long Lane knew that the march had been diverted, they formed their own procession, and shouting 'rats! rats! we gotta get rid of the rats!', met up with the head of the march further east in Jamaica Road, where there was another confrontation with the mounted police. At it turned out, Mosley did not reach his intended meeting place but was diverted to another site where, surrounded by mounted police, he briefly addressed his followers. He was inaudible to the crowd outside the police cordon; by this time they were chanting 'They did not pass'.

There were 111 arrests and the magistrate before whom some of them appeared was indignant. 'Not one of you has said "I am sorry to have behaved in this disorderly fashion",' he commented. 'You are not sorry. You came for the distinct purpose of creating disorder and must suffer for it.'[16]

It was true, they were not sorry. Bermondsey had shown that anti-fascism was as strong among the non-Jewish workers as it was among the Jews. Mosley's attempts to divide workers on racial grounds had failed.

[1]Skidelsky, op. cit., p. 331.
[2]Ibid., p. 388.
[3]*Fascism and Social Revolution*, p. 184 footnote.
[4]*Towards Soviet Power*, p. 29.
[5]*Daily Worker*, 2 October 1936.
[6]The London edition of the *Daily Worker* for 3 October 1936 was not in the file at the British Library's Newspaper Library at Colindale at the time this book was being researched. The only edition available there was the provincial one which did not include the special supplement. Lack of access to the London edition has led some writers to suggest that the Communist Party leaders were not anxious to mobilise a big anti-fascist demonstration – see, for example, Joe Jacobs, *Out of the Ghetto*, London 1978, p. 249. Such suggestions are manifestly untrue. The London edition was made available to the author by the Marx Memorial Library.
[7]See *Our Flag Stays Red*, Phil Piratin, London 1948, reprinted 1978. The author also had the benefit of discussions with Piratin and others involved in organising the demonstration.
[8]*Daily Worker*, 5 October 1936.
[9]*Daily Worker*, 12 November 1936.
[10]*Labour Research*, December 1936, p. 267.
[11]*Labour Party Annual Report 1937*, p. 83.
[12]Ibid., p. 215.
[13]*Daily Herald*, 25 September 1937.
[14]*Daily Worker*, 1 October 1937.
[15]*Daily Worker*, 4 October 1937.
[16]*Daily Herald*, 6 October 1937.

CHAPTER 13

Industrial and Trade Union Work
(1935–39)

Since the mid-1920s the Party's basic units of organisation had been of two kinds: 'factory' or workplace groups, and 'street' or area groups. Until 1936, the work of these groups was co-ordinated by the Local Party Committee which covered the area in which they functioned.

It had long been recognised that the primary aim of both types of group must be to get people into action, because the very experience of action changed their outlook. It taught them that solidarity means strength, it showed them who was their real enemy, it instilled into them lessons they never forgot, and broadened their ideas about the future. A victory, even on a minor issue, could encourage further organisation and open up possibilities for advance.

The factory or workplace was always held to be the most important area of work, since it was here that the struggle between capitalists and workers would emerge in a decisive form. As an early handbook on *Communist Party Training* explained, it was in the workplace that the 'antagonism of interests between the capitalists and the workers' was most evident, it was here that the least politically conscious workers could be reached, it was here that 'the fallacy of purely parliamentary methods of struggle' could be exposed, because 'in the workshop it is most evident that only the organised might of the workers can wrench concessions from the employers.'[1] To this end, where there were as many as three Party members employed at a particular workplace – whether a factory, mill, pit, rail depot, bus garage, building site, or office – they were expected to link up with one another, meet as a group on a regular basis, and organise their main political activity in the workplace concerned. The publication of special pit or factory papers – usually run off on a duplicator – had long been a part of such activity.

Each workplace group was supposed to have a representative on the Local Party Committee, which was expected to provide an 'instructor' to assist the work of the group from outside.

The Party also encouraged Party members in a given trade union to meet together in what was known as a 'fraction'. 'All our members, in any particular organisation, must work as a team,' said the handbook *Communist Party Training*. 'The reactionaries are united in their opposition, and to secure success we must organise fractions of Party members.'[2] There was nothing secret about the existence of 'fractions' – indeed it was common knowledge that people of right-wing views (in particular the Catholics) came together within the trade-union movement to co-ordinate their activities, and to make sure that right-wingers were elected to trade-union positions. But, inevitably, 'fractions' organised by Communists were denounced by the TUC leaders as a subversive device to disrupt the trade-union movement.[3]

From 1929 to 1935, the word 'cell' had been substituted for the word 'group' and the Party membership was, in theory, divided into 'factory cells' and 'street cells', their work co-ordinated as before by a Local Party Committee (known as a 'Local').

Despite the importance attached to workplace activity, it had been reported at the twelfth Congress in 1932 that less than 10 per cent of the membership was in factory cells.[4] In fact, after 1929, workplace organisation had fallen away. There were various reasons for this, as we have seen. Many of the Party members were unemployed, and devoted most of their active political work to the NUWM. The workforce as a whole was demoralised by the threat of losing jobs, and this tended to dampen down the possibilities of workplace activity. The Class against Class policy had been counter-productive.

At the thirteenth Congress at the beginning of 1935, when the industrial work of the Party had been recovering fast, mainly as a result of the change in attitude to the trade unions, the method of organising the Party came under scrutiny. It was decided that, wherever possible, isolated members working in factories on their own should be attached to the nearest factory cell in their industry, helping its work and themselves learning how to build such a cell. In January 1936, at an enlarged Central Committee meeting, further organisational proposals were made, and these were adopted after considerable discussion throughout the Party.[5] As a result, the word 'cell' was dropped in favour of the original word 'group', and all the groups in an area – whether 'factory', 'ward' or 'street', would be co-ordinated by a local 'Branch Committee' to replace the former

'Local Party Committee' and their members would all become members of the local 'Branch'.

The new organisation did not signify any change in attitude to workplace groups; on the contrary, they were still looked on as the most important form of organisation, and one of the objects of the change in structure was to facilitate the mobilisation of members who were not in such groups to help those who were.

Since masses of workers at this time were not even in a trade union, one of the first priorities of Communist workplace groups was trade-union recruitment. As the trade unions were, to a large extent, led by people who believed in class collaboration, the second major object was the transformation of the unions into organisations of class struggle. So the Party members tried to foster inner-union democracy in place of the bureaucratic structures which so often prevailed, aiming at maximum participation by workers in their unions' decisions. They fought for the election of militant and left-wing members to official positions in place of the right-wingers then in control. They strove to unite a trade union movement that was fragmented and weakened by sectional rivalries and demarcation disputes.

As one of the means towards changing the trade unions, the Party, as we have seen, had in the early-1930s initiated a number of 'rank-and-file' movements. These were usually regarded as a threat by the trade-union leaders. The most outstanding example of such a movement was that of the London busmen which was formed in 1932 and in 1937 was deliberately destroyed by Ernest Bevin, the right-wing leader of the Transport and General Workers Union.

The Party and the London Busmen

Between 1932 and 1937, Communist Party membership in the London bus fleet had grown from 12 to 98. The members were spread over some 29 bus garages. It was reported at a special meeting called by the Communist Party London District in April 1937 that about 15 of the 98 were 'individual members in scattered garages, and so far as we know, these have never done more than sign the form of application for the Party.' The remaining 83 members, however, were in some fourteen workplace groups at their respective garages.[6]

In the previous five years, the London Busmen's Rank and File Movement had flourished. Its regular monthly meetings were reasonably well attended, it had the support of the big majority of the union branches concerned; its paper, the *Busman's Punch* (still edited by Emile Burns who worked full time at 16 King Street) had a regular monthly sale of about 10,000.

The Movement had been built up on a union structure which did not exist in much of British industry, and offered unusually favourable opportunities for democratic participation. Thus, each garage had its own branch of the Transport and General Workers' Union; moreover these branches were grouped under a Central Bus Committee which had considerable autonomy. Shortly after the start of the Rank and File Movement its nominees won a majority of the positions on the Central Bus Committee and Bert Papworth was elected to the TGWU Executive Council. In short, the Movement had got beyond the stage of trying to prevent sell-outs by the union's leadership: it had begun the process of changing that leadership and with it the union machine.

The Movement's first priority was, of course, the defence and improvement of busmen's wages and conditions. It co-ordinated action for all-London demands, and mobilised support for any branch defending standards in its own garage. But the Movement was not limited to this. Firstly, it aimed to broaden its base, linking up with other sections, such as London tramwaymen and busworkers in the provinces. Secondly, it tried to get busmen into action on wider political issues – thus a sizeable contingent of busmen participated in the march against Mosley in September 1934. Later, bus garages were to be among the most energetic focal points for Aid for Spain activity.

The issue that brought about the confrontation with Ernest Bevin in 1937 was not 'political'; it concerned a claim for shorter hours. Busmen who worked an 8-hour day were suffering from increased strain and stress, brought about by bigger buses, a huge growth in traffic, tighter time schedules and irregular meal breaks. They put in a claim for a 7½-hour day. The London Passenger Transport Board turned this down; the Central Bus Committee thereupon declared itself in favour of strike action and, though Bevin advised against this, the TGWU Executive sanctioned it. So, on 1 May 1937, 25,000 busmen came out on official strike, just as London was crowded with visitors for the coronation of King George VI. Many thousands of busmen marched in their white summer uniforms to the May Day demonstration in Hyde Park.

The Minister of Labour appointed a Court of Enquiry which found that the men had established 'a case for investigation'. At this, the TGWU Executive, on Bevin's advice, recommended a return to work. Both the Central Bus Committee and the Rank and File Movement dissociated themselves from this recommendation, which was then overwhelmingly rejected at branch meetings called to discuss it.

Ostensibly, the TGWU Executive accepted this vote, but they refused to do the one thing which might have led to victory: they resisted calls to bring out tram and trolley-bus members, and, indeed, instructed them to remain at work. As a result many of the passengers who normally depended on buses were able to find other means of transport and the financial loss to the LPTB was much reduced.

After the strike had lasted for four weeks, Bevin struck his fatal blow. The TGWU Executive revoked the powers of the Central Bus Committee to conduct the strike, suspended the machinery of the bus section of the union, and ordered the men back to work.

Thereupon, the strike collapsed. An enquiry was then held under the chairmanship of one of Bevin's chief lieutenants, Arthur Deakin who was to be his successor as leader of the TGWU. Its report went to great trouble to establish something which had never been in doubt – the links between the Communist Party and the Rank and File Movement, which was then declared to be a 'subversive body, membership of which is inconsistent with membership of the Union.' Three of its leaders were expelled from the union: Bert Papworth, Bill Jones, and Bill Payne. Four others were debarred from holding office in the union; they included the Communists Bernard Sharkey and Bill Ware.

The response of non-Communist militant Payne and some other Rank-and-File activists was to establish a breakaway union. The Communist Party was strongly against this move, and the Party's Central Committee issued a special statement about it. Pointing out that 'the roar of approval in *The Times, Daily Telegraph* and *Morning Post* shows that the action of the Executive in expelling the busmen's leaders has the full approval of the capitalist class,' it nevertheless went on to say:

We are sure that the branches which supported the rank-and-file movement in its struggle for a stronger and more democratic union with a fighting policy will reject the suggestion of a new union which can only lead to the destruction of the splendid unity already existing in the bus section, and the division of this section into antagonistic groups with the consequent strengthening of reactionary influence.[7]

The breakaway union was to last for nearly a decade. All the Communists, including those expelled or penalised by the TGWU, refused to have anything to do with it, and some years later Jones and Papworth were allowed back into the TGWU, whereupon both of them were rapidly elected to the Union's Executive Council, and Papworth, in the end, to the TUC General Council.

The Party and the Engineers

During the first half of 1936 there was a prolonged discussion in the Party concerning the function and future of rank-and-file movements. A series of articles on the question appeared in *Discussion* (the Party's monthly 'journal for political controversy.)' The first of these was headed 'Why We Don't Want Rank-and-File Movements'. Signed 'PJ', it alleged that such movements represented a diversion of energy from the task of winning over the trade-union machine and could lead to serious splitting activities. 'A union is like an army which must go into battle as a single force.' In reply to those who pointed to the London busmen's rank-and-file movement as a model, the writer asserted that this organisation owed its success to the fact that the union branches concerned were based on the place of work and the branch leadership directly in touch with what was going on. In fact, it was not so much a rank-and-file movement as a conference of branch officials.

The article provoked a series of replies, among them one from Arthur Downton, who stressed the vital importance of the shop steward's movement in the engineering industry. He pointed out that this was in effect a rank-and-file movement under another name.

The shop stewards' movement in engineering had, indeed, begun to revive. Having made a considerable impact during the First World War, it had virtually disintegrated in the disastrous post-war slump and lockout of the early 1920s. The trade unions involved, notably the Amalgamated Engineering Union, still provided under rules for official union recognition of stewards elected from the workshop floor. In practice, in the early 1930s, shop stewards, where they still existed, were seldom more than dues collectors.

However, from about 1933 onwards, workshop-floor organisation began to spread, and much of this was due to the work of Party activists. In factories where the majority were unorganised, they set themselves the task of recruiting to the unions; in others, where perhaps the management refused to recognise the unions, they concentrated on strengthening the organisation. As a result of their efforts to promote unity in the workshop, Communist Party members were frequently elected as shop stewards, and received recognition from union headquarters. This was not because the workpeople concerned regarded themselves as Communist supporters but because Party members were often much the keenest and most experienced, and also because in that period of insecurity, when active trade unionists were under constant threat of dismissal, only the most committed were prepared to risk taking on the job.

In most engineering factories the workers were organised in more than one union, and it was the practice of the unions to conduct their affairs separately from one another. Party members campaigned for Joint Shop Stewards' Committees (JSSCs) on which stewards from every union in a particular factory would be represented. This was not easy to achieve, partly because the leaders of most of the unions involved, including those of the Amalgamated Engineering Union, were against such JSSCs.

Workshop-floor organisation was the first priority. But in addition the Party aimed to establish links between stewards in different plants belonging to the same company, and between shop stewards' committees functioning in different firms in the same district. Thus in South East London, where CP member Charlie Wellard was convener at Siemens electrical engineering factory, an unofficial shop stewards' organisation was formed covering quite a number of factories in the area. When, in April 1939, Wellard was dismissed, 9,000 workers came out on strike.

Perhaps the most significant results of the shop steward activity were in the aircraft industry. In 1935, at a Hawker aircraft factory in Gloucestershire a strike developed around several demands, one of which was an objection to the introduction of a non-unionist into a section that was 100 per cent unionised, and the demand for full trade-union recognition. The shop stewards involved contacted another Hawker factory at Kingston which came out on strike a few days later in solidarity. Soon after, other aircraft factories were circularised asking for financial support. The AEU Executive issued a call for a return to work and sent down an official to the Gloucester factory to get the strike stopped, but failed. The strike ended with certain gains made. Meanwhile, on 28 April 1935, a conference was called in West London at which thirty delegates were present from eleven aircraft factories. In an opening statement, Claude Berridge, a Party member who was on the London District Committee of the AEU, argued against the idea of forming a special trade union for aircraft workers. The Hawker's strike proved, he said, that the way to get grievances rectified and to overcome the 'deadening effect of interminable conferences under the York Memo' was through powerful Shop Steward and Works Committees[8]. (The York Memorandum was an agreement in 1914 between the Executive of the AEU and the Engineering Employers for avoiding disputes.) The upshot was the election of an Aircraft Shop Stewards' National Council (ASSNC), and the launching under its auspices in October 1935 of a monthly paper, the *New Propellor*. It was edited by Peter Zinkin, at that time industrial organiser for the London District Committee of the Party, and was sold throughout the aircraft industry. By 1937 its circulation was 14,000 spread around 49 factories; by 1938 this had reached 20,000.

One of the ASSNC's first actions was to organise publicity and collections in aid of a strike against dilution of skilled men by unskilled youths at the Blackburn Aeroplane Co. factory on the Humber. In 1936 a strike of the Fairey Aviation workers at Stockport over the introduction of trainees at low rates of pay was supported by 100 per cent solidarity strike at Fairey's in Hayes, Middlesex. The AEU Executive refused to recognise these strikes.

Dilution was one issue; time-and-motion study another. In the spring of 1938 there was a walk-out over this at Rover Aero Shadow Factory in Birmingham. Here the works convenor was George Crane, a member of the Communist Party Central Committee. A strike committee was elected and organised a highly successful campaign throughout other factories in Birmingham and Coventry, and the Rover management capitulated. The ASSNC acted as co-ordinator for strike action in the industry but this was not, of course, its only object. At its first annual conference, with delegates present from sixteen factories, the main concentration was on building trade-union membership, and reporting on the innumerable issues that had been tackled by shop stewards' committees. These were to become more firmly established in the years up to the outbreak of war, and the *New Propellor* carried regular information about their activities from aircraft factories all over the country.

At this time, Communist Party groups were becoming firmly established. In June 1937 *Aeroplane* – a right-wing technical journal – claimed that there was in the de Havilland aircraft factory at Edgware a Communist 'cell' of nine members, with a group of ten sympathisers, including members of the ILP, the Socialist League and Labour Party left-wingers. This report may well have been correct.

Among movements that had a major impact during the 1930s was that of the engineering apprentices. The Young Communist League was actively involved in this, and the Party took the lead in mobilising support for it among adult engineers.

The engineering employers had for many years been paying very low wages to young boys in return for training which was quite inadequate, so that at the end of the five years' nominal apprenticeship, the lad would get the sack without the skills he needed for an adult job. Dilution of adult labour with underpaid boys in this way had long been a cause of ill-feeling, but the employers refused to recognise the right of the unions to negotiate on behalf of the apprentices.

In April 1937 a few young boys working for a firm on the Clyde went on strike; they marched to other shops in the area and within a week had been joined by 13,000 young engineers. A committee of 160, representing every shop from which the strikers had come, in turn elected its Central Strike Committee which was chaired by Stuart Watson of the Young Communist League. An Apprentices' Charter was drawn up, and adult trade unionists supported the boys, even declaring a one-day general strike. After four weeks, there was a return to work on a promise from the employers that there would be immediate negotiations, while some firms conceded wage increases. Meanwhile the movement spread south; Manchester entered the fray in September and Coventry followed shortly afterwards.

In October, after joint discussions between the Clyde and

CLYDESIDE

APPRENTICES

STRIKE: FULL STORY

ONE PENNY

STRIKE!

Manchester apprentice representatives, a national conference of young engineers and apprentices was held in Manchester. This Conference had an effect on the engineering employers who at last recognised the trade union's right to negotiate on behalf of the apprentices. 'Youth Make History' was the headline in the *New Propellor* which issued a special number for young aircraft workers.

The whole campaign was followed in detail in the weekly journal of the Young Communist League *Challenge*, which by 1938 had a circulation of 20,000.

The Party and the Miners

The main industrial strength of the Party had always been in the coalfields. As we have seen, the United Mineworkers of Scotland, formed in 1929 as the answer to Adamson's right-wing breakaway union, made a major contribution to the election to Parliament of Willie Gallacher as representative for West Fife.

The formation of the UMS had been followed by a period of appalling difficulty. Pits were closed down, thousands of miners were unemployed; it was realised that a known member of the UMS would be the first to be laid off, and would probably find it impossible to get another job. 'The UMS period was the most difficult in my whole industrial and political life,' recalled John McArthur, one of the Communists who had been elected to an official position in the union.

> These were years of low wages, of being castigated as the Red Union, the hirelings of Moscow, in receipt of Moscow gold, etc. I felt many a time that I would have welcomed any distribution of Moscow gold, because as things got worse, many times there was no money in the UMS's hands to send out our wages, though we were full-time officials.[9]

Initially the UMS had had considerable support in Lanarkshire but, partly owing to 'Class against Class' tactics, the membership fell away. It also had a small following in Stirling and Ayr, but it was only in Fife that the majority of miners belonged to it. This was despite the fact that the coalowners were trying to smash it, and to this end granted recognition only to Adamson's breakaway union representatives, refusing to negotiate with UMS organisers. One of the ways in which the UMS was able to get round this was by securing the election of its own members as inspectors of mines. There was a statutory right to elect workmen's inspectors, and the UMS inspectors' reports on the inadequacy of the safety measures resulted in many visits from government inspectors, thus forcing the coalowners to improve safety.

By 1934 the UMS was firmly established in Fife. Its general secretary was a well-known Communist, Abe Moffat. By this time it was in a financially sound position, but it remained isolated from the Scottish county unions, and, therefore, from the Miners' Federation of Great Britain. It tried to get unity of action with the other county unions, but the Scottish Executive, under the influence of Adamson, rejected all advances. By the end of 1935, when Gallacher was elected to Parliament, the UMS had been trying to get a meeting with Adamson in order to propose a united union in Fife; though they had the support of Ebby Edwards, General Secretary of the MFGB for this aim, Adamson remained immovable.

It was clear that a united miners' union for Scotland was still as far off as ever, and the Party members came to the conclusion that if the working conditions of the miners were to be protected, the problem of a divided organisation had to be solved. After a lot of argument and heart-searching it was decided to dissolve the UMS and urge all its members to join the existing county unions. 'As Communits we felt it was a difficult time to argue for an attempt to unify all the forces of the working class if we kept this internecine struggle among the miners going,' recalled John McArthur. 'For these reasons we argued that, even though liquidation meant a period in the wilderness, it would be for the ultimate good.'[10]

It *did* mean a period in the wilderness. The leaders of the county unions hurriedly decided that no former official of the UMS was to be admitted to the county unions unless working in the industry; they simultaneously got agreement from the coal-owners that no former UMS official should be given a job. This meant that the leading Communists were all kept out of the pits and therefore out of the union for a considerable period. In the end, however, they won through, got jobs, and were elected, one after another, to posts in the county unions and, later, in the National Unio1 of Mineworkers.

In other mining areas, in particular South Wales, Communists were leading the fight against company unionism. The campaign for

100 per cent membership of the South Wales Miners' Federation referred to in Chapter 7 did not just involve a drive to recruit the unorganised, it meant a battle against the so-called 'non-political' unions – in reality company unions – which had grown up since the 1926 General Strike. At a time of heavy unemployment, where wages had been forced down, the coal owners were in a strong position, and at a number of pits membership of the 'Industrial union' (the South Wales Miners' Industrial Union) was declared to be a condition of employment; those who refused to join, or joined the SWMF were dismissed. One of the first serious actions against the SWMIU was at Taff Merthyr Colliery in 1934; it began with a campaign from outside led by Communist councillor, Edgar Evans, a local ironmonger, and a group around him consisting largely of unemployed miners. There was a prolonged strike, and in the end the company was forced to compromise.[11] At the same time Arthur Horner, in his capacity as elected SWMF agent, concentrated on the Emlyn colliery, near Ammanford, conducted mass meetings when the men came off work, and persuaded the majority to rejoin the SWMF. There was a strike, the industrial union was disbanded and the owners forced to recognise the SWMF.[12] The movement culminated in a series of stay-down strikes, notably that at Nine Mile Point in 1935.

One of the most dramatic struggles against company unionism was in the Nottinghamshire coalfield where a right-wing Labour MP, George Spencer, in agreement with the coal owners, had formed a breakaway union after 1926. In most pits only men who agreed to join the Spencer union could get jobs, with the result that by 1935, out of 43,000 men employed, only 8,500 still belonged to the genuine miners' union, the Nottinghamshire Miners' Association, affiliated to the MFGB.

A turning point in the struggle against Spencer was the Harworth dispute. The men working at Harworth Colliery had voted by 1,175 to 145 to belong to the NMA and not the Spencer union. The President of the Harworth NMA branch was a well-known Communist, Mick Kane. There was strike in the autumn of 1936 over a checkweighing question; the union told the men to go back pending negotiation, but the owners refused to let them back unless they agreed to join the Spencer union. They refused, whereupon over a hundred police were drafted into the village in order to escort scab labour, brought in day-by-day from other areas. The behaviour of the police was the subject of a special investigation by the National Council for Civil Liberties which exposed their hostile attitude to those on strike.

The dispute came to an end only in May 1937 after the MFGB had threatened a national mining strike. The owners gave in and a compromise was arrived at, whereby the Spencer union was fused with the NMA and all the Harworth strikers reinstated.

However, there was a sequel in the form of a trial at the Nottinghamshire assizes of eleven miners and one miners' wife. The accusation against them was that they, 'together with divers other evil disposed persons, unlawfully, riotously did assemble to disturb the public peace and then did make great riot and disturbance, to the terror and alarm of His Majesty's subjects.'[13] They received very harsh sentences; the worst case that of Mick Kane who was sent to prison for two years, though not accused of being armed, or striking anyone, or throwing anything. There was widespread protest at these sentences and finally the Home Secretary granted considerable remissions, Kane himself being released in August 1938.[14] He was named as a member of the Presidium at the Fourteenth Congress of the Communist Party in 1937, and again at the Fifteenth Congress in 1938.

Black Circulars and Official Positions

During these years, the Party made a major contribution towards building up the trade unions. 'Over one hundred of our members have been presented with the Tolpuddle medal for recruiting and scores of others are entitled to it if they would only apply,' reported the Central Committee to the Fourteenth Congress in May 1937.[15]

In its 'Black Circular' of 1934, the General Council of the TUC had asked its affiliated unions to prohibit the nomination of 'members of disruptive bodies' for any official positions. This circular had been endorsed at the 1935 TUC but only by a narrow majority – 1,869,000 to 1,427,000 – and many unions had refused to operate it. Listing these, which included those catering for distributive workers, engineers, building, railway and textile workers, the Party's Central Committee report said: 'In all these trade unions there has been a big increase in the number of official positions that have been won by our members due to their untiring work in factory and branch.'[16]

Referring to this during the debate on industrial work, J.R. Campbell said:

> Let our comrades be under no illusions. They are going into one of the most outstanding breeding grounds of reformism, and we hope they will go in as Communists and remain in as Communists, as comrades who are the most practical organisers in these unions, but who do not lose themselves in practicalism . . . they must see that their task is not merely to raise the level of wages, but to raise the level of class consciousness, is not only to make the workers see that their interests are opposed to the interests of the capitalists but to make them see that the capitalist system is a menace to the whole human race.
>
> Therefore we must make the trade-union machine not merely a machine for raising wages but one which organises the workers for the great historic task of overthrowing capitalism by mass action.[17]

The majority of the national trade-union leaders remained implacably hostile to Communists and made difficulties for them if they were elected to trade union positions. Thus Claude Berridge, who had been elected President of the London District of the AEU by ballot vote was, in February 1937, expelled from the union for addressing a meeting of Rolls Royce Shop Stewards in Derby where a strike was in progress. Although the strike had the support of the Derby District Committee of the AEU, the Executive ruled that Berridge's action was unconstitutional. However, at the union's final appeals court in July 1937, Berridge was reinstated.[18]

Again, when, towards the end of 1938, the representative of the Miners' Federation of Great Britain on the TUC General Council resigned his position, the MFGB nominated Arthur Horner, now President of the South Wales Miners' Federation, to take his place. But by a vote of 18–3, the General Council rejected Horner, and elected instead the nominee of the North Wales Quarrymen's Union, an organisation of 8,000 members compared with over half a million represented by the MFGB.

[1] *Communist Party Training*, published by the Communist Party of Great Britain, 1927 edition, p.105.
[2] Ibid., p.117.
[3] *TUC Report 1929*, p.103.

[4] *Resolutions Adopted by the Twelfth Congress of the Communist Party of Great Britain*, p.20, pamphlet, n.d.

[5] See the article by R.W. Robson on 'Communist Organisation' in *Discussion*, March 1936, the Party's 'journal for political controversy'.

[6] This information is taken from a report in the Burns papers headed 'Bus Fraction 6–4–37'. At this meeting there were reported to be present 17 bus comrades and 5 instructors. 11 garages were represented. The Burns papers are in the CP Archive.

[7] Burns papers.

[8] For further details see Edmund and Ruth Frow, *Engineering Struggles*, Manchester 1982, in particular pp.114–117 on which this account is largely based; see also Richard Croucher, *Engineers at War 1939–1945*, London 1982, pp.37–40 et seq.

[9] Ian Mac Dougall (ed.), *Militant Miners*, Edinburgh 1981, p.134.

[10] Ibid., p.136.

[11] *The Fed*, Hywel Francis and David Smith, London 1980, pp.211–43, 269.

[12] Ibid., p.207.

[13] See *Free the Harworth Prisoners*, pamphlet issued by the Communist Party, August 1937.

[14] See R. Page Arnot, *The Miners in Crisis and War*, London 1961, pp.205–40.

[15] See *It Can Be Done*, report of Central Committee to the Fourteenth Congress p.239.

[16] Ibid., p.242.

[17] Ibid., pp.114–5.

[18] See Edmund and Ruth Frow, op.cit., pp.123–4.

CHAPTER 14

Home Ground
(1936–39)

After the Thirteenth Congress in February 1935, membership of the Communist Party began to grow. The figures published at the time of successive Congresses were as follows:

February 1935 (13th Congress)	6,500
May 1937 (14th Congress)	12,250
September 1938 (15th Congress)	15,750
July 1939 (CC Report)	17,750[1]

The main reason for the Party's growth was, of course, its policies, which attracted many people deeply concerned about the objective situation; in addition, recruiting was made much easier by the changes in the form of organisation at the beginning of 1936.

As already explained, from 1929 to 1935 the Party membership was in theory divided into 'factory cells' and 'street cells', the work of these 'cells' being co-ordinated by a Local Party Committee. The theory on which this structure was based was elaborated by O. Piatnitsky (one of the Russian representatives on the Comintern Executive) in a pamphlet published in 1932, entitled *The Bolshevisation of the Communist Parties*. Piatnitsky stressed that Communist Parties needed a form of organisation different from that of the social democrats. The latter based their organisations on residential *electoral* constituencies, the main object of which was to gain *electoral* victories. But Communist Parties had a quite different purpose – 'to overthrow the bourgeoisie and establish the power of the proletariat' – and so must have an organisation suited to this aim, one based primarily on the place of work. One of the advantages of 'factory cells' was that they could continue to function in conditions of illegality, when members of higher Party committees might have been arrested. In this connection, Pollitt reported to the Central Committee early in 1934 that 38 of the Communist Parties belonging to the CI had been forced underground, and it was thought that in a year or 18 months, there would hardly be any legal parties left. The British Party, said Pollitt, must therefore also be prepared for illegality.[2]

In fact, the Communist Party had already suffered considerable harassment from the police and after 1925 (when, despite the fact that the Party was nominally a legal Party, its twelve leading members were arrested and imprisoned under the Incitement to Mutiny Act) the names of those elected to the Central Committee were never made public, while all minutes and records were destroyed except for those taken by hand to Comintern headquarters. (These exceptional circumstances are not usually appreciated by historians who occasionally complain that they cannot get access to Party archives, under the misapprehension that detailed minutes and records must exist in the same way as they do in the Labour Party.)

The main reason for the emphasis on factory organisation was, of course, political and had nothing to do with illegality. However, Piatnitsky criticised the Western Communist Parties – in particular the German Party – for the fact that the bulk of their membership was in street, rather than factory, cells. In Piatnitsky's view, street cells should rank as subsidiary organisations only, intended for those who were not eligible for membership of a factory cell, such as housewives, the unemployed, and the self-employed.

In Britain too, despite the emphasis on factory cells, some 90 per cent of the membership were during this period nominally in 'street cells'. These 'cells' were intended to consist of members living in the same or adjoining streets. In practice, the membership was not numerous enough for many of the so-called 'street cells' to function in this fashion; they were really small area groups consisting for the most part of unemployed members and those working in a factory or other job where there was not yet a workplace cell.

At the beginning of 1936, when it was decided that the word 'cell' should be replaced by the original word 'group', it was also agreed that the 'street cells' should continue as such only if they had a genuine membership in particular streets (in which case they were renamed 'street groups'). But those with fewer than six members were to be dissolved, and their members were to come together with others in ward or area groups. It was also agreed that all 'groups' whether street, workplace or area, should jointly form a 'branch' and should be represented on a Branch Committee which would replace the former Local Party Committee. (Plans to incorporate formally the new structure into the Party rules at the 1939 Congress, · after it had been in operation for three years, had to be abandoned when that particular Congress was postponed on the outbreak of war. The new structure was, therefore, not formally adopted until the first war-time Congress held in 1943. This has led certain historians to assume that the old structure prevailed until 1943 when the Comintern was dissolved; in fact the old 'cell' structure had been abandoned some seven years earlier.)

One of the arguments in favour of the change was that the old form of words sounded alien. 'We must be able to approach Labour Party organisations on an equal level and discuss questions in organisational terms common to both parties,' wrote R.W. Robson, then the Party's national organiser, in a special article outlining the new structure in the Party journal *Discussion* in March 1936.

But terminology was not the most important consideration. The new structure helped to overcome some long-standing problems and led to an enormous improvement in the Party's work. For one thing, contact between workplace groups and the· rest of the membership in an area became easier, which meant that the former got much more help in their work, leafleting, selling the *Daily Worker* at the factory gate, or setting up a pitch and holding a meeting during the dinner hour. But the main advantage was that members who had formerly been rather isolated in small 'cells', whether 'workplace' or 'street', now tended to gather together at branch meetings which were big enough to provide a stimulating political discussion. More and more, the Party was discarding its former somewhat conspiratorial style. Branch meetings of all members living or working in an area began to be held regularly with reports on the work being done in various spheres, exchange of experiences, proposals for expansion, and, usually, a speaker to open a discussion on some topical issue. The meetings were now often 'open' ones to which non-party sympathisers could be invited. Inevitably these sympathisers got drawn into whatever campaign was in progress; reception for a Hunger March, Aid for Spain, a peace meeting, a tenant/landlord confrontation, an anti-Mosley demonstration, a demand for a better bus service, a local strike, and so on.

There was an enormous rise in sales of Party literature.

We are able to record a sale of over a million copies of pamphlets issued by the Party, while Party organisations have also sold a further 400,000 copies of pamphlets and publications issued by other bodies.

So ran the Report of the Central Committee to the Fourteenth Congress in May 1937; it covered the two and a half years since the Thirteenth congress in February 1935. In the year 1937–8, the Party's Central Propaganda Department issued 17 penny pamphlets of which 300,000 were sold; this was in addition to others issued by the Districts (Lancashire, for example, sold 40,000 of its local pamphlets that year). The report of the Central Committee for the year 1938–9 mentioned 11 pamphlets of which 398,000 were sold in addition to district and branch pamphlets.[3]

The *Daily Worker* remained the chief area for concentrated sales work. By 1939 its daily sales had risen to between 40,000 and 50,000 and its weekend sales averaged 75,000 to 80,000. At times of crisis many extra copies were sold; for example, in September 1938, during the Munich crisis, the week-end sales exceeded 200,000.[4] Those years saw the formation of *Daily Worker* Readers' Leagues; by 1939, these numbered 55, of which 20 were in London.

Though the Communist Party was recruiting, the membership was still relatively small. However, the number of hours that the membership put in made up for its numerical weakness. Indeed, this deterred some people from joining the Party; they felt too much would be demanded of them. Day after day, the Communists with whom they were acquainted rushed home from work, hastily swallowed their tea, and dashed out again to attend a meeting, distribute leaflets, make contact with someone they had been asked to visit, or chalk slogans in the street. They could invariably be seen helping at outdoor meetings on Saturday evenings and canvassing the *Daily Worker* on Sunday mornings.

From time to time, Party leaders stressed the need to avoid putting pressure on new recruits, to explain to them, for instance, that they would not be required to devote more than a minimum amount of their leisure hours to Party activities. But in fact, the new recruits tended to consist of those who *wanted* to spend their time involved in political activity; non-active card-holders were proportionately much less numerous than in other organisations.

The Party and Women

The new structure at last gave a fillip to the involvement and recruiting of women into the Party. It had always been male-oriented, with women constituting a small minority of membership as was revealed by the composition of the delegates attending Congresses. At the Thirteenth Congress in February 1935 there were 294 delegates of whom 34 were women, some 11½ per cent of the total. At the Fourteenth Congress there were 501 delegates, of whom 71 were women: 14 per cent. At the Fifteenth Congress in 1938 there were 539 delegates of whom 96 were women – just under 18 per cent.

In theory the Party had always stood firmly for the emancipation of women and equality between men and women. But Communists believed that the inequalities were the product of the capitalist system, and that only the abolition of capitalism could achieve female emancipation. The programme *For Soviet Britain* set out the Party viewpoint on women in the society of the future in the following passage:

> For women, Soviet Power means full economic and social equality with men, with equality of opportunity in every trade and profession, in the Soviets, the Trade Unions, the Co-operatives, the whole of social life. For the first time, therefore, women will get equal pay for equal work; they will have ample time off at full pay for confinement, with special allowances and free medical service at all times; if working, they will have crèches, kindergartens and clinics for their children, with the best nursing staff, under supervision of working-class mothers. Adequate school dinners for all children will relieve the working mother of much unnecessary everyday toil, just as the assurance of full and free education up to the university standard will relieve her of the perpetual anxiety as to the future of her children. For housewives, the new houses to be built will contain all the latest appliances that lighten labour.[5]

Such a vision of the future seemed to be amply supported by the advances towards female emancipation – both in law and in practice – which appeared to be taking place in the Soviet Union.

Meanwhile, however, the concentration by the Party on industrial work as its first priority inevitably meant that more men

WILL SHE MARRY HER BOSS?

★ ★ ★ ★

So often on the films—dinner, working night and day for her boss—she finds he's fallen in love with her. So they get married and live happily ever after. How many women in real life do that—or want to?

★

She's not getting on very well with her trousseau. There's not enough left out of her wages! And the boy friend—not the boss—is too hard up to help her. Now she's wondering whether to trust that two bob or blow it all at once on two seats at the movies to cheer them up. Their future isn't very bright—with him likely to be stood off any time, now that the slump's coming.

Will she marry her boss . . . ? Judging by the affection the boss shows nowadays, she won't want to! The wages he pays and the speed-up methods he enforces in shop and factory are not exactly likely to make her fall in love with him!

Marry him? No! Make him treat her better? Yes! By trade union organisation and trade union action! Women and girls everywhere are more and more realising the value of trade unions. They can clean up conditions and put up wages—and that's what women want.

★ ★ ★
★ ★
★

joined the Party than women, who were not to be found among the miners, busmen, railwaymen, building workers, skilled engineers and dockworkers towards whom so much Party activity was directed. True, in some industries women played a major role and this was, here and there, reflected in the Party. As recorded in Chapter 7, Jessie Eden, a prominent trade-union activist in Birmingham, was elected to the Party Central Committee in 1935; earlier, Nellie Usher, a well-known figure in the Upholsterers Union, had served on the Central Committee from 1929–32. Such women were not very numerous, mainly because, except in the textile areas, the majority left industry when they got married – and indeed expected to. The result was that the female workforce consisted largely of young girls who were difficult to organise, partly because they regarded their work as temporary, intending to leave it as soon as they married. Such expectations were encouraged both in films and in women's magazines where a girl's marriage to a wealthy man – often her employer – furnished the typical happy ending. A Party pamphlet entitled *Women Take a Hand!* attacked this particular myth.

> So often on the films – after working night and day for her boss – she finds he's fallen in love with her. So they get married and live happily ever after! How many women in real life do that – or want to?

And beneath a photograph of a girl engaged in repetitive factory work

> Will she marry her boss? Judging by the affection the boss shows nowadays, she won't want to! The wages he pays and the speed-up methods he enforces in shop and factory are not exactly likely to make her fall in love with him! . . .' Marry him? No! Make him treat her better? Yes! By trade union organisation and trade union action!

It was not only child-care which caused most married women to leave work. Even without children, the standard of comfort in the home still depended largely on one person being there most of the time. There were few convenience foods and no refrigerators in most working-class homes, so that shopping and cooking had to be done daily. There were no laundrettes, so one full day a week – usually Monday – was devoted to washing. Most homes were heated by coal fires, which demanded constant attention, and in some cooking was still done on a coal range. A high proportion of working-class dwellings had no bathroom, let alone a hot water supply. If both husband and wife were out at work – and very long hours prevailed – life in the home could be cold and uncomfortable. The married woman whose husband did not earn enough to keep her was, understandably enough, an object of pity.

The relatively isolated lives they led helped to foster a tendency among housewives to regard politics as the man's sphere and refer all political questions to their husbands. At almost every Party Congress there was criticism of the failure to recruit housewives, and the husbands were frequently blamed for not recruiting their wives.

One obvious channel of communication with housewives was via the co-operative movement – in particular the Women's Co-operative Guilds. Though ever since its formation, Party members had been urged to become active in the co-operative movement, such activities had been directed during the Class against Class period towards setting up a separate organisation, 'The Guild of Militant Co-operators'. This organisation figured in the Labour Party pamphlet, *The Communist Solar System* published in 1933, though it was never listed by the Labour Party as a proscribed organisation. It did not get very far, and by 1934 had faded away.

Now, in the mid-1930s, housewives in the Party were encouraged to involve themselves in the work of the Women's Co-operative Guilds. These Guilds were in fact the nearest equivalent to a trade union for married women; those in England and Wales had a membership of 83,000 in 1938; those in Scotland 32,000. They usually met once a week in the afternoon at a time when children were at school and husbands were not yet home from work. Many of the Guilds were active on questions connected with women's rights, such as family planning and child-care, and concerned themselves in particular with the cause of peace, for example, selling white poppies on Armistice Day. The majority view was pacifist. As more Communist Party women became prominent in the Co-operative Movement, so the Co-op leaders became alarmed and in the English Guild movement (though not the Scottish) secured the adoption of a rule which banned Communists from election to office. In other aspects of work in the Co-operative movement, such as Management Boards and Education Committees, no such ban existed, and some Party women became well known in this sphere – for example, Esther Henrotte of the Royal Arsenal Co-op, who was elected to the Party Central Committee in 1935.

At the Fourteenth Party Congress in May 1937 a decision was at last taken to set up women's *groups*. These were to have the same status as workplace and street groups, were to meet separately and have a representative on the Branch Committee, though every member of such a group would, of course, be encouraged to participate in the general life of the branch. It was hoped that these women's groups would concentrate on issues particularly affecting women, while providing a training ground for developing their political understanding.[6]

Such groups were set up here and there, and some generated considerable activity. Irene Paynter reported from South Wales that in one village there had been a strong Party branch without one woman in it. There were women who helped with branch activities, but who refused to join because they felt out of place at branch meetings. After a talk, they agreed to join the Party and form a women's group with a representative on the branch committee. 'Today,' Irene Paynter wrote in August 1938, 'most of the women attend the full branch meetings able to take part in discussion and doing excellent work in the village.'[7]

She reported that women's groups in the Rhondda mobilised a thousand women to demonstrate on International Women's Day, 8 March; the Tonypandy Women's Group called a meeting and initiated a campaign against the cuts imposed by the Unemployment Assistance Board.

By far the most important area of activity to involve women turned out to be tenants' and residents' struggles. The Party had never agreed with Hitler's slogan 'Women's place is in the home', yet when it came to the defence of the home, women were always more involved than men.

Tenants and Residents

One of the initiators of activity around tenants' rights was a Party member from Stepney, Michael Shapiro, a London University lecturer specialising in land and town planning. At that time he wrote and carried on his political work under the name of Michael

Best. By 1937 he had become the first secretary of the Stepney Tenants' Defence League, and shortly afterwards was responsible for a newly established Federation of Tenants' and Residents' Associations, with headquarters in Chancery Lane, London. By 1938 he had produced a *Tenants' Guide*, published by the Labour Research Department at 6d, which provided an expert but very simple explanation of the Rent Acts.

These were incredibly complex. The vast majority of households were tenants of private landlords and about four and a half million of them were in houses which were, in theory, 'controlled' – in other words, the tenants had the legal right to security of tenure, their rents could not be increased, and they were entitled to withold 40 per cent of the rent if the local sanitary inspector certified that repairs had not been done. However, houses which had been vacated between 1923 and 1933 were 'decontrolled' which meant that the landlord could put up the rent and even evict the sitting tenant without legal hindrance.

In practice, a high proportion of the tenants of 'controlled' houses were denied their rights. There was widespread illegal overcharging by landlords, many of whom had registered their tenants as decontrolled when they were not so. Michael Shapiro himself alleged that half the two million controlled tenants in London were paying illegally high rents. A high proportion of them lived in insanitary slums.

Shapiro not only involved himself in tenants' work in Stepney; he visited other Party branches in and outside London, urging them to do the same in their own locality. In most cases these movements began in a small way. Party members would uncover a case of illegal overcharging by the landlord. The next step would be the formation of a tenants' committee to investigate and uncover other cases. The news would spread, and soon a tenants' association would have been established. The aim was not so much to set up advice centres to deal with individual cases – though this came into it – as to develop understanding among tenants on the need for organisation. By 1938, 45 local associations had joined the Federation of which Shapiro was secretary.

Soon some of the associations, particularly in East London, became the focus for great movements, including rent strikes. One of the first was in an East London block of 346 run-down flats in Quinn Square, Bethnal Green. The flat-dwellers had to share lavatories and water-taps; they had damp walls, peeling paper, falling ceilings, broken handrails on the stairs. In the summer of 1938 the property company owning the block attempted to evict a woman alleged to be in arrears with her rent. The local Party branch looked into her case and discovered she was a controlled tenant and the landlord had been overcharging her. Following this, on the suggestion of a Party member, Bob Graves, a tenants' meeting was held and a committee of 18 was elected, with Graves as its acting secretary. 90 of the 346 tenants turned out to be controlled, and most of them were being overcharged, and the process began – quite legally – of witholding rent until the excess paid over the previous six months had been recovered. But the Committee's main concern was to win reductions in rent for the 250 decontrolled tenants. They drew up a proposed scale of maximum rents, and put these to the company's agents; they were turned down. At a mass meeting of tenants, an all-out rent strike was then decided upon. Two days later, when the rent collector arrived, no one paid. Meetings of the tenants were held every day. Women picketed the estate office, and marched through nearby streets carrying posters: 'Quinn Square wants a Square Deal' and 'Our Landlord Has Made a Huge Fortune at our Expense'. Every time the agent tried to collect the rent, he was followed around and booed by huge crowds of women and children. After a fortnight, the company gave in and signed an agreement with the tenants association for greatly decreased rents, also promising repairs.[8]

After this victory, the struggle for decontrolled tenants began in Stepney. Here the Tenants' Defence League had become a big affair, with three full-time elected officials. They were all Communists: the secretary, 'Tubby' Rosen, and two organisers, Ella Donovan and Harry Conn. Tenants' committees were functioning in many streets and blocks of flats, and thousands of pounds had been recovered in repayment of overcharged rents. The movement for decontrolled tenants began in December 1938 when a rent strike was declared in Southern Grove Dwellings in Limehouse. It was successful, and was followed by rent strikes in more than twenty other blocks and streets. In most cases, the landlords gave in fairly quickly, but one company, which owned 320 flats in Langdale Mansions and Brady Mansions, decided on confrontation. The strike went on for 21 weeks, during which the tenants barricaded the blocks with barbed wire, bailiffs forcibly evicted families with the aid of foot and

GRAVES   One Penny

Quinn Square Tenants'
RENT STRIKE
VICTORY

Bob Graves, secretary of the Tenants' Association, speaking in Russia Lane during the strike

mounted police; but the families concerned were reinstated while thousands came out on protest demonstrations. In the end this company too gave in and signed an agreement reducing the rents.

In all these East London struggles, it was women who did the picketing, women who often dominated the committees making up the Stepney Tenants' Defence League, women who came out on demonstrations. It was, of course, partly because the men were at work, and the women were at home where the action was taking place. But Phil Piratin, by that time a Communist councillor in Stepney, later recalled that on the committees in which hundreds of people participated . who had never had any experience of organisation, the women were outstanding. 'There was nothing that the men could do that could not be equalled by the women, and, in fact, they were mostly more enthusiastic and hence more reliable.'[9]

The movement was not confined to the private landlord sector. There were two other, relatively new, areas in which it developed, and in which two women members of the Party were particularly prominent. One was Elsy Borders who achieved national fame in her legal battle against a Building Society on behalf of owner-occupiers.

The drastic cuts in subsidies for council-house building made by the National Government had resulted in a largely uncontrolled boom in small jerry-built houses erected by speculative builders for sale on the outskirts of towns. The sales were financed by Building Societies which, in agreement with the builders, would advance 95 per cent of the purchase price to the prospective owner-occupiers. After a few years these occupiers would too often find themselves trapped in a house which was literally falling to pieces.

One such estate was in West Wickham, Kent, and it was here that two party members, Elsy Borders and her husband, Jim, (a taxi-driver) organised the Coneyhall District Residents' Association. Like others, the Borders had moved into their new home, only to discover that they had been swindled. The house was damp, the roof leaked, the woodwork was infested, the electric wiring was faulty, there were cracks in the walls and other defects. In 1937, the Bradford Third Equitable Building Society claimed possession of the house from Mrs Elsy Borders on the grounds that she was three months in arrears with her mortgage payments. Elsy counter-claimed for the return of the money she had paid on the grounds that the Building Society had lent it to her on an insufficient security and had 'wilfully and fraudulently' misled her into believing that the house was built of good materials and in an effecient manner.

The proceedings opened on 13 January 1938, and Elsy Borders hit the headlines because she conducted her own case. She revealed a remarkable grasp of the legal and technical issues involved, and ended her court appearance with a six-hour statement, which earned her the name of the 'modern Portia'. Her case went on for many months; the following autumn she again made front-page news. The judgement left all the major issues unresolved, whereupon, in February 1939, some 3,000 owner-occupiers in outer London went on mortage strike. Some got their houses put right as a result, though the government brought in hasty legislation to safeguard the position of Building Societies. The Borders case dragged on throughout the first years of the war, but meanwhile, Elsy Borders had long since become a leading figure in the Federation of Tenants' and Residents' Associations of which Shapiro was secretary.

The Party had also been trying to build tenants' associations among council tenants, with some success. Such tenants were still in a minority, numbering less than a million. They were mainly skilled manual workers, amongst whom the habit of organisation was deeply ingrained. But in fact here again it was the women who were most closely involved and who, in the case of Birmingham, carried on a fight which ended in victory.

Birmingham had a Tory Council and one of its Parliamentary seats was represented by the Prime Minister, Neville Chamberlain. There were nearly 50,000 council tenants living on various estates. At the beginning of 1939, the Council announced increases in rents of between 1s and 2s 6d, together with a 'differential rent scheme' which meant that tenants who thought they could not afford the increases could apply for a rebate. To get his, they would be subject to a means test.

The Midlands District of the Party issued a penny pamphlet under the title *49,000 Tenants Say No* setting out the case against the increases. It showed that a 2s a week increase could mean 7 bottles of milk less a week or 6 loaves of bread less, or the ending of the weekly visit to the cinema. It exposed the reasons for high rents – such as the high cost of land and high interest rates – and said:

> The aim is to place the burden of housing on the shoulders of the better paid workers. It will divide the working class, set one

section against the other. Instead of seeing that the main enemy is the very rich, who, by their control of land are forcing up the capital charges for house-building, we shall have the fight against these diverted into a struggle against the comparatively better-off section of the workers and small shopkeepers.

The Birmingham Municipal Tenants' Association began its campaign with packed meetings on every estate, and hundreds of volunteers to collect signatures to a petition against the new scheme. General Secretary of the Association was Jessie Eden, a prominent Birmingham Communist who had served on the Party's Central Committee from 1935 to 1937.

Disregarding the petition, the Council announced that the new rent increases would come into force in May, and, in preparation for this, sent out a means test form to every tenant. By this time, the Association had 36 Committees in action. They collected the means test forms, announcing that they would all be returned uncompleted to the Town Hall. A ballot was taken and showed an overwhelming majority in favour of a rent strike. This started in the first week of May 1939. Every morning, the rent collectors were met by crowds of women who would escort them from house to house; they collected no rent. On 7 June, 10,000 women marched in protest to the City Council; a week later 15 bailiffs, escorted by police, made their first attempt to distrain on 175 tenants. The crowds prevented them from entering the houses.

The strike lasted ten weeks, and was enlivened by much original publicity. Thus, when the Lord Mayor went to conduct a ceremony to celebrate the opening of the Corporation's 50,000th house, he was met by a crowd of 8,000 women conducting the mock funeral of a dummy bailiff. Wreaths from Chamberlain and Hitler were on the coffin, a loud speaker played the Dead March, and the cortège marched to muffled drums, so that the Lord Mayor's words could not be heard above the noise.

On 4 July the City Council gave in. There were to be no rent increases; arrears were to be paid off in instalments; bailiffs were to be called off and no one victimised. And the Tenants' Association was recognised.

[1] This report was in preparation for the Sixteenth Congress, planned for October 1939, but postponed because of the outbreak of war.
[2] Central Committee meeting 5 January 1934, JK papers.

[3] *It Can Be Done* (report of 14th Congress), p.249. *Report of Central Committee to 15th Congress*, p.19. *Report of Central Committee to 16th Congress*, p.10.

[4] JK papers. See also *Report of Central Committee to 16th Congress*, p.26.

[5] *For Soviet Britain*, pp.40–1.

[6] *It Can Be Done*, p.307.

[7] *Party Organiser*, August 1938, p.23.

[8] Bob Graves, *Rent Strike Victory*, pamphlet published by London District of the Communist Party, September 1938.

[9] Phil Piratin, op.cit., p.46.

CHAPTER 15

Professional Workers, Students and Intellectuals (1932–39)

In the 1920s, 75 per cent of the employed population were manual workers, and the majority of Party members had been drawn from amonst them. There were few 'white-collar' workers or people with professional backgrounds among the members. Little more than a handful of those who joined the Party when it was first formed in 1920 and 1921 had been to university. They included R. Palme Dutt, Robin Page Arnot, Andrew Rothstein, Ivor Montagu, Emile and Eleanor Burns. Such people saw themselves as representing a trend forecast in the *Communist Manifesto* of 1848. According to this, the history of society was the history of class struggles and 'society as a whole is more and more splitting up into two great hostile camps, into two great classes directly facing each other – the bourgeoisie and the proletariat.' Further on it said

> When the class struggle nears the decisive hour . . . a portion of the bourgeoisie goes over to the proletariat, and in particular a portion of the bourgeois ideologists who have raised themselves to the level of comprehending theoretically the historical movement as a whole.

Nowhere was the division of society into two camps more apparent than in Britain where, unlike most continental countries, the peasantry had long since disappeared. Here it could clearly be seen that on one side there was a small capitalist class (the 'bourgeoisie') who were the owners of the means of production, distribution and exchange, together with their associates. On the other side was a huge working class (the 'proletariat') which owned no means of production, and was compelled to sell its labour-power to the capitalist class for wages.

Marxists understood that between these two camps there were middle strata which included small independent producers and 'white collar' workers. This class was referred to in the *Communist Manifesto* as the 'petty bourgeoisie.'*

According to the accepted theory, these middle strata could play no independent political role, but inevitably acted as allies of *either* the capitalist class *or* the working class, veering towards whichever of the two was showing signs of the greatest strength at any given moment. As R. Palme Dutt put it:

> The petit-bourgeoisie is by the nature of its position incapable of an independent political role, and can only follow in the wake of either the working class or the bourgeoisie. It is in character essentially vacillating, and tends to follow the stream of the moment.[1]

In fact the composition of the middle and lower-middle class in Britain was in process of rapid change. It was already beginning to be clear in Karl Marx's day that the advent of large-scale production and the growth of monopolies and giant companies would squeeze out small producers, and this had indeed taken place in Britain where small businessmen, small shopkeepers, small employers and even small farmers were disappearing fast.

But there was a second category of middle-class people which was growing by leaps and bounds. This consisted of the professional, technical and administrative salaried workers, including civil servants. Within this class, the upper layer – scientists, doctors, lawyers, university teachers, writers and the like – were habitually referred to by the Party as 'bourgeois intellectuals'. On the whole they were not classed as the 'petty bourgeoisie'; they were regarded as an integral part of the ruling capitalist class.

The 'bourgeois intellectuals' who were in contact with the Party during the 1920s were few – much fewer than in the Communist parties of other European countries.[2] This was partly the result of the attitude of some of the intellectuals within the British Party, expressed in its most extreme form in an article by R. Palme Dutt in

---

*R. Palme Dutt was always careful to refer to this class as the 'petit-bourgeoisie' or *small* bourgeoisie. In most Communist Party literature, including the English translation of the *Communist Manifesto* approved by Engels and reprinted by Martin Lawrence in 1934, the word 'petty bourgeoisie' is used. Since 'petty' means not only 'small' but also 'contemptible' this may have been a factor in creating a tendency among Party members to treat the 'petty-bourgeoisie' with some disdain. In the second half of the 1930s, the term was no longer used in Party literature.

the *Communist Review* of September 1932. While Dutt agreed that the best elements among the younger scientists, technicians and writers were beginning to realise that 'the future of all they care for lies with Communism' and that they should, therefore, be encouraged to join the Party, there were certain rules that such a recruit should observe. 'First and foremost, he should *forget that he is an intellectual* (except in moments of necessary self-criticism) *and remember only that he is a Communist*' (original emphasis). What this meant was that he should devote his activities to reaching out and influencing non-party *workers*. To those who said they had no contact with the workers, Dutt replied: 'But the good Party member will find and make opportunities.' Once he reached non-Party workers, then the intellectual's special skills would be particularly useful.

But Dutt wrote with withering contempt of a project initiated by some leading Communist intellectuals to organise themselves as a special group with sub-sections: 'Marxist Biologists', 'Marxist Physicists', 'Marxist Historians', and so forth. (One of the people involved in this project, though Dutt does not say so, was Maurice Dobb.) The project was, according to Dutt, 'nipped in the bud' by Party headquarters and the group dissolved.

Such was the attitude to 'bourgeois intellectuals'. A little further down the social scale were the school teachers, and among these certain Party members were already playing a part, not only as activists on the issues of teachers' pay and conditions, but in the fight for educational reform. Among them was G.C.T. Giles (one day to be President of the National Union of Teachers). However most of the Party teachers were making their name outside as well as inside the profession they practiced. Thus Nan MacMillan was a favourite speaker at Communist public meetings, while Kath Duncan in South-East London, had been prominent in the unemployed workers' movement and, after the 1932 Hunger March, had been jailed as a 'disturber of the peace'.

As with so much else, the coming to power of Hitler in 1933 was the starting point for a fundamental reappraisal. It was recognised that Hitler's major appeal had been to the improverished lower-middle class in Germany; it was here, above all, that his support had initially developed and grown. In the circumstances it no longer seemed adequate to go on expounding the theory that *if* and *when* the working-class movement grew strong enough to threaten .the overthrow of capitalism, the petty bourgeoisie would 'inevitably' swing behind that movement. On the contrary, positive steps must be taken to see that they did so, or at least to stop them turning towards the fascists. The issue was first raised by William Gallacher in June 1933 during a Central Committee discussion on the Reichstag Fire trial campaign and the fight against Mosley:

> Is the middle class going to be won for the support of workers' organisations in the struggle against capitalism or for the destruction of working-class organisations? This is the problem that confronts us.[3]

By 1934, those from the middle class who wanted to join the Party found themselves made rather more welcome than before. And though they were expected to involve themselves in the general work of the Party, and to devote their special skills to this work, where appropriate, they were no longer expected to turn their back on the circles from which they had emerged.

The new approach was underlined at the 13th Congress at the beginning of 1935. Pollitt in his report to his Congress stressed that the fascist attempt to win the lower-middle class must be countered. 'We must', he said, 'see in these students, intellectuals, authors, doctors, scientists and professors, valuable allies who can be won for the working class.'[4] And the Congress adopted a resolution stating that the anti-fascist front required not only the main body of the organised workers, 'but also small traders, working farmers, technicians, professionals, intellectuals and students.'[5]

Students

Initially, the biggest break-through was among university students. A high proportion of them came from among the well-to-do, since state support was very limited. The total number of students was small compared with the present day, and up to the early 1930s they had been regarded by the Party as an élitist and reactionary force – with some reason, since they were foremost among the 1926 strike-breakers.

But the great depression of 1929–31 brought about a change in the attitude of many at the universities. Graduates could not escape the economic insecurity which pervaded the whole of society. There were far fewer jobs on offer, even for highly qualified people. Moreover, job scarcity continued even after the worst days of the depression were over. As late as 1936, one commentator remarked: 'The number of ex-students peddling vacuum cleaners and toothpaste for a living is mounting up.'[6] It was clear that there was something basically wrong with a system which denied people the right to work and which failed to make use of the skills for which they had been trained, in which machinery was deliberately destroyed, and factories closed down, in which food was thrown into the sea, while thousands of people went hungry. In dramatic contrast came reports of industrial growth in the Soviet Union.

So, in 1931, a Marxist Society was formed in the London School of Economics; half a dozen of its members applied to join the Communist Party. At about the same time, a group of Communists began to function in University College, London. In the same year, a Cambridge student, David Guest, who had been in Germany studying mathematics and philosophy, returned to Cambridge and, together with Maurice Cornforth and four or five others, formed a Communist 'cell'. By 1932 it had grown to 25 members. In each of the universities at Reading, Durham, Leeds and Manchester there were Party groups of two or three members.[7] In Oxford, where there were ten in the Party, the October Club was formed in the summer of 1932, and grew rapidly to 200 members. That autumn, the Club organised a reception for the Northern contingent of the NUWM's 1932 Hunger March, with food and medical attention laid on for the marchers. It was announced that a student contingent would lead the marchers out of Oxford the following day. The University authorities threatened disciplinary action against any student who participated; nevertheless, 250 students did so and no action was taken against them.[8] Soon after this event, the Oxford Union was to cause a major sensation by adopting a resolution that 'this House will in no circumstances fight for its king and country.'

1932 saw the formation of a new national organisation, the Federation of Student Societies (FSS), to which some twenty organisations were affiliated, including that in LSE, the Oxford October Club, and the Cambridge Socialist Society, an old-established body on which left-wing students had won leading positions and majority support. The FSS was seen initially as an alternative to the University Labour Federation which had been formed in 1920 and was affiliated to the Labour Party. Although membership of the ULF was open to all types of socialist, it appeared to students on the left to be quite unsuitable for generating mass activity. The FSS – as was reflected in its paper, *The Student Vanguard* – was concerned with both political activity and Marxist analysis. Its General Secretary during 1933–4 was a party member, Dick Freeman, who spent much of his time visiting universities all over the country.[9]

For most of the Communist students of this early period, the Marxist analysis of society and interpretation of events was something quite new, and virtually unknown in the circles in which they moved. Inspired by their new vision of society, they adopted in their entirety the guidelines laid down by the Party in the Class against Class period, since these tallied with their desire to lose their class origins and 'go over' completely to the working class. They accepted the idea that their main task was to involve themselves in working-class struggles *outside* the universities. So the Cambridge Party students concentrated on canvassing the *Daily Worker* in the working-class streets, and in selling it outside the bus garage, and were, indeed, responsible for the formation of a Party group in the town. In Oxford also the Party students conducted their leafleting and *Daily Worker* sales outside factory gates as well as in working-class areas.

The new approach to intellectuals adopted by the Party after Hitler came to power and the development of anti-war and anti-fascist struggles brought about a change. It began to be suggested that the first job of a revolutionary student was to concentrate on winning *other* students over to the side of the working class. It was argued that the great majority of the student body could be so won. No longer should students be seen as a reactionary force out of which a few exceptional individuals would cross over to the workers. At the same time, the habit of denigrating and neglecting academic work began to be questioned and criticised. A memorable occasion for those in the Cambridge group – by this time growing fast – was a visit by Gallacher on behalf of the Central Committee in 1934 at which he expressed an attitude diametrically opposed to that put forward by Dutt only two years earlier. He said:

> We want people who are capable, who are good scientists, historians and teachers . . . We need you as you are; if you have a vocation, it's pointless to run away to factories . . . We want you to study and become good students.[10]

Out of this meeting came the slogan 'Every Communist student a good student.'

This did not mean that work among students was seen as an *alternative* to activities in working-class streets and outside factories. On the contrary, these activities continued, as did campaigning for special events, such as organising receptions for Hunger Marchers. The point was that the need to win other students over to the side of the working-class movement was now seen as an integral part of the political task. The new approach bore fruit. As more students joined the Party, so many more were involved in activities outside factory gates, going in groups to garages during a busmen's strike, giving help in the Pressed Steel strike in Oxford. In 1934, the Hunger Marchers received a huge welcome from students of Oxford and Cambridge, while early in 1935 Sheffield students were actively engaged in the great movement which ended in the defeat of the new regulations for the unemployed.

At the end of 1934, a British delegation of 90 attended an International Student Congress against war and fascism which took place in Brussels. Organisations from every university in Britain were represented in this delegation, and Party members returned with the aim of building a democratic student movement against war and fascism which would extend beyond the socialist society groupings and would include Christian and Liberal students, and those belonging to the League of Nations Union.

It was in this context, in 1935, that the FSS made a direct proposal to dissolve itself and allow its sections to reaffiliate to the ULF. The Cardiff conference of the ULF in January 1936 agreed to this, and John Cornford, a leading Cambridge Communist and at that time secretary of the FSS, was elected Vice-President of the united organisation. By this time membership of the Party among students could be counted, not in handfuls but in hundreds. 'Our Party has continued to grow among university students, and is now firmly entrenched in the most important universities' said the report of the Central Committee to the 1938 Communist Congress.

Professional Classes

The change in attitude to students was paralleled by a new approach to professional people working in all fields. The result was that a small but significant number of them joined the Party. Many of them were young; they included scientists, doctors, artists, musicians, writers, economists, historians, architects, lawyers and – above all – teachers.

Most of them joined the local branch where they lived and participated actively in the day-to-day branch work, doing their share of canvassing the *Daily Worker*, addressing open-air meetings, taking on responsibility as branch secretaries, literature secretaries and education organisers, representing their Party branch on local Peace Councils or Aid Spain Committees, and so forth. But they were also able to make a contribution of a special kind.

Firstly, their skills were of great practical value, both in educational and propaganda work, and in fostering movements on particular issues. Thus the Party architects and lawyers played a vital part in the work of tenants' defence leagues. Party doctors in that of the Committee against Malnutrition. Later, as we shall see, these doctors helped to organise the campaign for medical aid for Spain, and indeed many were to give their services in Spain. Scientists were also prominent in the campaign against malnutrition and were active in the agitation for protection against air-raids. The leader of this agitation was a well-known geneticist, Professor J.B.S. Haldane who, from 1936 onwards, contributed a regular column on scientific topics to the *Daily Worker*.

Party writers, actors, theatre and film directors, composers and musicians at this time fostered the growth of a new kind of entertainment, plays which aimed at representing the actual lives of working people, delivering a message of a very different kind to that of the orthodox theatre, and films which portrayed working-class struggle. The outstanding achievement here was Unity Theatre, which was established as a result of the growing co-operation between amateur workers' theatre groups and individual professional artists. Among the numerous Party members involved in Unity Theatre were Montagu Slater, author of two documentary plays, *Easter 1916* and *Stay Down, Miner*; Randall Swingler, who wrote and translated many revolutionary and socialist songs for choral singing; Alan Bush, the composer, and André van Gyseghem the theatrical producer. It was also in this period that giant pageants were staged, such as that produced by Montagu Slater and van Gyseghem for the London District of the Communist Party to celebrate the hundredth anniversary of the Chartist movement.

Secondly, the professionals in the Party worked to organise the non-Party members of their own profession and to involve them in movements of a progressive kind. Thus the scientists (among whom were Hyman Levy the mathematician and J.D. Bernal, an outstanding physicist) were active in reviving the Association of Scientific Workers which, after the war broke out, was to grow to 11,000 members and affiliate to the TUC. Again, mainly on the initiative of Bernal, the early 1930s saw the formation of the Cambridge Scientists Anti-War Group which by 1936 numbered 80 members; the group's activities were not confined to Cambridge, and it sent speakers to meetings all over the country.

Another example of organisation in the professional sphere was the Artists International Association. This was founded in 1933 by a group of Party members, in particular Cliff Rowe, Misha Black, James Boswell and Pearl Binder. As members, they had always contributed much in the way of posters and banners for demonstrations. But now, in 1935, the Association organised an exhibition entitled 'Artists against Fascism and War'. Many of the most distinguished painters and sculptors of the day lent work to this exhibition which was visited by 6,000 people, paying 3d each. [11]

In February 1934 a British section of the Writers' International was formed; in April it issued *Viewpoint*, 'a revolutionary review of the arts' which, in October, was published under another name, *Left Review*. [12] This journal lasted for four years; not all those who wrote for it were party members, but they all shared dissatisfaction with the state of literature at the time, both its content and its commercial basis. Among those who initiated it were Edgell Rickword, Christopher Grieve (Hugh MacDiarmid), Ralph Fox and Amabel Williams-Ellis. [13] Its first editor was Montagu Slater, followed by Rickword and then by Randall Swingler.

The period also saw the rise of the Workers' Music Association – one of its leading figures was Alan Bush – and the development of films and documentaries for the working-class movement. In this work, Ralph Bond and Ivor Montagu were to play an important part.

As well as endeavouring to use their skills in the service of the movement, and seeking to involve their fellow professionals, the Communist intellectuals during this period took some major steps towards establishing a Marxist approach in their own subjects. Thus in 1936, the Party publishers, Lawrence and Wishart, brought out a book, *Britain without Capitalists* – 'A study of what industry in a Soviet Britain could achieve'. It was compiled by a group of economists, scientists and technicians who remained anonymous, presumably because most of them would have put their jobs at risk if they had attached their names to it.

Among Marxist philosophers were John Lewis who edited *A Textbook of Marxist Philosophy* in 1937, and Hyman Levy, the mathematician, who wrote *A Philosophy for a Modern Man*, published in 1938. Among the scientists, J.D. Bernal produced a major work, *The Social Function of Science* in 1939 in which he explored the relationship between the development of science and the rise of capitalism which, he argued, was by now both holding back scientific advance, and distorting its use for war purposes. In the field of history, Leslie Morton wrote a pioneering work, *A Peoples' History of England* which appeared in 1937; it was followed by a study of the peasant revolt by Hymie Fagan entitled *Nine Days that Shook England*. The next year saw the formation for the first time of a group of Party historians.

The Marxist approach to literature was the subject of continuous discussion in the pages of *Left Review*. In addition, 1937 saw the publication of three contributions to Marxist literary theory: *The Novel and the People* by Ralph Fox; *Crisis and Criticism* by Alick West; *Illusion and Reality* by Christopher Caudwell. Two out of these three – Fox and Caudwell – were to be killed in Spain before their books appeared.

There was a vast expansion in the number of left-wing publications during the second half of the 1930s; many of them were brought out by Lawrence and Wishart, who published works by Communist Party authors, made the writings of Marx and Engels available to British readers and also published a 12 volume edition of Lenin's works. But the biggest breakthrough came with the formation of the Left Book Club.

The Left Book Club

The origin of the Left Book Club was an initiative by the leading Communist bookshop, the Workers' Bookshop, which in 1935 asked John Strachey – then a regular columnist in the *Daily Worker* – whether he would serve on the selection committee of a club that would choose left-wing books from any publisher's list. The scheme was put up to every publisher who handled left-wing books, but only Victor Gollancz replied. So it got no further, and in the end Gollancz decided to go it alone. [14]

Though Gollancz was a member of the Labour Party, his views at that time were much closer to those of the CP, and he had long been publishing books written by Communists. In 1933 he brought out *The Brown Book of the Hitler Terror* under the auspices of the World Committee for the Victims of German Fascism, whose British section had been banned by the Labour Party as part of the 'Communist Solar System'. In the same year he had published Emile Burns' book *Capitalism, Communism and the Transition* and in 1935, his *Abyssinia and Italy*. Burns, at that time head of the Communist Party's education and propaganada department at 16 King Street, had always kept contact with Gollancz; he had edited and selected *A Handbook of Marxism* (containing writings from Marx, Engels, Lenin and Stalin) which appeared in the Gollancz autumn list in 1935.

The announcement that a Left Book Club was to be launched under the auspices of Victor Gollancz Ltd came in February 1936. First among the books listed in a double-page advertisement in the *New Statesman* was *World Politics 1918–1935* by R. Palme Dutt 'the celebrated editor of the *Labour Monthly*'. [15] The Club offered a book a month at a price of 2s 6d – between a third and a half the normal price – to people who took out membership either with Gollancz direct or through their local bookseller. The book was to be accompanied by a brochure entitled 'Left Book News'. The selectors of the chosen books were to be Victor Gollancz himself, Harold Laski, a leading member of the Labour Party, though not yet on its Executive, and John Strachey who, although not a member of the Communist Party, was at that time one of its closest allies.

Those who were interested in the proposal for a Left Book Club were asked to send in a postcard to Gollancz. The results surpassed all expectations. By the time the first book choice was published in May 1936 (it was *France Today and the People's Front* by the secretary of the French Communist Party, Maurice Thorez) the membership had reached 9,000; by October it had risen to 28,000; by march 1937 it was nearly 40,000 and was to reach 57,000 by the Spring of 1939. [16]

Associated with this, Left Book Club discussion groups sprang up. By the end of 1937 there were 730 such local groups which met fortnightly to discuss the current month's choices; by 1939 the groups numbered 1,200. Many groups went into action, particularly in the cause of Spanish Medical Aid. In such groups, Labour Party members and members of no political party frequently met Communists for the first time. Giant rallies were held all over the country at which Communists, including Pollitt and Gallacher, spoke on the same platform with left-wing Labour members such as Cripps, Strauss and Aneurin Bevan.

The aim of the Left Book Club was expressed in its first announcement. It was intended 'for the service of those who desire to play an intelligent part in the struggle *for* World Peace and a better social and economic order, and *against* Fascism.'[17] To this end, the monthly book choices were intended to represent a wide spectrum of views. Among the 1937 choices was one by the leader of the Parliamentary Labour Party, Clement Attlee, *The Labour Party in Perspective.*

A high proportion of the Left Book Club members were white-collar workers and professional people. 'Our group consists of a draughtsman, a doctor of physics, a printer, a bank clerk, a dental mechanic, a road-mender, a school teacher, a painter, several clerks and sundry others,' said a letter received at head office from a group in Essex.[18] Of course, to some extent, the composition of the groups depended on the area concerned. In industrial locations, the group might be dominated by manual workers and staffed by long-standing members of the Labour Party who had previously played some part in WEA activities and the like. But there is little doubt that the movement made its chief impact on those from professional and clerical walks of life; for many such it provided their first introduction to Marxist thought.

It was made clear from the start that the Left Book Club was not a political party. Those who came into politics for the first time were advised to join the political party of their choice. The majority chose the Labour Party, and in some places moribund local Labour parties were brought back to life by an influx of new, keen members.

Clement Attlee, then leader of the Parliamentary Labour Party, sent a message of encouragement to the Club's first Albert Hall rally in February 1937:

Socialism cannot be built on ignorance and the transformation of Great Britain into a Socialist state will need the active co-operation of a large body of well-informed men and women. For this reason I consider the success of the Left Book Club to be a most encouraging sign.[19]

But Attlee's attitude was not shared by the dominant leaders of the Labour Party and TUC, who regarded the Club as yet another attempt by Communists to infiltrate and stir up trouble among their own members. Ernest Bevin, secretary of the Transport and General Workers' Union, said that the main object of the Club was 'to undermine and destroy trade unions and the Labour Party as an effective force', while Herbert Morrison, prominent throughout the decade as the Labour Party's chief witch-hunter, complained that the club was interfering with the Labour Party's 'consistent, ordered work'.[20] In a special memorandum which came before the Labour Party's Executive Committee in November 1938, it was alleged that of the 27 books issued by the Club in its first 12 months, 15 were written by Communists.[21] The rule that Labour Party members must not appear on the same platform as a Communist was being broken everywhere at Left Book Club rallies, and meetings, both national and local. In the end, a letter was sent out by G.R. Shepherd, the Labour Party's agent, to local Labour Parties telling them that unless their members refrained from buying Left Book Club books, they might find themselves liable to expulsion.[22]

Simultaneously an attempt was made to launch a rival organisation: the Labour Book Service, with Sir Walter Citrine, general secretary of the TUC and Francis Williams, editor of the *Daily Herald* on the selection committee. The rival body was not a success, however, and the Labour Book Service did not last long.

Ironically, a high proportion of those drawn into left-wing politics and into the Labour Party by the LBC's activities came from those very middle strata which the right-wing leaders, in particular Herbert Morrison, had long been most concerned to recruit. Morrison had always contended that Labour must concentrate on winning more votes from the middle class, and that, to do this, the Party must avoid left-wing militancy, and go for respectability. The Left Book Club proved him wrong. The young people who were coming into the movement were not at all attracted by 'respectability'; they wanted to clarify their ideas by means of argument and discussion; they wanted to feel part of a great movement which was going into action on the desperately important issues of the day: *for* peace, *against* fascism.

Myth and Reality

The growth of Party influence among professional workers during the 1930s led, both at the time, and later, to the promotion of various myths. One, fostered by the establishment, was that the group most attracted by the Party were poets and writers whose attachment was romantic rather than realistic and therefore short-lived. The main literary figure used to support this theory has been the poet Stephen Spender who joined the Party in 1937, but only stayed in it for a very short time, and has since done his best to denigrate those Party leaders whom he met, and to disparage the contribution made by the Party. No one is a greater hero in the eyes of the media than a Communist defector, and Spender's recollections have for many years now been used to supply a distorted view of the period.

In fact Spender was not at all typical. Many of the professional workers who joined the Party in the 1930s stayed in it for the rest of their lives, and most of those who, for one reason or another dropped out of it, remained committed to the socialist cause.

Another myth, promoted at the time by those who claimed to be the followers of Trotsky and repeated ever since is that the increase in recruits from among professional workers was a symptom of the Party's attempts, following the 1935 Comintern Congress, to damp down the class struggle, and so win the middle class over to the concept of a 'popular front'. We deal with the issue of Trotskyism in a later chapter, but on this particular allegation, certain points should be made clear.

If by the 'class struggle' is meant the struggle on the workshop floor, enough has been said in the chapter on industrial struggles – including the fight against company unionism and for the establishment of shop-floor organisation – to demolish the theory that Communists were 'damping down' the fight. If by the 'class struggle' is meant the mobilisation of great *political* movements such as that against Mosley or, as we shall see later, in support of Republican Spain and against Chamberlain's appeasement of Hitler, here again the allegation is obviously totally untrue.

What is true is that in this period, the Party ceased to suggest that the revolution and its sequel, the dictatorship of the proletariat, was on the *immediate* agenda, and this was seized on at the time and since by Trotskyists to argue that the Communist Party was no longer interested in revolution but was prepared to 'compromise' with the class enemy. The answer given by Communists at the time to this type of accusation was in two parts. Firstly, the dictatorship of the proletariat was still seen as the ultimate goal, and that this was so continued to be emphasized as, for example, in the draft programme drawn up for the expected congress in 1939. The second and more important part of the answer concerned the problem of how to reach this goal and how to make faster progress on the journey towards it. Unlike some smaller groups on the left, Party members had never spent much time preaching on the sidelines. Even in their most sectarian and isolated days of the Class against Class period, they had always understood that the way forward was to mobilise people for action on the key issue of the moment, the issue around which a great movement could be developed, which could in turn lead the struggle on to a higher stage. This was a conscious approach to the political task of the moment often referred to as the 'current link' and deriving from Lenin's writings. Thus at the 1937 British Party Congress, Pollitt, after referring to the need for the movement to base itself on Marxism, quoted a famous passage from Lenin:

> It is not enough to be a revolutionary and an adherent of Socialism or Communism in general. What is needed is the ability to find at any moment that particular link in the chain which must be grasped with all one's might in order to gain control of the whole chain and to prepare thoroughly for the passing on to the next link. [23]

Communists believed that the defeat of fascism and of fascism's plans to wage war on the Soviet Union was the crucial issue which the movement had to face. And in developing a struggle against this threat, every possible ally must be mobilised, including professional workers and those members of the middle class who were prepared to join in the fight and make their own specific contribution to it.

[1] *Labour Monthly*, October 1933, p.603.
[2] See *Communist Review*, September 1932. Article by R. Palme Dutt.
[3] JK 1933 folder. Report of Central Committee meeting, 16–18 June 1933.
[4] *Harry Pollitt Speaks*. Report of 13th Party Congress, p.33.
[5] Ibid, p.56.
[6] Pat Sloan (ed.), *John Cornford: A Memoir*, London 1938, pp.162–3.
[7] JK folder 16. Letter from Pollitt to Shields, 4 March 1932.
[8] See articles in *University Forward*, February 1941, by Ram Nahum and R. Freeman.
[9] See article by R. Freeman in ibid.
[10] See James Klugmann, p.32, Jon Clark, Margot Heinemann, David Margolies and Carole Snee (eds.), *Culture and Crisis in Britain in the Thirties*, London 1979.
[11] See *The Story of the AIA*, Lynda Morris and Robert Radford, Oxford 1983.

[12] See Samuel Hynes, *The Auden Generation*, London 1976, p.152.

[13] See the interview with Rickword in John Lucas (ed.), *The 1930s: a Challenge to Orthodoxy*, Hassocks 1978.

[14] See Sheila Hodges, *Gollancz: The Story of a Publishing House*, London 1978, p.126.

[15] *New Statesman*, 29 February 1936.

[16] See Sheila Hodges, op. cit., p.127; also *The Left Book Club*, John Lewis, London 1970, p.23.

[17] *New Statesman*, 29 February 1936.

[18] John Lewis, op. cit., p.27.

[19] Ben Pimlott, *Labour and the Left in the 1930s*, Cambridge 1977, p.160.

[20] John Lewis, op. cit., p.94.

[21] Ben Pimlott, op. cit., p.159.

[22] John Lewis, op. cit., p.94.

[23] *It Can Be Done* (report of 14th Congress), p.79.

CHAPTER 16

The War in Spain
(1936)

On the night of 17-18 July 1936, a group of Spanish army officers, among them General Franco, staged a rebellion against the Republican government in Spain. This government had come to power the previous February after an election in which Liberal and Left Republicans had joined forces with Socialists and Communists in a 'popular front' campaign to oust an oppressive régime of the extreme right. Many anarchist supporters voted for 'popular front' candidates, even though the anarchists themselves, as was their custom, refused to stand for election.

The new government began to carry out its election promises. 30,000 political prisoners were released, a plan for education was initiated, as was a programme of agrarian reform. The latter, however, was overtaken by a largely spontaneous movement of landless peasants who organised the occupation of many large estates in the spring of 1936.

From the first, the army officers plotted with the big landowners to overthrow the new government, and when the insurrection was mounted in the summer of 1936, it was supported by most of the church hierarchy, by monarchist groups and by the fascist Falange. The well-armed rebels expected a quick victory. In town after town they declared a state of war, seized and shot Republican and Popular Front supporters, took possession of public buildings and imposed military rule. But in town after town they were opposed by the people who, though largely unarmed and untrained in warfare, fought back; hastily formed militia, under socialist or anarchist auspices, forced the rebel troops to surrender. It soon transpired that the rebels were in control of only about one-third of the country; Eastern and Central Spain, including Madrid and Barcelona, were still in the hands of the Republic. At the same time, the defeat of the army rebels itself unleashed a mass movement. Factories and large enterprises were in many places taken over and put under workers' collectives; flats and appartments were municipalised and rents reduced.

There appeared to be every likelihood that, if left to their own resources, the Spanish people would defeat the military rebels. But the extreme right in Spain had for long been in close touch with Hitler and Mussolini and, on 19 July, General Franco sent an urgent plea for help to fascist Italy, followed by a similar request to Nazi Germany. The fascist powers responded. Within a couple of days, German planes were ferrying Moorish troops from Africa into Southern Spain, supplies of weapons, ammunition and troops from Italy and Germany began, and soon both countries were heavily involved in a war which was to last two and a half years, sending in army divisions and airforce units together with military advisers, while those parts of the coast controlled by the government were blockaded by Italian submarines.

Before the foreign build-up had become apparent, the Spanish government had approached its French counterpart, seeking to buy arms to put down the military rising, in accordance with a long-standing trade agreement. The French Prime Minister, Blum, agreed initially, but, after pressure from the British government, his decision was reversed. Instead, the policy of 'non-intervention' was introduced, under which all countries were urged to withhold arms from either side in the Spanish conflict. Thus, ostensibly the democratically-elected Spanish government was placed on an equal footing with the military rebels – on the face of it, a strange position for governments who boasted of their belief in democracy to take up. But, in practice, the Spanish government was not treated equally with its enemies, but was put at a terrible disadvantage, since Germany and Italy, though formally represented on the so-called non-intervention committee, openly continued to pour in arms and troops to help the rebels. On the other hand, the French, British and other governments forbade the export of arms to Republican Spain, and, indeed, enforced this with a naval blockade, thus making sure that the Spanish Republic should remain defenceless in face of the fascist attack.

The USSR initially agreed to be represented on the 'non-intervention' committee, but demanded that Italy and Germany cease aid to Franco; when it became clear that this aid was to continue, the Soviet government announced on 23 October that it no longer considered itself bound by the non-intervention agreement. From then on, the Spanish government was able to buy arms from the Soviet Union. But owing to the closure of the French frontier, and to the blockade imposed in the Mediterranean, these reached Spain only with much difficulty and were never equal in quantity to the weapons supplied to Franco by the fascist powers.

A curious international line-up thus emerged. A Republican government, elected by a democratic vote, was, by the other so-called democracies in Europe, denied the right to defend itself against fascist attack. The only government prepared to come to its rescue was the Communist government of the Soviet Union. (One other government, Mexico, also supported the Spanish Republic, but the arms which it could supply were very limited indeed.)

Inevitably, this line-up had far-reaching political repercussions, not only in Spain, but in the rest of the world.

In Britain, considerable sections of the establishment – including diplomats, businessmen, army chiefs and the Roman Catholic hierarchy – sided with Franco. They took the same view of him as they did of Hitler: he was a crusader against the 'reds'. Their hostility to the Spanish government was fortified by reports of mass movements taking place in Spain and, in particular, by accounts of the burning and closing of churches. Then, in September 1936, the Spanish government was itself reorganised. Before the rebellion, there had been no Socialists or Communists in it, but now the Socialist, Caballero was made Prime Minister and he invited two Communists to serve as ministers. Some months later it became known that the Russians were helping the Spanish Republic. All this confirmed the view that Franco was involved in a war against Communism. Support for Franco was reflected in certain British newspapers, in particular, Rothermere's pro-fascist *Daily Mail* (which had at that time the third largest circulation of any newspaper) together with the *Daily Sketch*, the *Morning Post* (a quality right-wing paper) and the Sunday *Observer*.

Most of the rest of the newspapers pretended to be 'impartial' or even to sympathise with the Republican cause, but this did not lead them to demand the lifting of the arms embargo which was proving such a help to Franco; on the contrary, the government's so-called 'non-intervention' policy was, in general supported. Only two national daily newspapers denounced 'non-intervention' and demanded that the Spanish government be allowed to buy arms. They were the liberal *News Chronicle* and the Communist *Daily Worker*.

The Labour Movement and Spain

The Communist Party made clear where it stood as soon as the war broke out. Weeks before any Communist had entered the Spanish government, the Party in Britain was demanding aid to the Republic and denouncing non-intervention. The Party's first pamphlet on Spain, produced immediately after the rebellion, sold 131,000 copies. 'We must force the national government to give assistance to the People's Government of Spain,' said the *Daily Worker* in a leader less than ten days after the rebellion began.[1] Reporting that Italy and Germany were sending planes to bomb the Spanish people, the paper demanded arms be sent to the Republic.[2] A few days later, it announced that its star reporter, 'Frank Pitcairn' (Claud Cockburn), had gone to Spain. On 12 August it urged every Communist Party member to report for an emergency distribution of a manifesto on Spain. The moment 'non-intervention' was mooted, it was denounced. 'Neutrality is Treason' ran a headline on 15 August. By 21 August the paper was expressing fears that the Labour leaders were planning support for 'non-intervention'.

These fears were justified. On 28 August the National Council of Labour issued a statement suggesting that the non-intervention agreement might lessen international tension, though the utmost vigilance would be required to prevent it being used to injure the Spanish government. This statement was endorsed at the annual Trade Union Congress on 10 September after Communist Bill Zak, speaking on behalf of the Furnishing Trades Association, had unsuccessfully tried to move an amendment which deplored the withholding of supplies from the Spanish government, and called for an international campaign against the 'deceptive policy of neutrality'. Zak said that this policy was

a further step along that road of retreat which started when Japan marched into Manchuria, which went on with the invasions of Abyssinia, which went on again when Hitler went into the Rhineland. This is a step which, in my opinion, far from preserving peace, draws us every day closer and closer to war, because it increases the audacity of the fascist powers.[3]

His amendment was defeated by 3,029,000 votes to 51,000. A month later, despite conclusive evidence of massive German and Italian help to Franco, the annual conference of the Labour Party also

upheld the statement endorsing 'non-intervention' though calling
for vigilance. On this occasion two delegates from Spain were not
given a chance to speak until after the debate was over.

Pressure of events, added to the indignation among rank-and-file
Labour Party members, was to force the leaders to abandon their
stand, if only on paper. On 28 October 1936, the TUC General
Council and the National Executive of the Labour Party adopted a
resolution demanding that the right to buy arms be restored to the
Spanish government.[4] But it was clear that the dominant leaders
were reluctant to contemplate action other than the formal passing
of a resolution. They were criticised for their attitude in a joint
appeal from Cripps and Mellor of the Socialist League, Brockway
and Maxton of the ILP, and Pollitt and Gallacher of the Communist
Party issued on 21 November:

> How long is the British labour movement going to stand aside
> without attempting to mobilise the mass of the British people to
> active struggle against the present arms blockade and for sending
> of arms to the Spanish people? . . . Almost a month has passed
> since the labour movement officially abandoned its support for
> non-intervention policy, and yet no campaign of any kind has
> been launched to force the government to lift the arms blockade.[5]

In the ensuing months, the Labour leaders seemed anxious to
confine themselves to occasional speeches in Parliamentary debates.
Harry Pollitt observed that

> It might have been thought that the Labour leaders in the oldest
> democracy in Europe would have rushed to give assistance to the
> Spanish people when their legally elected government and their
> young democratic institutions were threatened by fascism. But
> no! Pious expressions are allowed, but no action.

And he went on to say that the real reason was 'a mistaken fear of
losing the Roman Catholic vote in elections'.[6]

At international conferences called by the Labour and Socialist
International, the Spanish delegates appealed for industrial action
both to stop supplies going to Franco and to ensure that supplies
went to the Republic. The British TUC leaders firmly resisted these
demands. Meanwhile, the *Daily Herald*, Labour's official
newspaper, was less than enthusiastic about arms for Spain.

Soon local Labour Party members realised that it was not Labour's

Daily Herald but the Communist *Daily Worker* which was campaigning day after day for the Spanish cause. And, as in the case of the movements of the unemployed or against Mosley, they found that if they wanted to do something concrete in support of the anti-fascist struggle in Spain, it meant doing so in association with Communists who were in the forefront of local Aid-for-Spain activities. This, of course, could mean breaking the Labour Party's rules – for example, no Labour Party member was supposed to appear on the same platform as a Communist at a public meeting. Inevitably such rules got broken more and more often.

It was clear that the anti-fascist cause in Spain was arousing more feeling among British working people than almost anything since the 1926 General Strike. This was reflected in the vast numbers who turned up whenever a public meeting on Spain was called. Thus as early as 14 September 1936, the Newcastle Communist Party held a meeting on Spain at the Palace Theatre which could seat 3,000; it was packed out. On 31 November 1936 in London, 7,000 came to the Albert Hall in support of Spanish Medical Aid; among the speakers were Stafford Cripps and Harry Pollitt, while Isabel Brown took a collection of £2,000 in half an hour – in those days, a truly massive sum. Early in January 1937, 2,000 people assembled in the Leeds Town Hall resolved to set up a Spanish Aid Committee. All this was only a beginning; Aid-for-Spain meetings attracted unprecedented numbers throughout the two years of the war.

Aid for Spain

Initially, the Aid-for-Spain movement centred round medical supplies for which the Spanish government had appealed just after the fascist rising. Isabel Brown approached two young doctors suggesting that the Socialist Medical Association be asked to call a meeting. This was done, and the outcome was a Spanish Medical Aid Committee with Dr H. Morgan, medical adviser to the TUC as chairman, Dr Charles Brook, a Labour County Councillor, as secretary and Communist Christina Hastings as its treasurer. Isabel Brown represented the National Joint Committee for Anti-Fascist Relief on this Committee, and from that time on, was one of its moving spirits. The meeting sent out an appeal for funds, and before the end of August, two ambulances had been sent to Spain

accompanied by six trained nurses, four young doctors and eight dressers (including some medical students). It was the start of a continuous supply of medical equipment, vehicles and trained personnel: doctors, nurses and ambulance drivers. Among the Party members who gave outstanding service were Dr Colin Bradsworth, a general practitioner from Saltley, Birmingham, who worked behind the front line, organising the bringing in and treatment of the wounded, and who was himself wounded twice, and Dr Reginald Saxton, a general practitioner from Reading, who was in Spain from September 1936 to September 1938. Party women involved included highly-trained nurses such as Ann Murray from Edinburgh, Mary Slater of Preston and Margaret Powell; Nan Green, who was a hospital administrator, and Winifred Bates, a London school teacher, who became 'unofficial matron' for all the British nurses, co-ordinating and organising.

The Aid-for-Spain movement soon took other forms in addition to medical supplies. At the beginning of December 1936 a campaign for a Spanish Youth Foodship was launched, largely on the initiative of the Young Communist League; the aim was to collect 100 tons of food to send to the Spanish Republic. Young Communists in many localities went into action. 'West Ham Communist youth took a barrow round and collected 50 tins of milk, 35 lbs of sugar and 20 tins of coffee in 2 hours,' reported the *Daily Worker*.[7] By Christmas Eve the foodship was ready to sail; there was a packed 'send-off' meeting at the Shoreditch Town Hall with John Gollan, Young Communist League secretary, as the chief speaker. And the Southampton dockers, among whom was a well-organised Party group, announced that all the money they received for loading the ship would be given towards a second boat-load of supplies.[8]

It was the first of twenty-nine foodships sent to Spain. The response from families in working-class districts to food collections exceeded all expectations. Many years later Will Paynter recalled

> going into the streets of Trealaw and Tonypandy, in Trehafod and Porth, with a trolley, knocking on the doors of people, most of whom were unemployed and destitute, pleading for a tin of milk or a pound of sugar, and there wasn't a home, facing the impoverishment that they were facing, that wouldn't make a contribution, during that period, to help the fight of the Spanish people[9]

When, in the spring of 1937, Franco's forces closed in on the Basque country, cutting it off from the rest of Republican Spain, and subjecting it to heavy bombing, the Spanish Relief Committee in Britain organised the evacuation and reception of 4,000 Basque children. They were temporarily looked after at a tented camp near Southampton set up by the Southampton Trades Council; later they were put into the care of various organisations in different parts of the country, with local trades councils taking responsibility in several areas.

Before the end of 1936, local Aid Spain Committees had been set up in many areas. Usually the initiative for starting them came from Communist Party members. Typical was what happened in the South London borough of Battersea. Here the Communist Party branch called a Town Hall meeting early in the war and collected £45; this sum was offered to a Battersea Aid Spain Committee set up in November 1936 as a result of a proposal from a local Communist, David Guest, who was a delegate from the Shop Assistants' union to the Battersea Trades Council. The Aid Spain Committee was a loose sub-committee of the Trades Council to which organisations other than trade union branches could send representatives, including in particular the co-operative organisations and, initially, the Battersea Communist Party. When orders came down to stop the participation of Communists under the Labour Party rules, the Party took a formal decision to withdraw its own delegate, but its members went on participating as representatives of co-op guilds or union branches nevertheless. Shortly after its formation this Aid Spain Committee announced its aim of raising £750 to send a Battersea ambulance to Spain.[10]

In South Wales, the miners' lodges were usually the focal point for Aid Spain Committees. An outstanding example was in the village of Onllwyn in the anthracite coal field where a Spanish Aid Committee was set up on the initiative of local Communist miners who convened a meeting addressed by representatives from the Neath Spanish Aid Committee. The Committee elected at this meeting was representative of the whole community and of the adjoining villages. The local headmaster became the chairman, and among the organisations represented were the miners' lodge, the Communist Party, the Labour Party, miners' welfare associations, religious denominations, the local NCLC class, and even a knitting class. So widespread was the support, that only the colliery manager failed to contribute to the Committee's food and financial collections.[11]

Though Communist Party members usually provided the driving force in getting Aid Spain Committees set up, the aim was always that they should be as broadly representative as possible. Gone were the days of Class against Class when it had seemed important that every activity should be recognised as under Communist leadership. Now, on the contrary, the object was to encourage members of the Labour Party to take the lead. It was the level of activity that mattered, and the test was the number of trade union, Labour and Co-op organisations that could be persuaded to participate. In this process, Party members never tried to persuade Aid Spain Committees to undertake functions other than those for which they had been set up, or to pursue aims outside their stated objects. But since Communists emerged in many areas as the most dedicated activists in support of Spain, more and more of the non-Communists involved joined the Party. The Labour leaders looked on this process with dismay, and tried to enforce their ban on joint work with Communists; they found their prohibitions by-passed in one area after another.

The International Brigade

The most significant contribution made by the Communist Party was the formation of the British Battalion of the International Brigade. From the outset of the war, volunteers from Britain were playing their part. One of the first was a woman, Felicia Browne, a painter by profession, and a member of the Party. She happened to be in Barcelona when the rebellion broke out and immediately enrolled in one of the militia which were springing up to defend the Republic; she was killed in an advance into Aragon in August 1936.

An early move to organise a British group of volunteers was initiated by two Party members, East London garment workers Sam Masters and Nat Cohen. The latter had previously been imprisoned and then deported for organising workers in Argentina. Masters and Cohen were on a cycling holiday near the Spanish border at the time of the revolt. They went on to Barcelona and, in September 1936, joined a 'centuria' later known as the Tom Mann Centuria. Some other British volunteers were in it, though it consisted mainly of Spaniards. Tom Wintringham, who was in Barcelona as a reporter for the *Daily Worker*, wrote to Harry Pollitt on 5 September stressing the value of the Tom Mann Centuria and urging 'more volunteers to make it British in fact as well as in name'. He wrote again on 13 September spelling out what was needed: 'We want a respectable number of English comrades, CP, LP or TU, to make a centuria.'[12]

Meanwhile, John Cornford, a 21 year-old Communist, well-known in the Cambridge student movement, had gone to Spain with a journalist's press card immediately after the army rising; he made his way to the front, joined and fought with a unit of the POUM militia (about which more later). Coming back to England in mid-September, he discussed with Harry Pollitt the idea of recruiting a group to return with him to fight in Spain; Pollitt supported the idea, and promised that the Party would pay for the group's transportation. The group left for Spain at the beginning of October.[13]

At this time many Communists, refugees from fascism, living in Spain and other countries were joining units of the Republican army. The Secretariat of the ECCI decided to encourage the recruitment of anti-fascist volunteers and two representatives of the CI, Vittorio Codovilla and Jacques Duclos went to Madrid and on 12 October 1936 secured the agreement of Caballero, the Spanish Prime Minister, for the formation of International Brigades. Their base was to be at Albacete.

Once the Spanish government had agreed to the formation of such International Brigades the British Party, which had been quietly lending support to any members who wanted to go and fight, came out into the open with appeals for recruits. On 21 November, the *Daily Worker* devoted a page to Frank Pitcairn's account of the formation of the 'international legion' as it was initially called. On 5 December Harry Pollitt called for volunteers to go and join it, saying that the slogan of Marx and Engels, 'Workers of the World Unite!', was not a pious platitude but a call to practical action.

About thirty British volunteers, serving with French or German units, were with the International Brigades which stopped the fascists when they entered the streets of Madrid. These and others serving on the Aragon front soon made their way to Albacete, the new training base. On 12 December the *Daily Worker* reported that there were now 300 British volunteers; a week later, it said that another 150 men had left for Spain. Early in January 1937, the British volunteers came together to form the first British company and then the first British battalion of the International Brigade.

Until this time, appeals for volunteers could be made quite openly in Britain. Those who wanted to go to Spain went to 16 King Street and all the leading members of the Party, including Harry Pollitt, J. R. Campbell, R. P. Dutt and Emile Burns, were busy interviewing them, buying their tickets, instructing them on what would be expected of them, and handing out money for the journey. But on 10 January 1937, the Foreign Office declared that enlistment in the Spanish forces was illegal under the Foreign Enlistment Act of 1870. This meant that joining the International Brigade, or helping men to get to Spain, was illegal, and organising it had to go underground.

Illegal activity was not something to which the Communist Party was entirely unaccustomed and arrangements were quickly made to keep the recruitment process away from 16 King Street. A full-time member of the King Street staff – R. W. Robson – was put in charge and he set up a special apparatus. Every man who offered to go had to be interviewed to make sure he was a genuine anti-fascist and that he was medically fit. The interviewing had to take place in constantly shifting locations. Groups of would-be recruits from Scotland, Wales, the North, the Midlands, would come up to London escorted by a Party member who had special instructions on where to report. Sometimes communications broke down and frantic messages would be passed around that, for example, a group of Scots had disappeared somewhere in London. Once accepted, groups would be conducted to Paris (usually on weekend tickets which did not require passports) and handed over to organisers there who would see them on the next leg of their journey. After a train journey to a point near the Spanish frontier, this usually involved climbing the Pyrenees at night. Because the organisation was illegal, the Party members involved had to be changed if they became objects of interest to the authorities, or were thought to be so. Some volunteers were caught and turned back at Victoria Station or Newhaven; some were arrested in France and even spent time in French prisons. One way or another nearly all got through.

In the end, around 2,200 volunteers went from Britain to fight against Franco during the two and a half years of the war; they included Cypriots and Irish living and working in London. Between a third and a half of those who went were Communists, and others joined the Communist Party while in Spain. 526 of the volunteers were killed. Those who joined were a very typical cross-section of the men in the Party at that time. Though they included some young writers and scientists and intellectuals of great promise, between 80 and 90 per cent of them were industrial workers. There were skilled men who were already making their mark as trade-union activists, including engineers, miners, building workers, bus drivers, print workers. There were people who had been unemployed for years, active in the NUWM. Tom Wintringham, himself a Communist volunteer who became an instructor for the Brigade and later Battalion commander, said of them that they 'had spent their hours and their pennies on heart-breaking propaganda jobs that seemed sometimes to make little difference to the run of events; had endured prison and been black-listed from work'.[14]

Inevitably, Franco's sympathisers in Britain spread lies about their motives in going to fight in Spain. Thus the *Daily Mail* alleged that they were being lured by the promise of £6 a week – in those days an amount well above the skilled worker's pay. In fact they were paid 10 pesetas a day or about £3 a week, and were always told about this at the preliminary interview. More recently, some academic writers have tended to decry their motives, suggesting, for example, that personal problems were a major factor. Of course these always play a part, and the unemployed in the 1930s suffered severely from such problems. But the fact is that, just as in 1930, a judge refused to believe that anyone could distribute leaflets to the armed forces without being paid for it, so some academics have since appeared to be unwilling to face the truth: that there are people for whom the cause in which they believe is more important than their personal career, even their personal safety.

In this case, the cause had stirred the hearts of innumerable British people. With the help and connivance of the British ruling class, the fascist countries – Germany and Italy – were trying to smash a people's movement and a people's government. The spread of fascism had to be halted, the future depended on it. As Jack Jones, later secretary of the Transport and General Workers' Union, and himself a volunteer said, the men who joined were 'those who felt that international solidarity required something more than reading about it at home'.[15]

They wanted to *do* something, to get into action to strike a blow for freedom.

Initially the aim of the Party was to recruit men with experience either of service in the First World War or in the British armed forces since. Among those who played a leading role were Tom Wintringham who had seen service in the 1914–18 war; Fred Copeman, who had been involved in the Invergordon mutiny; Sam Wild, who had earlier served in the Navy; Jock Cunningham, formerly in the Argyll and Sutherland Highlanders; Harold Fry, from Edinburgh, who had served as a sergeant in the British army in China (he was killed in October 1937); George Fletcher, an ex-army sergeant and expert machine-gunner from Crewe. Later more stress was laid on political understanding than on previous military experience.

The Spanish people had not been involved in the First World War and had no experience of modern warfare. The object of the International Brigades was not only to demonstrate international class solidarity. They provided a force which combined knowledge of military techniques with high morale based on political understanding and which was able to hold the fascist advances while the new Republican army was being formed. As at the time of the French Revolution in 1789, and during the Russian Revolution of 1917, this involved the appointment of 'political commissars'.

In an article on this subject in *Inprecorr* in December 1936, Hugh Slater, at that time acting as a journalist, though a little later he joined the International Brigade himself, reported that some two months earlier the various political parties and groups making up the Spanish People's Front (Republican Union, Left Republicans, Socialists, Communists, Anarchists) had been asked to nominate suitable members to work as political commissars.[16] Slater contended that, whereas in a capitalist army, the attitude to the serving men had been summed up by Lord Tennyson as 'theirs not to reason why; theirs but to do and die', the needs of any people's army were obviously quite different, since there was no contradition between the individual personal interests of the soldiers and the cause for which they fought. Therefore, the clearer they were about what they were fighting for and why, the more unbreakable would be their morale. He went on to explain that the function of the commissars was not only to develop understanding and political conviction among the soldiers, but also to deal with manifold practical issues which had to be tackled if morale was to be maintained.

In practice, those appointed found themselves coping with the innumerable problems that arise when men are under an appalling strain, hungry, tired and always short of the weapons and supplies they needed. The British Party sent a number of its most trusted and experienced organisers to serve as Political Commissars. At Albacete, they included the writer Ralph Fox (who was killed just after Christmas 1936); Peter Kerrigan, the Scottish District Secretary and former engineering worker; Will Paynter, who went with the agreement of the South Wales Miners' Executive of which he was a member; John Mahon, who had formerly played a leading role in the Minority Movement in London. From November 1937, Bill Rust acted as base Commissar, though he was officially designated *Daily Worker* correspondent. Brigade Commissars included Dave Springhall, formerly a seaman, but now full-time London District Secretary; George Aitken, also with a Scottish engineering background, who had been a member of the Communist Party Central Committee during the 1920s. Battalion Commissars included Bert Williams, then full-time secretary in Birmingham and a former miner; Wally Tapsell, the former YCL leader who had helped to force through the 'new line' in 1929; since then he had been a manager for the *Daily Worker* (he was killed in April 1938); Jack Roberts, a Communist councillor and South Wales miner; Tom Oldershaw, a carpenter by trade and leading local activist in Battersea, London (he was killed in March 1938); Bob Cooney, from Aberdeen, originally an office-worker, member of the Scottish District Committee and well-known as a propagandist; Eric Whalley, leader of the NUWM in the Nottinghamshire and Derby area (he was killed in October 1937). Commissars in the British anti-tank battery included Hugh Slater, Bill Alexander, an industrial chemist, and Alan Gilchrist, a schoolteacher from London.

The Communist Party leaders in Britain kept continuously in touch with those who had gone to Spain. Thus Harry Pollitt, William Gallacher, Ted Bramley, John Gollan and Arthur Horner all made visits to Spain, some going several times. They made personal contact with the British volunteers, bringing out messages and parcels and interviewing the Republican political and military leaders on their behalf. On their return to Britain, they would be in great demand to speak at the numerous Aid Spain meetings taking place in every part of the country.

In support of those who went to fight in Spain a 'Wounded and Dependants' Aid Fund' was established with its headquarters at 1 Litchfield Street in London, and with Charlotte Haldane as its secretary. Actually, Charlotte was for many months playing a crucial role, acting as liaison in Paris. Local dependants' aid committees were formed to look after the dependants, and make sure they received the small allowances allocated to them. Day after day, the *Daily Worker* carried appeals for the Dependants' Aid Fund, very often on its front page, recording donations from busmen and taxi-drivers, printers and electricians, so that the practice grew up of making regular collections at work-places, factories and bus garages, as well as from trade union branches. No section raised as much as the miners.

'Everyone knows that it was only the work by the Party that made the Battalion possible,' commented Dave Springhall who was acting as Political Commissar, but who returned briefly to England in the spring of 1937.

> And yet, when our Party proposes to co-operate with the Labour Party and the TUC in order to bring aid to the Spanish people, we are told by Transport House that it is useless to co-operate with such an 'ineffectual' Party.[17]

He made a similar point at the 14th Party Congress held at the end of May 1937:

> We can say to our friends in the labour movement who, with the best of intentions, suggest that we should liquidate our Party, that without our Party there would have been no nation-wide campaign against fascism, and there would have been no immemorial British battalion of the International Brigade.[18]

The POUM and the ILP

While the vast majority of Britons who went to fight in Spain did so under the auspices of the International Brigade, about forty British volunteers fought with the POUM militia which was receiving support from the ILP. The POUM – or Workers' Party of Marxist Unity – was under the leadership of ex-Communists and former supporters of Trotsky.

The basic difference between the attitude of the Spanish

Communist Party and that of the POUM was that the Communists believed that if you wanted to achieve the socialist revolution, you must first defeat the fascists and that meant uniting with non-socialists and the preservation of the present Spanish Republican government. The POUM, whose militia was among those fighting on the Aragon front, argued that the basic aim of the moment was the dissolution of the bourgeois Parliament and its replacement by a constituent assembly which should not be elected by universal suffrage (regarded as a survival of capitalist democracy) but should consist of delegates from the front, from factory councils and from peasant assemblies.

The corollary to this was that the POUM opposed every move towards giving the Republican government greater powers. For example, when the government decreed that all troops must come under unified command, intead of being organised in independent workers' militias under various leaderships, the POUM opposed the decree. It also opposed a decision that workers in Barcelona should surrender the arms which had come into their possession so that these could be used at the front. Nobody in Britain had paid much attention to the POUM until May 1937 when news came of fighting in Catalonia behind the Spanish Republican lines.

The event which actually sparked off the fighting was an attempt by the Republican government to take charge of the telephone exchange in Barcelona. The majority of the industrial workers in this part of Spain belonged to anarchist trade unions, and the exchange had been staffed by anarchists ever since the beginning of the civil war. For months there had been numerous complaints that government communications were being disrupted. The takeover of the exchange by government forces in the first week in May was resisted, and fighting broke out which spread and went on for four days. The anarchist leaders implored their followers to stop fighting and go home. In the end they did so. But the POUM, unlike the anarchist leaders, urged everyone to remain at the barricades.[19]

Early on, the British Communist Party had had a first-hand account of the POUM's activities and attitudes from John Cornford who had fought with the POUM militia for a few weeks. On his return to England in September 1936, Cornford wrote a memorandum on Catalonia in which he criticised the POUM's

campaign for the arming of every man, woman and child in

Barcelona for the 'second revolution' at a time when all arms were wanted at the front.

He described the POUM's policies as 'provocative and utterly dangerous'.[20] Cornford himself returned to Spain to join the International Brigade; he took part in the defence of Madrid and was killed at the end of 1936. However, the ILP in Britain continued to encourage volunteers to join the POUM.

The issues raised by the POUM were discussed early in 1937 in a pamphlet by J. R. Campbell entitled *Spain's Left Critics* in which he argued against the theories put forward by Trotskyists in different parts of the world and by left-wing parties associated with the ILP, who alleged that the 'popular front' policy was one of class collaboration, and that the Communists in Spain were holding back the revolution. And at the British Party's 14th Congress in May 1937, which took place just after the Barcelona fighting, Campbell, who seconded the resolution on Spain, devoted most of his speech to the subject, saying that from the first moment of the struggle against fascism in Spain, there had been people who had sought to split the anti-fascist forces by striking an attitude, and shouting that they were not for the democratic republic, they were for the socialist republic. Yet it was clear that if the anti-fascist forces were divided, Franco could still win. Unity of the anti-fascist forces in Spain meant, among other things, a policy that would not separate workers from peasants. The land had been distributed to the peasants, and the important thing was the maximum production of food, not 'a premature policy of collectivisation'.

There had been an attempt in Barcelona to declare that democracy was not worth fighting for, said Campbell. But in Spain there was a new type of democratic republic, one that had given the land to the peasantry, one in which the newspapers were in the hands of the working class, in which the radio was at the disposal of the people, in which large-scale industry had been nationalised.

The POUM had opposed measures needed to win the war. It had resisted attempts to build a united army, to have one police force ('instead of each section having its own police force, sometimes arresting each other instead of the common enemy'). It had resisted attempts to centralise industry and convert peace industry into war industry.

In contrast, the Communist Party wanted a more vigorous war

policy, more order in the rear, 'not every trade union its own government, but one central government throughout Spain in order successfully to win the war.' It wanted better organisation of industry, 'workers' control – yes, but workers' control within the war plan . . . not workers' control irrespective of the war plan.' In conclusion, Campbell said that the Communist Party in Spain could not be 'a little irresponsible sect, indulging in phrase-mongering'. It was 'a great mass party which must justify the growing confidence that the working class has in it, by securing the operation of any policy that will defeat Franco'.[21]

There was no mistaking the mood of the 500 delegates at this Congress. To many of them, the anti-fascist struggle in Spain was the greatest cause in which they had ever been involved. They had worked for it with an energy and devotion not seen since the days of the 1926 General Strike. There was a roll of honour listing those who had been killed; at that time they numbered 122, of whom 52 had been members of the Party or the YCL. As the report of the Central Committee put it, the Party's campaign had constituted 'the proudest pages in our Party history; it had saved the honour of the British Labour Movement'.[22] In these circumstances it was hardly surprising that the POUM should be regarded as traitors, and that the behaviour of the ILP in supporting the POUM should be looked on with disgust.

[1] *Daily Worker*, 27 July 1936.
[2] *Daily Worker*, 1 August 1936.
[3] *TUC Report 1936*, pp. 371-4.
[4] *Labour Party Annual Report 1937*, p. 7.
[5] *Daily Worker*, 21 November 1936.
[6] *It Can Be Done*, pp. 47-8.
[7] *Daily Worker*, 1 December 1936.
[8] *Daily Worker*, 23 December 1936.
[9] See Francis and Smith, op. cit., p. 355.
[10] See Carmel Haden Guest (ed.), *David Guest: A Memoir*, 1939, p. 142. See also speech by G. Fineran, *Labour Party Annual Report 1937*, p. 214.
[11] Francis and Smith, op. cit., p. 356.
[12] See Bill Alexander, *British Volunteers for Liberty: Spain 1936–1939*, London 1982, pp. 52, 64.
[13] See Peter Stansky and William Abrahams, *Journey to the Frontier*, London 1966, p. 361.
[14] Tom Wintringham, *English Captain*, London 1939, p. 101.
[15] See foreword by Jack Jones to Judith Cook (ed.), *Apprentices of Freedom*, London 1979.
[16] *Inprecorr*, 24 December 1936, p. 1516.
[17] *Daily Worker*, 26 April, 1937.
[18] *It Can Be Done*, p. 146.
[19] See George Orwell, *Homage to Catalonia*, Harmondsworth 1970, p. 147.

[20]Jonathan Galassi (ed.), *Understand the Weapon, Understand the Wound*, Selected Writings of *John Cornford*, Manchester 1976, pp. 111–2.
[21] *It Can Be Done*, pp. 151–160.
[22]Ibid., p. 235.

CHAPTER 17

Trotskyism and the Russian Trials
(1932–38)

Until the appearance of the POUM on the Spanish scene, few British Communists had been particularly concerned about Trotskyism. That Trotsky had been expelled from the Soviet Union was, of course, well known; the Party had produced one or two pamphlets and articles arguing against his theory that socialism could not be built in one country. For Trotsky maintained that to foster the idea that the process of building socialism in backward Russia could be completed without the victory of the proletariat in other countries would encourage a down-playing of the need for international revolution; it would turn Communist Parties into 'border guards' of the Soviet state.

After his exile, Trotsky had been critical of the Communist International's policies during the Class againt Class period. He had, reasonably enough, denounced the characterisation of social democracy as 'social fascism' and the failure to make a proper distinction between fascism and bourgeois democracy. In relation to the German Party, he had attacked the insistence that the united front must be only 'from below'.

But as and when the Comintern began to change course, so Trotsky increasingly argued in favour of policies which would have meant no change. After Hitler came to power in March 1933, the ECCI recommended Communist parties to approach their respective social-democratic parties with proposals for joint action against fascism. From then on, as the Comintern little by little broke free of its former Class against Class fetters, culminating in the Seventh World Congress in 1935, so Trotsky gradually took over much of the old discarded theory, depicting the new anti-fascist peoples' front strategy as a betrayal of the world revolutionary movement. More and more he advocated immediate proletarian revolution as the only alternative to fascism. Whenever agreement on united action between socialists and communists on a limited issue was under discussion, he and his followers would put forward demands of an ultra-revolutionary kind, certain to be rejected by the socialist parties concerned, and, indeed, by their followers. For example, when, in July 1934, the Unity of Action Pact signed by the French Communist and Socialist Parties proposed measures for the defence of workers' meetings against fascist attacks, Trotsky put forward the slogan 'Arm the proletariat and the revolutionary peasants', which was not only unacceptable to the Socialists, but provocative in the circumstances prevailing in France at that time.[1]

In support of his revolutionary stance, Trotsky made assumptions about the mood of the masses which were not based on the facts. Just as the CI had talked in 1928-9 about the 'rising revolutionary upsurge of the masses' and accused its sections of 'tailing behind', so Trotsky now took a similar line. He wrote in 1938:

> In all countries the proletariat is racked by deep disgust. The multi-millioned masses again enter the road of revolution. But each time they are blocked by their own Conservative bureacratic machine.[2]

The 'bureaucratic machine' which was blocking the revolution comprised, according to Trotsky, not only the social democrats but also the Communist parties; the role of the Comintern he described as 'counter-revolutionary':

> The Third International has taken to the road of reformism at a time when the crisis of capitalism definitely placed proletarian revolution on the order of the day.[3]

Bit by bit, the myth was created by Trotsky and his followers that the 'popular front' policy was dictated by Stalin to damp down the class struggle in every country in the interests of Soviet foreign policy. This, despite the fact that in 1934 Stalin was persuaded only with very great difficulty of the need for the world Communist movement to change direction.

British Trotskyism

The first manifestation of Trotskyist activity in Britain had revealed a determination to stick to the Class against Class guidelines. In 1932, a handful of Party members in the 'Balham Group' in South-West London, were expelled for 'fractional activities in connection with Trotskyism'. Reg Groves, Harry Wicks and Henry Sara had been the leaders of this group. They had raised strong objections to the new approach to the trade unions embodied in the so-called 'January Resolution'. As recorded in Chapter 7, the Party had with some difficulty extricated itself from the Class against Class encumbrances in this field, and the result had been a formulation in the 'January Resolution' calling for the 'transformation of the trade union branches from organs of class collaboration into organs of class struggle'.

In the autumn of that year, 1932, there was to be some controversy with Dutt concerning the possibility of changing the unions *above* branch level. But long before this the Balham Group was on the warpath, denying that even union branches could be so transformed, and arguing that 'the whole history of the trade unions, their past as well as their present, makes them *unsuited* to be effective organs of class struggle'.[4] After a succession of aggregate meetings in South-West London, at which Groves and Wicks voiced criticism of the Party leadership but failed to win a majority of those present, they were both expelled.

From 1933 onwards, most of Trotsky's followers in Britain – initially no more than a handful – found their way into the ILP. That year, the ILP national conference had decided, against the wishes of its leadership, that the ILP should enter negotiations with the Communist International. It was from that year that Trotsky began to be given space in the ILP journal, *New Leader*.

> Frightened by the growing sympathy with Communism among the rank and file of the Independent Labour Party, the anti-Communist leaders of that organisation have sought the aid of Trotsky in stemming the tide.

was the sardonic comment of Andrew Rothstein in 1934.

> Something that looked like Marxism had to be employed if the ear of the rank and file was to be gained, and the ILP leaders were notoriously unversed in that. But Trotsky was a god-send; who so brilliant in the use of Marxist phrases, who so willing and anxious to employ them against the Communist International?[5]

Articles in the *New Leader* became increasingly critical of the Soviet Union's foreign policy and the association with the League of Nations. Thus, the Franco-Soviet Pact in 1935 was denounced as an example of the way in which 'Stalin repudiated the Leninist doctrine of the "enemy in your own country" and gave his blessing to the doctrine of national defence'.[6] The author of this article was C. L. R. James, an ILP member who was to become prominent as a follower of Trotsky.

This was the start of continuing disagreements between Communists and Trotskyists on the whole question of how to halt the fascist aggressors – Italy, Germany, Japan – and so avert – if only temporarily – a second world war. Communists believed that the fascist powers could be restrained by means of collective security through the League of Nations, which meant that governments should combine to impose sanctions on any nation that attacked another. It meant support for pacts, such as that between France and the Soviet Union, who had signed a treaty for mutual assistance in the event of unprovoked aggression. The French government had entered into this treaty because of Hitler's open threats. Communist belief in the possibilities of collective security did not imply any illusions concerning the imperialist nature of the French government, or most of the other governments concerned; it was based on the understanding that, unlike the fascist powers, France and Britain and the United States were not for the time being concerned to conquer new territories and wanted to avoid war if they could. Thus they believed they were adopting Lenin's approach in seeking to make use of the contradictions between the imperialists. Far from aiming to damp down the class struggle, as the Trotskyists alleged, they believed that 'collective security' would not be made a reality if left to the governments concerned. On the contrary, the workers must be mobilised for 'direct action' to enforce sanctions against the fascist aggressors.

For Trotsky and his followers, however, the slogan of 'collective security' was a deception of the workers, and the Communist International by its support for this deception had become 'a political agent of the imperialists among the working class'.[7] Trotsky did not think that the working-class movement should concern itself with the defence of national frontiers against fascist aggressors. He argued:

> The task of the European proletariat is not the perpetuation of boundaries but, on the contrary, their revolutionary abolition, not the *status quo*, but a Socialist United States of Europe.[8]

To British Communists, this sort of approach had become more and more unreal. For it seemed glaringly obvious that the British government was mainly responsible for *sabotaging* the possibility of collective seccurity. The government's behaviour had encouraged the fascist powers to grab territory – in Spain and China, and soon in Austria, Czechoslovakia and elsewhere. To stop this sabotage would not only frustrate the plans of the fascist powers, it would constitute a massive defeat for their best friends in the British government and raise the working-class struggle to new heights. It seemed to them that the attitude of the Trotskyists was playing into the hands of these pro-fascists, whereas the one thing which might avert another world war was the mobilisation of all possible people in the anti-fascist cause.

But it was the issue of the POUM that caused the greatest anger against Trotskyists among Communists. Ironically, the POUM was not a Trotskyist organisation in the strict sense – indeed Trotsky himself was to pour scorn upon it, alleging that 'under revolutionary conditions' it had 'proved completely incapable of following a revolutionary line' and that it had 'acted as a brake' in the 'heroic attempts' of the Spanish proletariat to take power.[9] However, the POUM's line – that of calling for revolution against the Spanish Republican government at a time when it was engaged in an anti-fascist war – was sufficiently close to that of Trotsky as to make little difference in Communist eyes.

In his closing speech at the 1937 British Party Congress, Pollitt called on members to give 'careful and painstaking explanations' about the POUM to the ILP comrades they met. Every argument had to be countered, he said, with clear answers, not with labels or phrases, so that they could see that what they had thought of as revolutionary was, in fact, counter-revolutionary.[10]

Everything said from the platform during this Congress was careful and objective. But shortly afterwards, allegations that the POUM leaders were *conscious* traitors acting on behalf of the fascist Franco, began to receive credence. Thus it was believed that Andrés Nin, the leader of the POUM, who was arrested and then disappeared, had gone over to the Fascists.[11] In fact he was almost certainly executed. But anger at the splitting tactics of the POUM was to lead to the acceptance of totally false allegations concerning Trotskyists.[12]

From 1936 onwards, Trotskyists were more and more frequently denounced as 'agents of fascism'. It was stated in a resolution adopted at the 1938 Party Congress that they were seeking 'to aid the reactionaries' by fostering the conviction that all attempts to stem fascist aggression, and to co-operate with France and the Soviet Union would bring war nearer. The Trotskyists, it was alleged, were spreading calumnies against the Soviet Union and the Spanish Republic, and were trying to disrupt movements aiming at aid for China and Spain. The 15th Congress noted:

> The Party must direct attention to the fact that those agents of fascism often work through other bodies – the ILP, and the National Council of Labour Colleges – in order to more effectively accomplish their objects. [13]

The Moscow Trials

By this time, many Communists had had some experience of disruptive activities by Trotskyists; the argument that they were 'agents of fascism' rather than horribly misguided seemed plausible to them. It was one of the reasons why the trials of Trotskyists in Moscow were accepted by Party members as just.

These trials took place in the years 1936–8. The initial event which sparked them off was the assassination of the Secretary of the Leningrad Communist Party at the end of 1934, allegedly by a terrorist group. Stalin, General Secretary of the Communist Party of the Soviet Union, used this as a pretext for a gigantic purge of members alleged to be 'opposition elements'. In August 1936, sixteen of them were put on trial, including two well-known former leaders, Zinoviev and Kamenev. They were charged with forming a Trotskyist terrorist organisation, and with plotting to assassinate other Party leaders. They confessed to these crimes and were executed. In January 1937, in a second trial, Pyatakov, Radek and 15 others were charged with wrecking, espionage, attempting to restore capitalism and with acting as fascism's fifth column. From now on, Trotskyist groups were depicted as fascism's *willing* tool. Again, the accused confessed, and 15 of them were executed. A third trial in June 1937 was held in secret, as those accused were generals, headed by Tukhachevsky, who were said to be planning a *coup d'état* which would precipitate an armed attack on the USSR by the fascist powers. On 12 June the execution of Tukhachevsky and his colleagues was announced. The last trial was in March 1938. Chief among the twenty-one accused was Bukharin, former Comintern leader. They were charged with murder, wrecking and sabotage and having contact with the fascist powers. Eighteen of them were condemned to death.

Simultaneously with the trials, hundreds of thousands of Russian Party members were arrested and imprisoned. One of those caught up in this was Rose Cohen. A former member of the British Party, she had married a Russian, Petrovsky, who had at one time acted as Comintern representative in the British Party under the name of Bennett. When he returned to Moscow, she went with him. Petrovsky, by this time in a high government position, was among those charged with spying, and executed. Rose Cohen protested at his arrest, was herself arrested and disappeared. Harry Pollitt went to Moscow, tried to find out what had happened to her, took the matter up with the other Comintern leaders, protested vigorously, but got nowhere.

According to a letter from R. Palme Dutt to *The Times Literary Supplement*, May 5 1966, in 1937

> at a meeting of a delegation, headed by Pollitt and attended by other leading comrades, including myself, with the international leadership, we were in conflict again over raising questions concerning the conduct of the security organs; and this dispute proved so intense that soundings were made to find support among us for the replacement of the General Secretary; but we all made clear that we stood by Pollitt on this matter.

Though Dutt never volunteered any further information on this matter, it has been assumed since that the dispute to which he refers must have been over Rose Cohen.

The trials and the mass arrests were, of course, an outward manifestation of Stalin's determination to eliminate anyone who might offer a challenge to his personal supremacy. But in Britain at the time, Communist Party members as a whole accepted the confessions made by those accused at their face value, firmly believed in the charges made and thought that those executed had met with their just deserts. Later generations were to find this attitude incredible, and accusations were made, both inside and outside the Party, suggesting that the leaders of the British Communist Party were fully aware of the terrible injustices perpetrated by the Stalin régime, but connived at a cover-up.

Those who make such accusations fail to understand the situation at the time. The fact that thousands were being detained and *not* being brought to trial but simply disappearing into prison camps was not known to the leaders of the British Party any more than to the rank-and-file members. Those who knew about Rose Cohen assumed that a mistake had been made in an individual case, and when this was recognised, Rose would reappear. Ignorance concerning the scale of the arrests contributed to acceptance of the verdicts on those brought to public trial, though here a number of factors were involved.

Fundamental to their approach was the belief – held by all Communists – that all persecution, tyranny and injustice had their roots in the capitalist system, and in capitalist property relations. It followed that, where the capitalist system was abolished, tyranny and persecution would wither away; insofar as they still manifested themselves in Russia, this was simply a hangover from Tsarist days, soon to disappear. The idea that the new socialist society, in which classes and the class struggle had been eliminated, could itself generate new forms of oppression was something which no Communist countenanced until after the Soviet party's Twentieth Congress in 1956.

The general standpoint that capitalism was the root of all evil was bolstered by a whole series of other considerations.

In the first place, some trusted English lawyers were present at the three trials held in public, and came back and testified that there was absolutely no sign that the prisoners had been ill-used in any way. They confessed, it was suggested, because the evidence of their guilt was overhwleming. Among the lawyers involved were Labour MP, D. N. Pritt and, perhaps more important, Dudley Collard who was on the Executive of the National Council for Civil Liberties and a leading figure in the Howard League for Penal Reform. He spoke Russian fluently and could hear for himself what was said by the prisoners and their accusers.

The second factor influencing the attitude of British Communists was that, ever since the revolution, lies and distortions concerning the Soviet Union had appeared in the capitalist press. And indeed, not only about the Soviet Union. Every Communist knew that you couldn't believe the newspapers. Look at how they suppressed the facts about British oppression in India! Look at the lies told about

International Brigaders being well-paid mercenaries! Look at the way trade unions were attacked and misrepresented! Why then should you believe what they say about the Moscow trials?

Thirdly, everyone knew that the Soviet Union was surrounded by hostile capitalist powers who had tried, in the 1920s, to smash it and who sent in spies and agents for hostile purposes. The idea that such agents could have penetrated the ranks of the Communist Party of the Soviet Union did not seem at all far-fetched – the tiny British Party, after all, had suffered its share of police informers, MI5 spies and *agents provocateurs*.

Fourthly, Trotsky, who had been exiled and was now living in Mexico, was known to be attempting to build the Fourth International and had boasted at the beginning of 1936 that it had its strongest, biggest and most hardened branch in the USSR.[14]

Fifthly, the notion that Trotskyists could be allied with fascists, or used as tools of the latter seemed plausible after the experience of the POUM in Spain. As already shown, it was assumed (not altogether correctly) that the POUM was a Trotskyist organisation; it was believed (with justice) that the organisation had betrayed the struggle against Franco, insofar as it had supported activities hostile to the Spanish government, and tried to split the anti-fascist ranks. But it was also alleged, this time with no justification, that the POUM leaders were acting as agents of the fascists.

Lastly, Communists were reluctant to believe that the government of the first socialist country could be responsible for such atrocities. For them, the Soviet Union symbolised a new world for which they were struggling. Wholly committed to the socialist cause, many of them had sacrificed a great deal in the course of this struggle. They could not accept the idea that a socialist system could be so deeply flawed. Some twenty years later, in 1956, they were to be forced to reconsider. But that day was still a long way ahead.

---

[1] See *Marxism Today*, October and November 1975, for articles by Monty Johnstone which deal in detail with Trotskyism and the Popular Front.
[2] See Leon Trotsky, *The Death Agony of Capitalism and the Tasks of the Fourth International*, 1963, p. 9 (pamphlet).
[3] Ibid., p. 48.
[4] *Daily Worker*, 14 April 1932 and 27 May 1932.
[5] R. F. Andrews, *The Truth about Trotsky*, pamphlet published 1934.
[6] *New Leader*, 25 October 1935.
[7] Leon Trotsky, *The Revolution Betrayed*, London 1937, p. 189.
[8] Ibid., p. 221.
[9] *The Death Agony of Capitalism*, pp. 9, 49.

[10]*It Can Be Done*, pp. 191–2.

[11]See J. R. Campbell, *Questions and Answers on Communism*, 1938, p. 92 (pamphlet).

[12]Nearly forty years later, the Secretary of the Spanish Communist Party, Santiago Carrillo expressed his disbelief in the suggestion that Nin went over to Franco, though at the time he himself had accepted the possibility. See Santiago Carrillo, *Dialogue on Spain*, London 1976, p. 53.

[13]*For Peace and Plenty*, Report of 15th Congress, p. 151.

[14]See article by Trotsky, 'The Soviet Section of the Fourth International,' published in the *Bulletin of the Opposition* (in Russian) Paris, February 1936.

CHAPTER 18

The Road to the Second World War
(1937–39)

A collective stand by the League of Nations against fascist aggression was seen by Communists as the only way in which peace could be achieved or preserved. Nobody can now say that this policy would have failed to avert a second world war, since it was never tried. The Chamberlain government took the opposite road: that of appeasement of the fascist powers.

Support for collective security was also the stated policy of the Labour and trade-union leaders, despite the fact that Labour's official organ, the *Daily Herald*, was frequently found to be on the opposite side of the fence. But the main criticism of the Labour leadership from those on the left was the refusal to take any sort of action to make collective security a reality. Just as Citrine suggested at the time of the 1936 Hunger March that it was wrong for a section of the community to subvert the will of Parliament, so, on international issues, the Labour leaders frowned on any sort of direct action, and where it occurred tried to stop it.

The Sino-Japanese Conflict

Early on, this attitude had been demonstrated over the war in Spain; it was to be shown again when Japan – a signatory with Germany of the 'Anti-Comintern Pact' – mounted an all-out offensive against China in August 1937.

Throughout the Sino-Japanese struggle, the line-up of forces in Britain conformed to a familiar pattern. The Labour Party annual conference in October 1937 called upon the British government to place an embargo on the selling of war materials, or the lending of money to Japan, and to co-operate with the League of Nations in imposing economic and financial pressure on Japan. But since Chamberlain was determined to maintain friendly relations with all the fascist powers, including Japan, it was a foregone conclusion that the British government would refuse to impose such sanctions.

The Labour Party leaders, urged on by their left wing, issued a call to British citizens to boycott Japanese goods. But they declined to participate in actions urged on them by their opposite numbers in Europe. Thus, the International Transport Workers' Federation proposed an embargo on the transport of war material to Japan, but the National Council of Labour rejected this on 7 January 1938. One week later, a proposal to call on workers to refuse to handle Japanese goods was strongly urged at a special joint conference of the Labour and Socialist International and the International Federation of Trade Unions. But Sir Walter Citrine, on behalf of the British delegation, resisted this demand, arguing that delegates must persuade their respective *governments* to impose sanctions on Japan; he ruled out direct action by trade unionists.

While this was going on at the top, British Communists had in practice successfully initiated industrial action here and there. One of the first such actions was at Southampton where, in December 1937, a Canadian Pacific liner, the *Duchess of Richmond*, arrived carrying 200 tons of Japanese goods as part of a 1,800 ton cargo. At the Southampton docks there was a lively and growing Communist Party group, and one of its members, Trevor Stallard, discovered the Japanese exports while the ship was being unloaded. He called a meeting of the men concerned, and it was agreed not to unload anything coming from Japan. In the end the Japanese cargo was taken off so that the rest could be discharged, after which it was put back again, and the *Duchess of Richmond* set sail for Canada with the Japanese goods still on board.[1]

The event made headlines, not only in the local press. As the *Daily Worker* of 6 December 1937, put it:

> Southampton dockers made history this weekend, giving the lead to the country in the fight for peace, against fascist aggression. They stopped and sent back across the Atlantic 200 tons of Japanese goods seeking to enter this country.

The London Communist Party distributed leaflets to London dockers calling on them to support the Southampton dockers; from then on the *Daily Worker* listed ships expected to dock under the heading 'Watch these Ships'.

Then, on 21 January 1938, stevedores at Middlesbrough refused to load a Japanese ship, the *Haruna Maru*, with a cargo of pig-iron.

After an official of the Transport and General Workers' Union had failed to persuade them to change their minds, and had tried, without success, to recruit casual dockworkers to replace them, the boat sailed away empty and made for the Royal Albert Dock of East London. Here the Party mounted a great campaign. Under the auspices of the China Campaign Committee, a public meeting was called at the Canning Town Public Hall on 30 January. The meeting was packed out and was addressed not only by such leaders as Ben Bradley, Tom Mann and Ted Bramley, but by representatives of the dockers from Middlesbrough and Southampton, including Stallard. That night, leaflets were hastily duplicated for distribution at the docks, and, early next morning, Stallard went with Tom Mann to address the stevedores at the call-stand to try and persuade them not to load the *Haruna Maru*. The stevedores responded. They refused to load the ship. A few days later the *Haruna Maru* left British shores with an empty hold.

The Southampton dockers who had taken part in the boycott were sacked and blacklisted as a result of their action, and Stallard could not get work again at the dock until 1939 when war was imminent. He and the others involved received letters of thanks from the Chinese embassy. The local dockers' branch of the Transport and General Workers' Union strongly supported their action. In later years, Stallard was to be elected to the union's Executive Council.

At the time, the *Daily Worker* recorded many resolutions from trade union branches, supporting the dockers and urging an all-out official embargo of Japanese goods. But the *Daily Herald*, Labour's official newspaper, on 15 February 1938, published a hostile article denouncing those who were calling for such industrial action.

Appeasement of Hitler

The British government's appeasement of Hitler had gone on ever since Germany left the League of Nations. In 1935, despite protests from the French, the British signed a naval agreement permitting Germany to build a submarine fleet in breach of the Versailles Treaty. In March 1936, when Hitler's troops occupied the demilitarised zone of the Rhineland again in breach of the Treaty, the Baldwin government made it clear that no action would be taken under the League Covenant and thus, as the *Daily Worker* put it, 'offered direct encouragement to Hitler to treat all such pacts and treaties as "scraps of paper".'

In February 1938, Hitler began to threaten Austria. By this time, Chamberlain was Prime Minister, and he made clear that nothing would be done to maintain Austrian independence. 'We must not delude small, weak nations into thinking that they will be protected by the League against aggression,' he said.[3] Thus given the green light, German troops invaded Austria on 11 March. A Communist statement the following day declared:

> The invasion of Austria by Hitler's armies has brought Europe to the brink of war. Unless fascist aggression is stopped now, fascist aeroplanes will be over Prague . . . Hitler's action has been taken in agreement with Chamberlain. Chamberlain has torpedoed the League of Nations . . .

It called for mass demonstrations and the formation of a Council of Action to drive out the Chamberlain government. The call met with some response; 40,000 joined in a protest march organised by the London Communist Party.

It was already clear that Czechoslovakia was next on Hitler's list. Here was a much richer prize than Austria. Her Skoda arms-works were the largest in Europe; geographically, she offered a means of access to territories farther east.

The main obstacle to Hitler's ambition was a mutual assistance pact between Czechoslovakia and France, whereby each country agreed to go to the help of the other if attacked. Czechoslovakia also had a pact with the Soviet Union, each agreeing to help defend the other *provided* the victim of aggression was assisted by France. Since the Soviet Union also had a mutual assistance pact with France, it appeared that Hitler could not take on Czechoslovakia without embroiling himself in a war on two fronts.

The argument of the Communist Party, and indeed of League supporters in the labour movement, had always been that Britain should join with France in these mutual assistance arrangements, drawn up under the auspices of the League, and thus deter the fascist powers, in particular Hitler, from aggressive action. But the British government, and Prime Minister Neville Chamberlain in particular, had always firmly refused to be associated with French and Russian guarantees to Czechoslovakia.

On 17 March 1938, just after the annexation of Austria, the Soviet government proposed joint discussions between French, Soviet, British and American statesmen to see what could be done to prevent further agression in Central Europe.

Chamberlain rejected this proposal, stating that the British government was not prepared to guarantee support to France if the latter was called upon to support Czechoslovakia against German aggression.[4] 'All clear signal given to fascist aggressors' was how the *Daily Worker* reported this statement. 'Chamberlain's policy can only be regarded as a deliberate encouragement to Hitler to annex the great steel industry and arsenals of Czechoslovakia,' said the Central Committee statement issued on March 26.

From then on it became increasingly clear that Chamberlain was not just refusing to be associated with pacts to protect Czechoslovakia, he was determined to undermine the pacts themselves.

The pretext for Hitler's threats to Czechoslovakia was the existence there of the Sudeten Germans, who formed a large minority within the population. Movements of German troops began and the situation became so threatening that on 20 May 1938, the Czech Government ordered a partial mobilisation. The *Daily Worker* called for support for the independence of Czechoslovakia alleging that Chamberlain was putting pressure on France to renounce its pact with the Czechs, and that this was encouraging Hitler to repeat his Austrian experiment in Czechoslovakia.[5]

In the event, German troop movements were halted and the threat of war diminished temporarily. This easing of tension was short-lived, however, and it grew up again over the next few months; it was to end in the disastrous Munich agreement.

In August the British government sent Lord Runciman to Czechoslovakia to act as 'mediator' between the Czech government and the Sudeten Germans. Ostensibly, the question of ceding territory to Hitler was not on the agenda. However, it had long since been rumoured in the American press that Chamberlain favoured the transfer to Germany of the Czech Sudeten territories.[6] On 7 September, a *Times* leader was urging consideration of this proposal, despite the fact that the Czech government had offered a wide degree of autonomy to the Sudeten Germans, including control of their local police.

At this stage the *Daily Worker* was the only paper which

SIDELIGHTS·ON·THE·CLIVEDEN SET

Hitler's Friends in Britain

From Cliveden House in Bucking-hamshire operates the Cliveden Set —making and breaking British Cabinet Ministers—bringing Britain to the verge of war—wielding the power of International Fascism.

ONE PENNY

consistently emphasised the need to stand by the Czechs. As it did so its sales rose, mounting to an extra 210,000 copies a week by the end of October. On 31 August it called on its readers to send telegrams to their MPs and get their organisations to adopt resolutions demanding a declaration from the British government that it would associate itself with France and the Soviet Union in resisting any German attack on Czechoslovakia. Day after day it alleged that the British government was about to make a deal with Hitler, and on 6 September it urged the Labour leaders to insist that there should be no such deal.

And that, at this stage, was what the Labour leaders did. On 8 September the National Council of Labour passed a resolution stating that the time had come for moves towards collective defence against aggression. 'The British government must leave no doubt in the mind of the German government that it will unite with the French and Soviet governments to resist any attack upon Czechoslovakia.'

On 12 September Hitler demanded the right of self-determination for the Sudeten Germans; the next day *The Times* again urged consideration of this proposal, and the day after it was announced that Chamberlain would fly to Berchtesgaden to meet Hitler. It was at this stage that Labour's *Daily Herald* showed itself in its true colours. For while the Labour leaders were making speeches against the dismemberment of Czechoslovakia the *Daily Herald* was saying 'Good Luck, Chamberlain'.[7]

'Chamberlain went to Hitler to betray peace, not to save it,' Gallacher told the 15th Communist Party Congress which happened to be meeting the weekend of 16–19 September. By this time, the message conveyed in newspapers and on the radio was that war was imminent, a message which seemed to be confirmed during the ensuing days, as the Fleet was mobilised, territorials were called up, gas masks were distributed and school children evacuated.

> No one who has followed the events of the past week can fail to see that the government has been deliberately encouraging a certain war atmosphere,

Dutt told the Congress. They were spreading the idea that tomorrow we would find Britain, France and the Soviet Union at war with Germany. 'Is it because they intend to make such a united stand?' asked Dutt. 'That is the last thing they mean to do . . . If there were such a united stand, that would not mean war but peace.' Their aim, said Dutt, was to betray Czechoslovakia, to betray peace, and 'to put it across in such a way that it is received as a triumph for peace, that Chamberlain is the saviour of peace.'[8] Dutt was to be proved right within a fortnight.

At Chamberlain's Berchtesgaden meeting with Hitler, the German leader proposed transference of the Sudeten territories to Germany. Chamberlain rushed home to secure the agreement of the Cabinet for the transference of Czech territories in which more than 50 per cent of the population was German; the French government concurred, in the hope that this might save them from carrying out their obligations to the Czechs. Under severe pressure, the Czech government then agreed to these proposals, on the understanding that the British and French governments would accept responsibility for the new frontiers and guarantee them if attacked. These Anglo-French proposals were made public, and on 21 September were condemned in a joint manifesto issued by the TUC, the Labour Party and the Parliamentary Labour Party.

Despite the fact that Labour's paper, the *Daily Herald*, hardly supported this call in its editorials and front-page headlines, some 3,000 'Stand by the Czechs' meetings took place. The Communist Party distributed 500,000 leaflets headed *Stop the Betrayal*.

However, when, on 22 September, Chamberlain returned to Germany to meet Hitler at Godesberg, he was faced with a list of demands much more extreme than those put forward before. The territories Hitler was claiming were even more extensive; moreover, he was insisting that all military and industrial installations within the territories concerned should be left intact and evacuated by the Czechs within a week. On 25 September the Czech government rejected this Godesberg plan, began to mobilise, and an official statement was issued that France and Russia would stand by Czechoslovakia if she was attacked, and that Britain would certainly stand by France.

It is now known (though it was not made public at the time) that Chamberlain tried to persuade the Cabinet to accept Hitler's Godesberg demands, but met with dissent and resistance within the cabinet.[9] However, shortly afterwards, Chamberlain was to get his way. On 27 September he made his famous broadcast to the nation:

How horrible, fantastic, incredible it is that we should be digging trenches and trying on gas masks here because of a quarrel in a faraway country between people of whom we know nothing.

By this time, the *Daily Herald* was using Chamberlain's arguments. It was no longer denouncing the dismemberment of Czechoslovakia. The only issue, it asserted, was whether the Czech territories should be subject to an 'ordered transfer' or whether Hitler should take them by force. And, on 28 September, when Parliament at last met, it became clear that the *Daily Herald*'s change of line was shared by the leaders of the Parliamentary Labour Party; their former call to 'stand by the Czechs' had been dropped.

On this occasion, Chamberlain explained that he had suggested to Hitler that he should once more come to discuss arrangements for the transfer of territory and that Hitler, who had previously threatened to march on Czechoslovakia by 2p.m., had held his hand. Chamberlain announced that Hitler had invited him to go to Munich to meet with himself, Mussolini and Daladier. In response, Clement Attlee, the leader of the Labour Party, welcomed Chamberlain's statement

> that even at this late hour a fresh opportunity has arisen of further discussions which may lead to the prevention of war. I am sure that every Member of this House is desirous of neglecting no chance of preserving peace without sacrificing principles. We wish to give the Prime Minister every opportunity of following up this new move.

Labour MP Lansbury then wished Chamberlain God-speed and said 'on behalf of millions of people how grateful we are that he has taken the initiative he has.' Even Maxton, the left-wing ILP member said he agreed with the step now taken.

Only one MP objected, and he had difficulty in making himself heard. This was Gallacher, Communist MP for West Fife, whose statement was largely ignored by the press the next day. He said:

> No one desires peace more than I and my Party, but it must be a peace based upon freedom and democracy and not upon the cutting up and destruction of a small state. I want to say that the policy of the national Government has led to this crisis (Hon. members: No) Yes, and if there is peace at the moment it is the determined attitude of the people that has saved it. Whatever the outcome, the National Government will have to answer for its

policy. I would not be a party to what has been going on here. There are as many fascists opposite as there are in Germany, and I protest against the dismemberment of Czechoslovakia.[10]

When Chamberlain returned from Munich on 30 September, and was met by cheering crowds, he waved a piece of paper and talked about 'peace in our time'. But it soon transpired that under the Munich agreement, Hitler would get even more than he would have done under the rejected Godesberg plan. It meant that Germany took over Czechoslovakia's massive defence fortifications and achieved virtual control of the Skoda arms-works, thereby considerably augmenting her armed strength.

The occupation by German troops of the Czech territories concerned was completed by 10 October. In the debate on 4 October, before the detailed terms of the agreement had been published, Gallacher said: 'if I were asked the question: "Did the Prime Minister save peace? I should answer with an emphatic No". The Prime Minister saved Hitler.' The point was reiterated in a Central Committee statement which said that the Munich agreement would 'open Europe and Britain to fascism and new wars.' A million leaflets calling for the repudiation of the agreement were printed and distributed, and a pamphlet entitled *Czechoslovakia Betrayed* by Harry Pollitt sold 95,000 copies.

A few months later, the reality of Chamberlain's Munich policy could no longer be hidden. For on 15 March 1939 German troops entered Prague, and Czechoslovakia disintegrated. 'Czechoslovakia ceases to exist' announced Hitler.

Fascist Victory in Spain

Munich was the beginning of the end. While the crisis was at its height in September 1938, Negrín, Prime Minister of the Spanish Republic, announced that foreign volunteers were to be repatriated. It was a last desperate bid to get the League to force withdrawal of German and Italian forces from Franco's side. So at the end of October 1938 over a hundred British members of the International Brigade, who had earlier been captured by Franco's forces, were released and arrived back in Britain. Finally, on 7 December 1938, the remaining 305 British International Brigaders returned home. The crowd that turned up to welcome them at Victoria Station was estimated at over 20,000. And on 8 January 1939, 9,000 people assembled in the Empress Hall, Earls Court, to welcome the returned Brigaders, hear Harry Pollitt and Isabel Brown speak, and Paul Robeson sing.

But Negrín's hope for the withdrawal of German and Italian troops was not fulfilled. The Italians launched a major offensive, so that by the end of January 1939 Barcelona had fallen. In Britain, supporters of Republican Spain continued their endeavours, here and there taking industrial action. Thus on 25 January, workers in thirteen London engineering shops imposed a ban on overtime, and joined with men on eight building sites to stop work at 4 p.m. and march to Downing Street. The next day, workers from aircraft factories, De Haviland and Handley Page, did the same. Communist Len Powell, later secretary of the National Aircraft Shop Stewards' Council, addressed the crowd, saying that some of the planes they were making were going abroad but not to Republican Spain: 'We feel they must go there, and we are going to have a voice in this.'[11] On 2 February, in response to a call from shop stewards, over 1,000 engineering workers assembled at Chenies Street, London, and were addressed by Gallacher before marching to Downing Street. Nine London building jobs set up an All-London Job and Shop Stewards' Action for Spain Committee; it organised a contingent of building workers on a march and deputation on 7 March. But that month, it all came to an end. Madrid surrendered. The war was over.

The Last Stage

Thus, by the spring of 1939, Spain and Czechoslovakia were both in fascist hands. Any illusions that this would satisfy Hitler and Mussolini were to be swiftly dispelled; the more they swallowed, the more their appetites grew. In April, Italy invaded Albania. Meanwhile, Lithuania had been forced to hand Memel back to Germany, and Hitler was laying claim to the Polish corridor, a narrow strip of land separating the German city of Danzig from the rest of German territory, which formed Poland's only outlet to the sea. Hitler moved troops up to the Polish border, at which the British government made a declaration of conditional support for Poland against immediate aggression. Announcing this in Parliament on 31 March 1939 Chamberlain stated that the 'differences' between Germany and Poland should be 'adjusted by way of free negotiations'.

In response to Chamberlain's announcement of support for Poland, Gallacher made the following observations:

> The Prime Minister has made a statement that if Poland is attacked we will go to war. May I draw attention to the fact that what everybody desires is the most immediate unification of the peace forces to *prevent* us going to war . . . with collective security peace could be saved . . . If Members on this side had stood with me and prevented the Prime Minister from going to Munich, we would not be discussing going to war now.

He asked the Prime Minister to resign and give those who believed in collective security an opportunity of forming a government and saving the people of Britain and Europe from the menace of war.[12]

But it was only too obvious that Chamberlain was opposed to the one thing that might have deterred Hitler: a mutual assistance pact between Britain, France and Russia. The Russians had been ostentatiously excluded from the Munich discussions. Every time they made a move towards a collective peace agreement, they were rebuffed. Thus on 18 March they proposed consultations between six foreign ministers: Soviet, British, French, Rumanian, Polish and Turkish. The Chamberlain government refused. On 17 April the Soviet government proposed a triple defensive alliance of France, Britain and the USSR; the British government took three weeks to reply, and then ignored the proposal, suggesting instead a simple guarantee to Poland. On 14 May the Soviet Union reiterated its proposal for a three-power pact and for a joint guarantee for the states bordering the USSR; on 27 May the British agreed to discuss mutual assistance, but wanted to restrict any guarantee to Poland and Rumania. By this time it was quite widely recognised that a mutual assistance pact with the Soviet Union offered the only hope of deterring Hitler from his aggressive designs and so avert war. This, indeed, was the argument put by Conservative Winston Churchill in a speech on 3 June 1939; it was reiterated in a resolution passed at the annual conference of the Labour Party at Southport which asserted that war could only be averted by pacts of mutual aid, and expressed concern at the delay in concluding such a pact with France and the Soviet Union.[13]

On 7 June it was at last announced that a Foreign Office official,

Mr William Strang, was to be sent to Moscow to discuss the proposal for a mutual aid pact between Britain, France and the Soviet Union. It soon became clear that the object of this announcement was to placate public opinion while continuing to avoid any link-up with the Soviet Union.[14]

The contrast between the behaviour towards the Russians and that towards Germany could not have been more marked. Chamberlain had personally flown to see Hitler three times within a fortnight. But when Strang left for Russia on 12 June the *Daily Worker* justly described his trip as

> a slow-motion demonstration of how to look like trying to have a pact with Russia without having it. Mr Strang, one of the Old School Ties who played in the Munich team, is about to commence to begin to get ready to start to think about considering to decide to rush off to Moscow – in a train.

It was, indeed a propaganda exercise. The weeks went by, while every kind of side issue was used by the British negotiators to drag the talks out. 'The Sands Are Running Out' was the headline in the *Daily Worker* on 23 June, alleging 'deliberate sabotage' of the negotiations. A month later it was asking 'How long, oh Lord, how long?'[15] and ten days later 'Chamberlain still stalls on pact', at which point Parliament adjourned for the recess. By this time, it was not only the Communist Party which was convinced that the object of the exercise was to leave the Soviet Union isolated if, and when, she was attacked by Hitler. The vision of Germany going to war with the Soviet Union, while Britain sat back, had always been treasured by some in high places, or so it was believed by many anti-fascists.

On 23 August, however, the Russians took a step which staggered friend and foe alike. That day a non-aggression pact with Hitler Germany was signed. It was not a mutual assistance pact or an 'alliance'. Under it, Germany and Russia undertook to refrain from attacks on one another and, if one of them were to 'become the object of warlike action on the part of a third Power', to refrain from supporting that third Power. There were also some clauses not made public at the time.

One thing became obvious on all sides: Chamberlain's policy was in ruins. There was violent reaction in the newspapers. Those which had previously been in favour of an Anglo-Soviet alliance were now bitter in their attacks on the Soviet Union. Those which had been supporters of Hitler, seeing him as a bulwark against Communism, now turned round and abused him. The *Daily Worker*, alone and very unconvincingly, argued that the non-aggression pact was a blow for peace.

The truth was that the refusal of the British to come to an agreement with the Soviet Union had left the latter with little alternative. This was indeed the point stressed by R. Palme Dutt in the September issue of *Labour Monthly*. The present dangerous situation, he wrote, arose because of the refusal to sign a pact of mutual defence with the Soviet Union. The responsibility rested with Chamberlain's policy

> which has continuously opposed and sabotaged the Peace Front, and assisted fascism and fascist aggression, because it has dreamt of playing off the fascist powers against the Soviet Union, and of solving the problems of British imperialism by diverting the attack of the fascist powers into war on the Soviet Union. The Soviet-German Non-Aggression Pact is the logical and inevitable answer to the treachery, double-dealing, sabotage of the Peace Front and counter-revolutionary war plans of British imperialism [and to] the spineless impotence, passivity, trust in Chamberlain and incapacity of leadership of the official democratic opposition in Britain and France.

The pact, he said, represented a heavy defeat for the whole Munichite camp; the supreme issue was for the labour and democratic movement to drive home the attack against Chamberlain, to secure his defeat, and to establish collaboration with the Soviet Union for a real peace system.

A few days later, Hitler attacked Poland, and on 3 September 1939 Britain declared war on Germany.

[1] The author is indebted to Allan Merson for the information concerning the Southampton dockers.
[2] *Daily Worker*, 10 March 1936.
[3] *The Times*, 23 February 1938.
[4] *Hansard*, 24 March 1938.
[5] Reprinted in *Report of Central Committee to 15th Party Congress*, pp.120–121, 129–30.
[6] *New York Times*, 14 May 1938, quoted in *Labour Research*, November 1938, p.242.
[7] *Daily Herald*, 15 September 1938.
[8] *For Peace and Plenty*, Report of 15th Congress, pp.90–91.
[9] See Maurice Cowling, *The Impact of Hitler*, Cambridge 1975 pp.197–200.
[10] *Hansard*, 28 September 1938.
[11] *Daily Worker*, 27 January 1939.

[12] *Hansard*, 21 March 1939.

[13] Labour Party Annual Report, 1939 p.240.

[14] It is now known that Chamberlain was opposed to continued negotiations with the USSR, but was obliged to let them go ahead because of the weight of opinion in the rest of the Cabinet. See Maurice Cowling, op. cit., p.303.

[15] *Daily Worker*, 20 July 1939.

CHAPTER 19

The First Weeks of the War
(1939)

On 1 September 1939 Hitler's troops invaded Poland. Some months earlier, Britain and France had declared that they would come to Poland's aid if her independence was threatened. But since neither of them had a common border with Poland, the main way in which direct aid could have become a reality was through an agreement with the Soviet Union. However, Chamberlain's government had spent months sabotaging any such agreement on the pretext that the Polish government would not allow Russian troops to enter Polish territory. It was not until 25 August, *after* the announcement of the Soviet-German Non-Aggression Pact, that an Anglo–Polish Agreement for Mutual Assistance was at last signed.

In line with this, on 1 September the French and British sent an ultimatum to Hitler stating that they would stand by their obligations to Poland unless German aggression stopped and the troops were withdrawn. The ultimatum was ignored, and on Sunday 3 September Chamberlain announced in a broadcast that Britain was at war with Germany.

An Anti-fascist War

The day before, the Central Committee of the Communist Party had published a manifesto. 'You are now being called upon to take part in the most cruel war in the history of the world,' it began.

> One that need never have taken place. One that could have been avoided . . . had we had a People's Government in Britain . . . We are in support of all necessary measures to secure the victory of democracy over fascism. But fascism will not be defeated by the Chamberlain Government.

The first and most vital step, it went on, was a new government in the hands of 'trusted representatives of the people who have neither imperialist aims, nor latent sympathies with fascism.' So it called for a war on two fronts: against fascism, and against the Chamberlain government. It listed fourteen demands for the defence of the people – including democracy for the armed forces and for colonial peoples, nationalisation of the arms industry and so forth.

By 12 September 50,000 copies of a penny pamphlet by Harry Pollitt entitled *How to Win the War* had appeared. It said: 'The Communist Party supports the war, believing it to be a "just war".' While stressing that the fundamental cause of war was the capitalist system, he emphasised that the victory of fascism would mean destruction of rights and liberties essential for the advance to socialism. Just as the Abyssinian and Spanish people had been right to fight the fascist invaders, 'so also the Polish people are right to fight against the Nazi invasion.' Taking up an argument, already being heard on the left, that the aims of the present rulers of Britain were to safeguard imperial interests, not Polish independence, he asserted that, whatever their motives, their action was helping the Polish people's fight and, for the first time, challenging Nazi aggression. Anti-fascists must be on their guard against attempts to use the war for imperialist aims; the first thing to fight for was a new government, because the 'Men of Munich' were not the enemies but the friends of fascism.

At the time this pamphlet appeared, Communist voices in some other parts of the world were delivering a very different message. On 11 September the Communist Party of the United States described the war as 'imperialist'; more important, a broadcast from Soviet Russia on 14 September referred to the war as ' "imperialist" and "predatory" on both sides.' The next day, at a meeting of the Political Bureau, R. Palme Dutt urged that the British Party's characterisation of the war as 'just' should be re-examined; but he got only small support.[1]

By the time of the next meeting of the Central Committee on 24 September, however, there had been dramatic changes on the Polish front. The German advance had been so rapid that major towns had already been captured; the Polish defence had collapsed, and on 17 September the Red Army crossed the Russian-Polish border, and within a few days had occupied the Eastern half of Poland. According to a statement issued in Moscow, the Soviet government had remained neutral until the last moment, but since the Polish state had disintegrated and its government virtually ceased to exist, it could become a fertile field for 'any accidental and unexpected contingency' which could create a menace to the Soviet Union. On 22 September a line of demarcation between the Russian and German armies was fixed; on 29 September an agreement between Germany and Russia on the partition of Poland was announced, and a joint declaration issued that it would be in the interests of all nations to stop the war.

Meanwhile, although a British Expeditionary force had been sent to France it had not been in action against the Germans. Something later to be known as the 'phoney war' period was just beginning.

When the Central Committee met on 24 September it was already known that the view of the war held at Comintern headquarters differed from that of the British Party. Nevertheless, Pollitt maintained that the general line of the 2 September manifesto was correct. He said: 'We have fought for peace and failed; we are now in the war – we cannot run away.'[2] He pointed out that the Communist International had long defined its attitude to three types of war: an imperialist war, a war for national liberation and a counter-revolutionary war against the Soviet Union, but it had not provided for a contingency like that of the present. He did not accept the argument that the present war was an imperialist war like that of 1914. For some years Communists had been saying that the second imperialist war had begun, but within this, the line had always been to support any country or people resisting fascist aggression.

Pollitt's view was challenged by R. Palme Dutt who argued forcefully that it was an imperialist war and the task of the Party was therefore to unmask its true character and mobilise opposition to those conducting it. But though, during the debate, some members expressed doubts, the majority supported Pollitt. However, that evening, Dave Springhall (who had been on the Central Committee since 1932) arrived back from Moscow where he had been acting as British representative at Comintern headquarters.[3] He informed the Central Committee that the Communist International believed the war to be an imperialist one to which the working-class movement should give no support.

The Line Changes

The Central Committee adjourned. They were, of course, in an impossible position. They could not, as on earlier occasions, appoint a delegation to go and argue the matter out in Moscow. The debate continued in the Political Bureau which, a few days later, received a short written Thesis from the Communist International stating:

> The present war is an imperialist and unjust war for which the *bourgeoisie* of all the belligerent states bear equal responsibility. In no country can the working class or the Communist Parties support the war. The *bourgeoisie* is not conducting war against fascism as Chamberlain and the leaders of the Labour Party pretend. War is carried on between two groups of imperialist countries for world domination.[4]

By the time the adjourned meeting of the Central Committee took place on 2 October, the majority of the Political Bureau had become convinced that the Comintern leaders must be right. Dutt took responsibility for moving a resolution which was identical to that adopted by the CI. Pollitt stuck to his guns, and his chief support came from Campbell who evidently thought that the Party was about to embark on the same kind of mistaken line which he had tried to resist in 1928–9, and which had been partly based on the conviction that world revolution was on the agenda. He argued that if we had the perspective of world revolution coming before fascism was defeated we might suffer the extension of fascism to Britain.[5]

There was a two-day debate, and many doubts expressed, but when the vote was taken on 3 October the resolution was adopted by 21 votes to 3, those who voted against being Pollitt, Campbell (at that time editor of the *Daily Worker*) and Gallacher. Pollitt then asked that Gallacher's name be registered as in favour of the resolution since, he explained, Gallacher did in fact accept it, but had been led by his personal feelings to vote against it.

On 4 October, the resolution was made public and on 7 October a new manifesto appeared. 'This war is not a war for democracy against Fascism,' it said:

> It is not a war for the liberties of small nations. It is not a war for the defence of peace against aggression . . . The British and French ruling class are seeking to use the anti-fascist sentiments of the people for their own imperialist aims.

Arguing that the British ruling class ('the enemies of democracy, the oppressors of the colonial peoples') had shown by their deeds that they did not stand for democracy, it said: 'This war is a fight between

imperialist powers over profits, colonies and world domination.'
For Chamberlain to pose as the man who would 'overthrow Hitler'
was a piece of colossal humbug and hypocrisy, since he and the
British reactionaries had helped to create Hitler fascism. They had
financed it and cleared the path for its aggression so long as they
believed this would be directed against the Soviet Union. The
manifesto alleged that Chamberlain had hoped that an easy Nazi
victory in Poland would lead to Germany and the Soviet Union
embroiling themselves in war. Instead, the Red Army marched,
Soviet power was advanced, and the Soviet Union was now
exerting its influence to promote peace in Western Europe. 'Let a
peace conference of the Powers be called immediately.' The
manifesto called for the election of a new government which would
carry on peace negotiations.[6]

In the October issue of the *Labour Monthly* Dutt developed the
argument that the war was the 'second imperialist war'. He made
clear his view that in analysing any war it was necessary to
distinguish the dominant factors which could be obscured by
subsidiary and seemingly conflicting trends. He admitted that

> the basic character of imperialist conflict for the redivision of the
> world appears intermingled with other factors, with questions of
> national liberation and with the question of the working class and
> democratic struggle against fascism in a tangled knot which
> requires the most careful unravelling.

But he pointed out that in the First World War, long since
characterised by Communists as an imperialist war, there were also
'myriad issues and conflicts' including national liberation struggles,
but these fell within the 'central antagonism' which was that
between British and German imperialism for the redivision of the
world.

He added that since the victory of the socialist revolution in
Russia, 'the central issue of world socialism and world capitalism
dominates all other issues'. From 1923 to 1938, he said, British
imperialism had aimed to rebuild German imperialism as the
supposed weapon against Bolshevism. 'Thereby it forged the
weapon which has been turned against itself. This is the basic cause
of the war.'

On 1 November a penny pamphlet was issued. In *Why this War?*
Dutt reaffirmed and explained the Party's new position. A few days

later was published a manifesto issued by the Executive Committee of the Communist International accompanied by a statement from Dimitrov, again asserting that the war was an imperialist one.

Meanwhile, on 11 October, it was announced that, in view of the differences of opinion, the Central Committee had decided that Harry Pollitt should not continue as General Secretary but should take on other duties. Palme Dutt then assumed the responsibilities of General Secretary. Pollitt stated that the decision was correct, and taken after discussion in which he had full opportunity to express his views. A few days later he told a miners' meeting in South Wales that 'it was a splendid thing for working men to know that the Communist Party was strong enough to depose leaders who disagreed with its policy – if the Labour Party had adopted a similar practice we should not be in the position we are today.'[7]

At the same time Campbell relinquished his job as editor of the *Daily Worker*; his post was taken over by William Rust, its first editor, who had not been back to it since 1932. Since the name of the editor was in those days never published as a protection against possible court cases, this particular change was not publicly announced. Campbell continued working at the paper, though a little later he went to Scotland. Pollitt went to work temporarily in the Manchester district.

What had happened down below in the ranks of the Party? Most Party members had initially accepted the Pollitt line of a war on two fronts. A few had rushed off and joined up, or endeavoured to do so; some, on the other hand, had disagreed with the Pollitt line. They did not express their disagreements in public – this, indeed, was not the practice, since it had always been considered necessary to adopt a united stance when facing the class enemy. But they did argue behind the scenes. One of them was Dave Priscott, then working in the naval dockyard at Portsmouth, who succeeded in winning over the Portsmouth branch to the view that it was an imperialist war before the Central Committee changed its line, and was well on the way to persuading his District Committee of the same thing.[8]

For the majority who originally accepted the Pollitt line the change announced on 4 October hardly came as a bolt from the blue. The real bombshell had been the Red Army's entry into Poland on 17 September. And though shock quickly gave way to relief that the thirteen million inhabitants of the Polish territory concerned would be protected from the Nazis and given the chance to build a new life, subsequent events had provoked uneasiness and a good deal of discussion. These included not only the Polish collapse and the joint declaration of Russia and Germany urging that the war be stopped, but the fact that the French Communist Party had been made illegal by the French government.

With air raids expected at any moment, and widespread evacuation, there was no possibility of thrashing the matter out at a special congress. Indeed, the Congress which had previously been scheduled for October had had to be called off. So the Party adopted the only practicable alternative. Directly after the new Central Committee Manifesto had been issued on 7 October, meetings were held of each District Committee and, shortly afterwards, aggregates which were attended by the vast majority of the members. And at meeting after meeting, the new line of the Central Committee was endorsed by overwhelming votes. Thus on the London District Committee, only one member, Jack Gaster, voted against; there was one abstention, while 26 voted in favour. The Scottish District Committee was unanimously in favour of the change of line, and at a Glasgow aggregate just after, attended by 400, only two voted against, and four abstained. Similar support was recorded in the North Midlands, Lancashire, Yorkshire, Wales and the Southern Counties.

Support for the Changed Line

Since that time some historians have sneered at this demonstration of support, using it to confirm their view that the Communist Party members customarily behaved like robots. Others have insisted that about one third of the Party members didn't agree, but voted with their feet and left the Party. Both these assumptions are untrue. Some did leave, as they had done, earlier, over the Soviet-German Non-Aggression pact, and later over the Finnish war. But they were few in number, and more than equalled by new members who joined. Indeed it was reported a few months later that the membership had risen from 18,000 in August 1939 to nearly 20,000 in March 1940.[9]

Many years later, some of the members of the Central Committee of that period – such as Ted Bramley and Idris Cox, District Secretaries of London and Wales respectively – expressed the opinion that the original 'war on two fronts' line had been right, and the change to 'imperialist war' was a mistake. This is not a view shared by all who were active at the time, or even necessarily of a majority.[10] But since a later generation has found it hard to understand the motives of those who so whole-heartedly supported the lead of their Central Committee after its declaration that the war was an imperialist one, it is useful to set out the main factors which influenced them.

First of all came solidarity with the Soviet Union which had called for an end to the war. The Soviet Union was the only country which had rid itself of capitalism and had been striving to build a new socialist society over the previous twenty years. The Soviet Union was not yet thought of as a strong country, but rather as one struggling to survive in the face of opposition from the entire capitalist world. If the ending of the war was in the interests of the only workers' state, it should be supported.

Secondly, the idea that any war declared by Chamberlain could be a just one was hard to swallow; it seemed obvious that he had declared war on Hitler because the latter had *stopped* acting as a useful anti-Soviet tool.

Thirdly, how could the British government pretend it was fighting for democracy when four-fifths of the people under its control throughout the Empire had no democratic rights at all, but were as much enslaved as people under a fascist régime? Indeed, organisations campaigning for colonial liberation were already protesting that India had been declared a belligerent without any consultation whatever with representatives of the Indian people.

But, more important than these last two political arguments was a deep-rooted anti-war conviction instilled by the experience of the First World War which had ended only a couple of decades earlier. It had not been, as alleged at the time, a 'war to end wars' but a struggle between imperialist powers for a redivision of the world. Before it happened, the Second International had declared that it was the duty of the working class to struggle to prevent war. But should a war break out, it was the duty of socialists to work for its speedy end, and to use the crisis produced by the war to rouse the people, and thereby hasten the downfall of the capitalist class. But when the 1914 war began, this decision had been betrayed by the British Labour leaders who, along with those of other countries, had lined up behind their respective imperialist governments. As a result, millions had gone to their deaths, while the handful of people who had taken a stand against the war – including many founders of the British Communist Party – had been imprisoned and persecuted. Since that day, the belief had grown up that the labour movement must never again fall into the trap of supporting an imperialist war.

It was not until November 1939, after most of the discussions had taken place, that the Communist International issued its public manifesto. The fact that it appeared together with a statement from Dimitrov served to reinforce opinion that the change of line was correct; if Dimitrov, the world-famous anti-fascist hero, said it was an imperialist war, it must be true.

Finally, there existed within the Party a habit of solidarity which was quite exceptional. Enemies of the Party have often portrayed this outward harmony as evidence of servile obedience to instructions from Moscow. On the contrary, the people who joined the Party were the opposite of servile; they were for the most part natural rebels who automatically questioned the orthodox attitudes they found in the world around them. But if there were fundamental disagreements with declared Party policy, it had long been the rule that you did not rush out and voice your disagreements in public; you conducted your argument within the Party organisation itself. To the outside world, you maintained unity with one another. You did not give the enemy the chance to make use of divisions in the ranks.

Once a decision was taken, it was your duty to go along with it, even if privately you disagreed; otherwise, it could split the Party. It was such motives which governed the behaviour of Pollitt and Campbell who, it was well known, had instigated and subsequently fought for the line of 'a war on two fronts' and had opposed the change to an anti-war line. Not surprisingly, their opposition had received considerable coverage in hostile newspapers. The Political Bureau – now headed by Dutt and Rust, but which at that time included Ted Bramley, Idris Cox, John Gollan, George Crane from Birmingham, Peter Kerrigan from Scotland, and Gallacher – was anxious to counter this type of publicity. So they persuaded the two to make statements admitting they had made a mistake; these appeared in the *Daily Worker* of 23 November. Pollitt said that his hatred of fascism had led to a position where he did not see the true role of British imperialism and that his strong personal feelings concerning the war in Spain had influenced his outlook, but that he now unreservedly accepted the policy of the Communist Party and the Communist International. Campbell's statement also declared his support for the new policy, saying that he had 'failed to see that the way forward for the British, no less than for the German workers, lay in a struggle with the main enemy – i.e. their own imperialists.'

Neither Pollitt nor Campbell ever really believed that their 'war on two fronts' policy had been a mistake, but they kept their counsel. In public and in private, they urged Party members who continued to think that the war-on-two-fronts policy had been right to give full support to the decision of their Central Committee in the interests of Party unity.

And that, in fact, is what happened. Most of those who still had doubts decided to stick by their Party. There was, after all, a war on; Britain could be bombed or invaded at any moment; the Party was under attack and could soon be made illegal like that of France. It was not a time for leisurely argument and debate. So, the solidarity within the British Party, which Manuilsky had joked about ten years earlier, in practice paid off; it guaranteed its survival and, indeed, its growth in the most difficult years of its existence.

[1] See John Attfield and Stephen Williams (eds.), *1939: The Communist Party and the War*, London 1984, pp.26, 53.
[2] John Mahon, *Harry Pollitt*, London 1976, p.250.
[3] Mahon, op. cit., p.251. But there is some evidence that Springhall may have returned a week later than this – see Ted Bramley in Attfield and Williams (eds.), op. cit., p.84.
[4] Ibid., pp.166–7.
[5] Ibid., p.162.
[6] Ibid., p.169.
[7] John Mahon, op. cit., p.252.
[8] Attfield and Williams (eds.), op. cit., pp.99–109.
[9] *The Communist Party in War Time*, pamphlet published March 1940, p.20.
[10] See Attfield and Williams (eds.), op. cit., pp.49–78 and 113–38.

CHAPTER 20

'Phoney War'
(1939–40)

During the first weeks of the war, a black-out was enforced, and millions of children were evacuated. But there were no air raids, and a British Expeditionary Force, which had taken over part of the front in France, did not appear to be doing anything. It was the beginning of what came to be known as the 'phoney war'.

There was a sensational rise in prices, and employers seized the opportunity to undermine wages and recognised conditions. 'All quiet – but not on the home front' was Gallacher's comment in a pamphlet *The War and the Workers* which sold 32,000 copies in a few weeks.

It was assumed by the Labour leaders that the membership of the Communist Party would crumble as a result of its anti-war stance. Herbert Morrison – always the leading anti-Communist crusader on the Labour Party's executive – declared in an article in *London News* that the CP's revision of policy would spell its doom: members would now be leaving it in large numbers. 'Facts tell a different story,' replied the *Daily Worker* on the 6 November. It reported that the North Midlands District had recruited 82 new members during October; Sheffield had made 22, Nottingham, 18 and over 30 had joined in South East Lancashire. A few days later, on 10 November, it recorded an increase in membership in the South Midlands: 30 new recruits had joined in Swindon, 10 in Oxford and a new branch had been formed in South Berkshire. During the early months of 1940 the rise in membership continued, particularly in Scotland and the Midlands, and was stated in March 1940 to be 'close to 20,000'.[1]

The growth in membership was accompanied by a rise in sales of Party publications. Malcolm Dunbar, then circulation manager of the *Daily Worker*, reported that the daily readership in January 1940 was 15,000 higher than it had been in January 1939.[2] Sales of the *Labour Monthly*, edited by Dutt, rose from 7,000 a month in September 1939 to 14,700 in March 1940 and to 20,000 by the end of that year, despite a total ban on exports.[3]

One explanation for the growth in membership and sales was undoubtedly the deep-rooted anti-war conviction that had dominated the minds of many Labour Party and trade-union activists ever since the 1914–18 war. As shown in the last chapter, when the 1914 war broke out, the British Labour leaders, along with those of other countries, had supported their respective imperialist governments. In later years anti-war campaigners looked back on this as a terrible betrayal of the cause of peace.

In 1939, it seemed to many such campaigners that the Labour leaders were doing the same. They had declared their support for the war, despite the fact that the Chamberlain government – the 'Men of Munich', the friends of Hitler – were still running the country. And they had agreed on an electoral truce whereby the Conservative and Labour Parties would not nominate candidates in by-elections for seats previously held by the other party. Though Labour's NEC emphasised that this electoral truce was not a 'political truce' it was widely referred to as such by worried Labour Party members.[4]

The result was that, from mid-October 1939 onwards the *Daily Worker* was regularly reporting anti-war resolutions passed by local Labour Parties, trades councils and trade union branches. By the end of the year, such resolutions had come from 84 Labour Party organisations, 24 trades councils, 97 other trade-union organisations, and 31 co-operative organisations.[5]

The trade union resolutions were mainly from branches, but the following Easter, both the Shop Assistants' Union and the National Union of Clerks supported motions at their annual conferences demanding the cessation of the war.

Among the co-operative organisations were a number of Women's Co-operative Guilds. The guild movement had long ago taken up a pacifist position, and there was an underlying belief that efforts to stop the war should be supported. But this view was by no means confined to woman co-operators.

At its quarterly meetings held in January 1940, the London Co-operative Society registered a vote of 1,063 opposing the war against 509 in support of it.

In this climate of opinion, meetings called by the Communist Party were receiving unexpected support. An example of this was the quite unprecedented success of a *Labour Monthly* conference held in London on 25 February 1940. 878 delegates came to it representing 379 organisations; among the latter were 132 trade-union organisations, 12 Labour Party organisations, and 32 co-operative organisations. As R. Palme Dutt said, the response to the conference had taken even the organisers by surprise and 'shows the deep desire of the rank and file of the labour movement to end the present bankruptcy and passivity.' The conference adopted a resolution stating that 'this war does not serve and cannot be made to serve, any interest or aspiration of the people' and went on to declare that the ruling class was saddling the masses of the people with the burdens of war through

> iniquitous taxes, higher prices without compensating wage increases, retrenchment in the social services, lengthened hours and suspension of Factory Act regulations and by the replacement of men by women employed at lower rates of pay.[6]

The trade-union leaders of course took action against those local trade-union bodies which refused to toe the line.

> Certain large trade unions, whose officials prefer flourishing the big stick to indulging in argument, are threatening to withhold affiliation fees from any Trades Council or local Labour Party which dares to come out against the war,

observed J.R. Campbell in February 1940.[7]

The threat was carried out by the Transport and General Workers' Union (of which Ernest Bevin was still secretary) in the case of the four biggest Scottish Trades Councils: Glasgow, Edinburgh, Aberdeen, and Dundee.[8] And, according to the TUC General Council's report for 1939–40, action was taken against twenty English trades councils which had been involved in 'disruptive activities' or associated with 'disruptive bodies'.[9]

The Russo-Finnish War

The anti-war views of Labour activists were not, as a whole, shared by the ordinary Labour voter. As Dutt himself pointed out, 'In our fight we have so far only reached the vanguard.'[10] And though, during the first three months of the war, the jingoism which had prevailed in 1914 was conspicuous by its absence, Communists found themselves the target of much hostility when, on 30 November 1939, Russian troops invaded Finland.

The purpose of this action was to protect Leningrad which was only twenty miles from the Finnish border and could be shelled from Finnish territory should the war spread to the Baltic states. The Russians regarded this as a potential threat, and asked the Finns to move the border back a little and to lease them a naval base north of the gulf of Finland to enable them to protect the sea route to Leningrad. In exchange they offered the transfer to Finland of extensive Russian territories further north. The Finns refused and, after a frontier incident, the Russians invaded. Simultaneously, they announced the formation of a so-called 'People's Government' at Terijoki, a few miles inside the Finnish border, thereby revealing a remoteness from reality reminiscent of the Class against Class period. This 'Peoples' Government' was headed by Otto Kuusinen, the Finnish representative on the ECCI.

Unlike the invasion of Poland, this was no walkover. Those Finns who thought the Russian proposals moderate and understandable and favoured accommodation with them (and there were such) could no longer argue their case.[11] The Finnish forces put up a strong resistance, and only acknowledged defeat on 4 March 1940, after the Russians had broken through the network of powerful fortifications known as the 'Mannerheim line'. A Peace Treaty was then signed giving the Russians far more territory than they had originally asked for. The so-called 'Peoples' Government' disappeared from view.

The behaviour of the Chamberlain government during the Finnish episode reinforced the view of Communists in Britain that its object was not to fight Hitler's Germany but to fight the Soviet Union. Both during and after the German invasion of Poland there had been no attempt to mount an attack on Germany from the West; on the contrary, the British Expeditionary Force in France appeared to be doing nothing at all. By contrast, when the Russians invaded Finland, the British government took immediate action. Large supplies of planes, guns, bombs and military equipment were sent to the Finnish forces. The Foreign Enlistment Act, which had been used against those who wanted to fight for Republican Spain, was now employed for an opposite purpose: to entice volunteers to fight the Russians. Under a special licence, a recruiting office was established in London and a British Major allowed to resign his commission in the British army in order to take charge of the volunteers. At the same time, a joint Franco-British expeditionary force was assembled from among men already conscripted for the

war against Germany; it comprised 100,000 men, but was delayed
from setting off partly because of the refusal of the Norwegian and
Swedish governments to authorise its passage across their
territories. Steps were taken to enlist the co-operation of the two
fascist dictators: Mussolini of Italy (who had yet to come into the
war) and General Franco of Spain. As Dutt observed: 'In this line-
up, the pretences of "war against fascism" are dropped.'[12]

Within the Communist Party there was no argument. Whatever
their differences had been concerning the war against Hitler, it was
beyond any question that the Soviet Union, the first socialist state
in the world, must be supported in her attempt to protect herself.
'Now once more the capitalist world is being mobilised against the
bastion of socialism,' wrote Emile Burns, and added: 'The attitude
to the Soviet Union is the ultimate test of where men stand.'[13]

The Party issued pamphlets and other material showing that
General Mannerheim, who was in charge of the Finnish forces, had
in 1918 put down a revolutionary uprising with the help of the
German Kaiser's army, and had slaughtered some 15,000 men,
women and children; subsequently, he had joined the West in its war
of intervention against Soviet Russia. Since then, the Finnish
economy had been dominated by British and American-owned
companies, while the Finnish Communist Party had been
consistently persecuted and its members arrested.

The *Daily Worker* was the only national newspaper to attack the
Chamberlain government's actions in support of the Finnish forces.
'Planes to "fight Hitler" diverted to fight Red Army' was the
headline on 8 December 1939:

> It is now admitted that British workers who have been asked to
> accept dilution and excessive overtime for the alleged purpose of
> beating Hitler have really been making armaments for the White
> Guards of General Mannerheim.

The *Daily Worker* was the first paper to expose the preparations
for recruiting volunteers, and as early as 31 January was asking
whether regular troops were going to be sent to Finland –
preparations for such a move had been hidden from the public.

During all this time, the newspapers were carrying on a violent
anti-Soviet campaign, expressing a good deal more hatred for the
Russians than had ever been directed at the Nazis. Labour's *Daily
Herald* was, if anything, more virulent in its abuse of the Soviet

Union than any other paper. The National Council of Labour had early on given it the go-ahead; on 7 December it had issued a call to the 'free nations of the world to give every practicable aid to the Finnish nation in its struggle to preserve its own institutions of civilisation and democracy.'[14]

In response, Emile Burns recalled the support given by the Labour leaders for non-intervention in Spain, and asked: 'Is this a change of policy now? No, it is the same policy as in 1936. It is the policy of following the lead of the British imperialist government.'[15] An official delegation, which included the Secretary of the TUC, Sir Walter Citrine, went to Finland, and on its return published a report expressing the belief that the Finns could have continued the struggle for much longer had they received more adequate supplies of armaments and greater numbers of volunteers. 'We believe that the Finns had a right to such assistance,' said the report.[16]

In such an atmosphere, Communist Party members were subject to a good deal of abuse, particularly when standing at street corners selling the *Daily Worker*. In February 1940, when the war with Finland was at its height, Harry Pollitt stood as Communist candidate in a by-election for the solid Labour seat of Silvertown in East London. There were some demonstrations of hostility and he received only 966 votes – just over 6 per cent of the poll. In the circumstances it was perhaps surprising that he got as many as he did.

Whatever the attitude of Labour voters as a whole, there were some on the left of the Labour Party who disagreed with the official line on the Finnish war. The University Labour Federation, at its annual conference in January 1940, voted by 49 votes to 9 for a resolution condemning the war against Germany as 'imperialist' and, by 46 votes to 5, expressed support for the action of the Soviet Union over Finland, stating that defence of the Soviet Union was of vital importance to the cause of world socialism and that the action had been taken 'to defend itself and that cause against the threat of capitalist intervention'.[17]

The ULF was among the Socialist Societies affiliated to the Labour Party. Its Honorary President was D. N. Pritt MP, a member of the Labour Party National Executive Committee and author of two books, published as Penguin Specials, *Light on Moscow* and *Must the War Spread?* which had earned the disapproval of the right wing. Soon after its Conference the Labour Party NEC took action. The ULF was disaffiliated and D. N. Pritt was expelled from the Labour Party on the grounds that 'he has shown himself to be in violent opposition to the declared policy of the Party on the question of the Russian invasion of Finland.'[18] The Executive action was endorsed at the Labour Party Annual Conference on 15 May 1940.

The Party and Industrial Struggles 1939–40

Building an anti-war movement among ordinary people was proving to be uphill work. By contrast, developing struggle on bread and butter issues offered quite new opportunities. The British Party had always in theory given priority to work-place organisation, and, after the war broke out, this approach was rewarded with quite unprecedented results.

The background to this was a growing resentment against employers who, as the Party constantly alleged, were engaged in a deliberate attempt to make the workers pay for the war while their own profits were protected and indeed greatly increased. On top of the discomforts caused by rationing and shortage of coal during one of the coldest winters for many a year, there had been a sharp rise in prices for which certain meagre wage increases failed to compensate. The employers imposed longer hours, breaking down established customs. Factory Act regulations were being suspended; the black-out regulations in factories meant lack of ventilation and discomfort; most skilled engineers were up against 'dilution' – the term given to the practice of allocating part of a skilled man's job to a woman or youth at much lower rates of pay. And, in all this, the trade union leaders appeared to be collaborating. As Arthur Upton put it in *Labour Monthly* in April 1940, 'the trade union leaders . . . because of their support for the war, have long since abandoned the defence of their members interests.'

Soon after the war started, D. F. Springhall (then National Organiser for the Party) reminded members that one of the principal factors enabling Russian Bolsheviks to overcome difficulties during the 1914–18 war had been their influence among workers in the factories. He stressed the need for the Party to build up factory groups, stating that in this respect there was considerable unevenness between Districts. 'London, with its 150 factory groups has far too big a lead on all others.' But even in London, he said, there were important 'localities literally abounding with factories where the Party has little or no contact.'

Springhall's article, which appeared in the *Party Organiser* for December 1939, was accompanied by another from Finlay Hart, the Party's Industrial Organiser, on workplace organisation. Admitting that there had been a considerable growth in Communist influence in the trade unions, and that many Communists had been elected to leading positions, while growing numbers had represented their branches and districts at national conferences, he pointed out that

> in very few instances can it be said that the influence of the Party has overcome the influence of the right-wing reactionary leadership that dominates the movement.

One result of this was that while most unions allowed within their rules for shop stewards, card stewards and collectors to function at the workplace 'most of them discourage active association with the shop stewards of other unions on a workshop basis.' Finlay Hart argued:

> This disunity of the trade unions on the job is the curse of the British trade union movement. It not only aggravates the rivalries between the unions, but strengthens the hands of the employers and the most reactionary trade union officials.

The *Daily Worker* emphasised the same theme. On 18 November 1939 an article by Wal Hannington (who was soon to make his way back into the engineering industry) urged the development of shop-stewards organisation in the factories and the co-ordination of the movement on a national basis.

As shown in Chapter 13, the Party had been the driving force during the 1930s in the creation of a shop-stewards movement in the aircraft industry. After September 1939 the imposition of disagreeable – and in some cases unacceptable – wartime working conditions had provoked much anger. At a meeting of representatives from aircraft factories called by the Aircraft Shop Stewards' National Council (ASSNC) in November 1939, it was reported that there had already been overtime embargoes, sit downs and go-slow movements. The influence of the ASSNC was clearly growing, and by December 1939 the circulation of its monthly journal *New Propellor* (still edited by Peter Zinkin) had reached

31,000.[19]

Early in 1940 came a major new development. The frontier between the aircraft sector and the rest of the engineering industry was increasingly hard to define, and in recognition of this it was decided at a meeting of aircraft shop stewards on 18 February 1940 to convene a conference with the aim of linking together shop stewards in all sections of the engineering industry. This conference took place on 6–7 April 1940 in Birmingham; it was attended by 283 delegates from 107 factories, and resulted in the setting up of the Engineering and Allied Trades Shop Stewards' National Council, thus merging those in aircraft factories with those in other sectors. The stated aims of the new National Council were to secure 100 per cent trade unionism in every plant, mutual co-operation between the various trade unions in each factory by the election of shop stewards in every section (who would hold regular Works Committee meetings) and the co-ordination of shop steward activity throughout the industry. Shortly after, the circulation of *New Propellor* rose to 45,000, and Len Powell, a well-known Communist, became the new National Council's full-time secretary.[20]

The Conference was almost entirely devoted to the practical issues of the workshop floor: wages, conditions, hours of work, the problem of 'dilution', the need to establish 100 per cent trade unionism, and so forth. A special statement on the position of women affirmed the principle of equal pay for equal work, stating that women substituting for men must receive the same rate for the job as men. It proclaimed the need to recruit women into the unions and to secure their election as shop stewards and their participation in meetings of work committees. It was resolved to 'campaign within the AEU for its ranks to be opened to females.' This had long been the declared aim of the Communist Party – in the event it took another two years to persuade the men in the AEU to admit women into their union.

There were no resolutions denouncing the war as 'imperialist'. In short, unity in the fight against the employers between all workers, whatever their views on the war, was the aim. However, in one place the main resolution did criticise the Executive Committees of the main unions involved without actually naming them. Speaking of the current struggle to defend standards and prevent the victimisation of active trade unionists it said:

In most cases, the efforts of the trade unionists are not supported
by the Executives, whose policy of support for this war has caused
them to abandon the defence and advancement of the members'
interests. Their policy endangers the very existence of our trade
unions.[21]

The Executive Council of the Amalgamated Engineering Union
(the largest union in the industry) was anxious to put a stop to these
developments, and three months later some fourteen shop stewards
were summoned to the AEU headquarters to answer charges that,
by attending the conference, they had rendered themselves liable to
expulsion from the union under its rules. They were accused of 'acts
detrimental to the interests of the AEU, of attempting to form a new
union, and fomenting strikes.'[22]

The preliminary answer to these allegations, published in *New
Propellor* was, firstly, that their policy and actions had been to *assist*
the trade unions; secondly, that the Shop Stewards' Council had
always rejected any proposals to form a new union, and thirdly that
the charge of 'fomenting strikes' was 'absurd.'

Among the Party members thus threatened with expulsion were
George Crane, a former convenor at Rovers in Birmingham – he had
been on the Communist Party Central Committee since 1935;
Edmund Frow, a member of the Manchester AEU District
Committee; Tom Sillars, a member of the Glasgow AEU District
Committee; Charlie Wellard, formerly convenor at Siemens.

The AEU Executive, however, committed one major blunder in
their attempt to use the Birmingham Conference to rid themselves
of a left-wing challenge. Among those summoned and threatened
with explusion was Joe Scott, who had not been at the Birmingham
Conference at all. Scott, who had also served on the Party Central
Committee, had in the summer of 1939 been nominated for a seat
on the Executive Council of AEU; the union officials at
headquarters had disqualified him from standing on a technicality.
Scott had taken legal action, and won his case, the Judge ruling that
no ballot could take place without his name being included. The
ballot had been indefinitely postponed, and the seat left vacant.

Confronting the AEU Executive Council, Scott made a lengthy
defence of the Birmingham Conference on behalf of the fourteen

threatened with expulsion, and then destroyed the Executive's case against him personally by proving that he had not been at the Birmingham Conference himself. After this embarrassment, the Executive Council refrained from pressing its charges against any of the other members, all of whom continued with their trade-union activities as before.[23]

[1] *The Communist Party in War Time*, op. cit. See also Chapter 22 below.

[2] *Daily Worker*, 12 February 1940. But see also the Poutney papers which provide figures of *weekly* sales for the period January 1939 to May 1940. These show that the average weekly sale was 308,000 in January 1939 and 362,000 in January 1940. There is no indication of how many were daily and how many weekend sales.

[3] See *Labour Monthly*, January 1941, p. 2.

[4] *Labour Party Annual Report 1940*, p. 19.

[5] *Daily Worker*, 27 December 1939. Angus Calder, in *The People's War*, London 1969, reports that over 70 Constituency Labour Parties were supporting the call for a truce by the end of November 1939. On paper there were 600 Constituency Parties but many of them were quite inactive; asked to make a survey of local activities, soon after the war broke out, 400 did so. (See *Labour Party Annual Report 1940*, p. 27.)

[6] *Labour Monthly*, March 1940, pp. 134, 137.

[7] *Labour Monthly*, February 1940.

[8] See *The Communist Party in War Time*, p. 14.

[9] The trades councils listed were: Bermondsey, Bethnal Green, Hammersmith, Hampstead, Islington, Paddington, Lambeth, Sheffield, Stepney, Southall, which had to be 'reorganised'; those trades councils which were made to bring themselves into conformity with the rules were named as: Bournemouth, Bromley (Kent), Croydon, Finchley, Hebden Bridge, Lincoln, Oxford, Shoreditch and Yeovil. *TUC Report 1940*, pp. 108 320-2.

[10] *Labour Monthly*, March 1940, p. 148.

[11] See Alexander Werth, *Russia at War*, London 1965, p. 84.

[12] *Labour Monthly*, March 1940, p. 137.

[13] Emile Burns, *The Soviet Union and Finland*, pamphlet published January 1940, p. 15.

[14] *Labour Party Annual Report 1940*, p. 13.

[15] *The Soviet Union and Finland*, p. 9.

[16] *Labour Party Annual Report 1940*, p. 14. See also Walter Citrine, *My Finnish Diary*, Harmondsworth 1940.

[17] *World News & Views*, 27 January 1940, p. 50.

[18] *Labour Party Annual Report 1940*, p. 20. See D. N. Pritt, *Light on Moscow. Soviet Policy Analysed*, Harmondsworth 1940, and *Must the War Spread?*, Harmondsworth 1940.

[19] *New Propellor*, December 1939.

[20] *New Propellor*, May 1940.

[21] *New Propellor*, April 1940.

[22] *New Propellor*, August 1940.

[23] For an account of this episode see Edmund and Ruth Frow, op. cit., pp. 147-8.

CHAPTER 21

Real War: the Party Under Threat (1940)

In April 1940 the 'phoney war' came to an end, and real war began. Following attempts by the British to lay mines along the Norwegian coast, the Germans invaded Denmark and seized certain Norwegian ports. Thereupon, British troops were landed in Norway, but they were soon forced by superior German strength to withdraw. As a result of this fiasco, Neville Chamberlain was obliged to resign as Prime Minister; he was replaced by Winston Churchill on 10 May. At the same time, the Labour leaders were asked to join the government, a proposal for which Attlee secured the agreement of the Labour Party annual conference, despite the fact that Chamberlain remained in the Cabinet.

The invasion of Norway was only the prelude. In May, the Germans swept through Holland and Belgium, both of which had declared themselves neutral at the outbreak of the war; within a few days they had surrendered and the Germans had crossed into France and mounted a drive towards the Channel ports. By the end of May, the bulk of the British Expeditionary Force had been cut off and over 330,000 men (including many French) had to be rescued from Dunkirk, an operation in which hundreds of small boats, sailed by the owners, took part. The men were saved, but practically all their heavy equipment, including hundreds of tanks, was left behind. The Germans continued their advance into France; by 14 June they had reached Paris. M. Renaud, the French Prime Minister, wanted to go on fighting, but the majority of his Cabinet colleagues were against him; Marshall Petain took over as Prime Minister, and invited the Germans to conclude an armistice. By the end of the month, France was out of the war; simultaneously, Mussolini's Italy came into the war on Germany's side.

It was clear that, once France, Britain's only ally, had been eliminated, the invasion of Britain could be close at hand. In fact, as is now known, Hitler had planned to invade, but postponed action, partly because of the failure of the Luftwaffe to deprive the

RAF of air superiority. As it was, the months of July and August saw mounting air combat over South East England, which was to culminate in the 'blitz' on London in September 1940.

Meanwhile, following the formation of the Churchill government in May, a new Emergency Powers (Defence) Act was passed, and many new Defence Regulations were introduced. One of these, Regulation 18B, was used to detain without trial Sir Oswald Mosley and over 700 members of the British Union of Fascists. However, it seemed possible that the government might use it to detain Communists. Another Regulation, 2D, threatened the future of the *Daily Worker* since it enabled the Home Secretary to suppress any newspaper which was systematically fomenting opposition to the war.

The Party's New Approach

To British Communists the French capitulation lent support to the view that this was not a war for democracy or liberty. For in France, the determination of the government to smash the Communist Party had been made plain even before the war broke out. As soon as the German-Soviet Non-Aggression Pact was signed in August 1939, the widely-read French Party newspaper, *L'Humanité*, had been suppressed. Despite the fact that the French Party – like the British Party – had initially expressed support for the war on 2 September 1939, many arrests of Communists had followed, and on 26 September the French Party had been declared illegal. After this Communist MPs (of whom there were seventy) were imprisoned or went into hiding, while hundreds of trade unions under Communist leadership were dissolved. All this had helped to strengthen the view within the British Party that the war was not one which workers should support. 'France on the Road to Fascism' had been the title of an article by Richard Goodman appearing in *Labour Monthly* as early as November 1939. In this, the author claimed that the events leading to the suppression of the French Party furnished 'unanswerable proof that the present war is not a war "against fascism".'

However, in June 1940 it became clear to the British Party that the threat of invasion called for a change in emphasis in their political approach. So long as the opposing forces were sitting behind their respective fortifications doing nothing, the denunciation of the war as 'imperialist' and the simple demand to end it, had seemed appropriate and had, indeed, commanded much support. Now such a call began to appear unrealistic. In fact, Pollitt's original line of 'a war on two fronts', in other words to try to bring down a reactionary government so as to conduct a real fight against the fascist aggressors, would have fitted the situation much more adequately. Nobody suggested that the Pollitt line should be revived, but it was all the same necessary to make clear that Communists were *not* in favour of surrender to Hitler – something of which they were frequently accused.

On 22 June 1940, the Central Committee issued a new manifesto calling for a People's Government that could guarantee the defeat both of the Nazi menace and of the danger threatened by the British representatives of fascism. 'The French catastrophe is the final warning,' it said. 'The same kind of leaders who brought France to defeat are in high places in Britain.' It said that the interests of the people required 'the speediest ending of the war, not by surrender to fascism at home and abroad, but by the strength of a free people organising their own defence.'

The gist of this manifesto was reproduced in a leaflet headed 'The People Must Act'. This called for a 'New Government' really representative of working people. The most urgent need, it said, was to

> clear out all supporters of fascism, the men of Munich . . . from all commanding positions. Secure the election of Workers' Control Committees in the factories. Arm the workers in the factories. Let the British workers take the destiny of their class and of Britain into their own strong hands. Only then can the danger of fascist invasion and tyranny be successfully withstood.

The call for the removal of the 'Men of Munich' commanded much support during the summer of 1940. The *Daily Worker* began to list organisations which had passed resolutions declaring that all those associated with the pre-war appeasement policy should go. Among them was the National Union of Railwaymen at its annual conference and the four district committees of the Amalgamated Engineering Union in the key war production centres of London, Sheffield, Birmingham and Glasgow. Sir Walter Citrine, General Secretary of the TUC, denounced the campaign against the 'Men of

THE PEOPLE MUST ACT

The appalling catastrophe that has befallen the French people is a final warning to us. We must learn the lesson or go under.

The same kind of leaders who brought France to defeat are in high places in Britain. They have the same record, policy and aims as those who are responsible for Hitler's victory over France.

The real defence of the people requires a complete break with the interests of the ruling class. The policy of the ruling class has led to disaster after disaster. Today the people are threatened with further disaster or an endless prolongation of the war.

Only the organised working class can lead and save the people. The responsibility falls on the Labour movement to break the present alliance of the leaders with the representatives of big business, and to lead the people in the present emergency.

The Labour movement must exert all its tremendous force and power to save the people of Britain from Fascism and the friends of Fascism.

A NEW GOVERNMENT

A new Government must come to power now, a Government really representative of the working people, a Government in which there shall be no representative of imperialism or friend of Fascism.

The Communist Party calls on all workers in the factories, trade unions, local Labour Parties and Co-operative Guilds to get together and develop such a mighty mass movement as can secure the formation of such a Government.

It can be done. It must be done. It is the only way for the people to preserve their independence and democratic institutions, and save themselves from the fate that has overtaken the people of France.

Let the British workers take the destiny of their class and of Britain into their own strong hands.

Only then can the danger of Fascist invasion and tyranny be successfully withstood.

Only then can a real People's Peace be established in Europe.

We of the Communist Party, who have consistently fought for the real defence and interests of the people, who have consistently given

(P.T.O.

Munich', but his opposition made little impression.[1] A book by Ivor Montagu entitled *The Traitor Class* appeared in September 1940. Within a month it had sold 10,000 copies and had to be reprinted.

The campaign against the 'Men of Munich' was supported by many who wanted to fight the war against Hitler, and this caused concern among certain of the Party's leaders who feared that it might lead to confusion over the attitude to the war. A letter from the Political Bureau sent out to branches on 15 July 1940 pointed out that the call for the removal of the Men of Munich was being voiced 'on other grounds than ours', and that among the shortcomings of the Party's campaign were 'tendencies to national defencism'. This had led to speculation inside the Party as to whether the line had changed: 'Such speculations are without foundation.'

Dutt at this time continually stressed the fact that despite the new turn in the war, it must still be regarded as one between imperialist powers. Pointing out that the 'new German Empire holds Europe in its grip', he said: 'The British Empire and the new German Empire now confront one another in the final conflict for world power'.[2] And Rust, in a somewhat critical review of Ivor Montagu's book, argued that the title 'traitor class' could be misinterpreted to mean that the ruling class were acting as traitors instead of carrying on a real People's War against fascism. The fact was that

> the war marked a turning point in international relationships, as a result of which the division of states into fascist and 'democratic' lost its former sense and the rival imperialists entered the path of open conflict in the struggle for world domination.[3]

The Party argued that if the British workers defeated their own ruling class, this would encourage the German workers to bring down Hitler. Indeed, in this respect they continued to think of the war in terms of 1914–18 rather than 1940. 'I am not for capitulation before Hitler or any other section of the capitalist class', Arthur Horner said to the 1940 Trades Union Congress, but he went on:

> I ask you, who in the end is to destroy Hitler – British arms from without or German workers from within? Who destroyed the Kaiser? The German workers, the German sailors, the German soldiers . . .[4]

This hope and belief that the Germans would rise against Hitler remained with British Party members right to the end of the war.

The extent to which Hitler had conquered the hearts and minds of the German working class, partially recognised during the Seventh World Congress, was never fully appreciated until the end of the war.[5]

That summer the Party leaders decided that the time had come to bring together all those outside the Party who were prepared to support the call for a 'People's Government'. Those local Labour Parties who opposed the war had been defeated at Labour's annual conference in May, and some had been disaffiliated. Among them was the Hammersmith Borough Trades Council and Labour Party which had continued its support for the expelled MP for North Hammersmith, D. N. Pritt. Now, after some informal discussions with Pritt and Harry Adams (London organiser of the Amalgamated Union of Building Trade Workers), a 'provisional committee' was formed which, jointly with the Hammersmith Trades Council, sponsored a conference at the Holborn Hall in London on 7 July 1940. The conference, which was unexpectedly well attended, set up a 'People's Vigilance Committee'. Besides Pritt and Adams, the Committee included W. J. R. Squance (former Secretary of the railwaymen's union, ASLEF) and Councillor Skilbeck (the London organiser of the Woodworkers' Union). Its stated aims were five: 1) the 'Men of Munich' to be driven out of office; 2) friendship with the USSR; 3) re-establishment of democratic rights; 4) defence of living standards and ending of profiteering; 5) 'a new government really representative of the people of Britain must come to power and provide the essential conditions of a real and enduring People's Peace.'[6]

The movement started in London, but soon spread to other towns, and became known as 'The People's Convention'. The response of the Labour leaders was speedy. Adams, Squance, and Skilbeck were all expelled from the Labour Party, while the People's Convention was outlawed as a Communist organisation.

The *Daily Worker* also took steps to broaden its base. The paper had always functioned as the organ of the Communist Party. The name of the editor had never been published, a practice which, as we have seen, was intended as a safeguard against prosecution. Actually, the identity of the editor – at this time William Rust – was always well-known to everyone in the Party. But in June 1940, for the first time, four of its best known contributors were invited to serve on an editorial board and their names were made public. The chairman was Professor J. B. S. Haldane, the scientist, who had long contributed regular articles to the paper, and had led the campaign for bomb-proof shelters. The other three were Robin Page Arnot, who had previously served for many years on the Party's Central Committee and was well-known as a Marxist lecturer and writer; Jack Owen, a Manchester engineer and Labour councillor of long standing (he was, of course, immediately expelled from the Labour Party); and Sean O'Casey, the celebrated Irish playwright. He said of the *Daily Worker*:

> It is in my opinion the only fearless and unpurchasable means by which the workers can make known their needs, their oppression and their resolution . . . It struggles against odds of ten thousand to one, against a multitudinous press devoted to the privileges and profits of a few. It stands like a ragged David facing a gold-plated Goliath . . . Its heart is a band of men and women, mostly young, whose eyes see a vision without which the people perish.[7]

The new editorial board members were well aware that if steps were taken against the *Daily Worker* under the new regulation 2D they might bear the brunt of any prosecution. They did not have long to wait before the government took action.

Government Moves Against the Party

Behind the scenes discussion was going on in government circles on whether or not to ban Communist propaganda. On 4 July Sir John Anderson, the Home Secretary, told the War Cabinet that a 'leaflet recently issued by the Communist Party and widely distributed was clearly designed to discredit the government and was calculated to foment opposition to the successful prosecution of the war.' (He was, of course, referring to the leaflet with the heading 'The People Must Act'.) Anderson thought that distribution of this leaflet ought to be stopped but that it would be 'both wrong and ineffective' to suppress it without also taking action against the *Daily Worker*. So he proposed making an Order under Regulation 2D prohibiting that paper. In the Cabinet there was some support for Anderson's proposal, but doubts were also expressed. According to the minutes:

> Ministers thought that it might well be unfortunate to suppress the *Daily Worker* at this juncture, since there was some feeling of

alarm in the country lest the government intended to suppress any expression of free criticism as had been done in France, with unfortunate results.[8]

The next day, this time with the Prime Minister present, the arguments were repeated, Anderson saying that if he stopped distribution of the leaflets but did not also suppress the *Daily Worker* he was open to a charge of inconsistency; others arguing that

> public opinion was, at the moment very sensitive in the matter of free speech. This was probably due, first, to the example of France, where rigid censorship had been followed by collapse.

In the end the cabinet agreed that distribution of the leaflet 'The People Must Act' should be stopped but that the *Daily Worker* should be given preliminary *warning* only; it should not be suppressed for the moment.[9]

So it was that on 12 July the *Daily Worker* received its warning in a letter from the Home Office which said:

> I am directed by the Secretary of State to say that he has had under consideration the question whether an order ought to be made against the *Daily Worker* under Defence Regulation 2D on the grounds that there is in that newspaper a systematic publication of matter calculated to foment opposition to the prosecution of the war to a successful issue.

The letter went on to say that Sir John Anderson, the Home Secretary, hoped that 'the paper is so conducted in future that it will not be necessary for him to take action under this Regulation.'

As chairman of the editorial board, Professor Haldane wrote back asking to which items in the *Daily Worker* the Home Secretary referred. In reply, he received a further letter saying that the Secretary of State could not attempt to give guidance by reference to particular items. Commenting on this, Haldane said:

> When I received his warning letter, I naturally asked which items he alleged were calculated to interfere with the war effort. The Home Office refused to tell me. Now this is something new in England. In the past, we have had some savage laws. Rebels were hanged, drawn and quartered. Heretics were burned. But at least evidence was called against them, and they were told what were their alleged treasonable acts and heretical statements. Sir John

Anderson has introduced a new principle into English law, a principle borrowed from Hitler and Mussolini.

What is the *Daily Worker*'s real crime? A very serious one indeed. It is the only daily newspaper which opposes the government.

Sean O'Casey poked fun at the Home Office language. 'It would be well if we got an explanation, or even a clue, to the meaning of "a matter calculated to foment opposition to the prosecution of the war to a successful issue",' he wrote. 'This seems to be Harrowing English, known only to a chosen few'. But he concluded that 'out of the cloudy gathering of words shoots out the order that the chosen ones are not to be criticised.'[10]

As some Cabinet ministers had anticipated, Defence Regulation 2D caused concern among many who feared that free speech would be undermined. The Central London branch of the National Union of Journalists called for it to be amended, and at a well-attended conference convened by the National Council for Civil Liberties on 21 July 1940, a resolution was passed demanding its withdrawal. Two Labour MPs, Sydney Silverman and Rhys Davies, denounced it as a 'danger to liberty', and when, on 31 July, the former moved an amendment to it in the Commons, he received support from a wide section of MPs. The Regulation was endorsed by only 98 votes to 60.

In this debate Gallacher said:

My idea of the successful issue of the war is freedom – freedom for the people of Europe and for the colonial people. Is that the conception of the party opposite? No, Sir, far from it. The *Daily Worker* is in danger, not because of the systematic publication of material that affects the successful prosecution of the war, but because of the systematic publication of political opinions that are not acceptable to the Executive in this country . . .

He went on to say:

Since these Regulations came into being, the one paper which has received a warning from the Home Secretary is the *Daily Worker*. What has the *Daily Worker* published which entitled it to this warning? As far as I can gather, the Home Secretary knows, but if he knows he will not tell.[11]

Following the outcry, the suppression of the *Daily Worker* was deferred for nearly six months.

The other Cabinet decision – that distribution of the leaflet 'The People Must Act' must be stopped provoked an argument with the Scottish Office. In England and Wales, the police were instructed to seize all copies of this leaflet wherever found, but the Scottish Office refused to send out such an instruction on the grounds that it knew of no law which would enable the police to take such action, and if such a seizure was challenged in court, there would be no hope of justifying it from a legal point of view.

The truth was that in ordering the seizure of the leaflet the Home Office had relied on the shaky legal grounds that leaflets which are thrust into the hands of persons who do not ask for them could lead to breaches of the peace. In the event, the seizures never were challenged in the courts, but the reaction of the Scottish Office made it inevitable that the government would later on give further consideration to the question of leaflets.[12]

Even before the government took action on this leaflet, Communist Party members had been subjected to widespread harassment by the police. The *Daily Worker* alleged that this was 'part of a campaign dictated from Whitehall to stifle by intimidation all criticism of the Men of Munich in the Government'. A special article stated that during the month of June alone, there had been '45 cases of political arrest'. These included speakers at open-air meetings, members distributing leaflets, others selling the *Daily Worker*. Most of those arrested were charged with 'insulting words and behaviour'; there had been only two acquittals out of the 45, and some defendants had received the maximum sentences.

> The survey of police prosecutions or, more accurately, persecutions, which we make today, shows that a systematic campaign is being waged against persons conducting propaganda for the removal of the Men of Munich and the establishment of a People's Government. These attacks are so persistent, similar and widespread, that they are obviously directed from a single source.[13]

The Cabinet decision on leaflets meant that police action against Party members was greatly extended. Until the first week in July it had been mainly confined to arrests of people engaged in outdoor activities; now there were many police raids on the homes of Party members. Thus on 13 July, the *Daily Worker* reported that the homes of a number of members in Leeds had been visited by CID men looking for the leaflet. Seizures were not confined to this leaflet; many other documents, pamphlets and even books were being taken away. In some cases, complete sets of Left Book Club titles were removed – and not only this; also taken were Shaw's *Intelligent Women's Guide to Socialism*, works by the Webbs on trade unionism and even John Stuart Mill's *Principles of Political Economy*.

The people whose homes were searched were taken to police stations to be questioned, and in many cases the police contacted their employers with the aim of securing the dismissal of Communists engaged in war production.

A survey of the kind of action taken was compiled by the legal adviser to the National Council for Civil Liberties, who reported:

Police broke into a closed branch meeting of a provincial Young Communist League and stopped the meeting. They took all the identity cards of those present and made lists of names and addresses from them and asked the names of employers. Several officials were taken to the police stations and interrogated for several hours. Afterwards, they were told they might leave, but must attend no meetings in future *of any kind*. Shortly afterwards, the police visited various employers, and later members of this group were dismissed from their employment.[14]

The pressures were such that in October 1940 the Party published a pamphlet entitled *How to Defend Yourself: a Practical Legal Guide for Workers*. It began by pointing out that the charges ordinarily brought against politically-active workers – such as 'obstruction', 'breach of the peace', 'insulting words or behaviour' – were in reality 'political charges brought for political reasons'. So knowledge of the law had to be supplemented by correct political understanding and activity. Since the rights available to the subject had been won by the vigilant activity of the mass of the people, those accused should do everything possible to enlist the support of their trade union branch, co-op guild and so on.

The guide went on to emphasise that 'you should never give the authorities any unnecessary opportunity.' When selling a paper, 'choose a spot where it seems unlikely you could cause any obstruction.' 'Do not thrust your paper or leaflet into the hands of passers-by. Do not shout any provocative slogans.' And it added:

Many courts have recently held that distributing leaflets, either in letter-boxes or to passers-by, is illegal if anyone objects to the political views contained in the leaflets, and is so annoyed that he is likely to commit a breach of the peace. This is probably quite wrong, but in war-time courts will go on coming to equally absurd decisions. Therefore, see that what is said in any leaflet is expressed in moderate language, and, if possible, take several friends with you when you go distributing, so that they can tell the court if in fact really nobody at all was annoyed.

The pamphlet said that the practice had grown up of searching the homes of people, whether or not they had been arrested; in the absence of a search warrant or written order, the police had no right to do this, and should be refused admission.

They often choose a time when you are not likely to be in, so that they can impose upon your wife or other relatives. You or your wife or other relative at home should *never consent* to having your home searched.

On the other hand, anyone arrested would almost certainly be searched, so readers were warned not to carry anything about which might give the police any information about themselves or anyone else. 'The emptying of pockets is better than the wringing of hands.'

The guide gave tips on how to behave in court – for example, the accused should not interrupt the prosecuting lawyer by shouting 'that's a lie' or 'you liar', but should make a note of any point which could be proved untrue in order to refute it later. If the case came to trial by jury, the accused should not only analyse the evidence in order to show that he or she should not be convicted, but should also explain what was the *real issue*. They had to try 'in a word, [to] bring out the political nature of the case.'

The Threat from 18B

One wartime measure appeared to pose a threat to the very existence of the Communist Party. This was Defence Regulation 18B. It enabled the Secretary of State to detain without trial the members of any organisation which was *either* 'subject to foreign influence or control' *or* had persons in control of it who sympathised with 'the system of government of any Power with which His Majesty is at war' *and* that there was danger of the organisation's utilisation 'for purposes prejudicial to the public safety, the defence of the realm, the maintenance of public order, the efficient prosecution of any war in which His Majesty may be engaged, or the maintenance of supplies or services essential to the life of the community'.

This Regulation was used during May and June 1940 to arrest and detain BUF members and sympathisers. Since they had always supported the Hitler régime, and Britain was at war with Germany, they clearly came within the second category of this regulation. Communists could not be accused under the second category but they could hardly deny that they came within the first – 'subject to foreign influence' – since the Party was the British section of a world organisation, the Communist International.

In the event, 18B was only used against a handful of Communists. One was T. E. Nicholas, well-known in Wales as a poet. A dentist by profession, his detention was clearly a blunder by the police, and he was released as soon as he came before a tribunal.[15]

The most notorious case was that of John Mason, who was arrested on 15 July 1940, and spent nearly 11 months in an internment camp. Mason was a shop steward employed by the English Steel Corporation; he had helped to form the Mexborough Trades Council in the West Riding of Yorkshire, and was still its secretary. At the outbreak of the war, he had joined the Communist Party. His arrest made headlines in the *New Propellor* which, for the next few months, listed hundreds of organisations – mainly shop stewards' committees, trade union branches and trades councils – which passed resolutions demanding his release. A 'John Mason Defence Committee' was set up, and the campaign gathered strength; meetings were held, the National Council for Civil Liberties took up his case. Questioned in the House of Commons on 20 February 1941, Herbert Morrison, Home Secretary since the previous October, said that he had decided that Mason's detention must be maintained because he was involved in attempts to slow down production. But he refused to give any particulars concerning this allegation, and, indeed, exactly what Mason was accused of was never made public. As with other 18B detainees, he was never brought to trial, and on 12 June 1941, after eleven months' campaigning, he was suddenly released.

It was the view of the Mason Defence Committee at the time that Mason, as a Communist trade unionist, had been selected as a 'test

case for punishment'.[16] But the truth was that, even before the
Mason campaign was under way, government circles had been wary
of using 18B against Communists since they anticipated that the
hostile reaction which such detentions might provoke would be
counter-productive. During the Cabinet discussion about
Communist leaflets and the *Daily Worker* on 5 July, Sir John
Anderson said that his expert advisers were 'against taking action
against Communists as such at the present time,'[17] and on 14 July
Regional Commissioners were informed in a letter from the Home
Office that orders under Regulation 18B 'should not be made against
persons merely because they are Communists'.

Moreover, the Home Secretary deemed it necessary to send a
further letter to the Regional Commissioners on 27 July, detailing
the reasons why much care should be taken in the exercise of 18B
against Communists.[18] Firstly, it pointed out that, although the
aims of the Communist Party were revolutionary, it also advocated
social reforms with which large numbers of non-Communists were
in sympathy. Therefore, action against Communists which could be
represented as victimisation of persons advocating the removal of
grievances was 'likely to win them support from people who have
no sympathy with their revolutionary projects.' Secondly, the
present line of the Communist Party was to argue that there were
fascist sympathisers in the government. 'If they can represent that
action has been taken against the Party because of this propaganda,
they might on this issue win sympathy from many people who are
entirely opposed to Communism.' The third point made in the letter
was a good deal more factual about the Party than were the public
utterances of government spokesmen. It said:

> While the Party is opposed to what it calls the 'Imperialist War',
> it has as yet shown no sign that it is prepared to give active aid
> to Germany. In no country which Hitler has invaded has evidence
> come to light that the 'Fifth Column' has been drawn from the
> Communist Party, and there is as yet no evidence that the
> Communist Party intends to act as a 'Fifth Column' here.

Fourthly, the letter stated that there was as yet no evidence of
organised attempts by the Party to slow down production in
industry; that if any individuals made such attempts, the trade union
leaders were generally willing to co-operate in their removal, but
difficulties were liable to arise if the trade union leaders were not

consulted beforehand.

Communists were an 'insignificant minority', said the letter, who had 'failed to shake the loyalty of the working people', but 'many members . . . would be quite willing to suffer the mild "martyrdom" of internment if by doing so they could advance their cause.'

It was for these reasons that the case of Johnny Mason remained an exception. The authorities preferred a more indirect method of trying to undermine Communist influence in war industry: that of victimisation. There were many examples of this; they were invariably highlighted in the *New Propellor* and in some cases the reaction of the workers brought about reinstatement of shop stewards who had been dismissed.[19]

[1] See *Daily Worker*, 29 July 1940.
[2] *Labour Monthly*, July 1940, p. 380.
[3] *Labour Monthly*, November 1940.
[4] *TUC Report 1940*, p. 280.
[5] Communists were not alone in this misconception, since the Fleet Street press also gave space to stories about growing opposition to Hitler within Germany. See the contribution by Chris Rubenstein in Attfield and Williams (eds.), op. cit., p. 53.
[6] See *A Call to the People* by D. N. Pritt (pamphlet published by the People's Vigilance Committee, 1940). Also D. N. Pritt, *From Right to Left*, London 1965, p. 245 et seq.
[7] Taken from an article in the American Communist magazine *New Masses*, reprinted in the *Daily Worker*, 11 September 1940.
[8] Cab 65/8. Meeting of War Cabinet 4 July, 1940. WM 193(40).
[9] Cab 65/8. Meeting of War Cabinet 5 July, 1940. WM 194(40).
[10] The correspondence and comments appeared in a pamphlet with a Foreword by J. B. S. Haldane, *Hands Off the Daily Worker*, n.d. (1940).
[11] *Hansard*, 31 July 1940.
[12] Cab 98/18 C. A. (41) 4
[13] *Daily Worker*, 2 July 1940.
[14] See article in *Labour Research*, September 1940, p. 134.
[15] See D. N. Pritt, op. cit., p. 231-2.
[16] See Edmund and Ruth Frow, op. cit., pp. 151-2.
[17] Cab 65/8 WM 194(40).
[18] Cab 98/18 C. A. (41) 4.
[19] See Richard Croucher, op. cit., p. 92 et seq. for an illuminating description of these incidents.

CHAPTER 22

Action during the Blitz and the Banning of the 'Daily Worker' (1940–41)

On 7 September 1940, the blitz on London began. Night after night, from dusk to dawn, the bombers were overhead. Sometimes they came in the daytime too. They dropped high-explosive bombs, incendiary bombs and land-mines. Initially, the heaviest attacks were on the densely populated districts of East and South East London, where a large part of dockland was set ablaze and continued so for many days, acting as a beacon for each succeeding wave of bombers. On the very first night, those killed and seriously injured numbered over 2,000, while the number of homeless mounted fast.[1]

'Yesterday, I walked through the valley of the shadow of death – the little streets of London's East End,' wrote Fred Pateman, a *Daily Worker* reporter, just after the raids began. 'Along the main roads is a steady stream of refugees – men with suitcases, women with bundles, children with their pillows and their own cot covers – homeless in the heart of London.'[2] By mid-November, four out of every ten houses in Stepney had been destroyed or damaged.

For some two years before the war broke out, the Communist Party had been agitating for adequate air-raid protection. As Dutt pointed out at the 1937 Party Congress, bomb-proof shelters were being provided for Ministers and government officials, and installed in luxury flats; they were there for the rich, but not for the poor.[3]

For ordinary people, the government had taken the cheapest way out; it had concentrated on the distribution of gas-masks and instructions on how to make one room in a house gas-proof. But the Spanish war had revealed that the major threat was not gas but high-explosive bombs. In his book, *Air Raid Precautions*, which came out in 1938, J. B. S. Haldane had argued for a system of tunnel shelters for London and other big towns; where this was impossible he advocated concrete shelters nearer the surface. An 'ARP Co-ordinating Committee' of architects, engineers and scientists, was established and chaired by Haldane. Making use of this expert help, the Party in 1938 brought out a penny pamphlet, *ARP: Act Now*, while, with the help of this same Committee, many Party branches drew up versions applicable to their own locality. These local pamphlets enjoyed large sales.[4]

Some local authorities had drawn up schemes for bomb-proof shelters, but in most cases the government had refused to sanction them. Instead, what came to be called the 'Anderson shelter' was provided for people with back gardens. These were made of corrugated steel and gave protection against blast and splinters, but not against direct hits. And since many people had no back gardens, about half the population had no protection at all.

Two months after the war broke out, on 2 November 1939, the ARP Co-ordinating Committee sent a memorandum to Sir John Anderson, the Home Secretary, urging the immediate construction of shelters which would be blast and splinter-proof in the first stage and could later be strengthened to give protection against heavy bombs. Sir John asked for details; later he informed the Committee that his experts had reported favourably on the type of shelter they had proposed and said that local authorities would be given grants for building them.[5] In practice, however, the money was spent on inadequate brick shelters. Meanwhile, the Labour Party Executive Committee banned the ARP Co-ordinating Committee as a subversive organisation.[6]

When the blitz started in September 1940, the London District of the Communist Party issued 100,000 leaflets and 5,000 posters demanding the immediate construction of bomb-proof shelters, the opening of the tube stations for shelter at night and the installation in these of lighting, ventilation, seating, bedding and sanitary facilities. They also demanded that private shelters be made available to the general public; that empty flats and houses be commandeered for the homeless who should be entitled to compensation for lost furniture and clothing.[7] With enormous difficulty, since the posts were disrupted and even telegrams took two days to deliver, the London District convened eight area meetings of branch secretaries to discuss proposals for action. The following week the police raided various offices and bookshops and seized such of the leaflets and posters as they could find. 'Plain clothes men swarmed about these places,' reported the *Daily Worker* on 19 September. 'Into one office they burst their way with violence, refusing to show search warrants until the search was completed. The place was turned upside down.'

Police action to seize the leaflets was accompanied by attempts to close the tube gates whenever an air-raid warning sounded. These attempts failed. Those in charge were defeated by thousands of people who occupied the tubes during the night and refused to move out. By the end of September, 79 underground stations in Greater London were being used as shelters by some 177,000 people. The London District of the Party got out and distributed another 20,000 leaflets, this time addressed to the people in the tubes saying 'stand firm and demand bomb-proof shelters' and advising the formation of shelter committees to act together to maintain tolerable conditions. A very large number of Party members were involved in these shelter committees, both in the tubes, and in the brick surface shelters which had never been intended for all-night occupation, and in which conditions were appalling.

Party members also promoted campaigns to get private shelters opened. Thus in St Pancras, they picketed Carreras, the tobacco factory, demanding that its shelter – capable of holding 3,000 – be opened to the public at night. The most spectacular of such activities was that led by Phil Piratin, the Communist councillor in Stepney, who mobilised some 70 people to occupy the deep shelter at the Savoy Hotel one Saturday evening.[8]

The mass movement for adequate shelters was causing consternation in govenment circles. On 3 October, following the resignation of Neville Chamberlain (who died shortly afterwards), it was announced that Herbert Morrison was to replace Sir John Anderson as Home Secretary. In his first speech in that capacity, Morrison told the House of Commons that the people who were demanding deep shelters were doing so for mischievous political reasons.[9] However, in private he told the War Cabinet that it was essential to counter Communist agitation on the issue but that he could not do so adequately 'if he adopted a wholly negative attitude towards the provision of deep shelters.'[10]

At the end of October it was belatedly announced that something was to be done to improve conditions in the tube stations for those very people whom the authorities had tried so hard to keep out. As the *Daily Worker* triumphantly put it on 2 November:

With a great flourish of trumpets it is announced that three-tiered bunks are to be built in the tubes and that hot food will be served.

Thus after weeks of agitation the authorities are compelled to announce measures which should have been instituted at the very beginning. This is a victory for the people and no credit to the powers that be.

The next day, 3 November, Morrison announced in a broadcast that the deep shelters provided by the London tubes would be extended by tunnelling.

From the second half of November, raids on London became more intermittent, while some other towns were singled out as targets. On the night of 14 November, Coventry suffered one of the most concentrated raids of the war; it continued for ten hours, during which 554 people died and over 800 were seriously injured; nearly one third of its houses were made uninhabitable; its telephones, water supply, gas and electricity services were put out of action. Unlike London, Coventry had no tubes, and there was no protection whatsoever; thousands fled into the countryside.

The Coventry Communist Party had at the time about 70 members; the day after the raid, supplies of the *Daily Worker* were rushed in and people queued up to buy it; it was the only paper on sale. The Party sent in Bill Alexander, former commander of the British Battalion in Spain, to be the town's first full-time organiser. The Midland District got out a pamphlet – *Coventry – What Now?* – while the trades council, which was chaired by Communist Bill Warman, a shop steward at Standard Motors, called an emergency meeting to organise action on housing, feeding and adequate protection. At special Party meetings it was agreed that the main concentration must be to build up the Party's strength in the factories. This met with some success; by the beginning of June 1941 the membership had risen from 70 to 150.[11]

With the coming of the blitz, distribution difficulties facing the *Daily Worker* became very acute. It was in November 1940 that a Scottish edition was successfully launched. 12,000 to 14,000 copies nightly were printed in Glasgow simultaneously with the London edition.

The Party and the Armed Forces

Another issue on which the Party was actively compaigning was that of pay and conditions in the armed services. This was highlighted on 8 October 1940, when a delegate to the annual Trades Union Congress appeared on the platform in his army uniform. He was a London Communist, Harry Berger, who had been called up not long since, but had been granted special leave to attend the TUC as one of the Shop Assistants' Union delegation to which he had been elected. He spoke in support of a resolution demanding improved pay and allowances for the armed forces, and his vivid description of life in the army, and how men – particularly those who had wives to support – could not afford 3½d for a packet of Woodbines, earned him the loudest cheers of the Congress, and was to hit the headlines in most of the newspapers on the following day. Berger blotted his copybook with the platform a little later when, in a personal capacity, he moved the reference back of the section of the TUC report on Finland. Not surprisingly, his appearance at the TUC provoked a hostile question in the House of Commons. [12]

It was at about this stage that the Party's activities in relation to the armed forces, which had been largely confined to propaganda campaigns conducted from outside, began to develop into work inside. Young men in their twenties formed a high proportion of the Party membership, so that by the autumn of 1940 many were in process of being conscripted into the army, navy and air force. Those called up left their Party cards behind them, and were indeed initially instructed to destroy them before they left home. This was, of course, intended for their protection, but in practice the advice to go 'under cover' was often disregarded. When they got into the armed services, most Party members went on behaving much as they had done at their former work-places. They contacted one another, met together unofficially in groups, recruited new members, and sent regular reports to the *Daily Worker* about life in the services. Already that paper was devoting considerable space to the subject, and by November 1940 was bringing out a regular 'soldiers' page' which soon became 'Our Page for Soldiers, Sailors, Airmen.' It appeared at least once a week – sometimes more often – and consisted largely of letters, signed only with initials, describing how men were treated in the armed forces, the problems they faced: low pay, the authoritarian structure, antedeluvian attitudes, the lack of democratic rights, the 'officer caste' system and the bureaucratic incompetence which made no use of the skills of those called up. All this was embellished with cartoons by the paper's cartoonist 'Gabriel'. 'Soldiers' letters pour into the *Daily Worker'* wrote Rust at the turn of the year. 'It has become the paper of the forces, passed from hand to hand in barracks, ship and aerodrome. A unique and proud position for a paper to occupy.'[13]

The People's Convention

All through that autumn, the People's Vigilance Movement was gaining ground. Following the London meeting in July 1940, conferences were held in a number of towns and at the end of September a call was issued on behalf of 500 signatories for a 'People's Convention' to be held on Sunday 12 January 1941 in the Manchester Free Trade Hall. 'The time has come for the people to unite in defence of their own interests,' it said, and went on:

> The present government is a government of the rich and the privileged, ruling the country in their own interests and against those of the masses of people. Behind it are the ruling class, the Tory machine, the Men of Munich, the friends of fascism, whose policy built up the power of Hitler, brought the nation into war, and is directly responsible for the unpreparedness which has sacrificed scores of thousands of lives. It protects the most shameless war profiteering, and seeks to place all the burdens of the war on the backs of the masses of the people.

It listed its aims as the defence of living standards, and of democratic and trade union rights; adequate air-raid protection; friendship with the Soviet Union and,

> A People's Government, truly representative of the whole people and able to inspire the confidence of the working people of the world. A people's peace that gets rid of the causes of war.[14]

According to its chairman, Harry Adams, when the Convention finally took place it 'surpassed all expectations alike in size, in character and in deep impressiveness.' This was despite the fact that, a few days before Christmas, the place where the Convention was due to be held, the Free Trade Hall in Manchester, was destroyed in an air raid. With only three weeks to go, a new hall had to be found, all arrangements for accommodating delegates changed. In the end, the organisers managed to book the Royal Hotel in London, as air raids on the capital had died down slightly. But since the Royal Hotel had a seating capacity of only 1,700, both the large and small Holborn Halls had to be booked as well, in order to accommodate the 2,234 delegates who finally attended. More than half these delegates were from outside London but, according to Adams, the offers by Londoners of overnight hospitality were more than sufficient and so were the numbers who volunteered as stewards to meet the visitors at railway stations during the Saturday evening.

665 of the delegates represented trade-union organisations, and another 471 were from shop stewards' committees, or factory committees. The remainder came from a variety of organisations including some Labour Parties, co-operative guilds, and tenants' associations. Twelve colonial organisations were represented, among them the India League on whose behalf Krishna Menon (later to be India's Foreign Secretary) spoke, saying that the Indian people and the British had a common enemy, and 'that enemy is imperialism', and reminding delegates that the leader of the Indian Congress, Pandit Nehru, was in prison. Nehru's daughter, Indira (later to be India's Prime Minister) was present at the Convention as an honoured guest.

After numerous speeches, the Convention adopted a programme which included the six points already mentioned, but added to them a demand for emergency powers to take over the banks, the land and large industries, and another calling for independence for India and freedom for colonial peoples.

The newspapers sent some of their leading political correspondents to attend the Convention which received unexpected publicity in much of the press. Since it was hard to deny that people felt strongly about many of the issues discussed at the Convention, the critics were obliged to fall back on the argument that the Communists were exploiting the grievances of the people for their own sinister purposes.

Labour's *Daily Herald* correspondent thought that the Convention was 'as clever a bit of political exploitation as I have yet encountered', and that the organisers had 'exploited a situation which puts even the Labour Party at a disadvantage'.[15]

The *Daily Mirror* made no bones about the dilemma. Observing that 90 per cent of the delegates were 'honest-to-God British citizens' with 'no wish to see Hitler victorious', it added:

> They have too many grievances the government leaves unanswered. They expected Labour ministers in the government to be their champions. They are disappointed in them. Labour ministers behave like pale imitations of Tory Ministers. So the people feel themselves leaderless. They are beginning to turn to the Communist Party.[16]

One week later the *Daily Worker* was suppressed.

The Daily Worker Banned

The suppression of the *Daily Worker* was hardly a bolt from the blue. It had been expected by Rust and his colleagues ever since the warning under Defence Regulation 2D. And when in October 1940 Herbert Morrison became Home Secretary, the writing on the wall was clear. For Morrison had long been the most fanatical anti-Communist in the Labour leadership, the chief witch-hunter at the time of the great purge, and ever since.

In fact, after taking up his new post Morrison had been met by a demand from Churchill for stiffer press censorship. Churchill had been angered by criticisms of the government appearing in the *Daily Mirror* and the *Sunday Pictorial*. Morrison successfully defended these two important Fleet Street papers in Cabinet discussions. But the *Daily Worker* was a different matter. On 27 December he proposed to the Cabinet that the paper should be suppressed under Regulation 2D.[17]

He set out his argument in a memorandum dated 23 December 1941.[18] The *Daily Worker*, he alleged, had done all that was possible to hinder the war effort short of open and frank incitement to obstruct that effort. Its general line was that the war was being waged by the capitalists for the purpose of benefiting themselves and robbing the workers of such rights and privileges as they had won in the past. He admitted that there was no evidence that the Party was engaged in *direct* attempts to frustrate the war effort by sabotage or refusal to handle munitions. But, he said, the *Daily Worker* had 'striven to create in the reader a state of mind in which he will be unlikely to be keen to assist the war effort.' This propaganda was 'calculated to have a bad effect on the morale of the people.' He thought there was little evidence that it was having much effect – indeed, the spirit of the people was still 'firm and high'. But he believed there was a risk in allowing Communist propaganda to continue into a period when circumstances might become more difficult. Morrison also suggested that *The Week* should be suppressed. 'A roneoed sheet published by Claud Cockburn,' it advocated the same views as the *Daily Worker* 'in a style which has a less popular and more "intellectual" appeal'.

On 13 January 1941, the day after the People's Convention. Morrison's proposal was discussed at a Cabinet meeting and, in the end, approved.[19] At the same time, again on Morrison's instigation, the Cabinet set up a special 'Committee on Communist Activities' 'to consider what further action, if any, should be taken in regard to the Communist Party'. Unfortunately for Morrison, certain newspapers got wind of these decisions before they had been implemented, and on 19 January, two days before the suppression of the *Daily Worker* was planned to take place, the *Sunday Express* carried a front-page story under the headlines 'Government to Stamp on Communist Trouble-Makers' and 'Criminal Charges May Follow Big Check-Up on War Factories Agitation.' 'The government has decided to take action to stop the treasonable activities of the Communist Party,' it alleged:

> It is probable that the Party as an organisation will be proscribed and dissolved. Action will be taken to stop the circulation of its propaganda literature. There is no desire to deal with Communists for mere political activity. They have as much right to freedom of speech within reasonable limits as any other citizen. [But] action has become necessary because of their open and deliberate campaign to cause disaffection in war factories . . . Some of them will find themselves in the Criminal Courts under the Defence Regulations.

The next day the story had been picked up by the other newspapers, some of which rushed in to supply a different version of it. The *Sunday Express* report, though not, as it turned out, a particularly accurate one, caused anger and embarrassment in the Cabinet Committee on Communist Activities which had just started its meetings. According to its minutes:

It was difficult for the responsible Ministers to make their plans which included carefully considered publicity if, as appeared to have occurred in this case, premature disclosures were to be made.[20]

The leak gave the *Daily Worker* the chance of a last shout of defiance. Pointing out that the *Sunday Express* was owned by Lord Beaverbrook, a member of the Cabinet and the Minister for Aircraft Production, it accused him of sharing responsibility with other Ministers for 'widespread economic chaos, now admitted even by the Government itself,' and of having made 'a most unholy mess of his own particular job.' 'So Beaverbrook attacks the Shop Stewards, the People's Convention and the Communist Party. He blames everybody except Lord Beaverbrook.' And it went on:

> The ruling class has got in its hands the BBC and the press; it exercises an almost complete monopoly of propaganda and news. But it is afraid . . . Gentlemen, you have good cause to be afraid. In face of the unity and determination of the people, the power of privilege will disappear as snow before the midday sun.[21]

Morrison was well aware that the suppression of any newspaper could cause alarm in Fleet Street. He was anxious to ensure that his reasons for taking action against the *Daily Worker* should be fully publicised. So, on the morning of 21 January, he called in the representatives of the Newspaper Proprietors' Association to inform them that he had that day issued orders for the suppression of the *Daily Worker* and also of *The Week*. He followed this up at 2 p.m. with an announcement to the editors of the national newspapers, summoned to his presence for the purpose. It was not until 5.30 p.m., some hours after this 'carefully considered publicity' had been set in motion that a posse of Special Branch men, supported by uniformed police, entered the offices of the *Daily Worker* and formally carried out the suppression. In addition, the paper's rotary press was sequestered.[22] The House of Commons was not informed until the day after, on 22 January.

The result of Morrison's endeavours was that most Fleet Street newspapers toed the line and expressed approval, though Liberal papers, like the *News Chronicle*, did so in a rather muted fashion. An exception was once again the *Daily Mirror* which at this time had a wide circulation among industrial workers. 'All suppression of *opinion* as distinct from falsification of *fact* is dangerous,' it declared.

'It is worth while to ask Mr Morrison whether a few silly opinions, violently expressed, in negligible publications, can ever be so dangerous . . . as muddle and mismanagement at the top.'[23]

In the House of Commons, Aneurin Bevan (formerly expelled from the Labour Party, but since readmitted) initiated a debate on 28 January. Bevan, who did not agree with the *Worker's* policy, argued that no newspaper should be suppressed without an opportunity to state its case. But Morrison had seen to it that the Party Whips were on, and, in the end, only fifteen MPs voted against the suppression.

One of Morrison's difficulties was that he was unable to furnish proof in support of the allegations he himself had frequently made in public that the *Daily Worker* was financed by Russian money. According to William Gallacher, before the debate took place, the leading Labour spokesman, Lees Smith MP, had requested the Home Office to supply him with evidence that the paper received money from abroad. But Sir Alexander Maxwell, the Home Office Permanent Secretary had replied:

We have kept a very close check on the Party and the *Daily Worker*. There is no evidence of any money from outside sources and we are quite satisfied that they are receiving sufficient financial support in this country to maintain the paper and the Party.[24]

Morrison was questioned on this matter by Labour MP Shinwell on 6 February 1941, but he failed to make any answer.

[1]A detailed description of the results of the bombing is contained in Angus Calder, op. cit., from which the figures in this chapter are derived. See pp. 158, 188.
[2]*Daily Worker*, 9 September 1940.
[3]*It Can Be Done*, Report of 14th Congress, pp. 132, 278.
[4]See Central Committee Report to 16th Congress, p. 23.
See also *ARP: Safety Now*, 1940, p. 5 (pamphlet).
[5]Ibid.
[6]*Labour Party Annual Report 1941*, p. 21.
[7]See the article by Ted Bramley in *Labour Monthly*, October 1940.
[8]See Phil Piratin, op. cit., p. 72 et seq.
[9]*Hansard*, 10 October 1940.
[10]Cab 65/9. War Cabinet meeting 30 October 1940. WM 280/40. See also Bernard Donoughue and G. W. Jones, *Herbert Morrison: Portrait of a Politician*, London 1973, p. 289.
[11]See James Hinton, 'Coventry Communism: A Study of Factory Politics in the Second World War', *History Workshop Journal*, No. 10, Autumn 1980.
[12]*TUC Report 1940*, pp. 287-9. Also Hansard October 15, 1940.
[13]William Rust, *It's Your Paper*, January 1941 (pamphlet). See also Gabriel, *We're in the Army Now*, pamphlet published by the *Daily Worker* Defence Leagues, 1941.

[14]The statement and its signatories were reprinted in *Labour Monthly*, November 1940.

[15]*Daily Herald*, 13 January 1941.

[16]*Daily Mirror*, 13 January 1941.

[17]Cab 65/9, War Cabinet meeting 9 October 1940. Cab 66/12 WP(40) 402. Cab 65/10, War Cabinet meeting 27 December 1940.

[18]Cab 66/14. WP (40) 482.

[19]Cab 65/21 War Cabinet minutes 13 January 1941 WM 5 (41).

[20]Cab 98/18, minutes of Committee meeting, 20 January 1941.

[21]*Daily Worker*, 20 January 1941.

[22]See William Rust, op. cit., p. 83.

[23]*Daily Mirror*, 22 January 1941.

[24]See William Gallacher, *The Rolling of the Thunder*, London 1947, pp. 124–5.

CHAPTER 23

Cabinet Deliberations and the Party's Response (1941)

The Cabinet Committee set up to consider further action against the Communist Party held its first meeting on 20 January 1941. This Committee consisted of six people, three of whom were Labour men who had been brought into the Churchill government in 1940. They were Herbert Morrison, Home Secretary; Ernest Bevin, Minister of Labour (he had formerly been secretary of the Transport and General Workers' Union and had, in that capacity, successfully put down the Communist-led Busmen's Rank and File Movement); A. V. Alexander, First Lord of the Admiralty (he had previously held that post under the MacDonald government of 1929–31). The chairman of the Committee was Sir John Anderson who had succeeded to Chamberlain's former post as Lord President of the Council, and its two other members were the Conservatives A. Duff Cooper, Minister of Information, and Sir Donald Somervell, the Attorney-General.

As background information, the Committee had before it a memorandum from Morrison as Home Secretary which was, in the main, factual and which disproved Morrison's own public statement at the start of the war that the Party would 'crumble'.[1] It said that membership of the Party had been rising before the war, reaching 17,539 in March 1939; that 'at the outbreak of the war, the Party itself claimed that its membership was 20,000 and there is reason to believe that this figure was approximately correct.' Since that date, no further membership figures had been issued, but it had been learned that the Party had ordered 20,000 membership cards to be printed for 1941. It could be assumed that 5,000 of these would be kept in reserve for new members won during the year, but, against this, it should be remembered that a considerable number of members were now in the armed forces and 'these men would not hold cards'. 'It can therefore be inferred that the strength of the Party has shown little change since the outbreak of war.'[2]

The memorandum went on to describe the Party structure and to review its publications, explaining that it was 'a branch of the Communist International' and 'yields obedience to its decisions.' 'The Party is not a secret society' and, except in the case of certain professional groups, 'membership is not concealed' said the memorandum. 'The strength of the movement lies in the open, working-class membership.' And it said:

> In industry the Communist Party has obtained a representation among shop stewards out of all proportion to the strength of the Party in the factories and has created a body called the 'Engineering and Allied Trades Shop Stewards' National Council' which claims to represent the workers whose interests the trade unions have betrayed.

The Committee held three meetings and discussed possible alternatives. Should the Communist Party be made illegal? If so, on what grounds? Should leading Communists be interned without trial under Regulation 18B? Or should they be prosecuted and, if so, what for? Should periodicals other than the *Daily Worker* and *The Week* be suppressed? And, if not, should there be any change in the rule which at present banned their export? How could circulation of anti-war leaflets be stopped? In the end it was only on the last issue – control of leaflet distribution – that the Committee recommended immediate action to the Cabinet.

The Question of Illegality

On the first issue, the Committee had in front of it a statement from the chairman of the Home Defence (Security) Executive (HD(S)E) which argued that, if further action was to be taken against Communists, 'it should be the proscription of the Party as an illegal organisation and the internment of a small number of the leaders.'[3] The HD(S)E had been set up by Chamberlain in May 1940 to deal with the 'fifth column' and, in particular, the 'control of aliens'. It was chaired by Lord Swinton who had been Chamberlain's Air Minister before the war and was an important figure in the Conservative Party; it was spoken of among MPs at the time as the 'Swinton Committee', although the names of its other members were kept secret. According to such information as has since emerged, its deputy chairman was Sir Joseph Ball (who worked for MI5 during the First World War and was subsequently the Tory Party's head of research, in which capacity he was involved in paying £5,000 to the man responsible for the Zinoviev letter forgery); its other members included the head of MI5, a senior member of MI6, two representatives of the War Office, a civil servant from the Home Office; a token Labour man – A. M. Wall, secretary of the London Society of Compositors – and a token Liberal, Sir Isaac Foot.[4]

The statement from the HD(S)E proposing the suppression of the Communist Party said that the aim of the Communist leaders was to 'destroy the authority of the government, of works' managements and of trade-union leaders, and to impede the war effort.' To this end, the Party had organised a campaign, the line of which was that the only hope of escape from hunger, disease and death lay in 'a People's Government which would inspire the setting up of a similar government in Germany, with whom negotiations for peace could be carried on'. It said that the Party's influence in the armed forces had so far been negligible, but this was not the case in industry where the position of the existing trade-union leaders was being gradually undermined. 'If no action is taken, there is likely to be an early crisis in their affairs, and the help they can give the government will correspondingly diminish.' The HD(S)E were, therefore agreed that, if further action were taken, it should take the form of making the Party illegal and interning its leaders. The HD(S)E believed that the grounds for such action should be the detrimental effect of the Party's campaign on the national interest and the war effort and *not* that the Party was subject to foreign influence and control. This would rule out action under Regulations 18AA and 18B.

In the discussion around the HD(S)E's proposal, Herbert Morrison expressed doubts about the wisdom of making the Communist Party illegal. He argued that if the Party were proscribed, or individual members of it interned, such action could not be confined to the small circle of intellectuals and leaders of the party, but must extend also to working-class members.

This might well lead to serious repercussions in industry resulting in labour disturbances such as had occurred on the Clyde in the last war. It would be most damaging if the government, having

committed themselves to strong action, were afterwards obliged
to give way. It would no doubt be possible to proceed by way of
prosecution rather than internment, but it was impossible to be
certain what the verdict of the courts would be and prosecutions
might be exploited for publicity purposes.[5]

A. V. Alexander said that the right course was to prosecute those
responsible for Communist agitation and not to intern them without
trial, which savoured too much of Gestapo methods. However, the
Attorney General, Sir Donald Somervell, said that the men behind
the Party's activities were too clever to expose themselves to
prosecution, and were careful to make use for the most part of
legitimate grievances for propaganda purposes. Under the existing
Regulations, it was doubtful whether any prosecution would
succeed. He thought that 'the grounds for prosecution would be
stronger if the Government were given powers similar to those
which existed in the last war'.

The chairman, Sir John Anderson, stressed that there was a
distinction between the fascists and the communists. It was believed
that the fascists had secret plans in the event of an invasion, either
to range themselves on the side of the enemy, or by a *coup d'état* to
seize power and make terms with the enemy. 'None of these
considerations could be urged against the Communists who had
proceeded in a perfectly open manner.' Nevertheless, it was
suggested that they should be dealt with by executive action instead
of by the normal processes of the law or by counter-propaganda. He
was apprehensive as to the ultimate effect of such a course on the
position of the constitutional leaders of the Labour Party.

Ernest Bevin, Minister of Labour, was initially disposed to agree
with the action proposed by the HD(S)E though he stressed at the
Committee's first meeting that it was 'difficult to distinguish
between subversive propaganda and the exposure of genuine
grievances'.[6] But after discussion with members of his production
executive, he came to the conclusion that 'if it was desired to
prosecute or intern members of the Communist Party, this action
should be directed against the intelligentsia and not against working
class members'.[7] His report on the 'effect of Communist activities
on production' revealed that he was in some difficulty for two main
reasons. First, there was no evidence that Communist activity had
had a serious effect on the output of war industries, though

Communists had probably in some cases, had a bad influence by discouraging working after an air-raid warning, or on overtime. (A not surprising conclusion, since sabotage of production had never been the Party's aim, as Gallacher pointed out in the Commons debate on 28 January 1941.) Bevin's second conclusion was that, though the workers were not likely to be aggrieved by action taken against Communists who were *not* working in factories,

> any action taken against workers in the factories on the ground that they are Communists would lead to complaints of victimisation and would cause discontent among workers who are not themselves in sympathy with communism. In particular discontent would be caused by any system of espionage to discover what workers are members of the Communist Party.[8]

At its final meeting on 5 February 1941, the Committee decided to recommend that 'no action of a general character should be taken at present against the Communist Party'.

The Discussion on Publications

The second major issue discussed by the Committee was whether periodicals other than the *Daily Worker* and *The Week*, should be suppressed. Duff Cooper, the Minister of Information, listed six of these. They were: *Challenge* (the monthly paper of the Young Communist League); *World News and Views*, a weekly published by the Party, which until 1938 had been known as *International Press Correspondence* (since the war, its coverage of the activities of Communist Parties in other countries had been necessarily much reduced, while concentration on British affairs had increased); *Labour Monthly* (of which R. Palme Dutt was the editor); *Russia Today* (a magazine issued by the Russia Today Society, the successor to the organisation known as Friends of the Soviet Union – like its predecessor, the Society had been instantly proscribed by the Labour Party);[9] *Inside the Empire* (published by the Colonial Information Bureau, set up in 1937 with Ben Bradley as its secretary) and *New Propellor* (the monthly organ of the Engineering Shop Stewards).

These periodicals were all legally produced in Britain, but there was a ban on their export. According to Duff Cooper's memorandum, the ban was originally imposed for a reason which was no longer valid – to meet the wishes of the French government, then Britain's ally.[10]

Duff Cooper thought that to forbid their export but permit their sale in Britain was illogical. He suggested that all the publications listed above be suppressed, but argued that if it was decided *not* to do this, he would prefer to avoid interfering with their export.

Herbert Morrison argued that it would not be easy to suppress some of these periodicals under Regulation 2D since it was difficult to hold that they were 'systematically fomenting opposition to the prosecution of the war to a successful issue'.

> Some of them are devoted to a glorification of the Soviet régime, and to contrasting the blessings enjoyed under such a régime with the sufferings imposed upon the people who live under 'capitalist conditions',

he said in his initial memorandum. 'Some of them purport to give world news and contain articles about the evils of "imperialist" rule in India and the Colonies.' It appeared that the references to 'imperialist war' in these periodicals were largely incidental.

> One of the papers, *New Propellor*, although edited and inspired by Communists, has been careful not to associate itself with the Communist Party as such. It is devoted entirely to the exploitation of industrial grievances and contains no direct references to the war.[11]

Morrison did tell the Committee that he was inclined to think that action against the *Labour Monthly* would have been justifiable. (He did not elaborate on this, but there is in fact little doubt that this journal could easily have been banned under Regulation 2D since, apart from any other articles, Dutt's 'Notes of the Month' never ceased to foment opposition to the war. But there seemed to be some muddle over the *Labour Monthly*: A. V. Alexander thought that if it were banned there might be protest from those who made use of the economic statistics it published; he evidently confused it with a quite different journal, *Labour Research* published by the Labour Research Department.)

In the end, the Committee urged that the ban on exports should continue, but made no recommendation concerning the suppression of further periodicals.

Leaflets

The only major decision reached by the Committee was to recommend a new Defence Regulation to stop the circulation of Communist leaflets. This was, indeed, Morrison's chief objective and it arose because, as shown in Chapter 21, there was doubt concerning the legality of the decision to confiscate the leaflet 'The People Must Act'.

None of the existing Defence Regulations provided for the seizure of leaflets, and it was this problem that Morrison was determined to tackle. But he was hampered by the experience of his predecessors. Just after the war broke out, the Chamberlain government had issued Regulation 39B which could easily have been used against Communist leaflets, since it provided that 'no person shall endeavour . . . to influence public opinion . . . in a manner likely to be prejudicial to the defence of the realm or the efficient prosecution of the war'. But this Regulation had met with such furious opposition from MPs of all parties – they considered it a threat to freedom of speech – that it had been withdrawn and another substituted for it which said that 'no person shall endeavour by means of any *false* statement, *false* document or report to influence public opinion in a manner likely to be prejudicial', etc. Since falsification of facts was not something of which Communists could be accused, the Regulation could not be used against them.[12]

Regulation 2D introduced later in May 1940, was confined to periodicals and newspapers, and did not include leaflets. Moreover, as Morrison pointed out, the words in Regulation 2D 'foment opposition to the prosecution of the war to a successful issue' – did not cover all the leaflets which he thought it was desirable to stop. He said that

> though the ultimate object of many of the Communist leaflets is undoubtedly to 'foment opposition to the prosecution of the war' there are many individual leaflets not covered by those terms. There are, for example, leaflets directed to specific objects such as criticism of shelter policy, which are intended to achieve indirectly the object of weakening the war effort.[13]

Morrison therefore proposed a new draft Regulation which would at last give the Home Office powers as sweeping as those exercised during the First World War. The draft Regulation –

numbered 2DA – said:

> Any person who publishes any leaflet which is calculated to undermine or disrupt the unity of purpose necessary to ensure the maximum war effort from all classes of the community shall be guilty of an offence.

Morrison admitted that these words might cover 'some forms of legitimate criticism', but argued that 'it is impossible to find a form of words to which this objection will not be taken'. In order to make his proposal more acceptable, he suggested that it should initially be limited to a three-month period only.

The Committee approved Morrison's draft defence regulation which was then brought before the Cabinet on 17 February 1941 by Sir John Anderson who explained that since the ban on the *Daily Worker* there were signs of an increase in the number of Communist leaflets distributed and the new draft regulation was intended to deal with this. The Cabinet gave the draft its blessing subject to discussion concerning its application to Scotland, and agreed that its operation should initially be limited to three months.[14]

But after this the whole project got bogged down. Asked on 27 March by a Conservative MP whether he was aware that since the suppression of the *Daily Worker* 'pamphlets of a similar nature' were being distributed, Morrison replied, 'This matter is receiving my attention. It would not however be right for me to make any further statement at present.' In the event, he never did make any further statement, and the new proposed Defence Regulation never saw the light of day. The Party continued to distribute 'subversive' leaflets including a massive number demanding the lifting of the ban on the *Daily Worker*.

New Methods of Work

The belief that the disappearance of the *Daily Worker* would lead to a decline in the Party's influence was soon shown to be without foundation. At the end of February 1941, a few weeks after the ban was imposed, the Party put up a candidate in a by-election in Dumbarton. It was a straight fight between Communist Malcolm MacEwen and an official Labour candidate. The latter got 21,900 votes; MacEwen 3,862 or 15 per cent of the poll – a much bigger proportion than in the two previous wartime by-elections contested by the Party. *World News and Views* welcomed this result as signifying a 'substantial swing of the politically advanced to the idea of a People's Government'.[15]

A few days later there was a furore over a BBC decision not to employ Peoples' Convention supporters as broadcasters. Though the signatories to the original call for a People's Convention were predominantly drawn from trade union circles, together with a small grouping of clergymen, there were among them some popular band leaders – Lew Stone, Ben Frankel, Phil Cardew – a number of writers such as Patrick Hamilton and Rosamond Lehmann, and some actors and actresses, including Michael Redgrave and Beatrix Lehmann. News about the BBC's decision was headlined on the front page of the *News Chronicle* on 4 March 1941: 'BBC Gives Stars an Ultimatum', 'Quit People's Convention or You Don't Broadcast'. According to this report:

> Michael Redgrave, the stage and film star, and more than a dozen other well-known actors, actresses, producers and musicians have been informed by the BBC that unless they state in writing that they withdraw their support of the Peoples' Convention they will not be allowed to broadcast again. They were given a week in which to think it over.

It was, however, the BBC which was obliged to 'think it over', for its move met with quite unexpected opposition. Many BBC broadcasters unaffected by the ban rushed in to support their colleagues. Thus Ralph Vaughan Williams, the most revered of British composers, withdrew from the BBC a specially commissioned choral work. He did this in protest against the ban on work by Alan Bush, a leading figure in the Worker's Music Association and a member of the Communist Party. The writer Rose Macaulay cancelled a broadcast previously arranged for her; E. M. Forster withdrew all his services; there were letters of protest signed by such well-known people as J. B. Priestley and David Low, the cartoonist, and no less than 40 MPs tabled a motion protesting against 'political discrimination' by an organisation associated with the State. In the end, Prime Minister Churchill announced that the ban was to be lifted. 'Anything in the nature of persecution, victimisation or man-hunting is odious to the British people,' he told the House of Commons on 20 March.

With the *Daily Worker* banned, the Party faced the loss of a vital organising medium. The paper's function had never been limited to political propaganda; for eleven years, it had fulfilled a crucial organising role. Its guidance to Party members and sympathisers – particularly shop stewards, trade union activists and others involved in progressive movements – had required the day-by-day collection and dissemination of information on political and industrial activities in a fashion quite unlike that of any other newspaper. The original aim of establishing 'worker correspondents', set in motion by Rust in the early days of the paper in the face of seemingly insurmountable problems, had by this time been achieved. There was now a long list of such correspondents who regularly sent in information to the paper.

The Party was much concerned that this two-way communication should not cease altogether with the banning of the *Daily Worker* and so made a move which had not been anticipated by Morrison or his Committee on Communist Activities. It was arranged that certain former members of the *Daily Worker* staff, in particular Walter Holmes, should be responsible for running a news agency known as 'Industrial and General Information'. The ostensible function of this agency was to supply industrial and general news to the national newspapers for a fee. For this purpose, it issued a duplicated bulletin every day to the press. But the bulletin was also mailed regularly to Communist Party offices, Party shop stewards, leading Party trade union officials and to the host of 'worker correspondents' who thereupon continued to send news from the factory floor and the localities as before. The agency was situated in Red Lion Court, just off Fleet Street; its nominal owner was G. J. Jones (a Party member who was a teacher); its bulletins often consisted of no more than both sides of a single sheet. For example, No 15 issued on 3 March 1941 contained seven items. The first concerned a campaign in the North East for a higher meat ration for men on heavy work. On this matter, it reported a meeting of shop stewards in 'the biggest shipyard on the Tyne'; resolutions passed by Newcastle Trades Council, one tabled to come before Gateshead Trades Council, one from a lodge of the Durham Miners' Association and one from the Darlington Labour Party. Another item described the successful resistance by the workforce of Rootes Securities Ltd (a big engineering factory in the North West) to a compulsory transfer-of-labour-scheme put forward by the firm and the Ministry of Labour. These two reports formed the major items in that day's bulletin, but were supplemented by five shorter notices: an answer to some untruths concerning the South Wales Miners' Federation and the People's Convention which had appeared in the *Evening Standard*; a campaign in America for the release of an imprisoned Communist, Earl Browder; some information on wages in Germany; how the profits of a certain textile firm had trebled. The last item was a report of a meeting of Birmingham Students Union which carried by 50 votes to 19 a motion against the ban on the *Daily Worker*.

Items in the next issue, 4 March, concerned the BBC bar on People's Convention supporters; a move by miners for higher meat and cheese rations; resistance to fire-watching arrangements imposed on the workforce at a power station; the profits of a well-known multiple store; a list of trade union branches protesting at the *Daily Worker* ban; an account of a People's Convention meeting at Welwyn Garden City; the campaign to release Nehru, the imprisoned Indian nationalist.

IGI, as it was called, posed a problem for Herbert Morrison. He could hardly ban it under Defence Regulation 2D for 'fomenting opposition to the war' since it hardly mentioned the war, nor indeed would it have been covered by his projected Defence Regulation to stop distribution of leaflets, since it didn't issue leaflets. On 16 March 1941, the Special Branch raided the premises and took away documents, disrupting the issue of the bulletin for a day or two, which then resumed as before. Two and a half months later, the documents seized by the police were returned, and no prosecution was ever brought against the agency or its staff. It seemed, indeed, that Morrison had been outwitted. IGI went on functioning until the ban on the *Daily Worker* was lifted in 1942.

The Party had long since made preparations for possible illegality. It was decided that certain leading members should go 'under cover'. Printing presses were set up in various places; the preparations were co-ordinated by William Rust. To prove that the *Daily Worker* was still alive, a couple of illegal issues were produced in duplicated form the day after the ban. But it was soon agreed that, having demonstrated what was possible, the major concentration must be the development of a mass campaign to lift the ban on the *Daily Worker*. This campaign rapidly gathered momentum. Former *Daily Worker* Readers' Leagues were turned into '*Daily Worker* Defence

One Million Trade Unionists Protest

OVER one million trade unionists have protested against the ban on the *Daily Worker* since it was imposed by the Government on January 21st. Among the organisations protesting are the following:—

National Union of Railwaymen (Executive Committee).
South Wales Miners' Federation (Annual Conference).
National Union of Scottish Mineworkers (Annual Conference).
Associated Society of Locomotive Engineers and Firemen (Executive Committee).
National Union of Clerks (Annual Conference).
National Union of Journalists (Annual Conference).
Engineering Shop Stewards and Allied Trades (National Conference).

At the Scottish Trades Union Congress in April, a resolution against the ban was defeated by only one vote (93-94). The Annual Conference of the Independent Labour Party has condemned the ban, and the Executive Committee of the National Council for Civil Liberties has protested in the name of the 1,800,000 people represented at its conference last August. In addition to the above, over 800 local and district organisations and factory committees have passed anti-ban resolutions.

Numbered amongst these are:—
64 trades councils.
68 shop stewards' committees and factory meetings.
48 local and divisional labour parties.
11 district committees of the Amalgamated Engineering Union.

Numbered amongst these are the following prominent personalities have expressed their opposition to the ban:—
Bernard Shaw,
H. G. Wells,
Lord Ponsonby,
Dean of Canterbury,
Sir Hugh Roberton,
Walter Hudd,
Hermon Ould,
Professor V. Gordon Childe,
Henry W. Nevinson.

A number of the above have constituted themselves into a Press Freedom Committee, which also includes Sir Richard Acland, M.P., and T. E. Harvey, M.P.

Is it not time that Whitehall paid some attention to this growing protest movement?

But the Home Secretary, Mr. Herbert Morrison, still refuses to raise the ban or even to receive a deputation from the Editorial Board. As the *Daily Worker* was suppressed without trial, there is no independent tribunal to which an appeal could be directed. Morrison is judge, jury, executioner and appeal court.

A reasoned memorandum from the Editorial Board, stating why the ban should be raised after a period of three months, was rejected by the Home Secretary without explanation beyond the statement that "the reasons for which it was found necessary to take action under the Regulation have lost none of their force."

These reasons may be satisfactory to the Home Secretary, but they are certainly not accepted by a large body of democratic opinion in this country. In fact, the reasons have never been explained to the people, and to this day they do not know why the *Daily Worker* was suppressed.

It has not been charged in a court of law, neither have any definite charges been brought against it.

The *Daily Worker* was the only paper in opposition to the Government. It was independent of the press monopoly, and it was maintained

PEOPLE'S PRESS
SPECIAL
PRICE - ONE PENNY

The
BATTLE OF THE NEWS
Serious Reverses for the People

THE battle of the news is on. We said it would come, and we were not wrong. When the *Daily Worker* was suppressed we predicted that this was a beginning of a "News Black-out." Now, rather late in the day, the rest of the press are discovering that we were right.

THAT DARK BROWN TASTE!

"The suppression of the *Daily Worker* may or may not have weakened the influence of the Communist Party, but it certainly has had a most serious effect on the independence of the Press as a whole," writes Mr. G. R. Strauss, M.P., in the *Fortnightly Review.*

Never has respect for truth and information been at so low an ebb in this country. The "News Chronicle" of April 30th, reported that "one of the two biggest American broadcasting companies . . . with an estimated listening audience of 35 million Americans, has cut the time it allows for its daily news broadcasts from London by half."

In a long article in the "World Press News" for May 8th, these words occur: "We are undermining the confidence of our people in our own affairs . . . The real danger of various Ministries are being covered by a spate of puff publicity which is receiving less and less credence from the public, and that public is actually beginning to turn to German radio and German communiqués for news."

The blame for this disastrous state of affairs does not rest with the Ministry of Information alone. In the same article it is made clear that the actual position is that the Foreign Office directs and is responsible for all information relating to foreign affairs and national propaganda abroad. Presumably the same responsibility is borne by other Ministries in regard to the affairs under their control.

In other words, the Government itself is indicted by the whole Press and public opinion on the count of spreading alarm and despondency.

This is the murk into which information and enlightenment have fallen directly as a result of the suppression of the "Daily Worker." Just so long as there was a paper determined to tell the truth without flinching, the Government

(Continued on page 4)

by the pennies of the people who subscribed over £4,000 every month to its Fighting Fund.

The *Daily Worker* has nothing to hide. Its hands are clean.

In Editorial Board, presided over by that famous scientist and servant of the British people, Professor J. B. S. Haldane, appeals to you to join in this great and growing movement for the lifting of the ban and for the freedom of the press.

Write to your M.P. Raise it in your Union Branch, Labour Party or Co-operative Guild. Take an organised part in the campaign by joining the "Daily Worker" Defence Leagues. THE PEOPLE NEED THE "DAILY WORKER"!

RAISE THE BAN NOW!
RESTORE THE FREEDOM OF THE PRESS!

(For further information regarding the fight against the ban, write to George Allison, National Organiser, "Daily Worker" Defence Leagues, Premier House, 150 Southampton Row, London, W.C.1.)

AN APPEAL

IF you are a believer in Freedom and Democracy, freedom in expression of opinion and the democratic right of the people to voice those opinions, then you cannot help but support the People's Press Fighting Fund.

The Fund exists to assist the publication of working-class and Socialist literature. Its objects are to further the cause of Socialism, defend trade unionism and the people's rights and privileges. It aims to rally the people, in every way possible, by means of the printed word, to a realisation of their strength and power to change this world of War and Poverty to a world of Peace and Socialism.

In the past, the money subscribed to the old Fighting Fund made possible the publication of the *Daily Worker*, despite the advertisers' ban and wholesalers' boycott.

That support has today been transferred to the People's Press Fighting Fund, which is collecting, on average of £1,500 per month for the above-stated objects. The trustees are Professor J. B. S. Haldane, Arthur Horner, Ben Frankel, Malcolm McEwen, George Allison and Violet Lansbury.

Our work goes on with the publication of literature which will educate and rally the-people, the organising of printing presses which will satisfy this demand. A contribution from YOU will assist in the building of this great movement.

Send a donation (no matter how small it may be) to me at the People's Press Fighting Fund, Premier House, 150 Southampton Row, London, W.C.1 or write for a supply of literature and publications dealing with our objects.
VIOLET LANSBURY

Leagues', with George Allison as their national organiser. By the end of March resolutions against the ban had been carried by over 600 organisations – mostly trade union branches, and shop stewards' committees, but including some local Labour Parties. At the end of May, the results of the campaign were set out in a *People's Press Special* – a four-page printed sheet issued by the former *Daily Worker* staff which reported that since the ban in January, over 750,000 leaflets dealing with the suppression had been distributed, and more than 250,000 pamphlets on the subject sold. By this time the number of organisations which had adopted resolutions protesting at the ban had reached 800. It included four annual conferences of trade unions (South Wales Miners, Scottish Miners, National Union of Clerks and the National Union of Journalists); two union Executive Committees (the National Union of Railwaymen and the railway drivers' union, ASLEF); eleven district committees of the Amalgamated Engineering Union; 64 trades councils, 48 local Labour Parties, 68 Shop Stewards' Committees. Soon after this, on 19 June, a resolution demanding the lifting of the ban was carried by a large majority at the annual conference of the Amalgamated Engineering Union – by far the largest and most influential union in the arms industry. It demonstrated all too clearly that government fears about the effect of its anti-Communist activities on the morale of the workers in war production were fully justified.

Just three days after the AEU passed its resolution, there came a dramatic change in the direction of the war.

[1]Cab 98/18. C. A. (41) 4.
[2]This calculation contradicts statements from historians such as Henry Pelling who estimated in his book *The British Communist Party: A Historical Profile*, London 1975, p. 120, that the membership of the Party in June 1941 was no more than 12,000. His guesswork has frequently been taken as fact by other historians see for example, A. J. P. Taylor, *English History 1914–1945*, London 1963, p. 458.
[3]Cab 98/18. C. A. (41) 2.
[4]The information on the Home Defence (Security) Executive is derived from Peter and Leni Gillman's, *Collar the Lot*, London 1980, p. 141 et seq. – a remarkable piece of research into the experiences and fate of the 'enemy aliens' – many of them anti-fascist refugees – in Britain during the war.
[5]Cab 98/18, minutes of Committee meeting 20 January 1941.
[6]Cab 98/18 C.A. (41) 3.
[7]Cab 98/18 minutes of Committee meeting 5 February 1941.
[8]Cab 98/18 C.A. (41) 8.
[9]Labour Party Annual Report 1940 page 27.
[10]Cab 98/18 C.A. (41) 9.
[11]Cab 98/18 C.A. (41) 4.

[12]Cab 98/18 C.A. (41) 5.
[13]Cab 98/18 C.A. (41) 6.
[14]Cab 65/17. 17 February 1941. WM(41) 18. Cab 66/14. 10 February 1941. WP(41) 27
[15]*World News and Views*, 15 March 1941.

CHAPTER 24

The Attack on the Soviet Union (1941)

At four o'clock on the morning of Sunday 22 June 1941, Nazi Germany invaded the Soviet Union along a 1,800 mile front. There had been no declaration of war, no renunciation of the German-Soviet Non-Aggression Treaty. Hitler's armies simply swept over the borders without warning, smashing the Red Army units facing them, and penetrating many miles into Russian territory. Within a few days, the Russians lost thousands of tanks and aircraft, and vast numbers of soldiers were encircled and taken prisoner, while the German armies continued their advance at unprecedented speed in a three-pronged drive to be aimed eventually at Leningrad in the north, Moscow in the centre, the Ukraine and the Caucasus in the south.

In Britain, first news of the German invasion came over the radio at breakfast time, a few hours after it began. To Communists it was totally unexpected; only a few days earlier the Russian news agency Tass had issued a statement maintaining that rumours, then current, of a coming German attack were without foundation. These rumours had been presented in the Communist weekly, *World News and Views*, as another example of the 'anti-Soviet dreams' of the British ruling class.[1]

It so happened that on that fateful Sunday, most members of the Central Committee were not in London; they were involved in public meetings or other activities in various parts of the country. Dutt and a handful of colleagues at the Party headquarters at 16 King Street were faced with the immediate necessity of getting out a press statement on the Party's attitude to the new situation. Two major considerations dominated their minds. One was the need to defend the Soviet Union. For it had always been understood that if the first workers' state was smashed it would put back the cause of world socialism for generations. So it had long ago been decided at Comintern Congresses that in any counter-revolutionary war against the Soviet Union, the workers of the world must be

329

mobilised to ensure victory for the Red Army.[2]

Now that Hitler's armies were attacking the Soviet Union, could the war between Britain and Germany any longer be characterised as 'imperialist', even though the aim of Britain's rulers might be the defence of their Empire?

The other thought dominating the minds of Party members was the fear that the British ruling class would now 'switch the war' – that the long-established plans of the 'Men of Munich' to give tacit support to Hitler while he attacked the Soviet Union, might now become a reality. Anxiety on this score had been rising ever since Hitler's deputy, Rudolf Hess, had suddenly on 10 May landed by parachute in Scotland and asked to see the Duke of Hamilton. It was widely assumed that Hess had come to try to negotiate a German-British deal against the Soviet Union. As Emile Burns observed just one day before Russia was attacked:

> When Hess arrived in Britain, there was a noticeable increase in the amount of anti-Soviet propaganda in the British press. It was obviously connected with the aim of those circles in the British ruling class who hoped for a return to the policy of Munich – collaboration with German imperialism against the Soviet Union.[3]

The statement issued on behalf of Central Committee on 22 June reflected these fears. Saying that Hitler's attack against the Soviet Union was fascism's supreme aggression against the people of the world, it demanded 'solidarity with the Soviet Union' and 'immediate military and diplomatic agreement between Britain and the Soviet Union.' But it also said:

> This attack is the sequel of the secret moves which have been taking place behind the curtain of the Hess mission. We warn the people against the upper-class reactionaries in Britain and the United States who will seek by every means to reach an understanding with Hitler on the basis of the fight against the Soviet Union.

It went on:

> We have no confidence in the present government, dominated by Tory friends of fascism and coalition Labour leaders who have already shown their stand by their consistent anti-Soviet slander campaigns.

So it reiterated the Party's call for 'a People's Government which can be trusted to defend the interests of the people and maintain close alliance with the Soviet Union'.[4]

The statement of 22 June had to be issued during the day. But it had already been announced that Prime Minister Churchill would broadcast to the nation at 9 o'clock that evening, and it was realised that much would depend upon what he said. Party members awaited the broadcast with trepidation. Churchill was known as the 'arch-imperialist' chiefly responsible for the attempt to smash Soviet Russia in its early days. Moreover, he had once said that if he had to choose between Communism and fascism, he would not choose Communism.[5] On the other hand, he had not been one of the 'Men of Munich' and, indeed, in June 1939 had urged a mutual assistance pact with the Soviet Union to deter Hitler. Churchill's broadcast that evening offered more than any Communist had dared to hope. It made clear that there was to be no sell-out, no deal with Hitler – far from it.

'No one has been a more persistent opponent of Communism than I have for the last 25 years,' said Churchill.

I will unsay no word that I have spoken about it, but all this fades away before the spectacle which is now unfolding . . . We have but one aim and one single irrevocable purpose. We are resolved to destroy Hitler and every vestige of the Nazi régime . . . Any man or state who fights against Nazism will have our aid . . . It follows, therefore, that we shall give whatever help we can to Russia and to the Russian people. We shall appeal to all our friends and allies in every part of the world to take the same course. The Russian danger is our danger . . . just as the cause of any Russian fighting for his hearth and home is the cause of free men and free people in every quarter of the globe.[6]

It was immediately clear to most Central Committee members that the statement of 22 June failed to meet the needs of the situation. If Churchill was prepared to show solidarity with the Soviet Union, and to take a stand against the known views of the 'appeasers', both in and outside his government, then surely the Party should stop campaigning for his downfall. Gallacher, who expressed himself as 'agreeably surprised' by Churchill's broadcast, said in a press statement issued on Thursday 26 June that the Communist Party would support the government in any steps it took to collaborate with the Soviet Union.[7]

That evening of 26 June, Pollitt addressed an open-air meeting in Montagu Place, London, attended by 8,000 people. Though he reiterated demands for the removal of pro-fascist reactionaries from the government, there was no call for a People's Government in his speech. And in a pamphlet sent to the printers on that same day – entitled, significantly, 'Smash Hitler Now!' – he made the same point as Gallacher:

> The people of this country should fully support every measure taken by the British government to secure the effective joint defence of the British and Soviet peoples against German fascism.

The Central Committee met on 4 July, and issued a new statement which was printed as a manifesto. It was headed 'People's Victory over Fascism', and said that the cause of freedom required the unity of all peoples against German fascism; that the Communist Party would support every measure of the government designed to secure victory in the common cause for the complete defeat and destruction of Hitlerism. Again, there was no call for a People's Government, but four urgent aims were listed:

1) A pact of alliance with the Soviet Union.
2) All friends of fascism to be cleared out of government posts.
3) 'Organise production for victory, end waste and disorganisation, ensure equal distribution of food supplies, give adequate air-raid protection.'
4) 'Mobilise the entire people for victory through the fullest democratic activity and initiative.'

At this same meeting, it was decided that Harry Pollitt who, in 1939, had wanted to support the war against Hitler, believing it to be an 'anti-fascist' struggle, should be restored to his old position as General Secretary of the Party. Since April 1941, Pollitt had been working in a London shipyard, and in the event he had some difficulty in obtaining release from his job, which was not granted until 8 August. He nevertheless assumed the major Party responsibility during the ensuing weeks.

The points in the new Manifesto ,were elaborated in a 'political letter' dated 8 July, signed by Pollitt and sent to all Party branches. This said that victory over Hitler was now 'the supreme issue before the whole of democratic and progressive mankind.' It followed that the Party's aim must be for a 'united national front' of all who stood for Hitler's defeat. 'In the light of this, our fight is not directed against the Churchill government but [against] those who are the secret friends of Hitler.'

Giving reasons for this new stand, the letter stressed that the situation had fundamentally changed.

It is an axiom of Marxism that the Communist Party formulates all its policies in accordance with the concrete situation that exists – not one that we imagine or would like to see exist, but as it actually is.

The letter admitted that there were still members of the Party who doubted the genuineness of the Churchill Government's statements, who were wondering how soon the war would be switched. But it asserted that any 'standing aside', 'not pulling our weight', 'putting forward impossible demands', would play into the hands of the 'dark forces' which wanted to take advantage of splits in the anti-fascist struggle.

In the event, any doubts among Party members quickly faded away. They had spent years swimming against the stream, and now suddenly found themselves swimming with it – a new and exhilarating experience.

In December 1941 yet further parts of the world were engulfed in the war. The Japanese attacked and sank most of the American Pacific fleet in Pearl Harbour, whereupon Hitler and Mussolini declared war on the United States in support of their Japanese ally. '1942 – and the whole world in arms,' wrote Pollitt at the turn of the year. 'The issue is clear: victory over the fascist barbarians and social progress; or defeat and a return to slavery.'[8]

The Party was, of course, jeered at for its 'somersault'. The answer given by Pollitt and Gallacher was two-fold. Firstly, that if the concrete situation changes, policies have to change too. But secondly, that every other political party had also somersaulted. This indeed was true. After being treated as the arch-enemy ever since 1917, the Soviet Union was suddenly acclaimed as a friend. Words of praise for the Soviet Union were not only voiced by politicians; they appeared in most newspapers – though here and there, expressed with some reluctance.

Most government advisers expected this new posture of friendliness to be short-lived. Convinced as they were of the weakness and inadequacy of any country which presumed to rid itself of the capitalist system, they believed Hitler's new drive to the East would offer no more than a few weeks breathing space to Britain, following which the Russians would capitulate, just as the French had done. They were wrong. Here, for the first time, resistance did not crumble; it grew. Even before the Japanese assault on Pearl Harbour, the German drive towards Moscow had been halted. The Russian people fought back, and were, in the end, to 'tear the guts out of the German army', as Churchill himself was to put it. And the Soviet Union, previously regarded with contempt, had at last to be recognised as a great power.

The Russian resistance had a significant impact on the outlook of the workers engaged in war production. Here, the Party had already achieved a considerable influence; now those members who had been elected as shop stewards had a new object in view. They had often been accused of wanting to sabotage war production. There had been no foundation for this accusation, but it was true that increased production had been of no interest to them; what mattered was the building up and strengthening of workplace organisation. From July 1941 onwards, however, increased production became a major aim. This did not mean that the Party supported the aims of the employers that everyone should work harder for less money. What it *did* mean was that obstacles to output, including waste and disorganisation due to mis-management, had to be dealt with – and were. To this end, the Party supported and played a leading role in the Joint Production Committees which were beginning to appear. The trade unions were, in the end, to emerge from the war in a greatly strengthened position; towards this, the Communist Party made a significant contribution.

On the political front, the central issue became once more the struggle against fascism, and as part of this, the campaign for a second front in Europe. The fight for the restoration of the *Daily Worker* gathered momentum and in May 1942 the Labour Party annual conference passed a resolution demanding the lifting of the ban, despite opposition from its National Executive. After this, Herbert Morrison reluctantly gave way, and, in September 1942, the *Daily Worker* reappeared.

'Our Party knows how to fight,' wrote Pollitt in June 1941: 'I know we are small – I know we are only 20,000 strong but I know when our Party goes into action . . . we can do great things'.[9] In the event, the membership of the Party was to rise over the next couple of years to more than 50,000. The people who joined were, as always, those who wanted to be active, not passive, who longed to participate in a movement to change society.

The End of the Comintern

In May 1943, the Presidium of the Executive Committee of the Communist International proposed that the Comintern should dissolve itself, on the grounds that the diversity of problems facing the parties in the different countries meant that guidance from a single source no longer met the needs of the situation. In a resolution placed before its affiliated sections in each country it recalled that the Comintern had been established in 1919 as a result of the political collapse of the majority of the old, pre-1914 workers' parties. It had aimed at 'preserving the teachings of Marxism from vulgarisation and distortion by opportunist elements', and had helped in a number of countries to 'unite the vanguard of the advanced workers into genuine working class parties'. But, it said,

> long before the war, it had become more and more clear that with the increasing complications of the internal as well as international relations of various countries, any sort of international centre was bound to encounter insuperable obstacles in attempting to solve the problems facing the working-class movement of each particular individual country.

And it said that the organisational form originally chosen by the Comintern had been 'outgrown by the movement's development and by the increasing complexity of its problems in the separate countries', and had 'even become a hindrance to the further strengthening of national parties'. The Central Committee of the British Party endorsed this proposal, as did other parties, and in June the Communist International came to an end.

Looking back over the previous 23 years, there had been two major occasions when the Comintern had overturned policies decided on by its British section. One was in 1928 when the politics of Class-against-Class had been introduced with devastating results. The other was in 1939, when the initial line of a 'war on two fronts' was changed on the insistence of the Comintern to one which characterised the war as 'imperialist'. Years later, many of the Party leaders were to regard this change as a major misfortune.[10] It certainly meant that the Party was to face quite unprecedented difficulties; it survived them primarily because of the solidarity of its members, one with another.

At last, in 1943, the Communist Party of Great Britain was no longer to function as a section of a world party. International solidarity would, of course, remain one of its fundamental aims. But it was finally to emerge as an independent political party, responsible to itself alone for its decisions, its policies, its strategy and tactics in the battles that lay ahead.

From the beginning, the Party had been confronted with problems very different from those facing Marxists in other countries. It had been born at the centre of a gigantic Empire, dominated by what was then the most powerful ruling class in the world, one which for many decades had been rich enough to grant concessions to its home population while savagely oppressing the peoples of its subject territories. The Party found itself part of a labour movement dominated by old-established trade unions whose potential for advance (which was immense) had been continually undermined by limited aims and sectional rivalries, and whose leaders, in the main, believed in class collaboration. These trade unions had founded the Labour Party, a federal body with a structure quite unlike that of the social-democratic parties on the continent. It was already firmly entrenched as the party representing the working class before the Communist Party was born or thought of. Though 'common ownership of the means of production, distribution, and exchange' was laid down as the Labour Party's goal in its 1918 constitution, its dominant leaders in practice aimed at the gradual improvement of conditions under the capitalist system rather than the abolition of the system itself. In furtherance of this, they eschewed extra-parliamentary action, preferring that their supporters should remain passive except when required to put a cross on a ballot paper.

In these circumstances, any party which aimed to base itself on Marxist principles faced formidable difficulties, certain to be treated as the supreme enemy, not only by the ruling class itself and its representatives, but by all those Labour leaders who thought in terms of modifying capitalism rather than demolishing it.

Despite these difficulties, the British Communist Party had a

considerable list of past achievements to its credit during the 23 years
of its existence. Its members had played a significant part in the
'Hands off Russia' movement when the British and other Western
governments were engaged in military intervention againt the first
socialist state. It had organised and led a powerful movement of the
unemployed; no other party had ever done this. It had been the
driving force in promoting community action: tenants' movements
against their landlords as well as resistance by owner-occupiers to
the building societies who had cheated them. In industry the Party
had done more than any other body to build up organisation in the
work-place, and its endeavours to mobilise support for the election
of left-wingers to union positions at district and even national level
were meeting with increasing success. As we have seen, the impact
of the Party's work in the industrial sphere had caused alarm in high
places. But its industrial activities were not limited to wages and
conditions; throughout it aimed to introduce a political perspective
into the industrial struggles in which it was involved.

During the 1930s, it had devoted considerable attention to work
among students and professional people, with outstanding results.
It had been largely responsible for the spread of Marxist ideas both
through its own publications and those of other organisations, not
least the Left Book Club.

It had been in the forefront of the battles for colonial freedom,
from the time of the 'Meerut Conspiracy' right through to the
'Hands off China' campaign, when its members had inaugurated
action in the docks to stop the movement of Japanese goods. Long
before there were any laws against racial discrimination
Communists were mobilising people to fight anti-semitism, and
had inaugurated a movement to combat Mosley's influence in
London's East End and elsewhere – at a time when the Labour
leaders preferred to look the other way. The Party had condemned
the government's 'non-intervention' policy on Spain which had
opened the door to the fascist aggressors, in contrast to the Labour
Party which began by supporting that policy. Communists had
done far more than others to promote aid for Republican Spain, and
had been solely responsible for establishing the British section of the
International Brigade in which a large number of Party members
had fought, and many had lost their lives.

The Party had been foremost in opposing the Chamberlain policy
of appeasement; Communist William Gallacher had been the only

MP to oppose Chamberlain's projected visit to Munich in order to arrange the handing over of Czechoslovakia to Hitler. These efforts failed, but this does not mean they were wrong. On the contrary, Communists were to be proved tragically right when a war which might have been averted finally broke out.

In all these struggles, Communist Party members had been targets for attack. Many of them had suffered terms of imprisonment, many more had been victimised. The reasons for this were obvious. Despite its small size, the Party was looked on by the ruling class as offering the greatest threat to its supremacy. And with good reason. For Communists viewed all these struggles on immediate issues, not as ends in themselves, but as part of a process in which people would be drawn into action; as a result their attitudes would change, and so would their view of the way ahead. Thus a new stage could be reached along the road to the final goal: the abolition of the capitalist system and the establishment of a socialist society.

[1] *World News and Views*, 21 June 1941.
[2] See Chapter 10 for the classification of wars at the Sixth World Congress. See also resolution on 'Tasks of the Communist International in connection with the preparations of the imperialists for a new world war', final paragraph at the Seventh World Congress.
[3] *World News and Views*, 21 June 1941.
[4] *World News and Views*, 28 June 1941.
[5] See *Industrial and General Information*, 27 June 1941.
[6] *The Times*, 23 June 1941.
[7] *Industrial and General Information*, 27 June 1941. *The Times*, 27 June 1941.
[8] Harry Pollitt, *The World in Arms*, 1942 (pamphlet).
[9] Harry Pollitt, *Smash Hitler Now!*, June 1941 (pamphlet).
[10] This is true not only of Pollitt and Campbell, but also Ted Bramley and Idris Cox, who were both on the Central Committee at the time. See Attfield and Williams (eds.), op. cit.

Appendix
Central Committee Members

Note. For reasons explained in the introduction the lists below are not complete; in particular, some of the first names are missing. Any information or corrections would be gratefully received.

1927, 9th Congress
Allan, William
Arnot, Robin Page
Bell, Tom
Brain, William
Brown, Ernest
Campbell, John Ross
Crawfurd, Helen
Dutt, R. Palme
Elsbury, Sam
Ferguson, Aitken
Gallacher, William
Glading, Percy
Hannington, Wal
Horner, Arthur
Inkpin, Albert
Jackson, Thomas A.
Joss, William
Kerrigan, Peter
Loeber, W. C.
Murphy, J. T.
Pollitt, Harry
Ramsay, Dave
Robson, R. W.
Rothstein, Andrew
Rust, William
Saklatvala, Shapurji
Stewart, Bob
Turner, Beth
Watkins, Nat
Wilson, J. R.

January 1929, 10th Congress
Allan, William
Arnot, Robin Page
Bell, Tom
Bright, Frank
Brown, Ernest
Campbell, John Ross
Cox, Idris
Crawfurd, Helen
Dutt, R. Palme
Gallacher, William
Glading, Percy
Hannington, Wal
Horner, Arthur
Inkpin, Albert
Jackson, Thomas A.
Joss, William
Kerrigan, Peter
Loeber, W. C.
Moody, C. J.
Murphy, J. T.
Pollitt, Harry
Pollitt, Marjorie
Robson, R. W.
Rothstein, Andrew
Stewart, Bob
Tapsell, Walter (YCL)
Turner, Beth
Watkins, Nat
Webb, Lily
Wilson, J. R.

December 1929, 11th Congress

Allan, William
Allison, George
Ancrum, Jim
Arnot, Robin Page
Campbell, John Ross
Cox, Idris
Coslett, R.
Collins, Enoch
Cree, Annie
Duncan, Kath
Dutt, R. Palme
Gallacher, William
Hannington, Wal
Herman, E.
Hoyle, Charles
Joss, William
McGree, Leo
Moffat, Abe
Moody, C. J.
Murphy, J. T.
Parcell, J.
Phillipson, Miss
Pollitt, Harry
Robson, R. W.
Rust, William
Rushton, J.
Scott, Joe
Shields, Jim
Short, George
Tapsell, Walter
Usher, Nellie
Walsh, Y.
Webb, H.
Williams, Garfield
Wilde, H.
Woolley, E.

1932, 12th Congress

Allan, William
Arnot, Robin Page
Bramley, Ted
Campbell, John Ross
Collins, Enoch
Cox, Idris
Dutt, R. Palme
Gallacher, William
Garnett, Jim
Jones, Lewis
Kerrigan, Peter
Lynch (YCL)
McGree, Leo
McIlhone, Bob
McClennan, Bob
McLean
Pollitt, Harry
Robinson, Trevor
Roberts, Tom
Robson, R. W.
Rust, William
Scott, Joe
Shields, Jim
Moffatt, Abe
Short, George
Smith, Rose
Springhall, Dave
Wesker, Sarah
Williams, Bert
Woolley, Ernest

1935, 13th Congress
Allison, George
Arnot, Robin Page
Bradley, Ben
Bramley, Ted
Brown, George
Burns, Emile
Campbell, John Ross
Cornforth, Maurice
Cox, Idris
Crane, George
Dutt, R. Palme
Eden, Jessie
Gallacher, William
Gollan, John
Hannington, Wal
Hart, Finlay
Henrotte, Esther
Horner, Arthur
Kerrigan, Peter
Lazarus, Abe
McIlhone, Bob
Moffat, Abe
Paynter, Will
Pollitt, Harry
Robson, R. W.
Rust, William
Shields, Jim
Springhall, Dave
Smith, Rose
Stewart, Bob

1937, 14th Congress
Allan, William
Allison, George
Arnot, Robin Page
Bradley, Ben
Bramley, Ted
Burns, Emile
Campbell, John Ross
Cornforth, Maurice
Course, Joe
Cox, Idris
Crane, George
Cunningham, Jock
Dutt, R. Palme
Gallacher, William
Gollan, John
Harrison, Tom
Hart, Finlay
Horner, Arthur
Jenkinson, Betty
Kerrigan, Peter
Mann, Tom
Pollitt, Harry
Rust, William
Scott, Joe
Kane, Mick
Smith, Rose
Springhall, Dave

1938, 15th Congress
Bramley, Ted
Burns, Emile
Campbell, John Ross
Copeman, Fred
Cornforth, Maurice
Cowe, William
Cox, Idris
Crane, George
Dutt, R. Palme
Gallacher, William
Gollan, John
Hart, Finlay
Horner, Arthur
Jessop, Marian
Kane, Jock
Kerrigan, Peter
Llewellyn, Mavis
Mann, Tom
Paynter, Will
Pollitt, Harry
Roche, Jim
Rust, William
Springhall, Dave
Whittaker, Bill
(Co-opted in 1939:
Bennett, Mick
Brown, Isabel)

General Index

Abyssinian war, 137–42
Air raid shelters, 302–6
Aircraft Shop Stewards' National
Council, 179–80, 260, 282–3 (See also
Engineering and Allied Trades etc)
Amalgamated Engineering Union, 14,
88, 93, 96, 98, 152, 154, 177–82, 186,
283–5, 288, 327
Armed forces, Party and, 60–72, 307–8
Arms manufacture, 132–3
ARP Co-ordinating Committee, 302–3
Artists International Association, 212
ASLEF, 152, 291, 327

Bakers' Union, 14
Balham Group, 241–2
Bermondsey, demonstration against
Mosley, 168–71
Boilermakers' Union, 14, 22
Boot and Shoe Operatives' Union, 14,
140
Builders Forward Movement, 88
Busmen's Rank and File Movement,
93–4, 174–7

Cable Street, Battle of, 162–8
Cambridge Scientists Anti-War Group,
212
China Campaign Committee, 252
China, Japanese invasion of, 250–2
Civil Liberties, National Council for,
168, 185, 247, 295, 297
Clerks, National Union of, 152, 276,
327
Colonial struggles, 58–68, 139, 309
Communist International, 1, 4, 7, 54;
constitution, 17–8; 9th Plenum
(1928), 19–30, 31–2, 37, 39, 40; 6th
World Congress (1928), 27, 30, 36,
40, 134; Discussion on British
position (1929), 36–7, 43–4; 10th
Plenum (1929), 27, 44–6, 48; 'January
Resolution' (1932), 79, 88–90, 242;
'unity manifesto' (1933), 111–2; 7th
World Congress (1935), 108, 124–8,
139, 148, 291; and outbreak of war,

1939, 267–8; dissolved, 335 (See also
'Moscow gold')
Communist Party of Great Britain:
membership, 1, 48, 74, 130, 188, 271,
275, 315, 335; dues, 154–5;
organisational structure, 43–4, 172–4,
188–90; method of electing
leaderships, 35, 49–50; literature sales,
191, 275; Congresses: 9th (1927,
Salford), 18–19, 28; 10th (January
1929, Bermondsey), 33–6, 41; 11th
(November 1929, Leeds), 27, 48–51,
52; 12th (1932, Battersea), 79, 90–2,
173; 13th (1935, Manchester), 98,
99–104, 130, 147–8, 173; 14th (1937,
Battersea), 185, 188, 196, 235, 237–8,
244; 15th (1938, Birmingham), 188,
245, 256; 16th (postponed), 218
Co-operative movement, 195–6, 276
Councillors, Communist, 146
Czechoslovakia, crisis, 253–9

Daily Worker: birth of, 52–7; circulation,
55–6, 130, 191, 275; editors, 57, 130;
court cases against, 64–5, 69–71;
Readers' Leagues, 191, 325–6;
editorial board set up, 291–2; Scottish
edition, 306; threats and suppression,
294–6, 310–3; campaign against ban,
325; ban lifted, 334
Defence Regulations 18B and 2D, 287,
292–4, 295–6, 298–301, 315–27
Duchess of Richmond, refusal to load, 251

Electrical Trades Union, 14
Engineering and Allied Trades Shop
Stewards' National Council, 283–5,
316

Fabian Society, 151–2
Fascism: activity against, 110–29,
159–73; fascist powers as war-
mongers, 134–7 (See also under
Germany, Spain, etc)
Fascists, British Union of (BUF),
117–24, 141, 159–71, 287, 299

343

Index of Names

346